'Chris Carr is analyzing globalization not on the level of firms or nation states, but on the level of industries. To this end, he has developed a rich and unique dataset that enable novel analysis industry structures worldwide. Most importantly, he shows that many industries develop oligopolistic structures not only nationally but globally. These insights and the data presented in this book provide essential insights for both businesses operating globally and for anyone interested in competition policy.'

Klaus Meyer, *Professor of International Business, Ivey Business School, Western University, Canada*

'While popular attention has focused upon ecommerce, Chris Carr reminds us that many mature sectors too are dominated by a few global firms. Combining statistics with intimate case study data, Carr offers fascinating insights into the extent of global oligopoly, the performance of leading firms, and the reasons for their rise and eventual demise.'

Robert M. Grant, *Professor of Management, Bocconi University, Italy*

'Oligopoly is an inadequately recognised fact of life in today's globalised business world, which is often overlooked. This book shines much needed light on it and its implications for decision making in a multitude of areas. It will be of great help to those searching for guidance on how to select the most suitable strategies.'

Sally Stewart, *formerly Head of the Department of Management Studies, The University of Hong Kong*

'What Japan used to call "keiretsu", we now see its evolution into "global oligopoly". This evolution in the relationships between global business, government and the marketplace is analysed in Prof. Chris Carr's book – an extensive review of global economic power to identify its roots. Essential reading for students, practitioners and policy-makers involved with global business.'

Sukhavichai Dhanasundara, *Visiting Professor, Lucerne University of Applied Arts and Sciences, Switzerland, and author of* The Global Manager and Leader, Second Edition

'The culmination of a lifetime of research, Carr achieves the best of both worlds, combining detailed data driven analyses with intensive field work and personal experiences in companies to enlighten our understanding of Global Competition.'

David Collis, *Professor, Harvard Business School, USA*

'Different approaches to understanding the role of global oligopolies resemble an Indian fable of the blind men and elephant where each man comes to a different conclusion by touching one part of the elephant. Professor Carr's comperehensive approach combines business strategy, economics and political economy aspects for holistic understanding of global oligopolistic competition. Global Oligopoly offers detailed accounts of different sectors as well as discussion of global competition through the theoretical lenses of Adam Smith, Karl Marx, John Maynard Keynes and Joseph Schumpeter. This book is a must read for students and scholars interested in global business, economics and political economy. A true masterpiece!'

Meelis Kitsing, *Professor of Political Economy, Estonian Business School, USA*

GLOBAL OLIGOPOLY

The era of globalisation brought waves of consolidation in business ownership alongside Leviathan-like state actors. Digital disruption too can leave market power in a relatively small number of hands. In organisational and economic terms, global oligopoly is now a fundamental idea for business and society, which this book explores and analyses.

This book focuses on global oligopolies, starting with an analysis of global concentration and profits in all sectors, before moving on to illuminate the geographical spread and global strategic orientation choices and performance outcomes of global oligopoly. Contemporary cooperation modes, such as cross-border M&A and strategic alliances, niche and Emerging Market champion strategies are also analysed in detail to move the reader towards understanding likely future directions for the field.

Presenting empirical data on strategies and performance outcomes, the book covers a range of industries to provide practical, research-based guidance for more effective global business strategies and policy perspectives.

Chris Carr is Professor of Corporate Strategy at the University of Edinburgh, UK.

Key Ideas in Business and Management

EDITED BY STEWART CLEGG

Understanding how business affects and is affected by the wider world is a challenge made more difficult by the disaggregation between various disciplines, from operations research to corporate governance. This series features concise books that break out from disciplinary silos to facilitate understanding by analysing key ideas that shape and influence business, organisations and management.

Each book focuses on a key idea, locating it in relation to other fields, facilitating deeper understanding of its applications and meanings, and providing critical discussion of the contribution of relevant authors and thinkers. The books provide students and scholars with thought-provoking insights that aid the study and research of business and management.

Titles in this series include:

Global Oligopoly
A Key Idea for Business and Society
Chris Carr

Luck
A Key Idea for Business and Society
Chengwei Liu

Feminism
A Key Idea for Business and Society
Celia V. Harquail

Hierarchy
A Key Idea for Business and Society
John Child

For more information about this series, please visit: www.routledge.com/Key-Ideas-in-Business-and-Management/book-series/KEYBUS

GLOBAL OLIGOPOLY

A Key Idea for Business and Society

Chris Carr

LONDON AND NEW YORK

First published 2020
by Routledge
2 Park Square, Milton Park, Abingdon, Oxon OX14 4RN

and by Routledge
52 Vanderbilt Avenue, New York, NY 10017

Routledge is an imprint of the Taylor & Francis Group, an informa business

British Library Cataloguing-in-Publication Data
A catalogue record for this book is available from the British Library

Library of Congress Cataloging-in-Publication Data
A catalog record has been requested for this book

ISBN: 978-0-367-31283-1 (hbk)
ISBN: 978-0-367-31275-6 (pbk)
ISBN: 978-0-429-31605-0 (ebk)

Typeset in Bembo
by Lumina Datamatics Limited

In honour of those who made this book possible: my former colleagues at BAe Systems and GKN, executives interviewed worldwide, my students and, most of all, my wife Jenny.

Contents

Figures

Tables

Preface

My study of global strategies has been a voyage of discovery encompassing almost 400 companies in 22 countries over the last 39 years. In terms of time and geography, the task has proved as onerous as Darwin's *Voyage of the Beagle* or Marco Polo's *From Venice to Xanadu*. Less dangerous, aside from a knife attack whilst researching in Rio. Prior preparation entailed over a decade from 1970 onwards working at BAe Systems and GKN. It was to explore global strategies, from truly worldwide perspectives (first in automotive, then later in other sectors), that I set out on my research travels so long ago. This is what I have learnt about one of the most fascinating and pertinent strategic questions of our age.

This book focuses on global oligopolies, first analysing global consolidation and concentration trends mapping sector after sector. Today, executives and business students have access to many excellent texts on both corporate strategy and on international business. Most appreciate intuitively that global consolidation processes are strategically crucial. Yet few understand what global oligopolies are; how they now dominate business competition and our everyday lives; what international and global strategies ensue; and with what outcomes in terms of survival prospects and performance.

Global consolidation occurs as the number of key players in any given sector falls, leaving a few players, usually four, dominating worldwide rivalry. This situation is termed a global oligopoly, drawing on the Greek word 'oligos' meaning 'few' (as opposed to a monopoly, drawing on the Greek word 'mono' for one). The simple measure for detecting such global oligopolies is the combined global market share of the top four companies.

Global competitive strategy today remains at the stage of introductory strategy texts, majoring on Strengths, Weaknesses, Opportunities and Threats (SWOT) analyses prior to Michael Porter's 1980 pioneering competitive strategy monograph. Check the indexes of most strategy, economics, or even international business books and texts and you will find virtually no hard data on global markets shares or global concentration levels. This though is the starting point for understanding global oligopolies, oligopolistic moves, and countermoves, the outcomes of which vary enormously from one sector to another. It is these global moves, on a scale frequently larger than nation states, which increasingly govern our lives and economic prospects. Even the global top 500, analysed in Chapter 6, alone had combined revenues of $28 trillion in 2016.[1] Economists can no longer ignore the 'black box', comprising top global oligopoly players who shape today's world economy.

Many academics, lacking knowledge of global oligopolies, fail to see the point of global strategy. Lacking direct experience of executing global strategies themselves, they see the issue as either 'obvious' or even downright 'wrong'. But there was nothing obvious about the vast, complex investments required for GKN to go global in constant velocity joints (CVJs). If obvious, then why didn't Britain's other major automotive suppliers do the same? The tragedy is that academics, consultants, and executives rarely know when it is right to go global and when it is not. Generalities about 'globalisation' are easy; harder, but more crucial, is to address and answer the question 'what about my specific sector and my company right now, and how should we do it?' Given the global rivals we are up against, which orientations and global strategic options are likely to give us the best outcomes?

No company can ignore the top four global players in their sector once they control around 40% of that global market; nor the trend in such global concentration metrics. Without such sector-specific data, strategists are blind: our trumped up overconfidence no more than whistling in the dark. To transpose Trotsky, *'You may not be interested in global competitive war, but war is interested in you'.*

Companies facing global competition are akin to animals engaged in evolutionary survival battles. Observing their evolutionary paths and occasional metamorphoses is a task on par with Darwin's, entailing systematic collection, classification, and codification. To do this, we must observe many species of companies and voyage more globally than Darwin. Patterns emerge. Repeatedly we see companies (like species), finely honed for familiar domestic environments, gradually rendered extinct through global rivalry. Adaptation through our more purposefully evolved '*rational brains*' is more sensible than '*muddling through*'.

Put simply, most neither understand the phenomenon of global oligopoly, nor how to handle it. After absorbing this book, you will. Others may wander 'eyeless in Gaza'; you, I hope, will not.

About the author

Chris Carr is and has been a professor of corporate strategy at the University of Edinburgh Business School for just over 20 years. He has previously lectured at Warwick, where he took his Ph.D. in business policy, Aston, Buckingham, Bath, and Manchester Universities; as well as researching and teaching at overseas universities including Harvard Business School, Wright State, HEC, University of Carlos III, Witten Herdecke, Moscow State, St. Petersburg, Yekaterinburg, Tomsk, Zhejiang, Shenzhen, South West University of Finance and Economics, China Academy of Social Sciences, Sao Paulo, Inbec, Ahmadabad, Bangalore, Calcutta, Delhi, Hyderabad, Madras, Bilgi, and Thammasat.

Prior to this, he worked for over ten years, first with BAe Systems as a student apprentice whilst studying engineering and economics at Cambridge University and subsequently with GKN following a master's advanced course in product and process management at Cambridge. At GKN, he worked in process and product development at GKN Forgings, and then on international turnkey projects at GKN Contractors. He worked on the project management team establishing GKN's United States constant-velocity joint factories at Sandford and Raleigh, liaising with GKN Hardy Spicer and GKN's Uni-Cardan team in Germany. He then worked for GKN for 13 months in Iraq, liaising for the head office in Baghdad and serving as administrator and project engineer on one of the three construction sites in Diwaniya. At GKN, he obtained full professional membership of the Institution of Chartered Mechanical Engineers and of the Chartered Institute of Management Accountants and a diploma in management studies from the Northwest Regional Management Centre. Whilst at GKN, between 1977 and 1979, he also served as a local district councillor and governor of three schools in Bromsgrove, providing some experience of the public sector.

Between 1980 and 1985, Chris completed a doctorate in global strategy research focused on the worldwide automotive components industry at Warwick Business School and one year there as a half-time lecturer in business policy. Since then, he has lectured at several universities in Britain and worldwide and undertaken some consulting. He has published 3 books and some 40 articles in top academic journals including *Strategic Management Journal*, *Journal of Management Studies*, *Management International Review*, *Management Accounting Research*, *Long Range Planning*, *Sloan Management Review*, *International Journal of Human Relations Management*, and *Business History*.

Acknowledgments

For my global field research undertaken since October 1980, I owe special thanks to around 400 companies from 22 countries, and to those 94 companies who afforded repeat visits to establish some genuine longitudinal perspective: especially GKN, where I worked for nearly seven years, with its incredible 260-year history and continuing global successes. The combined wisdom on global strategies of all of these chief executives, distilled over well over 30 generations, is probably unparalleled. *Financial Times* articles, systematically mined since 1980, have proved invaluable. I gratefully acknowledge Andrew Lorenz, former editor at the *Sunday Times*, for allowing me to draw in Chapter 13 on his excellent history of GKN and also Edgar Jones for his superb archival GKN histories going back to 1759.

Besides the University of Edinburgh Business School (at which I have been Professor of Corporate Strategy for 20 years), colleagues, and students, I also owe thanks to the Universities of Cambridge, Manchester, Warwick, Bath, Buckingham, Witten Herdecke (Germany), Carlos IVth (Spain), Wright State (USA), Sao Paulo (Brazil), Bilgi (Turkey), Shenzhen (China), Zhejiang (China), and Moscow State (Russia) and HEC (France), IIMB (India), and particularly Dr Katja Kolehmainen (Alto), Dr Benedikt Schwittay (Manchester), Dr Rehan Ul Haq (Birmingham) and his students Lucia Suliana and Saed Zuraikat, and, most especially Professor David Collis and the Global Strategy Group at Harvard Business School (particularly in relation to Chapter 2).

I am indebted to colleagues and remarkably capable students from the University of Edinburgh. I would like to thank all my Edinburgh colleagues including, especially, Dr Ling Liu (in Chapter 11) and Dr Lucy Liu. This book could not have been written without outstanding doctoral and dissertation contributions from several of the brightest students I have taught over the last 35 years from all over the world, and particularly: Dr Alessa Witt for her wonderfully diligent doctoral work included in Chapter 8 comparing both Britain's and Germany's top global niche champions, Dr Benedikt Schwittay in Chapter 3, and the late and sadly missed Dr Christine Soh. Among my undergraduate and master's students, I gratefully acknowledge special contributions by Olivia

Mason (in Chapters 1 and 14), Euan Robertson (in Chapter 2), Hanne Leknes (in Chapter 5), Shengming Shao (in Chapter 4), Qianli Ma (in Chapter 6), Anais Auriau and Patricia Ramos (in Chapter 12), and Suzanne Livingston (in Appendix B). I have also learned enormously from many global sectors and from cross-cultural contexts scrupulously examined by other exceptionally able Edinburgh students, most especially: Sasiya Supprakit, Nora Weisskopf, Anna Lauring, Zoe Gallon, Sophie Reed, Gigi Ruan, Beate Holzmann, Emma Thomson, David McLeod, Elena Hansen (Witteman), Shannon Robertson, Andrej Babace, Ravikumaran Govender, Marina Mukhina, Yuko Ogara, Dorothy Wilkinson, Wasni Caraccio, Paul Brown, Christina Lund, Georg Krubasik, Esther Khor, Simon Hughes, Kine Kjaernet, James Shepherd, James Bennett, Damianos Bouklas, Victoria Feldman, Louise Karlander, Maria Salgado, Jie Dang, Patricio Montiel, Lisa Birnie, Sunil Bazzaz, Tze Pun, Cory Pansing, Marcos Sanfiz, Oi Yee Ann Tung, Jordon Mitchell, Diala Khamra, Anastasia Mitina, Tessa Dunham, and Gwilyn Satchell.

Aside from my own work, all these additional and substantial contributions have been supervised by me. So, like all authors, I must admit that all faults, errors, and mistakes are down to me. The ground we have covered together is enormous, so for any points at which this might have happened, I can only apologise in advance.

Finally, I would like to thank Terry Clague for taking a sustained interest in these studies for over a decade. He was instigatory in bringing this book to fruition with Routledge who, in turn, published my first book *Britain's Competitiveness: The Management of the Vehicle Components Industry* 30 years ago in 1990. I would also like to thank Ajanta Bhattacharjee and Dolarine Sonia Fonceca for handling quite so many complexities in finalising this new book, and Dr Narayan Kanimozhi helping earlier with this manuscript. Sally Stewart, formerly Dean of the University of Hong Kong, has been invaluable, both in relation to early and later stage drafts, in terms of advice and extensive proof-reading, where I must also acknowledge the help of Jeanne Baird and my wife Jenny Carr.

Introduction to Global Study

The focus in this book is on the phenomenon of global oligopolies, their associated strategies, moves and countermoves, and on consequent performance outcomes. My aim is to provide experience and research-based guidance for executives or business students interested in more effective global strategies. Should you go global? When? What orientations should you adopt? How should you go global? Can you go it alone establishing your own greenfield sites internationally, or should you use international cooperation as through cross-border mergers and acquisitions (M&A) or strategic alliances? What performance outcomes result from different international orientations? How does this vary by sector and global concentration levels? To draw out lessons, we need to know which strategies and orientations pan out best. Finally, what are the implications for society and policymakers?

As shown in Contents, Part I begins with three chapters mapping global sectoral concentrations, then analysing trends from a dynamic evolutionary perspective. Some basic theory of outcomes, in relation to the emergence of global winners, niche players, alliances, or more negative exits, is evidenced in Chapter 3 based on the global spirits industry. Global oligopoly plays and counter-plays emerged in this sector even when Global Concentric Ratio 4s (GCR4s) were little above 10%. Part II then analyses geographical spread and global strategic orientation choices and performance outcomes, primarily for global top 500 firms. The impact of such choices is illustrated and evidenced in the global retail fashion sector, including Zara's essentially stand-alone greenfield site approach. Part III focuses on more global cooperation modes (cross-border M&A and strategic alliances), their patterns, performance outcomes, and lessons. Chapter 8 then switches attention onto focus and niche strategies, particularly pertinent to "Mid-Cap" players. It draws on 15 highly successful German Mittelstand global players, matched against 15 comparably successful firms from Britain's more typical shareholder-value driven context. Part IV focuses on emerging market global players, with Chapters 10 and 11 highlighting those from India and China, then illustrating their overriding impact in domestic appliances. Part V focuses on sustaining global success, as firms turn to global restructuring and turnaround measures to survive inevitable vicissitudes of fortune. Chapter 13 explores more resilient global strategies extracting lessons from GKN's 260-year history. Part VI examines the political economy of global oligopolies, recent trends, and policy issues arising and summarises key conclusions.

SUMMARY OF INTERNATIONAL FIELD RESEARCH AND FUTURE DIRECTIONS

During the decade up to late 1980, I gained experience at BAe Systems and then at GKN in relation to technology, international project management, and internationalisation. With hindsight, GKN was arguably the most successful British player going fully global. My subsequent global field research has spanned 22 countries, 39 years, and 392 companies, not only in the vehicle and vehicle parts industry (designated Auto), but also in relation to typically top companies from roughly similar numbers of companies from an extensive range of miscellaneous sectors (designated Misc). Each contributed typically one major in-depth strategic investment decision case story, including strategic planning approaches, all key financials techniques, and comments on strategic decision-making processes and cross-cultural differences globally. This excludes several companies visited, but not formally interviewed on strategic decisions (Table I.1).

Global oligopolies are complex and rapidly evolving, but we now have the tools to analyse them. Several huge sectors have now been examined globally, often repeatedly, as tabulated (Table I.2). Coverage further extended to include more globally fragmented sectors, such as international construction, as well as family vs public companies worldwide summarised in Appendix B. These studies typically analyse international orientations of 50–100 of the largest players, incorporating performance outcomes analyses as already illustrated. We need longer-term performance databases, since it proves surprisingly difficult to sustain oligopolistic advantages over successive five-year time periods. What's needed next is even more service sector studies, since they have become increasingly vital to wealth creation. Generally global data here are poorer and global rivalry more fragmented.

Table I.1 Summary of field cases on global strategic investment decisions, 1980–2019

	UK	*Ge*	*USA*	*Jap*	*India*	*China*	*Rus*	*CEur*	*Brazil*	*RoW*	*Total*
1980/4 Auto	31	9	5	18							63
1989/1999 Auto	33	49	12	15	7	3	2	3		10	134
1989/1999 Misc	21	24	10	2	6	13	5	7		15	103
2000/2016 Auto	1		1		9	5			5		21
2000/2019 Misc	2				7	5	3		7	37	61
Total	88	82	28	35	29	26	10	10	12	62	392

Table I.2 Sector studies of global oligopolies undertaken, 2000–2019

Sector	*Sector*	*Sector*	*Sector*	*Sector*	*Sector*
Banks	Insurance	Investment banks	Management consulting	Network airlines	Low cost airlines
FMCG	Beauty	Chocolates	Retail fashion	Groceries	Spirits
Wine	Brewing	Pharmaceuticals	Chemicals	Telecoms	Mobile phones
ICT	Medical equipment	Cameras/film	Domestic appliances	Metal packaging	Container shipping
Construction	Contracting	Oil & gas	Oil & gas equipment	Aircraft	Aero defence
Trucks	Cars	Vehicle parts	Steel	Iron ore	Aluminium
Photovoltaic	Wind power				

This book cannot do justice to the sheer variety of approaches to nearly 400 global strategic decisions worldwide over so many year and so many countries. Analysis of 100 such strategic investment decision cases in Britain, Germany, the USA, then extended to Singapore and Russia, has explored cross-cultural[2] and finance and accounting aspects of such strategic investment decisions.[3] In the future, I plan a companion volume *Global Strategies and Practices Worldwide*. This requires final updating on international field research conducted far and wide, over such a long period, and some extension to key new regions such as Africa, Australia/New Zealand, and the Middle East where I gained much early international experience. From my apprenticeship years at BAe Systems, this journey and exploration has taken 50 years.

This book has prioritised economics, strategy, and numerical performance outcomes. But as our early project managers rightly reminded us, in a global world, experience on the ground internationally is gold dust. There is no substitute for getting out there, seeing what is happening, talking to people and recognising inevitable differences across countries and business contexts.

NOTES

1 *Fortune*, July 2017, Global 500. This is over $7 trillion in terms of my value-added estimates, compared with world economic output of $76 trillion, or say, Japan's at just under $5 trillion.

2 Carr, C. (2005). 'Are German, Japanese and Anglo-Saxon strategic styles still divergent?' *Journal of Management Studies*, 42 (6), pp. 1155–1188; Carr, C. and Soh, C. (2014). 'Singaporean strategic investment decision making practices: Is culture or context more important?' *Review of Integrative Business and Economics Research*, 3 (2), p. 31; Carr, C. (2006). 'Russian strategic investment decision practices compared with those of Great Britain, Germany, the United States and Japan: Diversity, convergence and short-termism', *International Studies, Management and Organization*, 36 (3), pp. 82–110. Pudelko, M., Reiche, S. and Carr, C. (2011). 'Why international strategy and cross-cultural management matters in business research and education', *Schmalenbach Business Review*, Special Issue on International Strategy and

Cross-Cultural Management, 3, pp. iv–x. Piekkari, R., Reich, S., Pudelko, M. and Carr, C. (2010). 'A meeting of minds? Insights from intersections between international strategy and cross-cultural management research', *Scandinavian Journal of Management*, 26 (3), pp. 233–235. Carr, C. and Bateman, S. (2010). 'Does culture count? Comparative performances of top family and non-family firms', *International Journal of Cross-Cultural Management*, 10 (2), pp. 241–262. Reiche, S., Pudelko, M. and Carr, C. (2010). 'The role of culture at different levels of analysis', *International Journal of Cross-Cultural Management*, 10 (2), pp. 131–136. Harris, S. and Carr, C. (2008). 'National cultural values and the purpose of business', *International Business Review*, 17, pp. 103–117. Carr, C., Pudelko, M. and Henley, J. (2006). 'Globalization and its effects on international strategy and cross-cultural management', *International Studies, Management and Organization*, 36 (3), pp. 3–8. Carr, C. and Pudelko, M. (2006). 'Convergence of national practices in strategy, finance and HRM between the USA, Japan and Germany', *International Journal of Cross Cultural Management*, 6 (1), pp. 75–100. Pudelko, M., Fink, G., Hinges, P. and Carr, C. (2006). 'The convergence concept in cross-cultural management research', *International Journal of Cross Cultural Management*, 6 (1), pp. 15–18. Harris, S. and Carr, C. (2004). 'The impact of diverse national values on strategic decisions in the context of globalisation', *International Journal of Cross Cultural Management*, 4 (1), pp. 77–99.

3 Carr, C., Kolehmainen, K. and Mitchell, F. (2010). 'Strategic investment decision making: A contextual approach', *Management Accounting Research*, 21 (3), pp. 167–184. Carr, C., Tomkins, C. and Bayliss, B. (1988). 'Context, culture and the role of the finance function in strategic decisions: A comparative analysis of Britain, Germany, the U.S.A. and Japan', *Management Accounting Research*, Special Edition on Culture and Management Accounting, 9 (23), pp. 213–239. Carr, C. and Tomkins, C. (1996). 'From NPV to strategic management accounting? Strategic investment decision by U.K., U.S. and German vehicle component companies', *Management Accounting Research*, 7 (2), pp. 199–217. Tomkins, C. and Carr, C. (1996). 'Strategic management accounting', *Management Accounting Research*, 7, pp. 165–167. Tomkins, C. and Carr, C. (1996). 'Reflections on the state of management accounting', *Management Accounting Research*, 7 (2), pp. 271–280. Carr, C. and Ng, J. (1995). 'Total cost control. Nissan and its UK supplier partnerships', *Management Accounting Research*, 6 (4), pp. 347–365. Carr, C., Tomkins, C. and Bayliss, B. (1994). 'Financial or strategic controls? An Anglo-German case study', *European Management Journal*, 12 (1), pp. 102–113.

Part I

GLOBAL OLIGOPOLIES, CONCENTRATION, AND CONSOLIDATION PROCESSES

1

GLOBAL CONCENTRATION, OLIGOPOLIES, PROFIT APPROPRIATIONS AND PERSPECTIVES

GLOBAL CONCENTRATION, OLIGOPOLIES AND CONCERNS

Most are aware of global oligopolies such as the big four FAAGs, Facebook, Apple, Amazon, and Google, of their power to appropriate almost 'winner-takes-all' value and profits, and of their impact on societies. Even Apple, the first company that surpassed $1 trillion in terms of its stock market capitalisation value, is not a global monopoly where a single seller controls the whole market. An oligopoly is rather where just a few sellers pre-dominate the market.[1] In mid-2018, in smartphones, for example, Apple was only number three globally, after having been overtaken by China's Huawei. The number one Samsung had earlier overtaken Nokia, now virtually gone, having once sold 40% of all mobile phones. Yet such global oligopolies, where more typically four or so players control 10% or even 40% of the entire world markets, have become extraordinarily pervasive. Pervasive, though somehow evading adequate frameworks or empirical research to explain their behaviours or how to survive or succeed under such conditions. This chapter, therefore, includes ruthless analyses of all 158 8-digit-General Industrial Classification System (GICS) sector classifications, and fully 30,000 large public companies worldwide.

We cannot evade concerns over concentration. The rising economic and political powers of giant companies have returned centre stage in terms of public policy concerns. Mergers and acquisitions numbers in recent years have been running at over twice the rates in the 1990s. The five largest banks account for 45% of banking assets, up from 25% in 2000. The share of nominal GDP generated by the Fortune 500 went up from 33% of the GDP in 1994 to 46% in 2013. The share of Americans who hold 'very' or 'mostly' favourable views on big business has fallen from 73% in 1999 to 40% today, according to the Pew Research Centre in 2016.[2]

Such United States (US) concerns are not new. US concentration happened at the turn of the twentieth century, following the rise of giant steel, oil, and retail companies. Despite the anti-trust Sherman Act of 1890, consolidations in no fewer than 72 sectors had created giants controlling at least 40% of their industries. In 42 sectors, they controlled over 70%.[3] Roosevelt's anti-trust backlash in 1910 reined this back. Later policies proved inconsistent. A blind eye was turned to flourishing US champions like GM, Ford, General Electric, Westinghouse, Coke, and IBM in the 1950s, 1960s, and 1970s. In the 1980s and 1990s, public regulators again stepped in, privatising and breaking up giants such as AT&T. Management gurus, such as Peter Drucker, followed economists like Ronald Coarse[4] into believing that markets were more efficient than hierarchies, implying that large companies had had their day.

New technologies were supposed to lower entry barriers, spurring start-ups. Yet, already, more firms have been dying than being born. '*The numbers of listed companies in America nearly halved between 1997 and 2013... Profit margins have increased in direct proportion to the concentration of the market*'.[5] New entrepreneurial giants like Apple, Google, and Amazon have proven even more predominant than big businesses in the past: their cash piles were equivalent to 10% of the US's GDP. Facebook's market capitalisation per employee in 2016 was $20.5 million compared with $230,000 at General Motors and, from almost nowhere 20 years ago, the big four FAAGs, including Facebook, Apple, Amazon, and Google, have generated $23 billion of wealth, transforming all our lives.[6]

In the 4 years to 2017, the FAAG increased in value by some $1.3 trillion, or roughly Russia's GDP. In 2006, the largest five world corporations had been ExxonMobil, GE, Microsoft, Citigroup, then Bank of America, their market capitalisations totalling $2 trillion. In 2017, they were the FAAG with Microsoft squeezed in the middle, totalling $2.7 trillion.[7] New iconoclastic oligopolistic challengers are coming, not only from America (Tesla, Uber, LinkedIn, Airbnb), but also from emerging champions (Chapters 9–11). By 2016, Alibaba, for example, had surpassed Walmart, becoming the world's largest retailer with revenues of $485 billion: with just 20% of its revenues outside China, it had scarcely stretched its muscles globally.[8]

America's Department of Justice responded, blocking over twice as many deals as under George W. Bush. In 2017, US Senate Democrats pledged to make America competitive again, recognising that more than three quarters of its industries were more concentrated at home than two decades earlier. Averaged US Herfindahl indices rose between 1985 and 2016 as entry, exit, and investment rates declined and '*American consumers would have gained $65bn a year if they paid the same as Germans do now for mobile-phone contracts*'.[9] Even before President Trump's tax cuts, US corporate profits overall were higher in 2017 than at any point since 1929.[10] David Autor and colleagues at MIT found that '*superstar firms paid less of their profits in wages. As these firms have* *grown in importance, labour's overall share of GDP has fallen*'. The Economist found in 2016 that '*two-thirds of American industries became more concentrated in the 2000s*', concurring that consumers had suffered whilst corporate profits have jumped; and, in mid-2018, they found that in the previous ten years, 55% of Britain's sectors had similarly increased in concentration.[11]

Of even greater concern has been global concentration. Big corporations faced political backlashes triggered by anger at low-taxes/tax inversions and anti-austerity/anti-globalisation/anti-establishment/anti-trade movements. About 30% of global Foreign Direct Investment (FDI) flows passed through tax havens, encouraging transfer pricing and short-term profit manipulation.[12] Just over half of 1000 executives, surveyed worldwide, felt under pressure to deliver financial results within a year or less.[13]

According to McKinsey in 2016, 10% of the world's public companies generated 80% of all profits. Firms with more than $1bn revenue accounted for nearly 60% of total global revenues and 65% of market capitalisation. M&A were equivalent to about 3% of global GDP compared with 2% in 1990.[14] Firms with over 250 employees accounted for over half of value-added in every country monitored by the Organization for Economic Cooperation and Development (OECD).[15] In the USA, large companies created 58% of total employment; in Japan 47%; in the United Kingdom (UK) 46%; and in Germany 36%.[16]

Even US regulators though proved relatively powerless in the face of global oligopoly plays. They waived through, for example, Anheuser-Busch InBev's $107 billion acquisition of SABMiller. For the top 100 spenders, lobbying expenditure nearly doubled between 1998 and 2012.[17] A backlash seems likely, though arguably what is needed are global agreements or global regulators, the latter being merely national or regional. The issue is no longer just the USA. There are 156 of *Fortune*'s Top Global 500 that are now (like InBev) Emerging Market Champions, compared with 18 in 1995: McKinsey expects this number to rise to 45% by 2025.[18]

The traditional economist's adage that '*you don't need to open the box*', sullying your hands with what individual businesses do, looks antiquated. This held validity under Adam Smith's 1759 conditions of perfect competition, characterised by so many firms that single ones mattered little. Yet Marxist presumptions and prescriptions also appear antiquated. Monopolistic firms, whether working for the state or anybody else, degenerated into moribund, inefficient, unresponsive Leviathans, unable to compete against dynamic worldwide rivals. Not even Russia is considering reverting to old-style Soviet planning. Oligopolists like Rusal ripped up such former business models to compete on global markets.[19] Putin harshly re-emphasised political aims, including imperialism, but even he deferred from re-introducing state planning and re-instated Kudrin's economic pragmatism.

What we need to understand are global oligopolies, though not just those well-known big four FAAGs. The global top 500, further analysed in

Chapter 6, combined revenues of $28 trillion in 2016[20] (over $7 trillion in terms of my value-added estimates) compared with Japan at just under $5 trillion. Analysing the world's top 30,000 – that 'hidden economic continent' which enjoyed turnovers in 2016 of over $50 trillion – suggests their combined value-added was over $13 trillion, compared with the USA at $19 trillion, and the entire global economy at $76 trillion.

GLOBAL PROFITS FINDINGS

We analysed the entire global profits pool of the world's 30,000 large public corporations[21]. By ranking all 30,000 companies on Thomson One Banker by total earnings for all 6 years 2011–2016, just the top 10% took 87% of total earnings before tax and interest (EBIT) of all 30,000 major public companies worldwide.[22] The top 1% took 49%, ranging in individual years from 46% to 51%. Such global profit pool concentration has been stable, way beyond expectations from classic 80:20 patterns. Not to be in that top 1% ranking, is to be out of half of all such global profits.

The top 10% in terms of these 6-year total EBIT profit rankings accounted for 75% of all global sales in 2016.[23] They accounted for 86% of total assets, 78% of total research and development (R&D) expenditure, 76% of all capital expenditure, 74% of all sales and general administration expenses (a proxy for marketing expenditure), and 68% of all employment. Just the top 1% took 32% of all sales in 2016.[24] They accounted for 55% of total assets, 41% of total R&D expenditure, 33% of all capital expenditure, 31% of all sales and general administration expenses, and 23% of all employment. Ignore such global concentration impacts, and economic analyses risk irrelevance.

Global oligopolies, mapped and analysed further later in this book, have grown, extending to most major sectors, spawning yet more numerous subtler global niche oligopolies that are scrutinised in Chapter 8. The age of global oligopolies has arrived.

IN SEARCH OF GLOBAL OLIGOPOLY POWER: THE CHOICE OF MORE ATTRACTIVE SECTORS

From a dynamic Schumpeterian perspective, though, enduring oligopoly power is not so easy. Consider sectors sustaining greatest profitability, averaging all 6 years 2011–2016. All 158 8-digit-GICS sector classifications were analysed, using Thomson One Banker's data accessed in May 2017, focusing on the largest top 20 in each sector. Their averaged returns on capital employed (RoCE) for 2011–2016 were compared with averages for all 30,000 public companies' RoCEs.[25] As shown in Table 1.1, tobacco, household products, and retail clothing proved most profitable during 2011–2016.

Table 1.1 Most profitable sectors on 2011–2016 average RoCE, as %s of the average for all 30,000 firms worldwide

Sector	*Average RoCE T20/All*
Tobacco	458[a]
Household products	390
Apparel retail	372
Financial exchanges & data	312
Apparel, accessories & luxury goods	306
Data processing & outsourced services	303
IT consulting & other services	301
Home furnishing retail	295
Personal products	286
Automotive retail	269

Note

a i.e., tobacco is 4.57 × that average 30,000 firm figure. Sectors are here defined by the US GICS at the 8-digit level: being more refined than 4-digit standard industrial classifications (SICs). Data were from Thomson One Banker, accessed May 2017. RoCEs were calculated by dividing EBIT by capital employed, taken as total assets minus short-term liabilities. Sector figures based on top 20 only, but comparisons were taken against all 30,000 company averages. Again, I acknowledge gratefully the contribution of Olivia Mason who helped enormously with my analysis of these Thomson One Banker data sets on these tables/figures.

Economic theories of market structure, conduct, and performance emphasise traditional entry barriers, explored by Bain and Porter. Yet high levels of fixed asset formation (even including intangibles such as 'goodwill'), afforded only limited explanation. As in early studies conducted by Profit Impact of Market Strategies (PIMS), we found capital intensity per se often reduces sector profitability (Figure 1.1). As PIMS suggested, margins may not rise

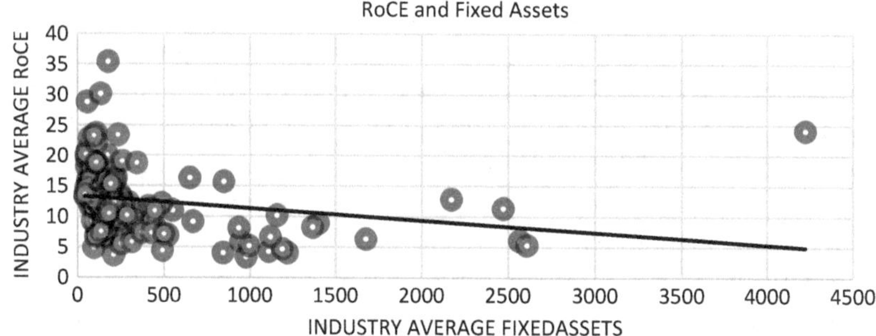

Figure 1.1 Relationship between sector RoCE 2011–2016 averages and their averaged fixed assets/sales ratios in 2016. RoCEs were calculated by dividing EBIT by capital employed, taken as total assets minus short-term liabilities. Sector figures are based on top 20 companies only.

sufficiently to allow better returns on capital, because high capital intensities incentivise vigorous rivalry – even variable-cost pricing aimed at ensuring high capital utilisation levels. Such intense rivalry is consistent with Adam Smith's classical economics perspective.

We also investigated the impact of global concentration, taking the cumulative sales shares of just the top 3 players, divided by those for all top 20 players, as initial crude surrogates for sector concentration levels. This suggested a positive relationship between higher concentration levels and profitability, though less pronounced and consistent, than expected based on traditional economic structure/performance theories.[26]

We re-checked sector 5-year RoCE rankings by re-running the analysis independently for an earlier 5-year period 2002–2006. None of these top-ranked sectors had been able to sustain such exceptionally high profitability in both 5-year periods. Thus, whilst Porter's '*Five Forces*' analysis places great emphasis on companies' sector choices, it may be that sector traits, per se, only rarely provide truly sustainable oligopolistic premiums.[27] Global success is not merely a matter of finding soft sectors where you can exploit higher profit premiums.

Whilst good news for consumers, this implies shareholders and executives must search further for more sustainable competitive advantages; pertinent metrics and benchmarking exercises need to be global; and few sectors exhibited gentle equilibria. As Keynes argued in his *General Theory*,[28] disequilibrium is the general case, not the exception. The oligopolistic challenge is global, dynamic, and Schumpeterian; rarely is it a matter of just higher prices, secured by collusion in naturally favoured sectors.

GLOBAL PROFIT POOLS FOR ALL GLOBAL TOP 4 LEADERS COMPREHENSIVELY

Global oligopolists' ability to dominate profits in their sectors varied according to a sector's level of concentration. The global concentration ratio 4 (GCR4) measures the cumulative global market shares of the top 4 players in each sector. Strictly, this can only be achieved adequately using high quality global market reports, as done later in this book; if not diversification, and family firms (analysed in Appendix B) become problematic. However, not all sectors afford such data, and global market research reports cannot extend to all 30,000 players analysed, so the aim first is to provide an extensive global overview.

Proxy global market shares were estimated by comparing revenues for all players with all other sector participants' total revenues taken together. A sector's GCR4 is then just the top 4 market shares added together, or we could take the sum of the squares of all players' global market shares to provide a similar proxy for global Herfindahl indices. We caution that basing global CR4s on just the top 30,000 companies risks overstating more accurate figures based on more precise market definitions. As compared with the next

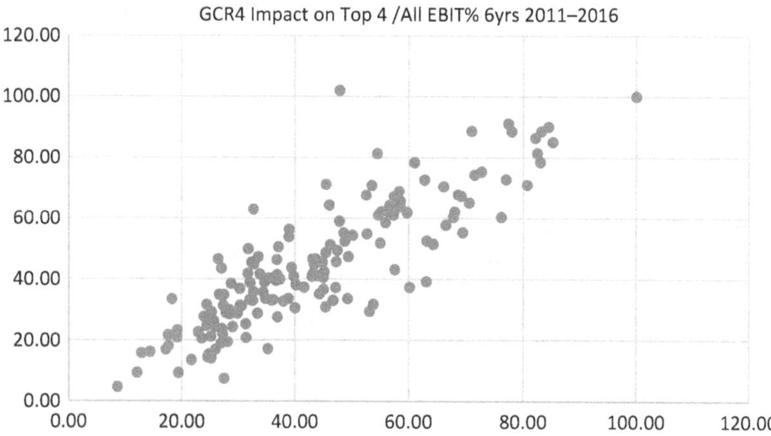

Figure 1.2 Global concentration level impact on global top 4 %s of all EBITs, 2011–2016. The GCR4 is again the cumulative share of the top 4 companies' sales divided by total sales. Please note that, in this case, sales of just the top 20 companies are taken as an extremely crude proxy for the global market: i.e., sales of the top 4/sales of the top 20. EBITs, sourced from Thomson One Banker (accessed May 2017), are averaged for all 6 years. The T4% is the averaged 6-year EBIT for all four top companies (in terms of 2016 sales values) divided by the same set of figures for all companies in the same GICS.

chapter, we are dealing with cruder GCR4 proxies.[29] Figure 1.2 investigates the impact of these (proxy) GCR4s on the ability of all four top players to appropriate disproportionate 2011–2016 EBIT profits in their given sectors. Re-checking these for just 2014–2016, the distribution was similar.

Based on such proxy GCR4s, 79 of all 158 GICS (based on 8-digit codes) corresponded to levels of 40% or above. A CR4 of 40%, even in just the US market was regarded by American economists such as Scherer as the point of unquestionable oligopoly – the point at which major players could no longer simply ignore each other's moves and countermoves – and at which greater tacit collusion was more likely. The difference in our studies is that we define markets globally. As markets globalise, they become more pre-dominated by emerging markets representing billions of new customers. Global market domination and GCR4s over 40% represents a challenge of a far higher order, so these represent extraordinary levels of concentration. Figure 1.2 highlights GCR4s as key determinants of profit pool appropriations.

Table 1.2 then sub-divides sectors into those with GCRs above 40%, those below 25%, and those in between. Only 12% of all 158 sectors displayed GCR4 levels below 25%. There remained numerous local sectors, such as utilities and local services, but, otherwise, the world of larger businesses has become highly globally concentrated.

Most remarkable was the emergence of a rough '4/40%' rule. On average, for every one of these key metrics, the top 4 companies globally controlled

Table 1.2 Global concentration drivers and EBIT profit pool impacts, 2014–2016 and 2011–2016

	Sector Nos	*1K/n Ind*	*T4/All SGA%*	*T4/All CX%*	*T4/All R&D%*	*T4/All Int%*	*T4/All 3-Yr EBIT%*	*T4/All% 6-YrEBIT*
Av GCR > 40%	79	29.3	53.4	52.3	53.1	64.5	58.4	58.8
Av 25%–40%	60	7.0	28.2	28.0	37.7	38.4	34.0	34.2
Av GCR < 25%	19	3.7	19.7	19.7	22.0	26.6	19.0	18.9
Av all	158	17.8	40.0	39.1	43.5	49.6	44.4	44.7

Note: The GCR4 is again the cumulative share of the top 4 companies' sales divided by total sales. Please note that, in this case, sales of just the top 20 companies are taken as an extremely crude proxy for the global market: i.e., sales of the top 4/sales of the top 20. EBITs, sourced from Thomson One Banker (accessed May 2017), are averaged, respectively, for all 3 and 6 years. The T4/All% is the averaged 3- or 6-year EBIT for all four top companies (in terms of 2016 sales values) divided by the same set of figures for all companies in the same GICS. T4/All% for sales and general administration (SGA) expenditures, though, show totals in just 2016 for top 4 companies divided by that for all companies in the same GICS sector. Akin to profit pool shares, this ratio examines top 4 player's shares of all SGA expenditures carried out in 2016. Likewise, we analysed and display capital expenditure (CX), R&D (research and development) expenditures, and international sales %s, as metrics illustrating their domination of these key drivers. 1 K/n is a cruder measure of concentration, dividing 1000 by the number of companies in the sector.

roughly 40% of everything related to their sector. They controlled 40% of all three key entry barriers, capital investments, R&D, and marketing expenditures. The top 4 also controlled half of all international sales. Correspondingly, they appropriated almost 45% of all EBIT profits, whether we take 2014–2016 or 2011–2016. We must strongly caution, though, that by taking Top 20 sales as a first crude proxy for the global market, this could exaggerate aggregation by at least 20%.

For those 79 sectors with higher global GCR4 concentration levels above 40%, constituting half of all sectors, this appropriation increased. Top 4 shares of key entry barrier investments increased to over 50%, and shares of profit pools correspondingly increased to just under 60%. Conversely, for that minority of 19 sectors with GCR4s below 25%, the appropriation effect weakened. Shares of both entry barrier investments and of profit pools reverted to around 20%. For our top half of more global sectors, the '4/40%' rule shifted to a '4/60%'; vs a '4/20%' rule for less global sectors where GCR4s averaged under 25%.

Given the interconnectedness of these variables, Table 1.3's left hand column analyses correlations suggesting key global CR4s drivers. Achieving high international sales was more important for high GCR4 sectors. But what mattered even more were investments in sales, and general administration (SGA), reflecting marketing and branding efforts. Capital expenditure correlations were the next strongest, followed by R&D investment correlations. Relationships appeared more pronounced in more global sectors. Sales revenue, per se, reflecting size, mattered less (exhibiting a correlation of 0.26), proving inconsistent at different concentration levels. We also checked out a weaker alternative concentration metric '1K/n', being 1000/number of companies in

Table 1.3 Global CR4 correlations with key drivers and EBIT profit impact, 2014–2016 and 2011–2016

Sector	*CR4%*	*T4/A Int%*	*T4/A R&D%*	*T4/A CX%*	*T4/A SGA%*	*T4/All 3 Yr*	*T4/All 6 Yr*
Count	158	149	110	158	156	158	158
Sum	6868	7397	4790	6181	6244	7017	7056
Average	43.5	49.6	43.6	39.1	40.0	44.4	44.7
Count top 10%	16	15	11	16	16	16	16
Sum top 10%	1211	1239	689	1119	1124	1352	1363
Average top 10%	75.7	82.6	62.6	70.0	70.3	85	85
Count bottom 10%	16	15	9	16	14	16	16
Sum bottom 10%	342	379	120	267	303	219	226
Av. Bottom 10%	21.4	25.2	13.4	16.7	21.7	13.7	14.1
Correl T6% vs Sales	0.26					0.20	0.20
Correl T6% vs R&D	0.41					0.46	0.45
Correl T6% vs CX	0.76					0.72	0.73
Correl T6% vs SGA	0.83					0.74	0.74
Correl T6% vs Int	0.75					0.63	0.64
Correl T6% vs CR4						0.86	0.86

Note: The GCR4 is again the cumulative share of the top 4 companies' sales divided by total sales. Please note that, in this case, sales of just the top 20 companies are taken as an extremely crude proxy for the global market: i.e., sales of the top 4/sales of the top 20. EBITs, sourced from Thomson One Banker (accessed May 2017), are averaged, respectively, for all 3 and 6 years. The (T4/All)% is the averaged 3- or 6-year EBIT for all four top companies (in terms of 2016 sales values) divided by these same figures for all companies in the same GICS sector.

sector. Unsurprisingly, this correlates positively with a GCR4 at 0.33. It likewise correlated positively with both 3- and 6-year profit pool %s, at roughly 0.27, and appeared to be a less useful explanatory variable than the GCR4.

Once achieved, high global CR4s seemingly enabled oligopolists to appropriate high 3- or 6-year profit pool shares, shown in the final two columns. The same key drivers determined how far they could do this: sales and general administration (SGA), capital expenditure, international sales, R&D, and finally some weaker size effect. This effect was more pronounced in more global sectors. Table 1.3 also contrasts top and bottom decile sectors: i.e., those sectors where appropriations were highest vs those where they were lowest. The top 10% of successful appropriators were in sectors averaging 75% GCR4 concentration levels. The same drivers such as marketing expenditures etc. again proved critical. And top 4s succeeded, on average, in appropriating 85% of all global 3- or 6-year EBIT profits. For top decile sectors, the '4/40%' rule became '4/85'! For weakest decile appropriators, which averaged only 20% GCR4 concentration levels, the '4/40%' rule deteriorated to a far less exciting '4/14'.

More reliable statistical correlations were strongest for GCR4s over 40%, but weakest during the transition between 25% and 40%. In highly concentrated, appropriating, sectors, these top 4 positions seemed strategically crucial. Global top 4s's international sales represented just over 50% of their total sales. The average EBIT/Sales (RoS) %s of top 4 leaders has been consistent in both recent 3- and 6-year periods to 2016 at just over 14%. Their international sales ratios averaged just over 50%, their R&D ratios 4%, and their SGA just under 20%.

TRAITS OF GLOBAL TOP 4s: ANALYSIS BY MAIN COUNTRIES OF OWNERSHIP

Given that top 4 sector leaders accounted for, on average, 40% of both sales and profit pools (or 60% for more concentrated sectors), Table 1.4 analyses appropriations by their countries of origin. Just three regions

Table 1.4 Global top 4s' % of all sales, international sales, R&D, and SGA expenditures in 2016 and of all EBIT profits 2011–2016, region and country analyses

	% Sales	*%6y EBITs*	*% of R&D*	*% of SGA*	*% of IntSales*	*% of all T4s*	*%GDPs/Gl*
Global	100.00	100.00	100.00	100.00	100.00	100.00	100.00
USA	41.19	45.97	54.04	35.96	28.34	39.78	24.62
Japan	12.39	5.45	14.05	14.88	12.15	13.10	6.53
China	9.37	16.93	3.16	7.31	2.41	7.83	14.83
UK	5.87	1.35	0.84	7.12	9.12	5.27	3.50
Germany	8.11	5.71	8.33	7.24	13.77	5.27	6.53
France	3.80	6.25	1.52	4.07	5.59	3.51	3.26
Switzerland	2.21	3.12	4.61	1.62	3.98	2.24	0.88
Canada	0.85	1.12	0.00	1.12	1.64	1.92	2.02
Australia	0.59	0.06	0.04	1.27	1.21	1.76	1.72
S. Korea	1.95	0.18	2.31	2.97	2.09	1.44	1.87
India	0.57	0.71	0.08	0.65	0.41	1.44	2.99
Cayman Isl.	0.77	0.60	1.44	0.82	0.18	1.44	0.00
Ireland	0.89	0.92	1.28	0.45	1.45	1.12	0.33
Hong Kong	1.22	2.21	0.07	3.51	0.77	1.12	0.36
Netherlands	2.75	1.21	2.75	2.84	4.00	0.96	1.03
Taiwan	1.14	0.81	1.25	1.13	2.55	0.80	0.77
Spain	0.32	0.46	0.30	0.50	0.56	0.80	1.64
Brazil	0.46	0.18	0.01	0.32	0.55	0.80	2.37
Bermuda	0.35	0.23	0.05	0.78	0.89	0.80	0.01
All above	94.79	93.46	96.12	94.56	91.66	91.37	75.25
Big 6 above	80.72	81.67	81.94	76.58	71.38	74.76	59.26
Big 3 above	62.94	68.35	71.25	58.15	42.90	60.70	45.97

Note: EBITs, sourced from Thomson One Banker (accessed May 2017), are again averaged for all 6 years. R&D and SGA total expenditures for all top 4 companies are analysed by country of ownership. GDPs/Gl% represents nominal countries' gross domestic products divided by total world GDPs, based on 2016 from *The Economist's Pocket World in Figures*, 2018.

(the USA, Japan, and China, accounting for 60% of nominal world GDPs in 2016) took two thirds of such appropriations. Six countries, adding the UK, Germany, and France (accounting for 75% of world GDP), took 80%. Global sales and profit pools were thus concentrated in the hands of global top 4 sector leaders, coming from just these six countries. In Chapter 14, Tables 14.1 and 14.2 analyse these national and regional appropriations further (adding wages and salaries) to bring out the value-added contributions of such leading corporations' global strategies to the wealth of nations in the twenty-first century.

WAS IT EVER SO? ANALYSIS OF GLOBAL OLIGOPOLIES AND OUTCOMES 2006–2010

Table 1.5 analyses 154 sectors allowing data for five earlier years up to 2010, drawing on Thomson's less extensive database of only 15,000 companies over this period. A smaller database risked overestimating the average GCR4 global concentration ratio at 53% in 2010, as compared with the 2016 figure of 43%. However, the share of the top 4s in total profits of sectors at 55% was probably slightly higher as compared with the 2016 figure of 45%.

This earlier less extensive Thomson data also provided additional 5-year sales growth and total investor returns (TiRs), being share price appreciations plus dividend yields. Table 1.6 also compares the relative performance of the top 4 companies as a % of the averaged performances of all companies within the same sector, whilst providing metrics for expenditures on R&D, capital expenditure (CapX), SGA, and for foreign sales (FSs) ratios. Thus, 100 corresponds to performances or expenditure %s on par with sector averages. This shows that Return on Invested Capital (RoIC)s were over 80% higher than sector averages, though at the slight expense of growth in terms of sales and particularly Total Investor Returns (TiRs). International sales ratios were over three times greater than average peers. R&D% levels were also three times higher, but, surprisingly, CapX%s were little different, and SGA%s were lower. Their main advantages again reflected global market shares and scale.

Coming down to only 15,000 companies earlier included far fewer Chinese and Asian companies, distorting geographical trends suggested by Table 1.6. With this reservation, just four big countries (the USA, Japan, France, and Switzerland) again accounted for around half of global sales and profits. Overall, high global concentration and appropriations, in terms of companies and of their countries of origin, have persisted over both 5-year periods.

Table 1.5 Global top 4s' average shares and relative performance metrics, 2006–2010

Sectors	*Nos*	*1K/n*	*GCR4*	*PFT4/All*	*RoIC5*	*SGrth5y*	*TiR 5*	*R&D*	*CapX*	*SGA*	*FS/S%*
Averages	154	20	52.8	54.9	187	94	78	284	104	88	363
Av > 40%	106	23	61.0	52.2	202	109	64	309	112	87	360
25–40	40	11	35.2	61.4	151	59	192	193	85	91	362
Av < 25	5	3	19.8	76.8	115	71	−538	504	49	96	188
Av > 50	72	28	68.7	46.4	202	115	119	275	132	93	340
Av > 60	54	32	73.4	45.5	206	84	74	285	120	101	340

Notes: Nos capped to + or – 1000.

Results show shares of top 4s in totals for all 15,000 cos.

PFT = earnings before interest and tax and GCR4 = share of global sales. Performance metrics are shown here as % of sector averages.

The GCR4 is again the cumulative share of the top 4 companies' sales divided by total sales. Please note that, in this case, sales of just the top 20 companies are taken as an extremely crude proxy for the global market: i.e., sales of the top 4/sales of the top 20. EBITs, sourced from Thomson One Banker (accessed May 2017), are averaged for all 6 years. The % (T4/All) is the averaged 6-year EBIT for all four top companies (in terms of 2016 sales values) divided by the same set of figures for all companies in the same GICS. 1K/n is simply 1000 divided by the numbers (Nos) of companies in any given sector, affording a weaker alternative global concentration metric. RoCEs were calculated by dividing EBIT by capital employed, taken as total assets minus short-term liabilities. They were then averaged for all 6 years and compared with averages for all companies' figures. Thus, 100 represents an average performance. 200 represents twice sector average performance metrics. Sales growth (SGrth) represent 5-year sales growth performances against sector pars, providing a proxy also for changes in global market shares. TiRs likewise show performances against sector pars: being increases in share prices plus dividend yields again over 5 years. R&D, CapX, and SGAs likewise benchmark research and development, capital, and sales and general administration expenditure ratios, again as compared with sector pars. FS/S is foreign sales to sales ratios, compared against sector pars.

Table 1.6 Global top 4s' averages for 154 sectors in 2006–2010 by top 4 countries of ownership

Sec Res	*Nos*	*No %*	*1K/n*	*GCR4*	*PRFT4/All*	*GDP%Wld*
Averages	154	100	19.7	52.8	54.9	100
USA	88	57	19.3	53.3	48.8	23
JAP	25	16	25.9	53.7	64.4	9
FR + CHE	14	9	21.3	54.4	55.2	5
BIG 4	127	82	20.8	53.5	52.6	37

Note: PRFT4 are the total EBITs, sourced from Thomson One Banker (accessed May 2017), which are again averaged for all 6 years, as a % of the same figures for all companies in the same sector. R&D and SGA total expenditures for all top 4 companies are analysed by country of ownership. Global refers to all T4 countries. GDPs/Gl% represents nominal countries' gross domestic products divided by total world GDPs, based on *The Economist's Pocket World in Figures*. The GCR4 is the cumulative share of the top 4 companies' sales divided by total sales. Please note that, in this case, sales of just the top 20 companies are taken as an extremely crude proxy for the global market: i.e., sales of the top 4/sales of the top 20. Sectors are based on the same GICSs. CHE is Switzerland.

IN SEARCH OF GLOBAL OLIGOPOLY POWER: HAS THE RULE OF 3 APPLIED GLOBALLY?

The '*Rule of 3*', derived from Sheth and Sisodia's research in the USA,[30] predicts that the top 3 players will outperform those next highest players, '*caught in the ditch*' between dominant oligopolists and much smaller niche players still able to make good returns, though making less overall impact. We, though, in line with companies such as GE, apply this rule globally since in most sectors the locus of rivalry has extended well beyond the USA. Table 1.7 compares 5-year RoCEs of just sector top 3 players with their sector averages, comparing them with just the top 20 players in each case.[31] With profit pool analyses, it makes sense to use data from all participants since smaller player data will not distort their overall impacts; with unweighted ratios such as RoCEs, this can be problematic.

Top 3 players in the marine sector were making RoCEs four times higher than other significant players in their sector, confirming some *Rule of Three* effect at the global level. Searching for more enduring evidence of superior leader performance, we repeated the same analysis for a much earlier 5-years 2002–2006. Just three sector industries retained their positions in the top 10 in both 5-year time periods: alternative carriers, communications equipment, and semiconductors. In terms of Boston Consulting Group (BCG)'s '*Environmental Matrix*', these would appear to be '*volume*' sectors where economies of scale underpin *Rule of Three* effects. Alternative carriers and communications equipment sectors also exhibit network externalities, commonly associated with winner-takes-all effects since offerings require compatibility. Sustaining relatively higher performances has proved feasible in relatively few sectors.

Table 1.7 Sectors where global top 3/global top 20 RoCEs 2011–2016 were highest, T3/T20 %s

Industry	*T3/T20 (%)*
Marine	408
Motorcycle manufacturers	384
Technology hardware, storage & peripherals	223
Alternative carriers	221
Communications equipment	212
Diversified real estate activities	210
Airlines	203
Commodity chemicals	181
Semiconductors	177
Systems software	174

Note: Sectors are here defined by the US GICS at the 8-digit level: being more refined than 4-digit SICs. Data were from Thomson One Banker, accessed May 2017. RoCEs were calculated by dividing EBITs by capital employed, taken as total assets minus short-term liabilities. T3/T20s show the ratio of top 3 companies' averaged results over all 6 years to that for the top 20 players in total. Thus, 408 implies that top 3 companies in the marine sector made just over 4× the RoCEs achieved by the full top 20 in that same sector.

Table 1.8 Sectors where global top 3/global top 20 RoCEs 2011–2016 were lowest, T3/T20 %s

Industry	*T3/T20 (%)*
Home entertainment software	55
Aluminium	55
Industrial REITs	55
Industrial machinery	54
Other diversified financial services	54
Trading companies & distributors	51
Thrifts & mortgage finance	35
Investment banking & brokerage	34
Department stores	22
Life & health insurance	−304

Note: Ibid.

Table 1.8 highlights many contrasting sectors where leaders became '*oligopolistic losers*', by achieving far lower than average 5-year Returns on Capital Employed (RoCE)s. Often these exhibited traits associated with BCG's '*fragmented*' sectors, as in numerous services and niches like home entertainment software, reducing scale economies or raising logistical costs (as in aluminium). Repeating this analysis for the much earlier 5-year period 2002–2006, we found no sector where such poor performance was sustained twice. Earlier movies and entertainment and biotechnology had proved appallingly unprofitable for oligopolistic leaders, but lower 5-year RoCEs may still have been a price worth paying for future returns.

Do sectors with higher international sales ratios allow global top 3 players to achieve superior 5-year RoCEs? Statistical correlations suggested an inconsistent, slightly positive linear relationship between the average profitability of the top 3/top 20 and averaged sector international sales ratios. More global sectors have, perhaps unsurprisingly, on average, shown relatively, slightly higher RoCEs for the top 3 players.

GLOBAL PROFIT POOLS FOR TOP 3 LEADERS NOW AND INTO THE FUTURE

Examining global oligopolies, profit pool appropriations can prove even more insightful than RoCEs.[32] Provided profitability remains above costs of capital, profit pool analysis yields evidence of the top players' ability to dominate markets commercially. Profit pool splits can also be compared directly with market capitalisation splits, which are effectively the stock market's view of discounted future oligopolistic profit expectations. Table 1.9 highlights that marine, technology hardware, storage, and peripherals sectors (having yielded higher RoCEs) afforded top 3 leaders the highest shares of '*profit pools*'.

Table 1.10 compares findings based on market capitalisation appropriations. Such future-orientated appropriation metrics were lower, presumably reflecting market scepticism about oligopolists' ability to sustain high

Table 1.9 Sectors where global top 3 players achieved highest % of global top 20 total EBITDA profit pools, 2011–2016 T3/T20 %s

Industry	*T3/T20 (%)*
Marine	97
Systems software	90
Home improvement retail	89
Diversified capital markets	86
Drug retail	86
Agricultural & farm machinery	84
Thrifts & mortgage finance	82
Technology hardware, storage & peripherals	78
Housewares & specialties	76
Insurance brokers	76

Note: Sectors are here defined by the US GICS at the 8-digit level: being more refined than 4-digit SICs. Data were from Thomson One Banker, accessed May 2017. T3/T20 %s show the ratio of top 3 total EBITs for all 6 years divided by the total figures for all 20 companies.

Table 1.10 Sectors where global top 3 players held the highest %s of total global top 20 company market capitalisations in 2016, T3/T20 %s

Industry	*T3/T20 %s*
Internet software & services	69
Home improvement retail	63
Commodity chemicals	55
Hypermarkets & super centres	53
Technology hardware, storage & peripherals	51
Marine	49
Communications equipment	44
Fertilisers & agricultural chemicals	39
Personal products	39
Apparel retail	35

Note: Sectors are here defined by the US GICS at the 8-digit level: being more refined than 4-digit SICs. Data were from Thomson One Banker, accessed May 2017. T3/T20 %s show the ratio of top 3 total market capitalisations as divided by those of all 20 top companies in their same sectors.

levels of profit appropriation. Internet software and services ranked highest, results proving consistent with earnings before interest, tax and depreciation (EBITDA) share rankings. Marine, home improvement retail, technology, hardware, storage, and peripherals emerged as sectors where top 3 leaders dominated current and future expected profit pools.

APPROPRIATIONS FOR TOP OLIGOPOLISTS' OVERALL AND PERFORMANCE OUTCOMES GLOBALLY

Table 1.11 shows that top 4 companies, in their respective sectors, consistently appropriated roughly 35% of all global sales and EBIT profit pools of all top 30,000 companies analysed. In 2016, they also accounted for 33% of all employment; 44% of all international sales; and 44% of all value added (comprising 'employee salaries' and 'gross profits').

Table 1.12 shows that top 4 companies achieved such shares of sales, profits, and value-added, through commensurate investments in R&D, SGA expenses, and intangibles, all at over 40%, as well as broader capital expenditures and capital employed, at around 30%. This endorses Haskel and Westlake's argument on the increasing importance of the 'intangible economy', and of associated metrics, relating to technology and brands for which R&D and SGAs are proxies.[33]

In terms of 6-year returns on capital employed and returns on sales, shown in Table 1.13, leading top No 1s typically outperformed No 2s, No 3s, and No 4s, but were (all four) lower than other top 20 companies. On 6-year sales growth, all top 4 players were well outperformed by smaller companies.

Table 1.11 Appropriation of sales, EBIT profit pools, salaries, gross income, value added, employment, and international sales 2011–2016. Analysis of 30,000 companies worldwide

2011–2016%s	*Sales 16*	*Sales 11*	*EBIT 16*	*EBIT 11*	*EBIT Av*	*Sales 16*	*GrInc 16*	*Val-Added*	*Emps*	*Int. Sales*
TotalAll30K	100	100	100	100	100	100	100	100	100	100
Total 1s	15.5	14.8	16.1	13.5	15.1	7.7	18.0	12.9	13.1	16.7
Total 1s, 2s	25.1	24.4	26.1	22.8	24.7	14.7	28.5	21.6	21.8	29.5
Total 1s, 2s, 3s	32.1	31.5	31.1	29.1	30.5	19.0	35.7	27.4	28.0	36.9
Total 1s, 2s, 3s, 4s	37.6	37.5	36.1	34.7	35.8	46.3	40.6	43.5	32.8	44.3
Total 1–20s	71.9	72.3	69.6	71.1	70.3	72.7	74.8	73.7	66.0	81.0

Table 1.12 Top 1s, 2s, 3s, 4s, and 20s' appropriations of all R&D, capital expenditure, sales and general administration, intangible expenditures, and capital employed: analysis of 30,000 companies worldwide in 2016

2016%s	*R&D%*	*CapX%*	*SGA%*	*Intang%*	*CapEmp%*
TotalAll30K	100	100	100	100	100
Total 1s	21	13	17	16	12
Total 1s, 2s	32	21	28	28	20
Total 1s, 2s, 3s	41	28	36	34	26
Total 1s, 2s, 3s, 4s	46	33	41	41	30
Total 1–20s	79	70	75	78	64

Table 1.13 RoCE and RoS profit and sales growth performances of top global oligopolists vs 30,000 companies, 2011–2016

2011–2016	*6yRoC%*	*6yrRoS%*	*6yrSG%*	*Nos*	*~Rule %*	*Nos %*
AvgAll30K	21.3	13.2	44.7	300001		100
Avs 1s	14.7	18.3	9.3	169	15	0.06
Avs 1s, 2s	13.8	17.9	7.6	328	22	0.11
Avs 1s, 2s, 3s	13.2	17.6	9.4	487	30	0.16
Avs 1s, 2s, 3s, 4s	13.0	17.5	9.6	645	35	0.22
Avs 1–20s	17.0	16.9	20.8	3160	70	1.05

Overall, leading companies were only modestly more profitable than smaller players. However, even slight performance margins may prove important, particularly if they have achieved lower weighted averaged costs of capital (WACC). Our data on these were extremely patchy. Against this, it is generally easier for smaller companies to achieve mathematically higher growth rates. Small company survivors, at least, have been gaining global market share over this six-year period.

Taking Tables 1.11–1.13 together suggests some rough rules of thumb, as delineated in the penultimate right-hand column. Leading oligopolists may not be exploiting profit margins as extortionately as many imagine; but their ability to appropriate sales and profit pools is nevertheless appreciable globally. Leading top 1s appropriate roughly 15% of all global sales, profit, and value-added pools; top 1s and 2s 22%; top 1s, 2s, and 3s 30%; top 1–4s 35%; and top 20s 70%. And as we've seen, in sectors with above average GCR4% levels, such figures go very much higher.

Tables 14.1 and 14.2 in Chapter 14, examining political economic effects, analyse all 30,000 companies' appropriations (including value-added) by country affiliations. Their impact on wealth creation across nations worldwide is such that corporations from just four top countries, the USA, Japan,

China/Hong Kong, and Great Britain/Ireland in 2016, appropriated around 60% of all sales, gross profits, employment, R&D, capital, and marketing related expenditures.

Strategically, though, we next examine when and how to deploy effective global strategies; how to interpret global concentration GCR metrics and trends using world class market share data, rather than crude proxies from large financial databases as used in this chapter; mapping sectors systematically; and finally synthesising towards some more universal theory.

NOTES

1 Oligopoly comes from the Greek word 'oligos' meaning 'few' and monopoly from 'mono' meaning one.
2 Special Report: The Rise of the Superstars, *Economist*, 17 September 2016, pp. 12 and 14.
3 Ibid., p. 4.
4 Coase, R. (1937). The Nature of the Firm. *Economica*, 4 (16), pp. 386–405.
5 Numbers fell from 6797 to 3485 according to Gustavo Grullon of Rice University. Source: *Economist*, ibid., p. 4.
6 Galloway, S. (2017). *The Four: The Hidden DNA of Amazon, Apple, Facebook and Google*. London: Bantam Press, pp. 1, 6, & 7.
7 Ibid., p. 7.
8 Ibid., p. 206.
9 *The Economist*, 29 July 2017, p. 19. 'Free exchange: Too many quiet lives Uncompetitive markets have macroeconomic consequences'. Sources: G. Gutierrez and T. Philippon, *Declining Competition and Investment in the US*, based on Census Bureau US data.
10 *The Times*, 19 December 2017, p. 45.
11 *The Economist*, 28 July 2018, pp. 6 and 17–18. 'Concentration problems' and 'Britain. Business. More money, more problems', citing the Resolution Foundation's extremely fine-grained analysis; Haskel, J. and Westlake, S. (2018) *Capitalism without Capital*.
12 In 2012, the British Virgin Islands' FDI inflows were $72 billion, compared with Britain's at $46 billion. Ibid., pp. 12–13. Google effective tax rate was 2.4% of 2007–2009 non-American profits.
13 Source: Focusing Capital on the Long Term (FCLT), cited by the 'Management Horizons: Quick and Dirty', *The Economist*, 8 October 2016, p. 66.
14 *The Economist*, 17 September 2016, ibid., p. 4.
15 Ibid., p. 5.
16 *Financial Times*, 2 October 2017, p. 1.
17 Ibid., p. 13.
18 Ibid., p. 6.
19 Rusal's HRM director personally interviewed in Moscow in 2010.
20 *Fortune*, July 2017, *Global 500*.
21 I acknowledge gratefully the enormous contribution of Olivia Mason helping to analyse Thomson One Banker data sets, used in this chapter and later in Tables 14.1 and 14.2.
22 For individual years, the variation was ±1.5%, figures ranging between 86% and 89%.
23 Individual year figures ranged from 68% to 86%.
24 Individual year figures ranging from 23% to 55%.
25 The danger with larger samples, though, is that huge numbers of tiny players distort any impact on overall profits.

26 For a summary of market structure, conduct, and performance theories, see Besanko, D., Dranove, D., and Shanley, M. (2000 or latest edition), Chapters 7–11; Scherer, F.M. and Ross, D. (1991). *Industrial Market Structure and Performance*. New York: Houghton Mifflin; Porter, M.E. (1980). *Competitor Analysis: Techniques for Analysing Industries and Competitors*. New York: Free Press; Bain, J. (1956). *Barriers to New Competition: Their Character and Consequences in Manufacturing Industries*. Cambridge, MA: Harvard University Press.

27 Porter, M.E. (1980). ibid. and Porter, M.E. (1998). *On Competition*. Cambridge, MA: Harvard Business Review Press. Porter advocates taking 10 years of RoCE data in assessing industries and competitors, though here we have taken two independent and separate 5-year periods. It would be worthwhile extending this analysis over even longer time periods. Even larger company data sets risk dangerously including massive numbers of potentially strategically irrelevant companies distorting results and statistical correlations.

28 Keynes, J.M. (1936). *The General Theory of Employment, Interest and Money*. London: Macmillan.

29 An alternative measure is to take the inverse of the number of significant companies recorded in Thomson One Banker's database, as defined by say '1000/number of companies': a lower number of companies signifies greater concentration, but this is unsatisfactory in fragmented sectors where excluding highly numerous smaller players becomes even more problematic.

30 Sheth, J. and Sisodia, R. (2002). *The Rule of Three: Surviving and Thriving in Competitive Markets*. New York: Free Press.

31 When handling such large data sets, it is sometimes easier technically to focus on the top 20. Numerous tiny, often niche companies frequently play insignificant roles as genuine competitors, and their inclusion risks distorting performance relationships. This chapter will, nevertheless, move on to a more extensive analysis of all 30,000 firms. In estimating global market sizes and share and in analysing profit pools, we do then need to include all players, not just the top 20 in each sector.

32 RoCE performance relationships tend to over-weight numerous small players.

33 Haskel, J. and Westlake, S. (2018). *Capitalism Without Capital: The Rise of the Intangible Economy*. Princeton, NJ: Princeton University Press.

2

SECTOR GLOBAL CONCENTRATION TRENDS AND PERFORMANCE OUTCOMES

WHY DO GLOBAL STRATEGIES AND SECTOR GLOBAL CONCENTRATION PROCESSES MATTER?

Competing globally requires huge commitment, backed up by strategic investments – foreign direct investments (FDI), not merely trade. In their absence, puffed-up 'strategic visions', global or otherwise, count for little as competition becomes global.[1] Committing too late, almost no other major United Kingdom (UK) automotive supplier, aside from GKN, succeeded in going fully global.[2] Associated policies are surprisingly complex, automotive suppliers being among the first into the firing line. Key United States (US), European, and Asian vehicle manufacturer customers, being semi-global, all required geographical support from suppliers having to serve all of them. Other sectors are now encountering similarly global competition and having to catch up fast.[3]

The critical problem arises from global concentration and associated oligopolistic strategies, global moves, and countermoves. Even those of us trained in economics did not understand these issues in the 1960s, 1970s, and 1980s when companies like GKN went global. Their strategic decisions were not merely 'muddling through', but they were pragmatic and partly intuitive. Basil Woods, a professional economist and GKN's powerful strategic planning director struggled to engage his charismatic chairman in analytical conversations 'beyond five minutes'. I don't believe any of us involved in going global in the late 1970s were deploying pertinent economic frameworks. It is hard to integrate the two fields. Few economists relate easily to this global concentration phenomenon. Aside from some international trade and FDI theory, the closest many come is perhaps game theory. However, ask these same economists to apply game theory to a single global sector (let alone around 200 analysed here) and most struggle or decline to answer.[4]

Fortunately, we've learned much since 1980 from a few applied economists, such as Porter, Yip, and Ghemawat, straddling strategy and economics fields related to market structure, behaviour, and performance. Porter (1980), influential at the start of my PhD, was and still is applicable to those facing strategic and global choices. As Porter recognised, competition is not always global, nor are sectors all concentrated. To avoid catastrophic strategic investment decisions, we must understand the economics underlying such differences. In genuinely fragmented industries, typified by heterogeneous demands, low scale economies and entry barriers, overinvesting may be dangerous. Prelude Corporation's attempt to become the 'General Motors of the [naturally fragmented] lobster industry' culminated in bankruptcy.[5] In sectors where local adaptation pressures outweighed global traits, global strategies sometimes proved unprofitable.[6]

Global strategies, though, won out in automotive components.[7] Initially, this was only true of segments, like automotive bearings, conducive to trade; but later this happened across the board as multi-nationals learned to sidestep trade barriers by deploying FDI. As global drivers changed, most other business sectors have begun following suit.[8]

GLOBAL DRIVERS, LOCALISATION ADAPTATION PRESSURES, AND IMPLICATIONS FOR GLOBAL STRATEGIES

When and how fast sectors go global hinge on the balance of pre-conditioning global and localisation drivers; going too early can be as dangerous as going too late. Principle global forces are scale economies, driven by specialisation and the need to spread fixed costs (product development, for example) over the widest possible market base. Yip and Hult distinguished four global drivers: market drivers, cost drivers, government drivers, and competitive drivers for 12 illustrative sectors, ranging from book publishing and pharmaceuticals to civil aircraft production.[9] Adverse localisation pressures, by contrast, reflect the requirement to adapt business models to heterogeneous customer needs worldwide and international market entry barriers.[10]

Andersen and Hallen (2017: 30[11])'s more recent analysis, shown in Figure 2.1, positions 14 major sectors by global integration (and hence the requirement for international integrative planning) and decision autonomy (and hence local responsiveness capability), suggesting two contrasting integrated, more global strategies.

For example, when working earlier for BAe Systems on aircraft manufacture in the 1970s, our scale economies and learning curve effects were huge. Trade and exports sufficed to serve global markets. VC10s and 1-11s were assembled just in UK factories and Concordes either there or in Toulouse for Aerospatiale. High up-front investment commitments precluded adaptability, aside from our smallish aircraft services department handling just minor

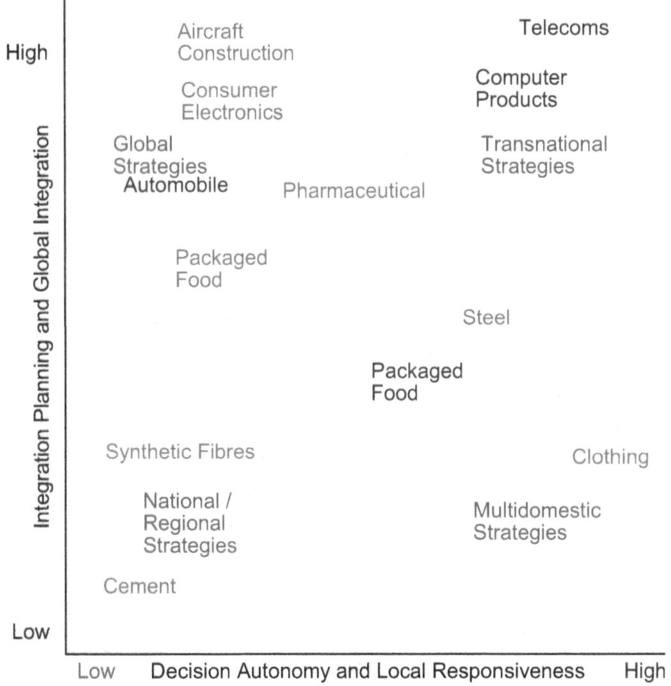

Figure 2.1 Global integration orientations and industry contexts. (From Andersen, T.B. and Hallin, C.A., *Global Strategic Responsiveness*, Routledge, London, p. 30, 2017.)

customer required adjustments. The industry was so globally oligopolistic that customers accepted exports, with little FDI support. The alternative global strategy, labelled transnational, by contrast, allows for far greater adaptation to differences worldwide. This is achieved by huge FDI commitments (sometimes requiring organisational adaptations such as matrix structures). In the absence of exceptional scale economies (as in aerospace and ecommerce sectors) such transnational global strategies are arguably more pervasive, committed, and effective globally.

We should next check whether consolidation has occurred domestically. Has the home market concentration ratio (CR4) already exceeded 10% and company numbers fallen? Consolidation processes, first nationally and then more globally, are akin to a game of musical chairs: as chairs get withdrawn, participants run faster and faster, anticipating further chair withdrawals and other players' responses. Once we then see signs of any big successful international cross-border moves, global consolidation becomes likely. Global versus localisation drivers should be re-checked, but unless analysis unambiguously confirms localisation drivers as dominant (as in lobster fishing), take recourse to Carr's first law. This states that the 'see-saw' will ultimately tip, favouring global consolidation processes; with the net balance of economic forces now evident, future consolidations will not stop at half-way regional or continental levels. The matter resolves to one of timing. Global, not mere national or regional, concentration metrics, and *global* rivals must now be examined.

Who has the resources to go global successfully, and who must reposition defensively? Thanks to Birfield's acquisition in the 1960s, GKN Drivelines had plants in Britain, Italy, France, and Germany (though Uni-Cardan was initially only a joint venture). Our team had to build two major plants in the USA, each costing around $100 million – no mean sums in 1978/9. Only a licence deal was feasible in Japan. In the late 1980s, huge plants followed in Delhi and Shanghai, and later, similar (40% equity) joint venture plants in some 36 countries.

You need a business model enjoying global competitive advantages. GKN had a cast iron 30-year patent for constant velocity joints, crucial to fuel-efficient smaller cars now needed globally. However, the main entry barriers stem from well developed competences and from scale, fostered by FDI commitments globally, and not just exports; though green-field site investments are slow and expensive, whilst cross-border alliances or mergers and acquisitions (M&A) often prove even more difficult to implement effectively.

Zara spent decades incubating its radical, innovative fast-response business model at home, before going global exceptionally fast, solely through FDI. They used greenfield sites, eschewing M&A, but deployed joint ventures solely for highly problematic major countries such as Japan and India, and franchises for minor countries. Invent a new mouse trap and the world will *rarely* beat a path to your door, facilitating exports; but you *can* take your better business model worldwide to customers if you commit to FDI.

Yip and Hult further emphasise managerial and organisational global readiness tests relating to organisational structure, people, culture, and managerial processes,[12] though neither GKN nor Zara quite passed their criteria. People and corporate culture issues prove crucial on cross-border alliances and M&A, scrutinised in Chapter 7.

However, no strategy is easy; or others would have already done it. As Chandler's major business histories demonstrated,[13] bold diversifications (whether horizontal or geographic) usually resulted in performance dips, until organisational adaptations and learning later restored profitability. Initially poor performance outcomes for globally orientated appliance manufactures, discussed in Chapter 11, have since turned around; whilst national and regional players have now been weeded out[14]: as happened, two decades earlier, in cars and parts.[15]

Other sectors seem set to follow. Drivers, trends, and concentration processes then merit examining globally; collecting data nationally or regionally (as sufficed economists and policy makers traditionally) will no longer be enough.

GLOBAL CONCENTRATION MAPS

Global concentration metrics are so patchy that executives may find themselves in unfamiliar global terrains lacking data. Ghemawat and Ghadar highlighted controversial strategic issues arising from global GCR5 and the Herfindahl index (HI) concentration metrics in automotive, oil production and refining, and aluminium sectors, followed by a further ten sectors in 2011.[16] Economists and regulators (concerned over pricing power) often favour HIs, which emphasise the impact of leading players, by taking the sum of the squares of market shares. Such metrics need now to be calculated globally. To guide executives further, Carr and Collis published the first summarised 'map' in 2011, based on Figure 2.2, showing patterns of global concentration across 50 sectors, together with secondary trend change metrics.[17] Global concentration data are scarce, so years for recent data are necessarily varied, but the average date for our more recent data was then 2004, compared with 1996 for earlier data.

Figure 2.2's 45-degree diagonal line represents GCR4s unchanged over the period. Above that diagonal lie sectors where GCR4s had increased GCR4s, and below are those where they had decreased. Where GCR4 levels

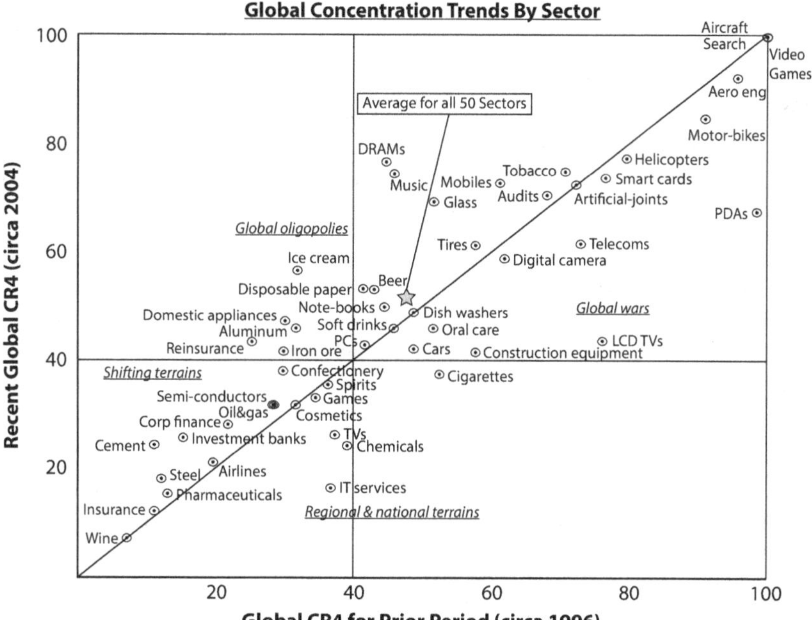

Figure 2.2 GCR4s in 2004 vs 1996 by sector. *Note*: The contribution of Professor David Collis, Harvard Business School, is gratefully acknowledged. We worked together on this data over five months at HBS and published an abbreviated summary of this figure and of our ideas in Carr, C. and Collis, D. "Should you have a global strategy?", *Sloan Management Review*, 53, 1, 21–24, 2011.

are well below 40%, sectors below this diagonal are classified as '*regional and national terrains*' internationally. Here, international competition is more fragmented, and we then would concur with Ghemawat that executives should be extremely cautious in pursuing aggressive global strategies, or indeed cross-border mega-mergers; this would be Porter's Prelude cautionary tale, writ globally. Information technology services reflected this scenario. Not all sectors studied were displayable. GCR4s were lowest in wine, having fallen slightly from 7.4% in 2004 to 6.8% in 2011, though this figure subsequently returned to 7.3% in 2013. Any trend in wine has been ambiguous. In fact, even at such low concentration levels, we are in fact now already seeing several substantial global moves in wine and IT services. This reinforces our hawkish view that global moves and countermoves set in as we approach double-digit levels of GCR4s.

'*Shifting terrains competition*' scenarios occur where GCR4s are above the diagonal and rising, but still below 40% levels designating more powerful '*global oligopolies*'. Sceptical economists, such as Ghemawat, recognise contexts conducive to more aggressive global strategies, only when GCRs or HIs are rising. However, economic theory rightly places far more emphasis on absolute levels of concentration (as depicted on the y axis). Trends are interesting, but less fundamental; even upwards trends cannot keep rising forever. Global concentration levels in most sectors, for example, are far lower than in piston engine airplane manufactures, where the GCR4 in 2010 at 78% has fallen from 86% in 2000; nor would we equate dairy products (up from 11.7% in 1998 to 14.5% in 2009) with civil helicopters (up from 79% in 1987 to 92% in 2009), simply due to rising trends. Increased global concentration metrics may though reflect cross-border M&A as occurred in spirits or when pharmaceuticals likewise pushed up towards a 20% GCR4.

GCR4s above 40% indicate increasingly powerful *global oligopolies*, when GCRs are rising (depicted above the diagonal). Global strategies and mega-mergers may be on strongly positioned players' strategic agendas, anticipating returns beyond costs of capital through economies of scope and scale. More common, though, are '*global wars*' scenarios, where the GCR4 having once approached 40% level, now reverts below that same 45-degree diagonal. It is then tempting, but wrong, to interpret the falling GCR4 as a sign of global fragmentation. GCRs tend to dip as huge emerging markets like China come into their own and as challenger disruptors gain share. Global rivalry intensifies and margins fall. Some players may even need to retrench to survive. Yet *not* to invest sufficiently in response to such global challengers can lead to bankruptcy, as General Motors discovered in the case of cars.

Figure 2.2 gives just a preliminary overview of the main different types of internationally exposed sectors. It highlights four global concentration scenarios, meriting distinctive global strategy orientations and suggesting different performance outcomes. Sweeping generalities advocating polar extremes, whether for national, regional, or global strategies, are seductively simple, yet misleading. Executives need to analyse their own sectors. Where their own data are weaker, it makes sense to draw lessons (recognising performance outcomes) from those illustrated sectors discussed later, most akin to their own.

INTERPRETING GLOBAL CONCENTRATION TRENDS

Interpreting these global concentration trends is not straightforward. Past industrial economists linked CR4s of 40% in US markets to oligopolistic interactions between companies, likely to generate above average returns[18]; but note they specified the CR4 *level*, not the *change* per se. Scale economies advantaged top three US players.[19] However, this logic relates to the locus of competition, now far more global. By the 1990s, GE under Jack Welch already pressed business units to achieve top 3 positions globally, not domestically, or regionally[20]; though one robust alternative (discussed in Chapter 8) is just to niche globally. As analysed in Chapter 3, such concepts fit well with experiences in the worldwide spirits sector.

Rising GCR4 trends can signal global consolidation moves and an end to international fragmentation. Where low GCR4s (under 5%) suggest global fragmentation, falling trends imply this will not be reversed anytime soon. At such low levels, sceptics would be right to warn against herd-like 'go global' moves and megamergers. However, our evidence suggests that initial moves and countermoves occur at around 10% GCR4 levels. It would therefore be dangerous to infer that falling GCR4s then signal waning globalisation, endorsing more cautious national or regional strategies. The range of 40%–50% has proved almost as far as GCR4s ever go in most sectors; after that, Schumpeterian counter-challengers emerge. Our data suggest that fluctuating cycles become the norm. We designate this scenario '*global wars*'. Radically different from '*global fragmentation*' scenarios, this calls for diametrically opposite global strategy orientations. For such global scenarios, Figure 2.2 provides an initial helpful framework, leading on to a more universal theory later in this book.

ANALYSIS OF CONCENTRATION LEVELS ACROSS 100 SECTORS AFFORDING CONSISTENT TREND DATA

Trends for all 100 sectors analysed, which provided consistent global market research-based trend data, showed average GCR4s rose from 49% in 1994 to 55% in 2009. GCR1s, reflecting just global leaders, though remained flat at 25% throughout, so the issue has been one of rising global oligopolies rather than monopolies. From a Schumpeterian perspective, such GCRs are already so high that at some point levels must fall; mathematically such figures cannot keep rising. Yet whether rising or finally falling, executives would be foolish to ignore top four global players, controlling over half their markets; scale economies and experience effects leave others hugely disadvantaged, thus deterring many potential entrants.

Sectors differ. The lowest GCR4 in 2009 was 6.8% for these 100 sectors compared with 7.3% in 1994; the highest was 99.6 compared with 96 in 1994. The lowest GCR1 in 2009 was 1.5% compared to 1.3% in 1994; the highest was 82% compared to 74% for 1994. It is therefore naïve to overgeneralise, whether for or against global strategies. Executives, consultants, and academics, not conversant with specific sector GCRs are like 'Samson eyeless in Gaza', blind as to key competitors or how to direct companies internationally. GCRs' levels are the 'elephant in the room' strategically, ignored even by academics. Search indices of pre-eminent textbooks on strategy or even international business and few contain the term global market share, let alone global concentration metrics; but quite how such academics could pronounce on strategies, without any knowledge of GCRs in sectors being examined, remains unclear.[21] This implies ignorance of leading players' market shares, of changes in such shares, and of even the most basic knowledge of competitive strategies.

MORE RECENT CONCENTRATION LEVELS IN A MORE EXTENSIVE RANGE OF SECTORS

This section[22] reviews and partially updates GCR data for 214 sectors, affording reliable global market share data between 2006 and 2012, though only 173 afforded GCR4s (as opposed to GCR1s, GCR2s, and GCR3s); some were already down to just three major players. Average GCR1s, GCR2s, GCR3s, and GCR4s were, respectively, 25%, 39%, 46%, and 53%. GCR4s, displayed in Figure 2.3, averaged 53% for all 173 sectors examined. Only

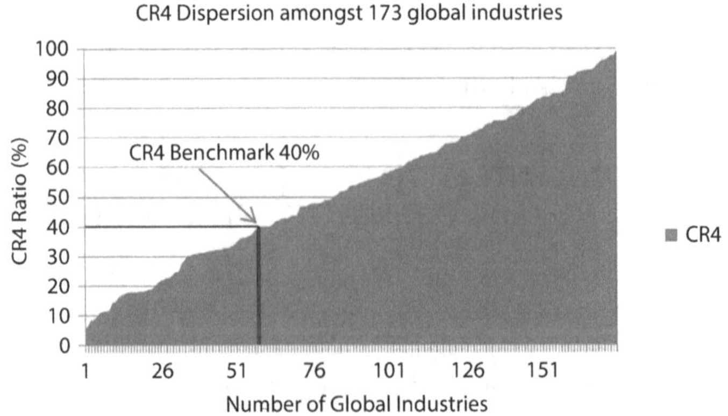

Figure 2.3 GCR4 dispersions across 173 sectors, 2006–2012.

61 sectors (35%) fell below 40%. Only 26 (15%) were below 20%, where we had already seen major cross-border M&A in sectors such as pharmaceuticals.

CR1s ranged from Microsoft's 92% in desktop operating systems in 2012 down to McDonalds 1.5% share in the highly fragmented restaurant sector (based on gross revenues). Even so, positions have been highly dynamic since: by 2018, Microsoft's share was down to 40%, whilst Google's Android position rose to 35% and iOS's to 13%, implying a GCR3 of 89% (Statistica). Defining the market more narrowly as fast food though, including also pizzas and Asian fast food, McDonalds' GC1 was 10% in 2016.[23]

Dominant firm scenarios then included the online search engine market (Google 82% in Quarter 1, 2012), microprocessors (Intel 82% in 2010), and debit cards (Visa 78.5% in 2010). By April 2019, Google's share had risen to 92% and the GCR4 to 98%. Google's share of smartphone operating systems, represented by Android, likewise rose to 88% by 2018, quarter 2, the balance of 12% being taken by iOS and implying a GCR2 of 100%; this compares with 2001, quarter 1, when shares were Symbian 49%, RIM 21%, iOS 11%, and Microsoft 10%, implying an earlier GCR4 of 91%. Visa's share fell back to 66% in 2016, the GCR2 remaining high at 97%; but Intel fell back to 31% in 2018 (GCR2s and 4s being, respectively, 41% and 62%). Such sectors were characterised by scale advantages, network effects, learning effects, homogenous products, and complemented by high entry barriers.

Less dominant leading firm scenarios included commercial banks (Bank of America Corporation holding only 2.8% in 2011), coal[24] (ShenHua Group, 2.7% in 2010), and the wine industry (E & J Gallo, 2.5% in 2011). In wine, such volume-based estimates have varied wildly, though in stark contrast to Coca Cola's 50% global market share of the global carbonated beverage market or Anheuser-Busch's 28% in global beer.[25] On a value-basis, Gallo's share in 2017 (the GCR1) was only about 2.8%. These more fragmented sectors were characterised by situations where local customer preferences mattered more or where products exhibited low value-to-weight ratios, rendering wider geographical coverage less economic.

GLOBAL COMPETITION FORCE – A NEW TERMINOLOGY FOR GLOBAL STRATEGISTS

Modern industrial organisation theory classifies markets into six types, characterised by market power and concentration: monopoly (CR1 of 100%); dominant firm (CR1 40%–99%); tight oligopoly (CR4 60%>); loose oligopoly (CR4 less than 40%); monopolistic competition (many firms with only slight market power); and finally pure competition (many firms, none of which have any market power).[26] Global monopoly cases will not always allow for four players and data may not always be available for every type of GCR. A more universal system of classification could be helpful.

On the same principle as the Beaufort wind force scale, I devised a novel global competition force (GCF) scale. No sailor of sound mind would embark on the world's oceans without regular updates on Beaufort wind forces: single reefs would be taken in, typically, at wind force 4 or 5 for smaller boats or at 6 or 7 for larger yachts, and at gale forces 8s and 9s, we are down to storm gibs or even bare mast poles at hurricane 10–12s. Pity poor executives, beset by global competition, with nothing more than polarised notions of national vs global strategies to guide them. GCF scales, are simple enough to be readily interpreted. GCF scales, in Figure 2.4, enable us to leverage knowledge from the internationalisation experiences of hundreds of sectors, categorising on a simple 12 point 'force' scale.

This is directly akin to the Beaufort wind force scale, where 10 is a very high concentration and a 12 is the most extreme 'hurricane' force level imaginable, corresponding to the highest degree of monopoly conceivable. GCR4 is the main method of categorisation, but where such data are inherently unavailable (as in the case of just two firms existing in a global sector), we can still assign a GCF scale based on just the GCR1 or the GCR2; or in other cases, we might draw on the GCR3 or GCR5 depending on data available. It is useful just to be able to articulate the key international concentration metrics: Okay, my sector right now is in a force 4, this being on a neutral trend, or force 4+ if the trend is rising, or force 4 – if it is falling.

A force 4+ tells us a lot and suggests a '*transitional*' scenario, but, knowing the long-term context can aid interpretation just as in weather forecasting. Say your

GCF	**CR1**	**CR2**	**CR3**	**CR4**	**CR5**	**CR6**	**CR7**	**CR8**	**CR9**	**CR10**	
12	80	90									Global Monopoly
11	70	80	90								Global Duopoly
10	50	60	70	80							Global Quadopoly
9	30	40	50	60	70	80	90				Tight Oligopoly
8	20	30	40	50	60	70	80	90			
7	10	20	30	40	50	60	70	80	90		Loose Oligopoly
6	-	10	20	30	40	50	60	70	80	90	
5	-	-	15	20	25	30	35	40	45	50	
4	-	-	7.5	10	12.5	15	17.5	20	22.5	25	Transitional
3	-	-	-	5	6	7.5	8.5	10	11	12	Competition
2	-	-	-	2.5	3.5	4	4.5	5	5.5	6	Fragmented
1	-	-	-	<2.5	<3.5	<4	<4.5	<5	<5.5	<6	Competition

Figure 2.4 Global Concentration Force (GCF) scales.

sector's position used to be a force 3.5 (the half-way position between 3 and 4) even further back, say 20 years ago. Okay, so there's a steady rise towards more globally oligopolistic patterns, and it may be profitable to invest to gain greater dominance. Or okay, so the sector used to be a force 5, so concentration metrics are now cycling Schumpeter style. Under such a '*global war*' scenario, we are likely to need a robust strategy to counter new global challengers; but it doesn't imply a comfortable ride and some refocusing may prove necessary.

Knowing our own force 4+ context enables us to compare experiences from other sectors in similar positions. Instead of just comparing the widget industry (because let's face it, that's just the sector we used to work in), we can pick out from our now extensive database those sectors also around force 4+. Alternatively, we can deploy 'straddling' as when warships fire a salvo short then long, facilitating final targeting. Okay, so let's check our judgements. So, at force 4, other sectors typically suggest these sorts of international strategies and is this what we're really seeing or not? If not, why not? Consider perhaps other sectors already at force 5s. What international strategies do they use, and do these pay off commercially?

GLOBAL CONCENTRATION FORCE LEVELS IN 214 SECTORS EXAMINED

Global concentration force (GCF) scales facilitated analysis of 214 sectors, as displayed in Figure 2.5. Only sectors significantly exposed to internationalisation yield data on global market shares or corresponding concentration ratios and a further bias results from 'niche segmentation' – the tendency for firms to create sectors narrow enough to 'shield them against' bigger global rivals. Even so, sector concentration levels proved pervasively high: no sectors could

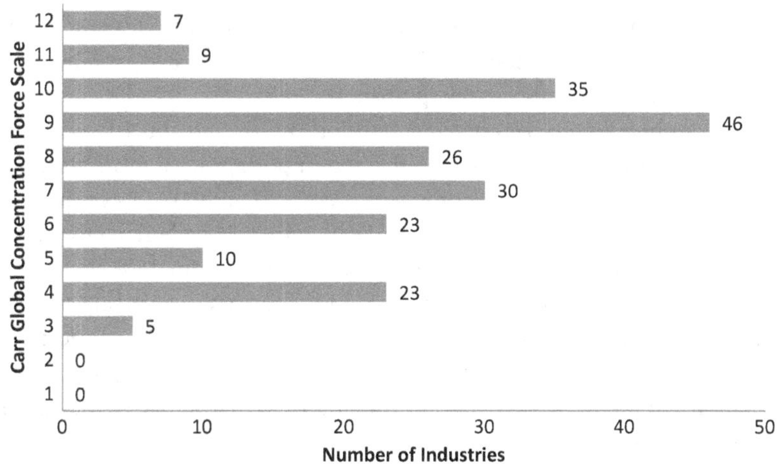

Figure 2.5 Carr's GCF distribution across sectors.

be categorised as global concentration forces GCF1 and 2 '*fragmented global competition*'; 13% were '*transitional competition*' GCF3s (2%) and GCF4s, (11%); and almost 30% were GCF5, 6, and 7 '*loose oligopolies*'. There were 57.5% that were above GCF7, corresponding to at least 40% GCR4s. By this point, global rivalry was unambiguous, yet with GCR4 levels typically beginning to cycle. '*Tight oligopolies*', being GCF8s (12%), GCF9s (21.5%) constituted 33.5% of sectors. There were 16% that were GCF10 '*global quadropolies*'; 4% were GCF11 '*global duopolies*', and 3% GCF12 '*global monopolies*'.

Most services still lack global data causing them to be excluded. Several remain naturally early stage, but have started to change. Hairdressers (just two bits of intersecting metal, as used by Delilah on Samson or Cleopatra on Mark Antony!) lack scale technological scale economies and would have perhaps rated a GCF1. Yet here, Toni & Guy has successfully begun taking its hairdressing brand across borders. Trade is inherently impossible in such service sectors, so Toni & Guy (like Zara) just committed to FDI.

Fast-food restaurant services at GF3 was the least globally concentrated of sectors sampled. This included burgers, pizzas, and Asian takeaways, excluding smaller restaurants and cafes lacking data. Low concentration reflected heterogeneous tastes and lower scale economies, though figures varied depending on market definitions. McDonalds became the new global number (No) 1 as Sodexo fell back to No 3. Top players marginally increased global shares between 2003 and 2010, but huge, growing emerging markets have perhaps made it harder to achieve oligopolistic domination worldwide. Even McDonalds merely increased its global market share from 1.3% in 2003 to 1.5% in 2010, despite rising revenues from middle class emerging market consumers attracted by McDonald's iconic American service brand.[27] Like Toni &Guy, McDonalds deployed FDI in place of trade, through its own sites; but about half its income came from franchises. In 2017, prioritising China, McDonald's global sales jumped 6.6% in the second quarter, hitting their highest in more than 5 years, as profits climbed to $1.4 billion.[28] As discussed in Chapter 12, global No 2 Compass is also highly global.

Aside from investment banking and auditing at GF9 and above, services have generally proved slower to globalise, reflecting important local relationships and lower entry barriers. GCR4s in consulting were 20% in 2007 (down from 28% in 2003 as demand rose in emerging markets), with relatively few cross-border megamergers. By contrast, GCR4s in advertising rose from 11% in 1960 and 1970 to 38% in 2001 (though only 19% on an agency basis), reverting to 25% in 2012.[29] Omnis/Publicis attempted further megamergers as they strived to rival WPP, the global leader – itself the outcome of several mergers. Bain Capital's $1.3 billion bid for Japan's No 3, ADK, prising it away from its alliance partner WPP, hinted at cross-border battles to come.[30] By 2019, WPP's market valuation had fallen back, hit by its former chief executive officer (CEO) Martin Sorrell's new challenger and on-line disrupters Google and Facebook.

Force 9 sectors, the most frequent classification, included: athletic footwear (market leader Nike with 31% Global Market Share, GMS, in 2009); cereal makers (market leader Kellogg Co. with 37% GMS in 2010); digital cameras (market leader Canon with 19% GMS in 2010); M&A advisory (market leader Goldman Sachs with 29% GMS in 2011); music distributors (market leader Universal Music Group with 23% GMS in 2010); nickel mining (market leader Norilsk with 20% GMS in 2008); oral care (market leader Colgate-Palmolive Co. with 21% GMS in 2009); smartphone microprocessors (market leader Qualcomm with 26% GMS in 2009); and tobacco (market leader Chinese National Tobacco with 38% GMS in 2009). Nike's GMS rose to about 33% in 2018 (GCR2s and 4s to 55% and 63%, respectively). 'Global quadropolies' force 10s included: acetates, chewing gum, computer peripherals, DRAMs, E-Readers, lithium, platinum, and world cruise lines. Auditing accountants' GCR4s have since moved from 67% in 2013 to 71% in 2017, but remain over 95% for just global top companies' audits.

Overall, 71.5% of sectors reviewed were at force 7 'loose monopoly' levels or beyond. For such sectors, global concentration levels argued for globally integrated strategies. In just those 100 sectors affording consistent trend data (whose GCR4s were illustrated earlier), GCF forces rose on average from 7.3 in 1994 to 7.7 in 2009. The average sector had moved up to a virtual force 8+ (the plus indicating a rising trend) 'tight global oligopoly'.

LONGITUDINAL GLOBAL CONCENTRATION WAVES ACROSS 15 OTHER SECTORS

Figure 2.6 shows evolutionary concentration trends in 15 further sectors, providing more longitudinal data. These wave patterns, exhibiting peaks and troughs, were consistent with Schumpeter's 'gales of creative destruction' model (discussed earlier), though not all sectors moved together. Some consolidated quickly; some reverted. Complex to untangle, patterns are best understood in relation to their GCF levels and associated performance outcomes, discussed in the next section.

CONCENTRATION AND PERFORMANCE

Figure 2.7 analyses a sample of 25 industries, categorised by GFC levels 3 to 12, examining their 5-year average returns on invested capital (ROIC)[31] up to 2011, a profitability metric comparable against the opportunity cost of capital. Oligopoly theory would anticipate some positive correlation between market leadership (No 1 or at least top 4) and ROIC performance vs average sector performances. Most empirical work here has previously been carried out only in national markets such as the USA. This may be relevant for GF3 level sectors like restaurants, but, in most sectors, competition has been

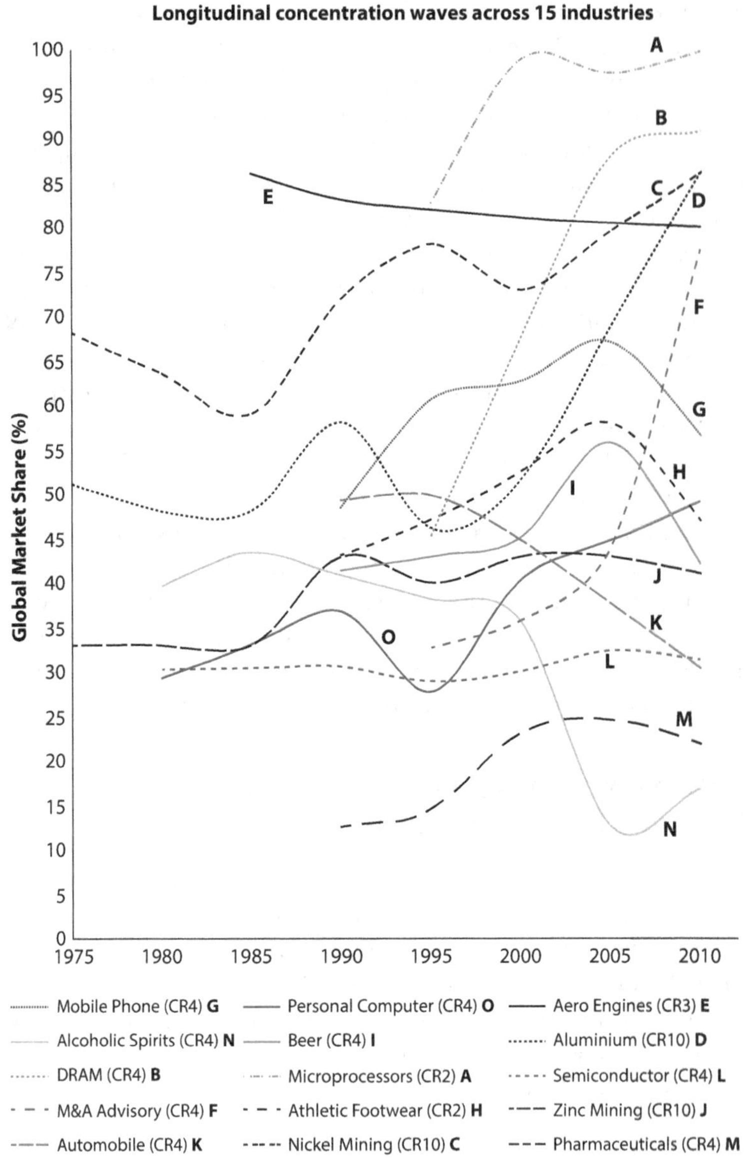

Figure 2.6 Longitudinal concentration waves across 15 sectors.

more typically global: Any superior profit performance should only be anticipated for top global (not national) players.

A weak relationship has been apparent between global concentration and average sector RoCEs invested capital (shown in green). Sectors displaying oligopolistic characteristics tended to report higher returns on capital.

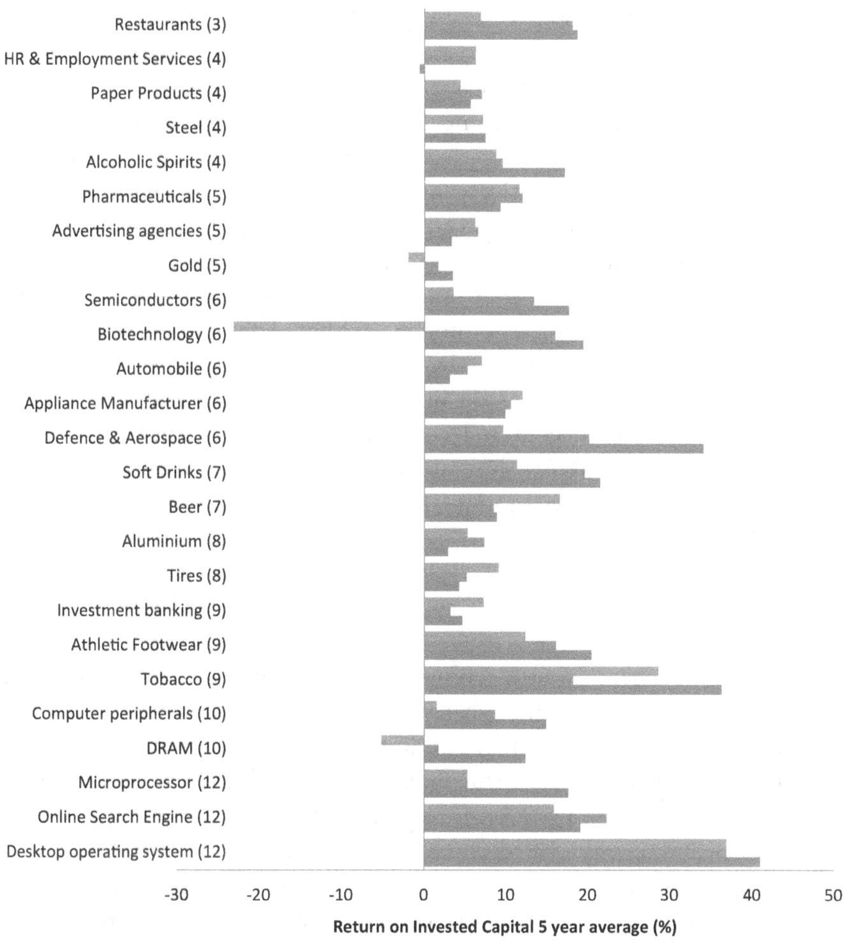

Figure 2.7 Market leaders versus sector averages: 5-year returns on invested capital, 2007–2011. *Note*: Sequential order each time: first ROIC Industry average, then Top 4, then Leader.

Tobacco (tight oligopoly scenario) and desktop operating systems (monopoly scenario) displayed the highest returns of the 25 sectors sampled. The positive relationship though has not proved consistent. DRAMs, with the fourth highest GCR4 of 91% in 2011, averaged negative 5-year ROICs of −5.2% due to oversupply and depressed prices, though profitability later recovered as the GCR4 reached 99% in 2012.[32] Nonetheless, sectors where GCR1 levels exceeded 80% have generally been extremely profitable as in desktop operating systems (Microsoft CR1 92% in 2012) and online search engines (Google CR1 82% in 2012). Increased market power has perhaps allowed such global leaders to become price setters, rather than takers.

Even more important from a competitive strategy perspective is whether or not top global leaders outperform sector average ROICs.[33] The M&A advisory sector exhibited a decisively negative performance outcome. Some negative outcome also occurred in automobiles and beer. This reflected the demise of former incumbent leaders, General Motors in cars and Anheuser-Busch, as their positions became usurped by new global challengers from Japan and Brazil. Other sectors, though, exhibited far more positive performance outcomes for top 4 global leaders: particularly in semiconductors, DRAMs, athletic footwear, on-line search, spirits, pharmaceuticals, PCs, aluminium, and even in gold and restaurants despite greater international fragmentation. 2017's GCR4 in semiconductors had dropped back to 28%, reflecting the rise of Huawei (3.5%), HPO (2.5%), and China's Oppo/Vivo (2.8%).[34]

SALES GROWTH

Executives simultaneously seek revenue growth, justifying higher valuations, and to increase global market shares. Five-year average sales growth figures are imperfect (since they may also just reflect diversification), but important proxies, indicating which firms are gaining or ceding global market share. Figure 2.8, therefore, shows average sales growth figures for the sampled 25 sectors, in ascending order based on GCF concentration levels.

Sales growth rates exhibited little correlation with industry global concentration levels. Gold and biotechnology were perhaps outliers,[35] but, otherwise, sector sales growth displayed no trend (one way or the other) with global concentration; they mainly reflected demand trends varying enormously between sectors. Declining consumer demand for personal computers, for example, had knock-on effects also on DRAM, microprocessors, and computer peripherals, which displayed some of the lowest 5-year sales growth industry averages in the sample (shown by the grey bar).

The comparison between market leaders and industry averages presented a stark contrast to ROIC outcomes. Only in three sectors – soft drinks, beer, and online search engines – were market leaders able to exceed industry sales growth over these 5 years. Large, mature already global companies naturally faced growth challenges. Market leaders often needed to buy that growth through acquisitions and merging. Intuitively, market leaders also faced the challenge that their top line starting point is higher and, inherently, they couldn't just go on growing market share. Smaller followers inherently

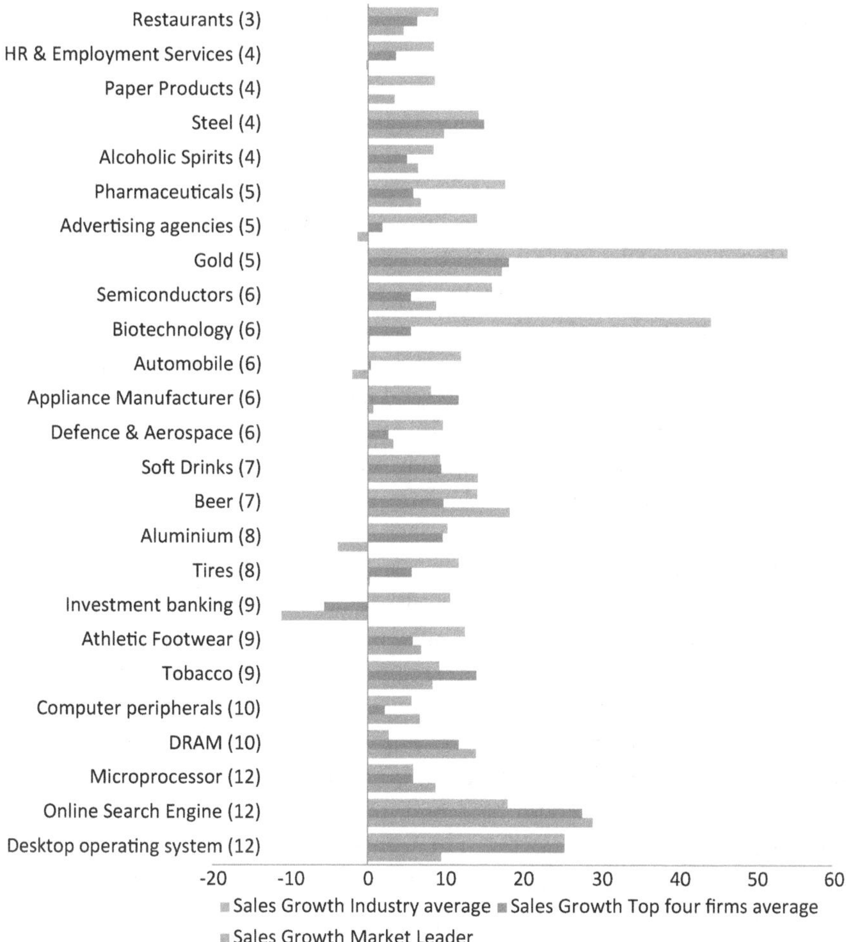

Figure 2.8 Market leaders vs. sector average 5-year sales growth, 2007–2011. NB: Sequential order each time: first ROIC Industry average, then Top 4, then Leader.

have greater potential for outstanding growth. Where scale matters, though, leaders may be harvesting profits through ceding market share.

ADAM SMITH, MARX, AND SCHUMPETER AND UNIVERSAL THEORETICAL PERSPECTIVES

We need to understand the fundamental processes leading to such global concentration, from the perspective of classical equilibrium economics, dating back to Adam Smith's *Wealth of Nations*, but also of alternative paradigms of thought such as Marx and Schumpeter.[36]

Smith well understood economies of scale brought about by the division of labour. His famous pin industry case described 400-fold productivity increases in automated factories, as compared to small traditional craft producers. He recognised the contribution of trade and geographically expanding markets and would have understood the logic of the division of labour in today's worldwide markets. Laggard companies would be akin to traditional craft manufacturers. Would they really accept pittance wages as prices inevitably plummeted reflecting far higher levels of productivity achieved by others with modern technologies, securing vastly greater scale economies based on global – no longer village – markets? For Smith, one thing was clear: ultimate prices would be set by the [global] market, not us, our aspirations, or what we feel we deserve. This powerful idea has implications, strategically for companies, and for all societies failing to come to terms with global competition. The wealth of nations depends on responding positively to global markets; mercantilism and protectionism are self-defeating and leave nations all worse off.

Smith eschewed 'Jeremiah' economists, yet saw no easy pickings even for world-class players. There was no likely natural monopoly, no natural process of concentration, globally, any more than locally. Once companies hit upon superior methods offering potential profits beyond their cost of capital, he expected profuse new entrants. Even efficient global winners would likely see profit return falling right back to their costs of capital. Smith envisaged we would still have thousands of pin manufacturers. 'Commodity markets' would be preserved and even global players would all be price-takers. In rare cases of concentration and monopolies, governments would justifiably intervene, maintaining more numerous rivals and essential market disciplines.

Truth lies in such insights. In Chapter 1, we saw it was rare for sectors to sustain superior returns on capital in successive 5-year periods. Yet, if Smith's classical model was entirely correct, why would executives bother getting up in the morning? Why not just stick shareholders money in the bank? Why worry about global winners or their strategies? Today's databases finally enable us to address these non-trivial questions. Between 1879 and 2015, *The Economist* in January 2018[37] highlighted equity returns averaging just slightly below housing returns at 7% globally, though proving far more volatile. They were far higher than bonds averaging 2.5% or bills averaging 1% returns. Smith did not anticipate sustained 145-year equity returns so far in excess of interest levels; nor should you have just stuck your money in the bank. More important, though, is the opportunity cost of capital. A safer way to achieve wealth has been putting your money into less productive property investments. This has policy implications, as discussed in Chapter 14, but implies that only highly appropriate and usually global strategies are likely to sustain returns beyond such opportunity costs.

From an evolutionary perspective, such classical economic models provide just a partial picture. In every exceptionally attractive territory (as in every sector) rivals arrive, battling each other, until higher final numbers do destroy easy pickings. As in Malthus' bleak model, every time productivity rises, populations increase, offsetting sustained wealth per capita growth, as indeed happened for centuries prior to the Industrial Revolution. Yet even this is no pointless game for winners. Winning brings hard-fought-for pickings and resources; losers get little and may not survive. Every day sees bold, capable entrepreneurs taking their ideas out into the world and making fortunes; others struggle, sometimes desperately. Outcomes are not trivial strategically, for society or for entire communities as for Michigan or Detroit.

In evolutionary terms, Smith's conjectures have not always proved correct; Marx's critique attacking Smith's logic cannot be dismissed lightly. If scale economies were as large as demonstrated in pins, why would concentration not just continue increasing? The largest players might eventually dominate, deterring and debarring Smith's potential entrants lacking similar scale. In other sectors, scale economies remain even higher. Between 2001 and 2016, the cost of sequencing human genomes, for example, fell from $3 billion to under $1000, but requiring investments, which rose from $0.5 billion to $1.7 billion.[38] Such global scale economies have constituted far more formidable entry barriers than former local ones. In 2016, Google and Facebook together captured 90% of online advertising revenue growth[39]; 'commoditisation' in such sectors is unlikely any time soon.

By 1980, even Smith's famous pin industry, exhibiting more modest scale economies, was a global oligopoly. Concentration had reduced numbers to only about four, including one in North America, one in Scandinavia, and one in Germany.[40] Notwithstanding classical economics, one of the few routes to sustained profits, beyond costs of capital, has been through market leadership in sectors where scale economies have applied. Increasingly, this has meant globally; even national champions have often proved tragically disadvantaged.

Smith's and Marx's paradigms are diametrically opposite polarised extremes. The former implies fragmented markets, global or not: GCR4s would be virtually zero, rendering global strategies impotent, unexciting to investors. At the other Marxian extreme, even GCR1s approach 1.0, facilitating creating omnipotent, potentially demonic global monopolies. This would raise spectres of unacceptable inequality (as Piketty argues is happening today[41]), chronic, extreme demand-supply imbalances, unemployment, '*sowing the seeds of capitalism's own self-destruction*'. The 2008 financial crisis, for example, may have been exacerbated by concentration within global finance.

Yet reality has lain between such extremes. None of our sectors analysed scored GCR1s approaching zero or 1.0. Fortunately, Schumpeter's more dynamic theory of industry evolution has been closer to the truth than either

Smith or Marx, taken in isolation. Innovation has warded off polar extremes. As one new, superior technological 'paradigm' has risen to pre-eminence, exploiting scale economies, other entrepreneurs have devised yet more novel technological paradigms, heralding new challengers – even entire new markets and previously unheard-off niches (discussed in Chapter 8).

For Schumpeter, predominant technological 'paradigms' often originating from advanced economies risk becoming supplanted by novel paradigms incubated in other large advanced economies, or later, in more emergent economies (aided by relative comparative advantages as theorised first by Ricardo). Unlike classical economic models, Schumpeter's precepts, like Keynes', were based on dynamic 'disequilibria'. Yet, whilst Keynes had emphasised macro-level issues, Schumpeter highlighted novel technological paradigms, arising to topple former incumbents, creating deeper, more violent dynamic 'disequilibria'.

'*Gales of creative destruction*' clear out marginal incumbent capacities – much as forest fires clear out dead wood, creating new space for more vigorous entrepreneurial shoots. This process, so damaging to some, regalvanises rivalry, reinvigorating, and rejuvenating companies. Sclerotic global monopolistic tendencies are turned upside down, as a macabre game of musical chairs gathers pace. Where once there had been almost enough chairs to go around, market leaders had scarcely had to stir; but as vigorous new players arrive, all eye chairs being removed or taken. All players want to survive. In oligopolistic competition, companies react to moves by others, seeing even slothful rivals responding, all accelerate. Moves provoke countermoves. That formerly quietly controlled game of musical chairs degenerates into whirling dervishes style chaos, power drains from formerly confident players.

High GCRs now fall as top incumbents cede market share to usurpers. I term this vicious down-cycle *global wars* to distinguish this scenario from increasing international fragmentation, when GCRs are negligible and falling, such that global rivals scarcely matter. Global consolidation can, confusingly, occur even when high GCRs are falling, as weaker capacity is weeded out. We should therefore complement our global concentration analysis, adding one further concentration metric: simply the number of significant players. Are we down to just four major global players, from thousands as happened in pins? Is this number rising or falling? We should also distinguish incumbent numbers (typically from advanced countries) and newcomer numbers (typically from rising nations). As former numbers fall, the latter numbers typically continue rising for a time, disguising any ultimate contraction in total participant numbers. Later, once these global gales have completed their havoc, weeding out marginally competitive capacity, both numbers may fall. As new leaders, in turn, consolidate their new positions in the pecking order, GCRs may again rise. They usually fluctuate longitudinally (as in Figure 2.6).

During *global wars*, such sinusoidal dynamic effects are non-linear and hard to predict. At pain of survival, oligopolistic responses may prove more emotional than rational, especially in relation to megamergers (discussed in Chapter 7). As in war, is now the time to '*disguise fair nature with hard-favoured rage*'? As discussed in Appendix B, family firms, guarding future generations, often prove more steadfast than public companies insistent upon shareholder value; but no one wants to be driven out. All must raise their games (ideally looking to global not local performance standards), anticipating others doing likewise. Now is also the time when even powerful global players necessarily take recourse to retrenchment and turnaround policies, as elaborated in Chapter 12. This is no gentle process of Walrasian prices re-adjusting to happy new equilibria, as theorised in traditional 'equilibrium economics'.

Falling GCRs can beguile economists into suspecting international fragmentation; yet now is the time when global competition has become crucial. Ghemawat and Ghadar warned that cars, aluminium, and oil had undergone falls in global CR and Herfindahl indices; but I would caution against their inference that aggressive global responses were correspondingly misplaced.[42] These are not fragmented domestic industries, where only fools overinvest internationally.[43] In sectors surpassing double-digit GCRs, competition is already global. There is a global ratchet effect. Even where GCRs fall back, competition does not revert to being simply local or fragmented. Wolves pounce on incumbents displaying less than total international commitment. It was General Motor's under response to global competition, not over aggressive global moves or megamergers, which led to its bankruptcy; it owes its salvation to its superb position in the ever more important Chinese market. Rugman's advocated regional/bi-regional strategies likewise risk downplaying China.

CARR'S 'UNIVERSAL' THEORETICAL FRAMEWORK RELATING TO OLIGOPOLIES

There is a difference between sectors where the locus of effective rivalry remains essentially local and those characterised by more global competition, depicted on the y axis in Figure 2.9. The debate between Adam Smith's classical economists and Karl Marx's critique can be depicted on the x axis, based on sector CRs. In Smith's day, the locus of competition for pins was changing from being the local town or even village, characterised by craft skills, to becoming national. This transition facilitated modern factories, using the market more extensively, to achieve 400-fold scale economies as compared with tiny craft shops. Positive about such market benefits, Smith was equally positive about incipient international trade. Entrepreneurs should exploit such an efficient division of labour as extensively as possible; in contrast to mercantilists, Smith advocated governments encourage trade and freer domestic and international markets.

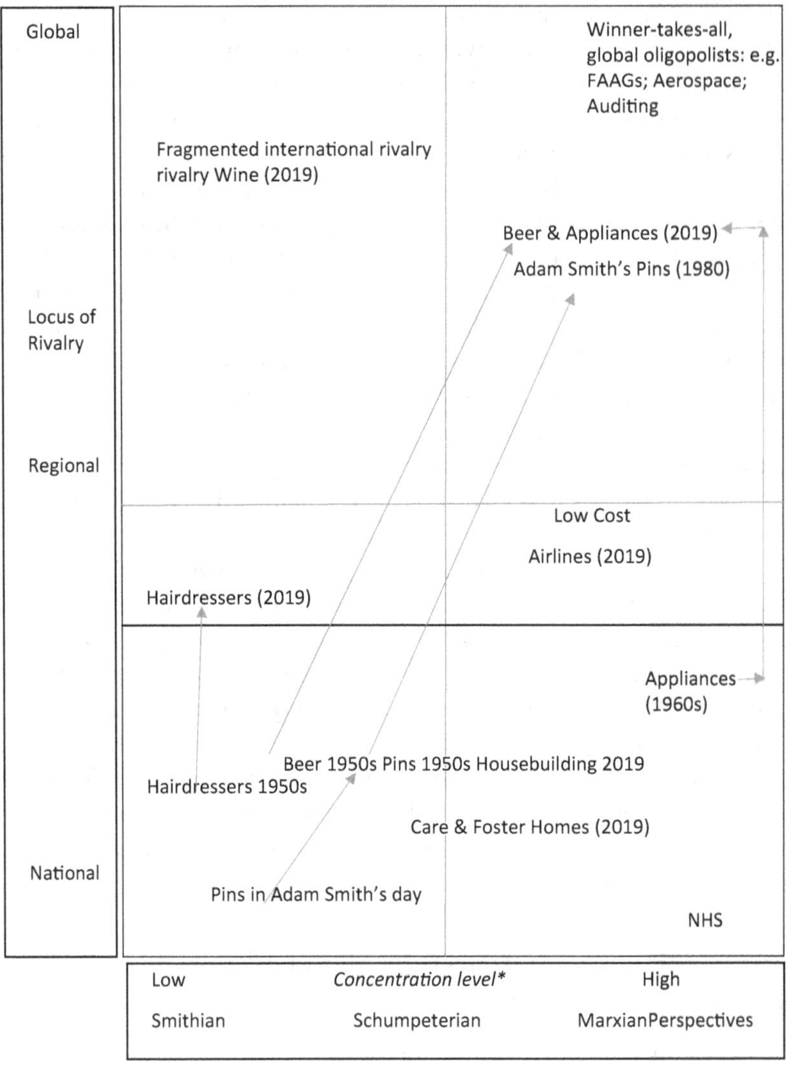

Figure 2.9 Carr's universal theory of oligopolies: Smith, Schumpeterian, and Marxist influences related to sectors' loci of rivalry and concentration ratios. *Note*: *CR metrics here need to be calculated at appropriate loci of rivalry. At the top, this means global CRs; in the middle, regional CRs; and at the bottom, national CRs.

Many entrepreneurs today, like Ortega at Zara, wisely exploited this division of labour, writ global, as this became more feasible. Yet, Smith would have been perplexed by Ortega's oligopoly power and wealth, rivalling that of many nations – the subject of his book! In Smithian classical economics, new entrants (attracted by superior profits) appear in such numbers as to render fast fashion once again a commodity market, akin to his experience of the pin industry. Were this so, CRs whether CR1s, CR4s, or even CR10s, whether calculated globally or domestically, would return to zero. Facing so many rivals, entrepreneurs find their quest for superior profits beyond their cost of capital returned to zero, aside from perhaps a slight risk premium. Entrepreneurs collectively find themselves like foolish rats on a wheel, running faster and faster, yet getting nowhere.

A neat consistent theoretical model; yet entrepreneurs are not quite so stupid. Why would they work so passionately all their lives? Why indeed bother to get up one single morning? Wise entrepreneurs do not altogether ignore this Smithian paradox. They know that rivals will ultimately come at them, even were regulators tardy in measures against undue monopolies. A good question in any boardroom is always 'if this business opportunity is so good, why hasn't someone else already done it'?

Entrepreneurs need to consider potential entrants. As Marx argued, if scale economies were as strong as argued by Smith, why would players not prioritise scale, as the obvious counter to any such threat? Appropriate high market share and entrants, with more limited shares, may struggle to compete. Such is the strategic logic behind sector consolidations. By taking his better fast fashion model to the world faster than even rivals as strong as H&M, Ortega at Zara has consistently outperformed minor rivals for over two decades, securing a fortune. In fact, GCRs remain relatively modest in fast fashion, though certainly not zero; paradoxically, even the GCR4 in Smith's famous pin industry has become remarkably high. Even by 1980, there were only four major pin manufacturers globally, including one in Scandinavia, one in Germany, and a couple in North America. Global top players do consolidate sectors, thereby achieving top four market positions which, in turn, do appropriate on average around 40% of all global profits (as evidenced in Chapter 1). This appropriation effect is even stronger (at around 60% of all global profits) as sectors (such as beer) have often moved towards Figure 2.9's top right-hand box, as GCR4s exceed 40%.

Whether we should take rather more Marxian as opposed to Smithian theoretical perspectives must depend upon which sectors we are dealing with, or which (from a macro-policy perspective) sectors dominate our economies or not. Ideological extremes are apt to overgeneralise, favouring one pole or the other. More pragmatic realities lie somewhere mid-way, though the weighted average has shifted more towards the right-hand side (contributing to rising levels of appropriation and potential inequalities and Piketty's recent concerns).

Yet Marxian perspectives are also inadequate. Most sectors have not sustained ever-rising GCRs. As we have just seen, once GCRs get into double digits or remotely approach 40% levels, diminishing Smith's pertinence, instead of moving inexorably towards Marxian, sclerotic global monopolies, they more typically revert towards the left. The most pertinent theoretical perspective is more dynamic and Schumpeterian, with GCRs fluctuating as depicted in Figure 2.6. Wise entrepreneurs recognise such dynamics. Having invested massively in new products, services, and developments, they know it is reckless *not* to attempt to spread such costs over the greatest possible customer bases, maximising scale economies; but they also know that advantages cannot last forever. Even gains from arbitraging, say China's lower wage costs are short-lived: a once twenty-fold gap as compared with the West is rapidly closing. To survive Schumpeterian rivalry and still make money, they must be dynamic, constantly striving to stay just one step ahead. As Chinese wages rose, Honda, for example, has shifted to strategic alliances in Vietnam where wages remain far lower.

Strategists, like policymakers, need to be pragmatic. The locus of competition in some sectors, especially those linked to regulated public services, remains far more local, and are positioned in the lower quadrants in Figure 2.9. Just rarely we found sectors, such as groceries or low-cost airlines, where the locus of competition really was still regional, not global: in 2018, the European regional concentration ratio (RCR2) was around 40% (Ryanair and EasyJet). In sectors where the locus of competition is still more local, we can find powerful domestic oligopolies, such as those positioned on the right-hand side: In the public sector or cases of services which have yet to be de-regulated, it is not uncommon to find virtual monopolies. Oligopolistic issues may prove just as important locally and appropriations just as great, but these are local, not global, oligopolies, and other critical issues arise. Strategists engaged internationally, to whom this book is addressed, though, require insights into performance outcomes as next discussed.

NOTES

1 As psychologist, coach, and former surgeon, Professor Steve Peters questions the use of motivation statements: '*My motivation may be good or bad one morning, but you don't want your surgical operation's outcome to depend on how I'm feeling. Oh, I'm really sorry: I'd like to do a good job on you, but I'm just not feeling that motivated today! The thing which matters is "Commitment" – the professionalism and commitment to do a great job whatever the circumstances and however you are feeling*'. Source: 'Chimp Paradox' presentation, Buxton 8.9.2017. The same applies for world class multi-national teams going global: they commit to huge strategic investment over decades.

2 A British exception is Johnson Matthey, which is a major global niche player in chemicals and precious metals, including environmentally crucial catalysts and catalytic converters. Established in 1817, it had plants in Belgium, the USA, and Australia by 1989. It had 13,000 employees in 2016/17, 53% in Europe, 25% in North America, 18% in Asia, and 4% in the rest of the world. Sales increased from £1.4 billion in 1989 to £11 billion in 2013 and £12 billion in 2017. In the latter 5 years, its RoCE averaged 19%. Like GKN, it has arguably survived and flourished through exceptional global commitment, though in 2019, it too faced pressure from hedge funds.

3 In Chapter 2, I acknowledge gratefully the contribution of Euan Robertson on several global concentration and performance analyses and research cooperation from Professor David Collis and Harvard Business School's Strategy group over five months in 2006.
4 All those I've met retreat behind claims of just being '*theorists*', but based on what? We can all have theories, but if these are not evidence based, their value is questionable.
5 Porter, M.E. (1980). Ibid., pp. 191–214.
6 Bartlett, C.A. and Ghoshal, S. (1981). *Managing Across Borders: The Transnational Solution*. Cambridge, MA: Harvard Business School Press; Baden, F.C. and Stopford J. (1991). 'Globalisation frustrated: The case of white goods', *Strategic Management Journal*, 12, pp. 493–507; Yip, G. and Hult, G.T.M. (2012). *Total Global Strategy*. Upper Saddle River, NJ: Pearson.
7 Carr, C. (1993). 'Global, national and resource-based strategies: The case of automotive components', *Strategic Management Journal*, 14, pp. 551–568.
8 To be discussed further, but for an extensive list of recent changes in general globalization drivers, see Yip, G.S. and Hult, G.T.M., ibid., p. 12.
9 Yip, G.S. and Hult, G.T.M., ibid., pp. 12, 30, 41, 50, 55.
10 Ibid., but see also Bartlett, C.A. and Ghoshal, S. (1981) ibid.
11 Andersen, T.B. and Hallen, C.A. (2017). *Global Strategic Responsiveness*. London: Routledge.
12 Yip, G.S. and Hult, G.T.M., ibid., pp. 22–23.
13 Chandler, A.F. (1962). *Strategy and Structure: Chapters in the History of the Industrial Enterprise*. Cambridge, MA: Harvard Business School Press.
14 Liu, L. and Carr, C. (2009). Globally frustrated? Revisiting the case of domestic appliances, *Strategic Management Society Annual Conference*, 11–14 October 2009.
15 Carr, C. (1993). Ibid., pp. 551–568.
16 Ghemawat, P. and Ghadar, F. (2000). 'The dubious logic of global megamergers', *Harvard Business Review*, (July–August), pp. 65–72. For some further sectors, see also Ghemawat, P. and Ghadar, F. (2006). 'Global integration is not equal to global concentration', *Industrial and Corporate Change*, 15 (1), pp. 595–623.
17 Carr, C. and Collis, D. (2011). 'Should you have a global strategy?', *Sloan Management Review*, 53, 1, pp. 21–24.
18 Scherer, F. and Ross, D. (1990). *Industrial Market Structure and Economic Performance*. Boston: Houghton Mifflin; Stigler, G.J. (1950). 'The development of utility theory', *Journal of Political Economy*, 58 (4), pp. 307–327.
19 Sheth, J. and Sosodia, R. (2002). *The Rule of Three: Surviving and Thriving in Competitive Markets*. New York: Free Press.
20 Welch, J. (2002). *Jack: What I've Learned Leading a Great Company and a Great People*. London: Headline.
21 When challenged on an evident lack of knowledge on global concentration levels, common defences are '*ah well, all business is global these days*' or '*ah well, globalisation is anyway grossly exaggerated*'; but such overgeneralities serve to disguise ignorance and superficiality. A more credible defence would be for 'strategy experts', unversed in this international field, simply to acknowledge that their strategy expertise relates merely to dwindling numbers of sectors (such as many public services) still conducted domestically.
22 This section draws heavily on a supervised MSC dissertation by Euan Robertson, whose contribution here is gratefully acknowledged.
23 Source: Statistica and Profit Works CA accessed on line 9 May 2019. McDonalds' US fast food market share was 43% on the same basis.
24 Between 2009 and 2012, Peabody Energy, for example, led US coal output controlling 18%, but held only 0.7% of global output, and ranked only fifth globally.
25 Richard Hemming 11 November 2018 showed volume-based estimates from 0.5% in 2016, from 2.8% in 2012. Zion Markets Research market $ figures suggest 1.7% for 2017.

26 Shepherd (1997, pp. 15–16). See also Harford, T. (2005). *The Undercover Economist*. New York: Little, Brown.
27 Mujtaba, B. (2009). *Workforce Diversity: Challenges, Competencies and Strategies*. Carrollton, KY: iLead Academy.
28 Hipwell, D. 'McDonald's is knocking at the door of vast new home delivery market', *Times*, 29 July 2017, p. 63.
29 Sources for GCR4s: Andrew von Nordenflycht, 'Firm size and industry structure under human capital intensity: Insights from the evolution of the global advertising industry', *Organisational Science*, March 2010, p. 5, Table 2; 2005 estimate from an unpublished update by von Nordenflycht was 45% on a holding companies basis. *The Financial Times*, 13 August 2012, p. 2 had the top five agencies as accounting for 25% of gross global revenues, though other estimates might well be lower, depending on precise industry definitions.
30 *Financial Times*, 3 October 2017. p. 16. 'WPP to fight Bain bid for ad agency'. '*With only about 7% of the domestic advertising market, ADK lies behind Dentsu and Hakuhodo*, [but exhibits] *growing success in digital advertising*, [and aims to] *look more broadly* [than WPP] *for partners on the digital advertising side*'.
31 Performance data are from Thomson One Banker for RoCEs, sales growth, and total investor returns discussed later in this section.
32 http://www.pcworld.idg.com.au/article/416622/elpida_world_third-largest_dram_maker_files_bankruptcy/.
33 Sheth and Sosodia, ibid., argue, however, that market share and profitability relationship are non-linear. Market share correlated strongly with profitability among US larger companies, but smaller niched specialists also sometimes generate supernormal profits. The worst 'ditch' position was No 7s, 'stuck-in-the-middle' between highly profitable leaders and tiny niched specialists. Their data were solely for the USA, but their logic is arguably better explored using global market share data, except in more domestic sectors.
34 Source: Gartner and Bernstein analysis; Canalys. *Financial Times* 17 May 2019, p. 6.
35 Biotechnology and gold averaged 5-year returns on capital were, respectively, –23% and –2%, amongst the worst performing sectors.
36 Smith, A. (1776). *The Wealth of Nations*. London: W. Strahan and T. Cadell; Marx, K. (1867). *Capital. A Critique of Political Economy*, reissued as Oxford's World Classic paperback 1999, Oxford; Schumpeter, J.A. (1954). *Capitalism, Socialism, and Democracy*. London: Allen and Unwin.
37 *The Economist* 1 January 2018, p. 55. Source: National Bureau of Economic Research.
38 Source: *Financial Times* 25 September 2017, p. 19. Investments were expected to double again by 2017 to $3.2 billion. Falling DNA sequencing costs towards about $100 should allow cancer diagnoses to be individualised. Such scale economies, affecting all our lives, are huge.
39 *Sunday Times Business Section*, 24 September 2017, p. 9.
40 Pratten, C.F. (1980). 'The manufacture of pins', *Journal of Economic Literature*, 18 (1), pp. 93–96.
41 Piketty, T. (2013). *Capital in the Twenty-First Century*. Boston: Harvard University.
42 Ghemawat, P. and Ghadar, F. Ibid. For some further sectors, again see Ghemawat, P. and Ghadar, F. (2006). Ibid.
43 Ghemawat, P. and Ghadar, F. Ibid., cautioned Global HIs were falling by around the year 2000 even in seemingly global sectors, like oil production and refining, cars, and aluminium, arguing for more conservative regional strategies, eschewing global mega-moves/mergers. Global HIs and CR4s rose subsequently in all four sectors examined, following consolidation moves. In aluminium, Russia's Rusal leapt to global No 1 and Canada's Alcan (previously global No 2) was acquired by Rio Tinto. Though misinterpreting underlying globalisation trends, Ghemawat and Ghadar rightly highlighted notorious M&A integration risks: Rio Tinto's Tom Albanese later resigned as CEO after writing off some $10 billion on his Alcan acquisition. Over the

same period, Rio Tinto and equally acquisitive BHP Billiton, nevertheless, delivered average annual shareholder returns of 9.5 and 17% p.a., compared with the FTSE's average of 4%. Subsequently, both companies overdiversified and overinvested, destroying shareholder value in the wake of a commodity price downturn. Likewise, global CR5 trends have not followed Ghemawat and Ghadar (2006)'s downward trajectories. However, the real problem lies with their interpretation of *changes* in such metrics as key; in economic theory relating to conduct and performances, it is rather the *level* of CRs (or HIs) which is critical. Change measures are secondary and indicative; if levels are high, they cannot keep rising forever. Global CR4s already ranged from 30% to over 60% in their sectors, rendering downs, as well as ups, inevitable. The thesis that global oligopolies' impacts are dispelled by minor fluctuations is contradicted by historical studies in the case of oil: see, for example, Anthony Sampson (1975). *The Seven Sisters. The Great Oil Companies & the World They Shaped*, New York: Viking Press.

3

GLOBAL WINNERS, OLIGOPOLISTIC MOVES AND OUTCOMES IN SPIRITS SECTOR 1939–2019

Chris Carr and Benedikt Schwittay[1]

INTRODUCTION

How do global winners emerge to transform sectors, and what is the impact on moves and countermoves as global concentration ratios (GCRs) begin rising? Between 1982 and 1995 spirits, Britain's most successful export sector, underwent an instructive transition from a multi-domestic to a global industry, the premium spirits sector's GCR4 (based on volumes) rose from 29% to 52%.[2] This chapter presents a historical analysis, developing a theoretical model of global winners, and then gives updates in the light of subsequent moves and countermoves.

The 19 United Kingdom (UK), United States (US), and German companies investigated all had sales volumes of at least £100 million in 1995.[3] They controlled on average over 70% of these national markets in volume and value terms and 71% of the global spirits market. Cluster analysis,[4] followed by 'strategic group' (SG) analysis[5] were done at national levels for 1982–1986, and then at a global level for the period 1987–1995 as GCRs rose higher.

A century ago, the first phase of the spirits industry's evolution had been local regional at a sub-national level: competition was fragmented, even atomistic. Even national markets had not yet consolidated. In phase 2, as powerful players began to consolidate national markets, national CRs rose and strategies became nationally orientated. These SGs are shown in Figures 3.1 and 3.2, and this evolutionary perspective is depicted in Table 3.1. In phase 3, by 1982, several players dominated national markets, but faced an added ambivalent, transitional shift more internationally as rising GCR4 metrics approached 30%.

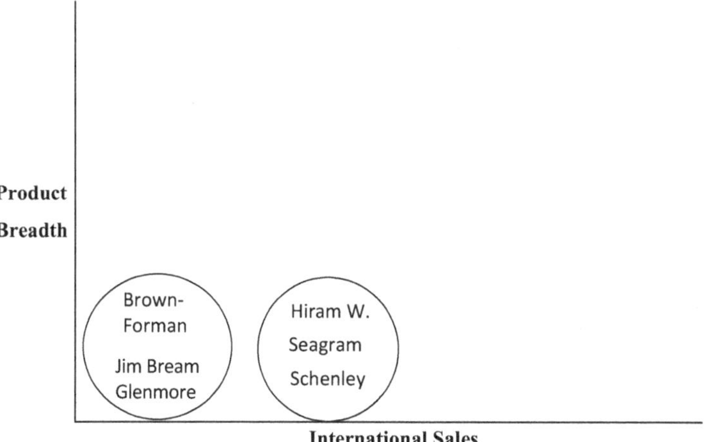

Figure 3.1 Strategic groups in the spirits market (Phase 1, atomistic, until 1939). *Sources*: Schwittay, B. (1999). *Globalisation and Strategic Groups: the Case of the Spirits Industry*. Doctoral thesis, Manchester: University of Manchester, Faculty of Business Administration, Table 7.8, p. 201.

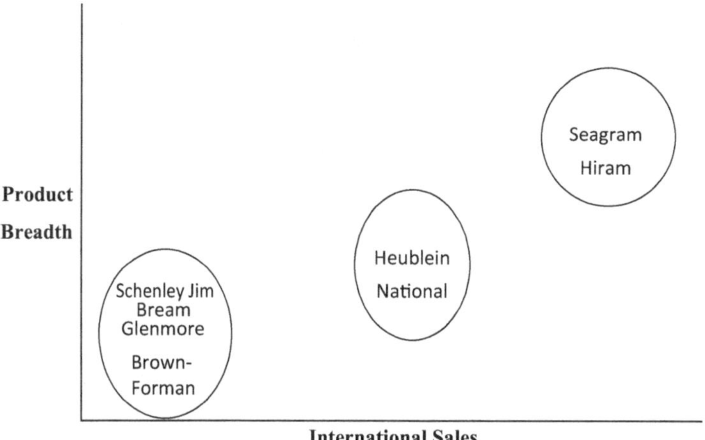

Figure 3.2 Strategic groups in the global spirits market (Phase 2, national, 1945–1981). *Source*: Schwittay, B. (1999). *Globalisation and Strategic Groups: the Case of the Spirits Industry*. Doctoral thesis, Manchester: University of Manchester, Faculty of Business Administration, Table 7.8, p. 201.

At this point, our interviews permitted cluster analysis, revealing, five statistically significant SGs in the UK, four SGs in the US, and two SGs in the German market during the period 1982–1986, as shown in Figures 3.3–3.5. In the UK, we analysed all ten spirits companies with over £100 million in sales and identified five SGs[6]; in the German spirits market, all nine such companies were divided into just two SGs[7]; in the US spirits market, ten such companies were divided into four multi-member SGs.[8] Statistical analysis endorsed such SG clusters and helped to explain differential averaged profitability and sales growth outcomes, as between SGs, thus indicating better performing strategic choices (as regarding scope and internationalisation) for players, over this 1982–1986 period.

Table 3.1 'Four-phases' framework

Phase	*First*	*Second*	*Third*	*Fourth*
Concentration/ geography	Pre-national consolidation	National concentration	Pre-global consolidation	Global concentration
Competition	Atomistic	Concentrated	Atomistic	Concentrated
Strategic orientation	Regional	National	International/ transnational	Global

Source: Schwittay, B. and Carr, C. (2001). 'New strategic group concepts in the transition to a changing global environment – A dynamic analysis of strategic group behaviour in the world-wide spirits industry', in McDonald, F., Tuselmann, H., and Wheeler, C. (2002, Ed.). *International Business: Adjusting to New Challenges and Opportunities.* Basingstoke: Palgrave, Table 17.1, p. 225. Reprinted by permission.

Note: For further elaboration, see also Schwittay (1999). Globalisation and Strategic Groups: the Case of the Spirits Industry. Doctoral thesis, Manchester: University of Manchester, Faculty of Business Administration.

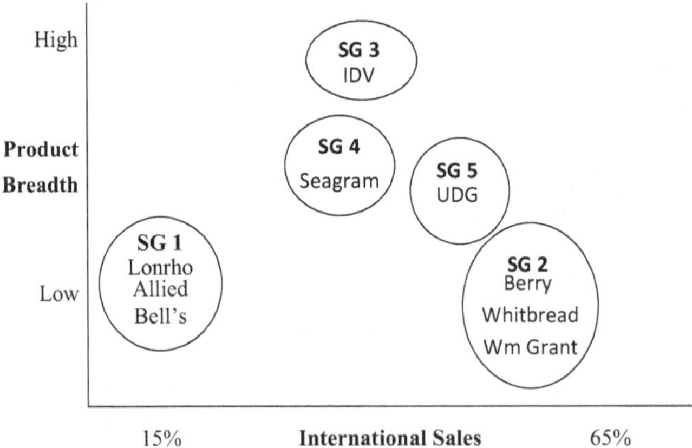

Figure 3.3 Hierarchical cluster analysis of the UK spirits market (Phase 3, 1982–1986). *Source:* Schwittay, B. and Carr, C. (2001). 'New strategic group concepts in the transition to a changing global environment – A dynamic analysis of strategic group behaviour in the world-wide spirits industry', in McDonald, F., Tuselmann, H., and Wheeler, C. (2002, Ed.). *International Business: Adjusting to New Challenges and Opportunities*. Basingstoke: Palgrave, Figure 17.1, p. 229. Reprinted by permission. *Note:* Based on Hierarchical Cluster Analysis. For further elaboration, see also Schwittay (1999) ibid.

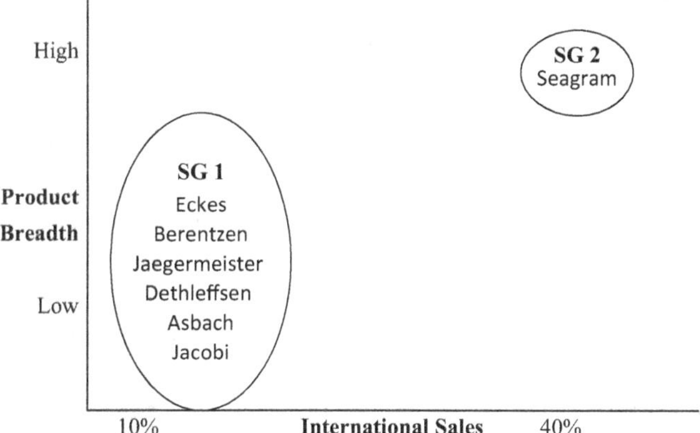

Figure 3.4 Hierarchical cluster analysis: German spirits market (Phase III, 1982–1986). *Source:* Schwittay, B. and Carr, C. (2001). "New strategic group concepts in the transition to a changing global environment – A dynamic analysis of strategic group behaviour in the world-wide spirits industry", in McDonald, F., Tuselmann, H. and Wheeler, C. (2002, Ed.). *International Business: Adjusting to New Challenges and Opportunities.* Basingstoke: Palgrave, Figure 17.2, p. 230. Reprinted by permission. *Note:* Based on Hierarchical Cluster Analysis. For further elaboration, see also Schwittay (1999) ibid.

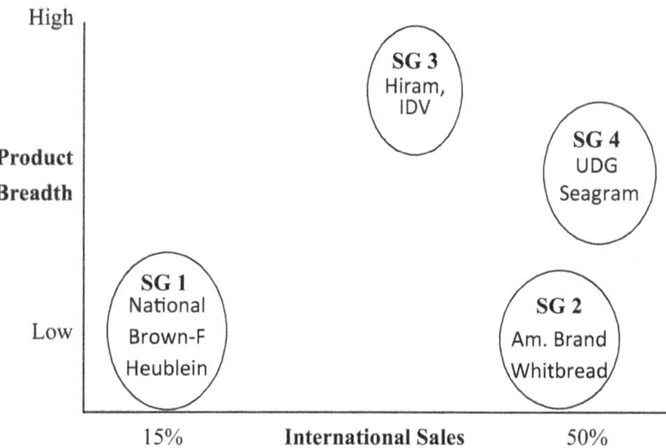

Figure 3.5 Hierarchical cluster analysis: US spirits market (Phase 3, 1982–1986). *Source:* Schwittay, B. and Carr, C. (2001). 'New Strategic Group Concepts in the Transition to a Changing Global Environment – A Dynamic Analysis of Strategic Group Behaviour in the World-Wide Spirits Industry', in McDonald, F., Tuselmann, H., and Wheeler, C. (2002, Ed.). *International Business: Adjusting to New Challenges and Opportunities.* Basingstoke: Palgrave, Figure 17.3, p. 230. Reprinted by permission. *Note:* Based on Hierarchical Cluster Analysis. For further elaboration, see also Schwittay (1999) ibid.

STATISTICAL STRATEGIC GROUPS ANALYSIS OF OLIGOPOLISTIC INTERNATIONAL COMPETITION 1987–1995

After 1986, these SG clusters conducted nationally no longer discriminated meaningful firm behaviour or consistent SG performance outcomes – a cautionary warning for SG analysis, using merely national data, once the locus of competition has gone global. Reclustering through factor analysis for all 19 US, UK, and German companies on a new global basis, however, now produced three multi-member SGs, distinctive from each other in terms of choices in respect to product breadth and international sales, as shown in Figure 3.6.[9]

SGs and group memberships changed between both time phases, reflecting instability during this transition phase. Aside from two, the other nine companies joined new SG constellations as compared to the pre-global period. SG membership patterns also reflected countries of origin and national competitive advantages. Spirits companies chose their strategies (and thus their SGs) by joining or forming groups with competitors they had known well before, using from their same home markets: companies from the same country dominated two of the three SGs. This, taken together with a fully 100-year historical analysis, confirmed the importance of national competitive advantages (as discussed in Porter 1990). This emerged as a phase 3 transitional effect on route to globalisation.[10]

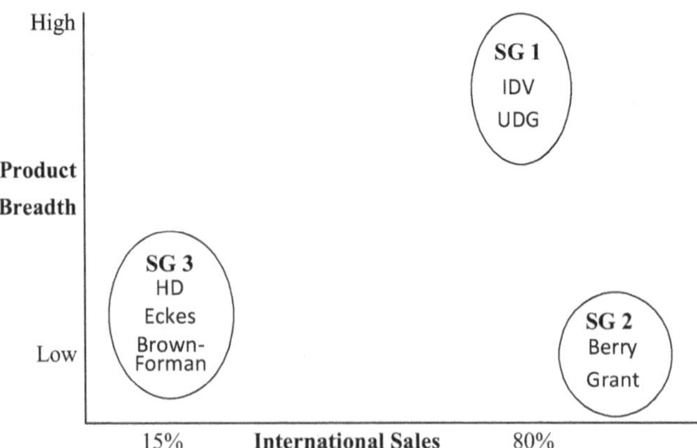

Figure 3.6 Hierarchical cluster analysis: global spirits market (Phase 4, 1987–1995). *Source:* Schwittay, B. and Carr, C. (2001). 'New strategic group concepts in the transition to a changing global environment – A dynamic analysis of strategic group behaviour in the world-wide spirits industry', in McDonald, F., Tuselmann, H., and Wheeler, C. (2002, Ed.). *International Business: Adjusting to New Challenges and Opportunities.* Basingstoke: Palgrave, Figure 17.4, p. 231. Reprinted by permission. *Note:* Based on Hierarchical Cluster Analysis. For further elaboration, see also Schwittay (1999) ibid.

Differences of friendly and hostile behaviour between members of the same SG and members of different SGs proved less significant. There were 79% of executives that considered intra-SG relationships predominantly neutral, with most (77%) describing extra-group-relationships as friendlier. There were 92% of senior executives that considered that strategy imitation played a highly significant role within their industry. Strategy imitation played an important oligopolistic role in global strategic group interactions, implying at least some tacit collusion.

Globalisation was triggered initially by the launch of a global strategy by UDG's visionary chairman Ernest Saunders, countered by similar moves by its UK' rival IDV, likewise motivated by declining UK profit levels. Both suddenly acquired former distribution partners in the US and other sizable foreign spirits companies, building up global distribution networks and full-line product portfolios. The UK No 3, Allied Breweries, and the US-Canadian company Seagram followed suit shortly afterwards, and all four companies followed each other from continent to continent between 1987 and the early 1990s, acquiring or forming joint ventures (JV)s with local spirits distribution companies. Table 3.2 delineates merger and acquisitions (M&A) and extensive strategic imitations.

By 1995, these four companies together controlled 52% of the world's one million cases of spirits brands. Since the formation of their most globally orientated SG in 1987, this SG continuously increased its world market share year by year. Economies of scale and scope, resulting from full-line brand portfolios, achieved major cost savings in production, distribution, and marketing. Owning distribution networks allowed them independence, full brand marketing control, and to survive ensuing global shakeouts. Nevertheless, no statistically significant relationships were found between such strategic group-memberships and financial and market performance during the sample time period of 1987 to 1995. Whilst this global SG was the best performing SG in terms of returns on sales (ROS) and market share growth, we could not confirm this at a statistically significant level. The second best-performing SG, companies pursuing an international strategy, came close. Early global SG short term profitability outcomes were positive, but not conclusive statistically.

SG analysis, applied globally rather than nationally, thus provided a useful tool for competitive analysis, allowing performance outcomes to be assessed for key strategic choices. Does greater scope pay off, or should we go for greater internationalisation, or perhaps both? Once such consistent SGs have been established, at the appropriate geographical level, performance databases aid up-to-date assessments and guidance for such strategic choices. We need at least 5-, if not 10-, year up-dated performance data sets for all key players, some historical evolutionary perspective, and periodic updating of SG classifications.

Table 3.2 Major international acquisitions of UDG, IDV, and Allied, 1986–1995

Year	*US/Canada*	*Europe/Far East*	*L. America*
1986	UDG => Schenley/US	UDG => Alliance with LVMH/Fra (1986)	
1987	IDV => Heublein/US	Caldbeck-Dodwell/HK (1987)	
1988	Almaden/US (1987)	JV with Jardines/Jap (1987)	
	La Salle/US (1989)	JV witch Inchcape/HK (1987)	
	Allied => Hiram/US	IDV => Far East JV with Martell (1987)	
		JV with Cinzano/It (1987)	
		Allied => JV with IDV/Aus (1987)	
		JV with Suntory/Jap (1988)	
1989–1990	UDG => Schenley/ Can (1990)	UDG => Asbach/Ger (1991)	UDG => Pampero (1991)
		IDV => Metaxa/Gre (1989)	
1991	Glenmore/US (1991)	AED/Spa (1990)	
1991		Emmet/Ire (1991)	
	Allied => Corby/Can	Allied => JV with Spirit/It (1989)	
		JV with Costa Pina/Por (1989)	
		JV in Thailand (1990)	
		JV with Genka/Gre (1990)	
1992–1995		IDV => Cinzano/It (1992)	IDV => JV in Colombia (1994)
		JV with Ekpac/HK (1992)	
		JV with Young/Kor (1992)	
		Gonzalez & B./Spa (1992)	Allied => JV in Venezuela (1993)
		Buton/It (1993)	
		Picon/Fra (1995)	
		Allied => JV in India (1993)	JV in Chile (1993)
		PJBG/Fra (1993)	
		P.Domecq/Spa (1994)	
		Jacobi/Ger (1994)	
		JV in China (1995)	

Source: Schwittay, B. and Carr, C. (2001). 'New strategic group concepts in the transition to a changing global environment – A dynamic analysis of strategic group behaviour in the world-wide spirits industry', in McDonald, F., Tuselmann, H., and Wheeler, C. (2002, Ed.). *International Business: Adjusting to New Challenges and Opportunities*. Basingstoke: Palgrave, Table 17.2, p. 232. Reprinted by permission. Based on annual reports, industry journals, and *Financial Times*. For further elaboration, see also Schwittay (1999) ibid.

CHARACTERISTICS OF 'GLOBALISATION SURVIVORS'

As the spirits sector consolidated globally, we observed a process akin to Schumpeter's '*gales of creative destruction*'. Just a few companies metamorphosed into global winners, their moves and countermoves intensifying rivalry and shakeouts. Fewer were able to compete across all market segments; some focused on global niches. Some leveraged their assets and hedged their bets through international strategic alliances. Weaker players struggled, lacking cash flows to match investments required to remain globally, and ultimately exited. Many were acquired as global winners sought to consolidate and integrate new assets.

Anticipating such processes requires analysis of 'globalisation preconditions, delineated in international business texts'[11] including scale economies of scope or specialisation; convergence of consumer requirements; exploiting brands or technology; and arbitrage exploiting wage differences worldwide. Constraints include government tariffs, controls, and regulations, as well as transportation, storage, and communication costs. Less appreciated is that companies have increasingly turned to foreign direct investment (FDI), as their principal internationalisation strategy, to circumvent such trade constraints. Whilst trade theory has become insufficient, FDI investment appraisals entail more far-ranging considerations.

The balance of forces is inherently difficult to determine. As in football matches, nothing appears to happen for ages, but, like cognoscenti, we must 'read between the lines' and sense that tipping point. One company makes a novel global move; another (often from the same SG) retaliates and suddenly 'the game's afoot'. A moment ago, all had appeared so stable, uneventful, and dull. Now security evaporates; global consolidation threatens; only world-class stars seem set to survive. Anyone still in doubt would be wiser anticipating relentless global evolution, prompted by scale economies and Smith's division of labour writ globally.

Figure 3.7 suggests techniques to help map and comprehend these global transformation processes and likely outcomes. First, strategy texts[12] help elaborate notions of 'strategic fit'; survivors do proactively exploit distinctive strengths matched to international opportunities; and they do reposition to circumvent competition and other threats, whilst addressing weaknesses and crucial issues relating to global market shares and scale. Strategic groups analysis helps map international players, their strategic behaviour, rivalries, and likely future scenarios: adding performance analyses for SG groups likewise aids strategic choices.

National competitive advantage (NCA) analysis proves especially pertinent in that third transition stage on route to globalisation, though Porter's a temporal NCA theoretical model[13] needs amending by adding some four-phase evolutionary perspective, as suggested by Table 3.1. At phase one, NCA has, anyway, little impact as competition is local; at phase four when multination corporations (MNC)s have globalised completely, they become rootless. Eventually, the coherence of a firm's (global) strategy has more impact than NCA on success or failure. Figure 3.8 depicts this by folding-in Porter's four key NCA 'diamond' drivers, appreciating their significance in phase three.

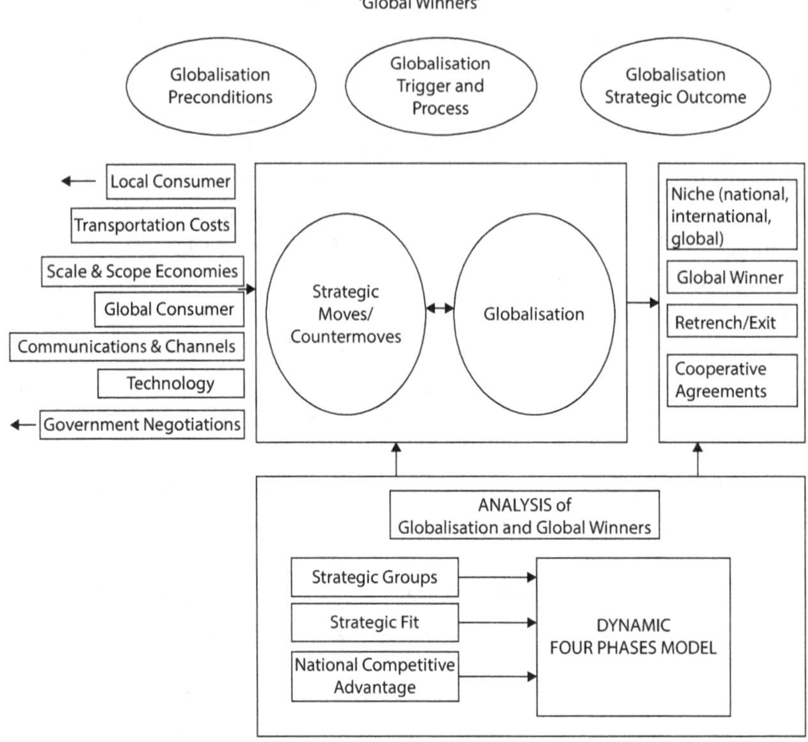

Figure 3.7 Global winners outcomes model. *Source:* Schwittay, B. (1999), ibid., Table 2.8, p. 81.

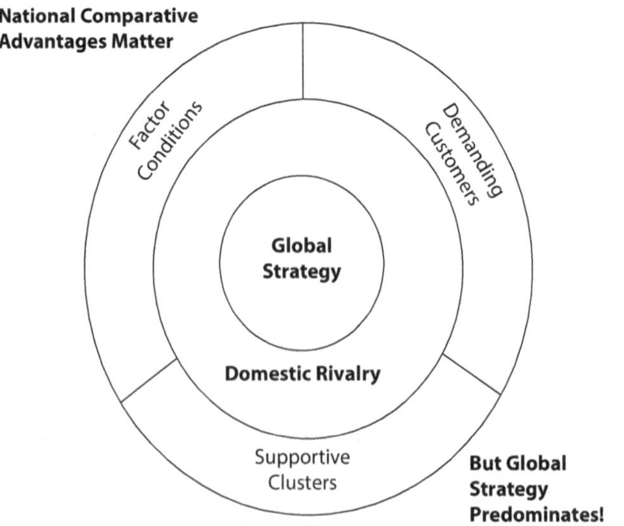

Figure 3.8 Global winners and national competitive advantage drivers.

TESTING OUR 1999 GLOBAL WINNERS MODEL: UPDATED DEVELOPMENTS TO 2019

Schwittay's global spirits doctoral study supporting our global winners model shown in Figure 3.7, published in 1999, was endorsed by events, within about 18 months. UDG and IDV, Britain's major players, still charted separately in Figure 3.7, merged creating Diageo, the sector's first global winner. Its moves triggered countermoves and global consolidation, reshaping the sector. Spirits have emerged, in trade terms, as Britain's most successful sector.

France's Pernod Ricard, as a far-sighted family firm interviewed in Paris in 1998, proved equally bold subsequently. Like two globally aspiring lions, they and Diageo then worked together, taking out North America's biggest beast, Seagram. US spirits brands never quite recovered from Prohibition in the 1930s, allowing Seagram (in Canada just over the border) to dominate the North America market. Yet Seagram's younger family generation now held other business interests. Could they best 'parent' spirits, matching Diageo's investments as this mature industry consolidated?[14] Or should they prioritise media, promising sexier, faster growth? Funding both raised crucial questions of strategic focus, whilst stretching funds. Today's globally orientated investors rarely any longer favour unrelated diversification. The Seagram family therefore took the money for their spirits business and reinvested further in media/entertainment; whilst Diageo and Pernod Ricard both stepped up North American and global market shares,[15] keeping their merger and acquisition (M&A) investments within bounds.

Maintaining pace globally with Diageo, Pernod Ricard went on to acquire Britain's second largest player, Allied Lyons, whose parent group likewise enjoyed alternative investment opportunities. Regulatory concessions dictated some divestments for Pernod Ricard, who sold to Fortune Brands, the group formerly known as American Brands controlling Jim Beam. Both American Brands and Brown-Forman, formerly North American-centric, were finally emerging as a strategic group, slightly more international than other former SG3s depicted in Figure 3.5.

Akin to 'crack propagation' or 'earthquake-after-shock' theories, global mega-moves provoked further instabilities. Others targeted divested opportunities, then realigned to counter up-scaled global rivals. In 2005, Fortune Brands spent $5 billion acquiring Jim Beam and increased investments in 18 further brands, rising to No 4 globally. Beam Global was renamed in 2007, as they divested wine activities and refocused as a 'spirits pure-play' company. In 2010, Fortune split into three, refocusing as internationalisation continued. In 2014, Japan's Suntory acquired Beam creating Beam Suntory, the new No 3 globally, which enjoys strong complementary Asian and US positions. Based again on the Impact Databank Top 100 premium brands, the global concentration GCR4 figure rose to 57% in 2016, as shown in Table 3.3, higher than for the car sector, formerly so far ahead.

Table 3.3 Global premium spirits market shares and CR4 concentration trends, 2011–2016

2011: Diageo 27%; Pernod Ricard 18%; Bacardi 11%; Beam Suntory 6%; Brown-Forman 6%
2016: Diageo 25%; Pernod Ricard 16%; Bacardi 9%; Beam Suntory 7%; Brown-Forman 6%

Source: Impact Databank February 2011 and March 2016, based on volumes.

Global CR4 2016 = 57% compared with 2011 at 62%, 1995 at 52%, 1987 at 41%, and 1982 at 29%.

As in cars, GCR4s will likely fall at some point as in global wars scenarios. Growth comes increasingly from protected emerging markets calling for greater resources. Schumpeterian theory suggests that large new regions may also spawn and incubate newer business paradigms of their own, aided by their national competitive advantages.

An updated strategic group analysis for 2019 in Figure 3.9 depicts global winners Diageo, Pernod Ricard, Beam Suntory, and Bacardi-Martini at the top right given their wide spirits portfolios. Formerly America-centric Constellation Brands and Brown-Forman shifted modestly geographically, whilst broadening brand portfolios. Eckes and Berentzen (from Germany) remained conservatively in the bottom left-hand quadrant.

By contrast, Bacardi, the world's largest private spirits company, originally from Cuba, but now based in Bermuda, shifted radically to join the other three global fuller-line players in SG1. Countering others' moves, Bacardi, in 2008, initiated a 30% equity-based strategic alliance with Patron Spirits

Figure 3.9 Strategic groups in the global spirits market (Phase 4, global, 2019). *Source*: Author, updating earlier strategic groups analyses, though unsupported by hierarchical cluster analysis.

International, complementing top-end niche brand positions in rum, vodka, blended whisky, and gin with Patron's tequila. In 2014, it acquired Martini for $4.6 billion, forming Bacardi-Martini, further extending top-end brands to Martini's vermouth and sparkling wines. On 30 April 2018, its successful strategic alliance with Patroni was transitioned to a fully 100% acquisition. By 2019, with 20 production sites (including vertical integration into bottling and distribution in addition to production), Bacardi-Martini's sales extended to over 170 countries and 200 brands, moving it fully into the top right-hand SG1, alongside Diageo and Pernod Ricard.

Ten-year metrics up to 2017, shown in Tables 3.4 and 3.5, reflect recent retrenchments following a slow down in China; but, overall, global players have outpaced the spirits Financial Times stock exchange index since the end of the 1990s. Aside from Kweichow, whose market capitalisation at $84 billion reflected China's high potential, Diageo's market capital (reflecting future profit pool expectations) predominated other advanced country players at $73 billion as of 7 July 2017. Prior market capitalisations were reported at, respectively, Kweichow $72 billion, Diageo $71 billion, Constellation Brands $33 billion, Pernod Ricard $31 billion, Wuliangye Yibin $23 billion, Brown-Forman $18 billion. Suntory's market capitalisation on 21 June 2017 was Y1.60 trillion ($14 billion).

In summary, global players have consolidated successfully, their mega-mergers having been generally well integrated. In contrast, national champions have gone; even the largest regional players, Seagram and Jim Beam, have succumbed to takeovers. By 2019, in contrast to 1997, just before Diageo's formation, the sector had transformed following the emergence of four major global winners. Our intuition, at the start of Schwittay's Ph.D., that spirits might follow the car sector's much earlier path to globalisation, appears

Table 3.4 Global top spirits companies: 10-year shareholder returns, % p.a. compound

Brown-Forman 14%; Diageo 11%; Pernod Ricard 7%; Comparable Co.s 10%; S&P 500 7%

Source: FactSet as of April 30, 2017, Source Brown-Forman 2017 Annual Report.

Table 3.5 Global top spirits companies: 6-year returns on capital employed, sales, and sales growths 2010–2016

	6y RoC	*6y SG% pa*	*6y RoS*
Average Top 10	20.60	2.37	35.63
Diageo/Top 10%	94.02	−143.20	98.20
Pernod/Top10%	49.33	−63.16	89.97
Average Top 4	14.15	6.20	27.54
Av Top 4/Top 10%	68.71	261.65	77.29

Source: Thomson One Banker accessed May 2017.

vindicated. Figure 3.7's global winners model, likewise, has proven robust over two subsequent decades since, and looks promising for future-orientated judgements.

NOTES

1 This chapter draws partly on Schwittay, B. and Carr, C. (2001). 'New strategic group concepts in the transition to a changing global environment – A dynamic analysis of strategic group behaviour in the world-wide spirits industry', Manchester: Manchester Business School Working Paper, and also partly on Benedikt Schwittay's unpublished doctoral thesis, University of Manchester (1999), where I gratefully acknowledge Benedikt Schwittay's copyright, having sadly been unable to locate him in recent years. To honour his contribution, I have added his name as effectively a co-author of this chapter.

2 Source: *Impact International*, which provides consistent global markets share data for premium spirits, based on volumes represented by the numbers of 9 L bottle packs sold. Metrics for just premium spirits metrics overstated global concentration levels for spirits overall, it was important to use consistent global data over time. In 2016, whisky was Britain's most successful sector with exports of £4 billion compared with imports of £200 million.

3 A minimum sales volume of $100 million was chosen as the cut-off for sample companies for quantitative analysis and, for qualitative field research, at 47 comparable companies worldwide. The latter entailed semi-structured interviews at corporate headquarters and in national subsidiaries, and trade organisations.

4 Six strategy variables were used to conduct a hierarchical cluster analysis (at a 95% confidence level) for all three separate national markets.

5 As developed by Porter, M. (1980). *Competitive Strategy: Techniques for Analysing Industries and Competitors*. New York: Free Press.

6 The three single-member SGs (SG3, SG4, SG5) of the five SGs were closer to each other in terms of 'strategic space' than the multi-member SGs (SG1 and SG3). Analysis focused on two key strategic drivers – scope, in terms of product breadth, and scale, taking as a proxy the number of cases of brand sales – versus internationalisation taking as a proxy firms' international sales ratios. For further elaboration of the concept of strategic space, see McGee, J. and Segal-Horn, S. (1990). 'Strategic space and industry dynamics: The implications for international marketing strategy', *Journal of Marketing Management*, 6 (3), pp. 175–195.

7 The 'strategic space' (McGee and Segal-Horn, ibid.) between the multi-member SGs (SG1) and the single-member SG (SG 2) was significant.

8 In terms of 'strategic space' (McGee and Segal-Horn, ibid.), no significant differences existed between the four multi-member SGs.

9 In terms of 'strategic space' (McGee/Segal-Horn, ibid.), no significant differences existed between the three multi-member SGs.

10 In 2019, in phase 4, global MNCs in 2019 depended little on their countries of origin.

11 Yip, G. and Hult, G.T.M. (2012). *Total Global Strategy*. Upper Saddle River: Prentice Hall; Cavusgil, S.T., Knight, G., and Riesenberger, J. (2017). *International Business: The New Realities*. London: Pearson; Peng, K. and Mayer, K. (2016). *International Business*. Boston, MA: South-Western. Cengage; Hill, C.W.L. (2015). *International Business: Competing in the Global Market Place*. 9th edition, Global Edition. New York: McGraw-Hill.

12 See e.g.: Grant, R. (2019). *Contemporary Strategy Analysis*, 10th edition. Oxford: Blackwell.

13 Porter, M.E. (1990). *The Competitive Advantage of Nations*. London: Macmillan.

14 This is a common dilemma for family firms addressing global oligopolies and

consolidation processes, as going globally requires deep pockets. Whilst exporting is usually cash generative, achieving double-digit market shares in major international markets generally requires foreign direct investment, through either new expensive factories (GFS), cross-border joint ventures, or M&A. Such investments take time to pay off, stretching even those families (such as those interviewed in Germany) willing to look longer term. Keeping pace with global oligopolists simultaneously demands investments in new technologies, product generations, and world class manufacturing and distribution facilities. It takes but a single performance dip or economic downturn for families to put themselves at risk. For example, Leigh Paints' former owner and chief executive officer interviewed on 10 July 2017 recounted their similar strategic dilemma in 2015. Following a fine 150-year history they held a niche position in fire-resistant paints. Trade opportunities in Middle Eastern niche markets, encountered rivalry from global players complementing positions with more and more international facilities. Profit margins fell, forcing exits. Following suit and going global would have meant huge investments, so they succumbed to acquisition by Sherwin Williams, a major US player, aiming to extend and reinforce its international position. This was a win-win, rolling out Leigh's excellent fire-resistant paints globally facilitated by this MNC's deeper pockets and complementary geographical facilities, distribution, and relationships.
15 Likewise, history repeated itself a decade later in beer, as Heineken and Carlsberg combined to acquire and break up Scottish and Newcastle, Europe's number 2 top player.

Part II

GLOBAL STRATEGY ORIENTATIONS AND PERFORMANCE

4

GLOBAL GEOGRAPHICAL COVERAGE CHOICES AND OUTCOMES

INTRODUCTION AND METHODOLOGY

How far top global multi-nationals spread, or should sensibly spread, their sales and assets around the world has proved contentious.[1] Those, sceptical about global strategies, have argued that extensive global geographical coverage has been rare and anyway undesirable, though their methodologies have been questioned.

Rugman's analysis[2] of *Fortune*'s world top 500 in 2001 delineated their geographical sales splits by region. Companies were classified as home-regional where domestic sales were 50% or above; bi-regional, where sales were under 50% domestically, but exceeded 20% in two regions; global, where sales exceeded 20% in three regions[3]; or host-regional, where sales in a region other than the home region exceeded 50%.[4] Such (arguably artificial) criteria resulted in only nine companies meriting Rugman's 'global' classification.

Yet, on such criteria, even a tiny firm, with just $1 in three regions, would be classifiable as 'global'; by contrast Wal-Mart, with 60% of revenues from North America in 2011, was classed absurdly as merely home-regional; Exxon Mobil, with 40% of sales from North America, 24% from Europe, and 10% in Asia just scraped into Rugman's bi-regional classification.[5] Arithmetical %s may belie any genuine global impact. Rugman's criteria are not even appropriately normalised to avoid problems of unequal regional markets.[6]

Geographic spread choices are, nevertheless, strategically crucial. This chapter therefore accepts Rugman's criteria, updating his 2001 *Fortune*'s Global 500s data to 2011, to provide consistent analysis of trends and performance outcomes, again in terms of 5-year return on capital employed (RoCE); sales growth (SG), and total investment return (TIR). Geographical data for *Fortune*'s Global Top 500 companies were obtained from 2011 annual reports with classifications being matched against Rugman's for 2001. As for

Rugman's earlier study, information on geographic sales was unavailable for several companies; some companies may also have changed their orientations over the 5-year period. Disaggregating sector results, using General Industrial Classification System (GICS) codes, then helped clarify how differential global concentration levels resulted in distinctive international choices.

FORTUNE GLOBAL 500 INTERNATIONAL ORIENTATIONS 2001 TO 2011

Figure 4.1 shows global top 500 company numbers by major geographic regions, updating Rugman's 2001 figures to 2006 and 2011. United States, European Union (EU), and Japan numbers declined from 86% in 2001, to 70% in 2011, as emerging market region numbers rose. With rising global concentration and new regional players, multinational corporation (MNC) geographic sales choices have changed.

Figure 4.2 updates Rugman's 2001 classifications of *Fortune* 500 companies to 2011. Even on Rugman's remarkably conservative criteria, the number of

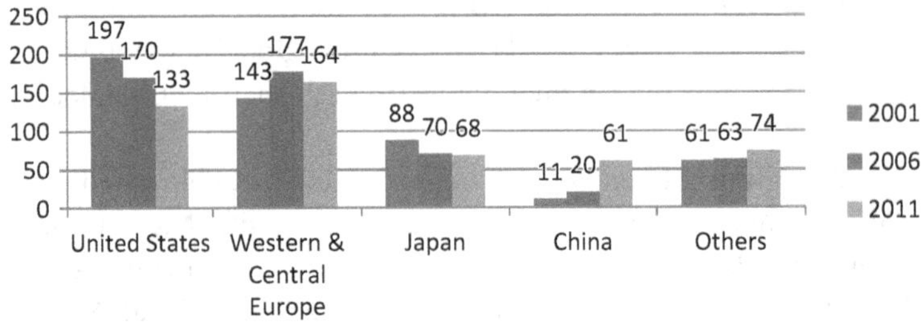

Figure 4.1 Global top 500 analysis by major regions 2001, 2006, and 2011. *Sources:* Rugman (2005), CNN/*Money Fortune* 500 List data for 2001, 2006, and 2011. *Note:* Sequence order: first 2001, second 2006, third 2011.

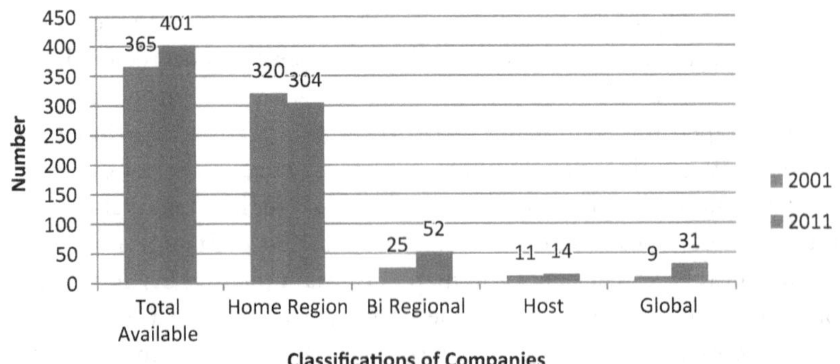

Figure 4.2 Rugman's 2001 global top 500 classifications, updated to 2011. *Source:* Rugman (2005), CNN/*Money Fortune* 500 List data for 2001, 2006, and 2011. *Note:* Sequence order: first 2001, second 2011.

global firms roughly tripled from 9 in 2001 to 31 in 2011; bi-regional firms doubled from 25 to 52; whilst home-regional numbers fell from 88% to 76%. Average foreign sales %s for global top 500s increased over the same period, whilst average intra-regional sales declined from 75% to 70%.

Though falling, home-regionals still pre-dominated, reflecting differences in consumer tastes and limited access to national markets. Of 304 home-regionals in 2011, 39% originated from Asia Pacific, 32% from North America, and 29% from Europe.[7] Collinson and Rugman's (2006) study of Asian regionals found that large Asian firms were already exploiting competitive advantages honed at home in neighbouring, fast-growing Asian markets. Given such huge opportunities in their home regions, they were perhaps less motivated by market-seeking foreign direct investment (FDI)[8]: Chinese firms had the highest levels of intra-regional sales and assets, but had so far proved less ambitious in terms of foreign markets.

Bi-regionals doubled from 6% in 2001 to 13% in 2011: of these, 50% originated from Europe, 35% from North America, and just 15% from Asia Pacific (ibid). Only about 3% of firms were classifiable as host-regionals either in 2001 or in 2011: examples included Intel and Standard Chartered, but were otherwise rare.[9]

Global companies tripled from 2.5% to 7.7%, undermining Rugman and Verbeke's central argument that '*The home region orientation of most MNCs implies that reality of globalisation has been vastly exaggerated*'.[10] There were 58% of global firms in 2011 that were from Europe, 29% from North America, and only 13% from Asia-Pacific. Such trends again reflected FDI flows: In 2011, European firms accounted for 26% of FDI inflows to Association of South Eastern Asian Nations (ASEAN) regions, compared with 13% for the USA, and 13% for Japan.[11]

Performance by types of regional strategies

To explore Rugman's unsupported assertion that '*A firm does not need to use global strategy to be successful*',[12] Figures 4.3–4.5 show averaged 5-year RoCE, sales growth, and TIR performance metrics for all four types of international orientation. To simplify performance analysis, we further weighted these 5-year RoCE, SG, and TIR metrics at 50%, 25%, and 25%, respectively. RoCEs are generally weighted higher because they are directly comparable with the cost of capital, independent of biased base-year effects; sales growth may also prove pointless unless RoCEs can be achieved beyond the cost of capital.

In contrast to Rugman and Verbeke's earlier conjectures, global companies achieved the highest profit ratios in terms of RoCEs at 14%, followed by bi-regionals, the second most profitable group, whilst home-region proved the least profitable at 7%. In terms of sales growth, though, host-country companies performed best, followed by home-regionals, growing much faster than globals or bi-regionals.

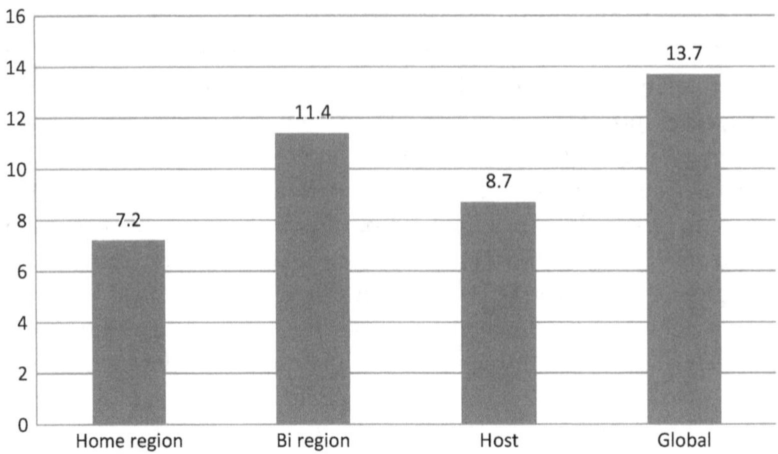

Figure 4.3 Rugman's global top 500 classifications: average RoCEs, 2006–2011. *Source:* Thomson One Banker database, *Fortune* Global 500 List.

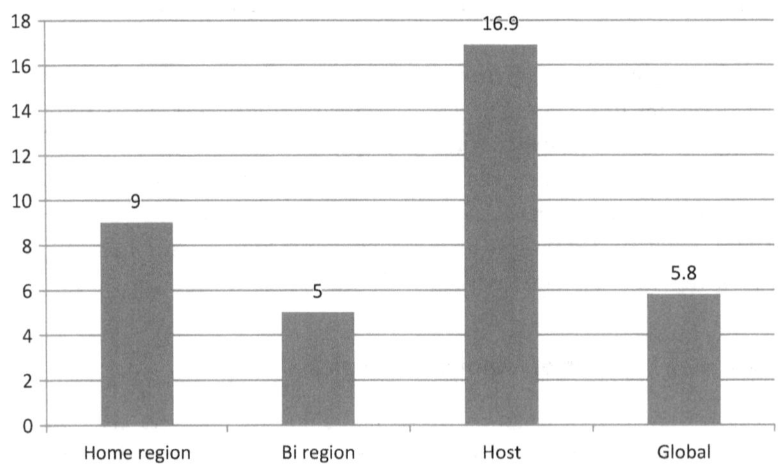

Figure 4.4 Rugman's global top 500 classifications: average sales growth, 2006–2011. *Source:* Thomson One Banker database, *Fortune* Global 500 List.

Global, followed by host-country, companies performed best on an averaged TIR; whilst home-regionals demonstrated the lowest and indeed negative TIRs. Bi-regional companies did rather better, but still made negative TIRs: These resonate with city perspectives, but risk subjectivity and distortion when poor base years, for example, exaggerate subsequent performance figures.

Figure 4.6 finally takes the weighted average of all three metrics, based on the formula: '*50% x RoCE + 25% x Sales Growth + 25% x TIR*'. Global and

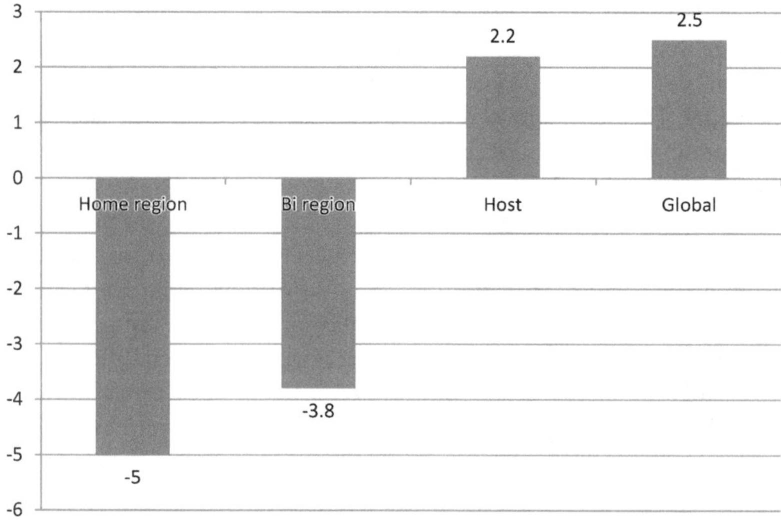

Figure 4.5 Rugman's global top 500 classifications: average total investor returns, 2006–2011. *Source:* Thomson One Banker database, *Fortune* Global 500 List.

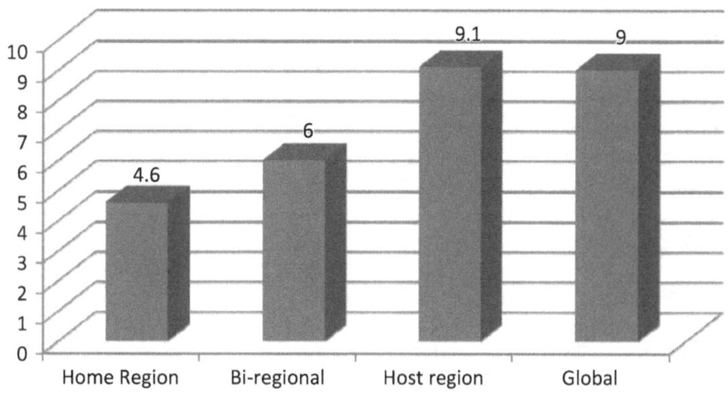

Figure 4.6 Rugman's global top 500 classifications: weighted average performances, 2006–2011.

host-countries orientations performed best in terms of these overall weighted averages: Their scores double those of home-regionals. Bi-regionals performed midway between these two extremes.

Analysis by sector: Top 500 up to 2011

Rugman and co-researchers conducted some sector studies further arguing that most strategies were essentially regional,[13] though without offering performance metrics. To analyse this situation systematically, we used GICS sector classifications, first sub-dividing companies into 24 sub-sectors, though full data were only available for 393 of the top *Fortune* 500 companies. Performance metrics and regional ratios are shown in Table 4.1, followed by sector positioning in terms of globalisation and performance levels in Figure 4.7.

In Figure 4.7, the horizontal axis shows the percentage of sales outside home region; the vertical axis shows the weighted averages (as just discussed) of RoCE, SG, and TIR of each sector. Figure 4.7 portrays the relationship between the degree of globalisation and average overall performance of different sectors. From this perspective, pharmaceutical companies emerged as some of the most global (in terms of sales outside home regions) and also best performing players among *Fortune* Top 500 companies.[14] Beverage & tobacco firms were also quite global and strong performers. Automobile and technology hardware players were also relatively global, but had not performed strongly. By contrast, top players in banks, insurance, and transport tended to

Table 4.1 Global top 500: General Industrial Classification Sector analysis

GICS[a]	*Sectors*	*No. of Companies*	*Avg % of Sales Outside Home Region*	*Avg Weighted RoCE, SG, TIR*
1010	Energy	39	21.5	9.3
1510	Materials	37	33.8	6.4
2010	Capital Goods	44	32.4	8.4
2020	Commercial Services	1	43	1.4
2030	Transportation	16	24.3	1.2
2510	Autos & Components	22	44.8	0.7
2520	Consumer Durables	6	39.6	0.4
2530	Consumer Services	4	32.3	11.8
2540	Media	6	28.9	5.7
2550	Retailing	9	29.3	8.6
3010	Food Retailing	22	19.4	4
3020	Food, Bev. & Tobacco	16	49.5	9.9
3030	H'hold & Personal Prod	3	54	9.3
3510	Health Care	14	11.8	7.5
3520	Pharmaceuticals	12	57.9	10.3
4010	Banks	32	14.1	-0.2
4020	Diversified Financials	16	38.6	2.1
4030	Insurance	31	17	0.9
4040	Real Estate	2	0	−0.8
4510	Software & Services	2	52.8	20.3
4520	Technology & Equip.	20	47.6	0.7
4530	Semiconductors	2	59.5	12.8
5010	Telecommunication	14	17	5.5
5510	Utilities	23	12.5	2.9
Total	Averages	393	32.6	5.8

Source: 2011 *Fortune* Global 500 List, Company Reports for FY 2011, Thomson One Banker Database 2006–2011.

Note: [a] Standard & Poor's GICS.

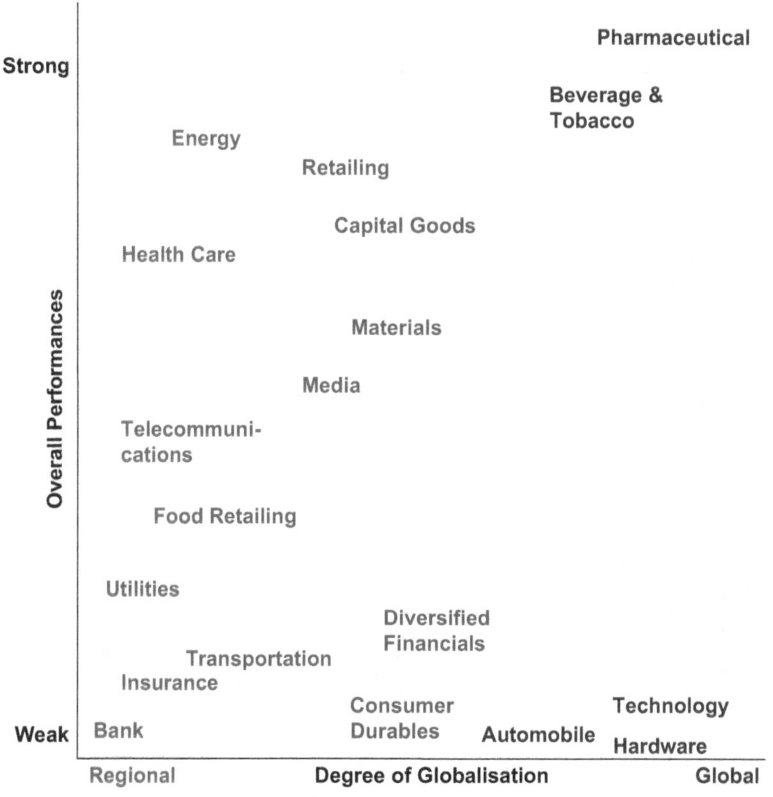

Figure 4.7 Regional and global performances of global top 500s by sectors.

limit themselves to home regions and performed poorly. Regional players in health care and energy industries, on the other hand, performed well.

Interestingly strong performers, whether global or regional, tended to be providers of life's necessities such as drugs, tobacco, oil, electricity, or such services as health care; profitability was lower in sectors more vulnerable to economic turbulence, such as banks, automobile, and technology products, which perhaps can be considered as more discretionary. Beyond this, any relationship between performance and globalisation appeared to reflect sector traits including global concentration levels discussed earlier.[15]

Analysis by sector: Top 5500 companies, up to 2012

For even more extensive coverage of 66 sectors, Thomson One Banker was re-accessed in 2014, using foreign sales ratios as proxies for globalisation levels and updated 5-year performance figures for RoCE and SGs (TIRs being unavailable) up to 2012. Tables 4.2 and 4.3 analyse the global top

Table 4.2 Global top 500 performance analysis of sectors, ranked by average international sales %s, 2008–2012

Int Sales%	*RoC5y*	*SG5y*	*Sector*	*Perf**	*R&D%*	*CapX%*	*Rev/Emp*	*Sales% AV*
55.93	0.06	0.08	Semiconductors	0.066	11.60	–9.16	3.70	95
50.71	0.12	0.24	Biotechnology	0.160	28.26	–7.84	1.31	66
49.05	0.41	0.05	Tobacco	0.288	0.47	–3.38	2.99	149
45.36	0.07	0.10	Oil & Gas Drilling	0.083	0.73	–17.66	3.05	67
44.01	0.10	0.12	Automobiles	0.108	2.49	–6.18	3.25	457
43.25	0.06	0.05	Machinery	0.055	1.76	–4.19	3.70	67
42.59	0.08	0.11	Communications Equip	0.091	9.46	–4.10	4.03	91
42.21	0.11	0.06	Healthcare Equip	0.095	5.85	–5.38	3.99	53
42.12	0.07	0.10	Electronic Equip	0.082	2.34	–4.01	4.42	85
42.01	0.25	0.01	Household Prdts	0.160	1.35	–3.51	2.43	148
41.12	0.00	0.11	Technology	0.038		–8.30	3.26	146
40.77	0.08	0.12	Auto Components	0.095	1.83	–6.42	4.38	79
40.63	0.07	0.05	Containers/Packaging	0.066	0.53	–5.31	3.27	59
40.32	0.14	0.03	Leisure Prdts	0.102	4.04	–4.39	2.72	35
40.01	0.10	0.08	Airlines	0.093	0.00	–11.70	3.78	112
39.92	–0.04	0.02	Marine	–0.017	0.00	–12.48	2.25	83
39.13	0.12	0.14	Apparel, Luxury Gds	0.126	0.64	–4.32	6.08	58
38.79	0.07	0.06	Household Durables	0.071	1.35	–3.21	3.67	81
38.62	0.14	0.08	Software	0.120	4.98	–3.30	6.63	77
38.31	0.03	0.05	Paper & Forest Prdts	0.035	0.29	–7.95	2.74	53
38.17	0.06	0.10	Chemicals	0.077	1.67	–7.40	2.35	78
38.16	0.12	0.10	Food Retail	0.11	0.15	–6.33	3.22	111
38.11	0.10	0.07	Aero & Defence	0.090	3.45	–4.42	4.04	154

(Continued)

Table 4.2 (Continued)

Int Sales%	*RoC5y*	*SG5y*	*Sector*	*Perf**	*R&D%*	*CapX%*	*Rev/Emp*	*Sales% AV*
36.68	0.07	0.08	Ind. Conglomerates	0.072	1.06	–8.06	4.65	180
36.65	0.14	0.06	IT Services	0.112	0.95	–3.29	8.07	22
36.62	0.13	0.18	I'net/Catalog Retail	0.150	1.35	–3.84	2.21	88
36.33	0.14	0.09	Personal Products	0.126	1.43	–4.76	3.59	77
36.01	0.06	0.09	Construction Mtls	0.073	0.23	–9.63	3.99	66
35.55	0.12	0.11	Pharmaceuticals	0.118	10.16	–6.24	3.58	127
35.16	0.05	0.10	Electrical Equip	0.063	1.99	–4.88	4.46	84
35.12	0.05	0.04	Airfreight/Logistics	0.047	0.00	–4.48	4.96	138
34.81	0.00	0.07	Metals & Mining	0.024	0.34	–12.47	3.18	105
34.48	0.06	0.15	Transport/Infrastruc	0.091	0.04	–15.44	3.51	28
34.46	0.07	0.10	Gas Utilities	0.077	0.06	–12.36	2.18	64
34.12	0.03	0.12	Food Products	0.061	0.45	–5.16	3.54	83
34.07	0.09	0.07	Life Sciences	0.082	4.99	–4.50	4.73	41
34.05	0.06	0.13	Oil & Gas Services	0.079	0.17	–21.55	1.62	293
33.55	0.09	0.08	Hotels/Leisure	0.088	0.15	–8.65	6.92	61
33.26	0.07	0.08	Cap. Markets	0.075	0.00	–2.88	1.94	99
33.25	0.07	0.09	Trading/Distribn	0.077	0.04	–2.66	1.22	118
32.09	0.12	0.05	Profess. Services	0.098	0.09	–2.50	5.46	55
31.43	0.13	0.29	I'net S'ware Serv.	0.183	7.82	–11.20	2.81	78
25.44	0.06	0.06	Telecom Services	0.057	0.26	–18.49	3.19	197
24.89	0.09	0.08	Specialty Retail	0.088	0.02	–3.42	3.05	74

(Continued)

Table 4.2 (Continued)

Int Sales%	*RoC5y*	*SG5y*	*Sector*	*Perf**	*R&D%*	*CapX%*	*Rev/Emp*	*Sales% AV*
24.36	0.05	0.04	Consumer Finance	0.045		–3.29	3.12	71
24.04	0.03	0.14	Distribn (Retail)	0.066	0.04	–1.02	2.03	57
21.62	0.09	0.05	Consumer Prdts	0.078	0.09	–3.65	6.79	31
21.53	0.06	0.06	Road & Rail	0.060	0.06	–14.46	4.63	71
20.62	0.08	0.08	Insurance Multiline	0.083	0.00	–2.39	1.40	205
19.94	0.05	0.05	Divers Fin Services	0.047	0.64	–12.81	2.86	182
19.46	0.00	0.10	Healthcare Tech	0.031	5.73	–8.57	5.14	31
18.88	0.04	0.15	Power/Renewables	0.079	0.05	–20.58	1.90	68
18.64	0.03	0.14	Electricity Utilities	0.068	0.09	–19.49	1.94	123
16.42	0.13	0.10	Telecom Services	0.121	0.12	–18.67	2.25	168
15.37	0.05	0.07	Real Estate Trusts	0.056	0.03	–33.41	1.45	27
15.09	0.03	0.03	Mortgage Fin	0.031	0.00	–29.57	2.27	0
14.84	0.10	0.09	Multiline Retail	0.097	0.01	–4.87	3.72	80
6.45	0.04	0.09	Water Utilities	0.060	0.07	–29.45	3.45	36
6.18	0.07	0.05	Banks	0.066		–3.74	3.73	158
	0.03	0.11	Construction/Eng	0.057	0.43	–4.22	3.12	95

Note: Weighted performance = 2 * RoC + 1 * SG (averaged over 5 years to 2012).
RoC and SG figures in absolute terms (i.e., multiply by 100 for %s).

Table 4.3 Global top 500 performances by sectors, ranked by average international sales %

Int Sales%	*RoC5y*	*SG5yr*	*Int' Sales %s*	*Perf**	*R&D%*	*CapX%*	*Sales / Emp*	*Sales%AV*
32.61	0.08	0.09	Average	0.084	1.97	−8.78	3.52	100
42.33	0.10	0.08	Top Third	0.096	3.80	−6.66	3.51	102
34.45	0.08	0.11	Next Third	0.090	1.58	−8.21	3.68	101
20.50	0.06	0.08	Lowest Third	0.065	0.47	−11.47	3.38	97
15.13	0.05	0.09	Lowest Sixth	0.065	0.72	−16.85	2.89	97

Note: Weighted performance = 2 * RoC + 1 * SG (averaged over 5 years to 2012).
RoC and SGs require multiplying by 100 for %s.

5500, increasing our average sector sample sizes from 16 to 83 for our refined 6-digit GICS codings. All 66 sectors are ranked in terms of average foreign sales ratios, adding 5-year averaged RoCE and other metrics including research & development (R&D)/sales ratios.

Statistically, there was a consistent monotonic relationship with more international sectors tending to perform better, both in terms of 5-year averaged RoCEs and on overall weighted performances, taking some account of sales growth. R&D/sales ratios followed the same pattern, with the top third in terms of international sales ratios exhibiting R&D ratios twice the average. Capital expenditure/sales ratios surprisingly moved in the opposite direction: suggesting that technology intensity rather that capital intensity drove internationalisation. Productivity displayed a less consistent relationship.

Examining drivers of profitability, only two sectors displayed 5-year RoCE averages above 15%: tobacco at 41% and household durables at 25%. Both sectors' international sales ratios, at 49% and 42%, respectively, were well above the overall average of 34%. Tobacco again stood out as both highly international and exceptionally profitable; though household durables were only slightly less profitable. In terms of RoCE, next came cosmetics, software, information technology consulting, and toys at 14%; catalogue retailing, mobile phones services, internet, and software services at 13%; pharmaceuticals, professional services, biotechnology, food retail, and consumer luxury goods at 12%; health care equipment at 11%; and retailing, airlines, automobiles, and capital goods at 10%. Aside from mobile phone services and retailing, these sectors all had above average international sales ratios. All these other double digit RoCE sectors, plus tobacco and household durables, formed a cluster of sectors both more international and more profitable.

Sectors yielding 7%–9% RoCEs likewise included fairly international sectors, several with the high global concentration ratios discussed: at 9%, consumer products, hotels/restaurants & leisure, specialty retail, and life sciences; at 8%, insurance, auto parts, communications equipment, and consumer services & supplies; and at 7%, real estate management, household durables, oil & gas drilling, containers & packaging, investment banks & capital markets, electronic equipment and instruments, banks, trading companies, gas utilities, and industrial conglomerates.

At the other extreme, three sectors (slightly above average in terms of internationalisation) achieved losses or negligible profits: computers, materials, and shipping lines. Health care technologies made negligible RoCEs and were less international. Below 5% average RoCE, down to a minimum of 3%, came sectors with well below average internationalisation ratios: water, power utilities, media, mortgage finance, utilities, distributors, food products, and capital goods and materials. Slightly more profitable, but still below 7% average RoCE came: commodity chemicals, health care services, building products, construction materials, road & rail, semiconductors, machinery, transport infrastructure, telecom services, oil & gas services, airfreight & logistics, consumer finance, real estate investment trusts, financial services, and electrical equipment.

Low profitability reflected sector maturity and capital intensities. Some, more domestic, sectors had less need for ambitious global strategies. Performance relationships were influenced by short-term economic cycles and by longer-term cycles, such as in commodities. Such relationships need to be regularly monitored.

A broad analysis of major sector traits is crucial to judgements about internationalisation strategies. Extending global reach is risky and resource intensive; in banking and retail groceries, Royal Bank of Scotland and Tesco internationalisation strategies certainly proved a '*bridge too far*'. Safer, more domestic, sectors, such as utilities, have proven less profitable. Yet, here major players still found they could not entirely escape global consolidation pressures, nor completely eschew requirements to respond. Even they have substantially extended their geographical spreads since Rugman's analysis a decade earlier. Companies clearly need an appreciation of the subtler differences and performance relationships applying to their own specific sectors, as delineated in this chapter. Overall, however, top companies radically extended their geographical coverage, achieving positive performance outcomes.

NOTES

1 In Chapter 4, I acknowledge with thanks the enormous contribution of Shengming Shao in combining research from many of our studies to analyse the geographical spread choices, orientations, and performance outcomes for most of the global top 500 group of companies.
2 Rugman (2005).
3 In 2011, Daimler, for example, would be classed as 'Global' having 24% of sales in North America, 43% in Europe, and 21% in Asia. Rugman's 2001 study identified only nine 'global' firms: IBM, Sony, Philips, Nokia, Intel, Canon, Cola-Cola, Flextronic, and Louis Vuitton.
4 Intel, for example, in 2011, had 57% of sales in Asia, classifying it as host-country orientated; but arguably companies should be classified according to their prime markets.

5 Rugman's classifications were criticised by Aharoni (2006) for ignoring global outsourcing and longitudinal perspectives and by Osegowitsch and Sammartino (2008) for adopting artificial criteria levels, but persisted, nonetheless. Rugman and Verbeke's (2004) argued intra-regional sales accounted for 80% in their home-regionals, 43% in bi-regionals, 31% in host-regional, and 38% in global firms, bolstering their scepticism regarding 'the reality of globalisation' (Rugman & Verbeke 2008). Rugman and co-authors published several further sector studies similarly arguing that multi-nationals were more regionally than globally orientated: Rugman and Girod (2003) (retail multi-nationals); Rugman and Collinson (2004) (automotive sectors); Rugman and Chang (2006) (cosmetics); Rugman and Collinson (2005) (MNCs in New Europe); Rugman and Yip (2007) (MNCs in UK); Rugman and Li (2007) (China's multi-nationals); Collinson and Rugman (2007) (Asian MNCs).

6 Many markets and customer service requirements split asymmetrically worldwide. For example, an aero-engine manufacturer serves dual markets. Selling to aircraft manufactures, based primarily in Toulouse for Airbus or Chicago for Boeing, requires highly concentrated geographical sales even from the most global strategy conceivable; selling to multiple airliners worldwide direct, however, requires far greater support and asset dispersions, but even their demands are highly asymmetric.

7 Source: *CNN/Money Fortune* 500 2011; Company Annual Report for FY2011.

8 More prevalent initial motives might include 'technology seeking' as discussed by Dunning (2008) in relation to Lenovo's acquisition of IBM's PC business in 2005.

9 Intel, the US based chip maker, has more than half of the total sales (57%) in Asia because Japan and China are the two largest PC consumers in the world. See Ye (2011). Chips and PCs are complementary goods, so that most of Intel revenue derives from Asia. Other types result from headquarter locational choices. Standard Chartered, for example, is headquartered in the UK, but most of its customers are from Asia and Africa. Headquarter choices are often symbolic. This classification may be less pertinent for firms making international strategy choices.

10 Rugman and Verberk (2008, p. 398).

11 Source: *ASEAN Foreign Direct Investment Statistics Database.*

12 Rugman (2006), ibid.

13 See, for example: cosmetics (Oh & Rugman 2006); automobile (Collinson & Rugman 2004); and retail multi-nationals (Rugman & Girod 2003).

14 Ogura (2012) argues pharmaceutical firms' strong profitability reflect aggressive global strategies.

15 Schile and Yip's (2002) likewise argue that the macro forces of globalisation and regionalisation, which differ by sector, affect any optimal international strategy choices.

5

GLOBAL CONFIGURATION ANALYSIS

THE CASE OF RETAIL FASHION

Chris Carr and Hanne Leknes[1]

CALORI'S INTERNATIONAL CONFIGURATIONS

The need for global rather than domestic or regional strategies remains controversial,[2] so it makes sense to consider subtler, less polarised international variations. In more globally orientated sectors, Bryan et al. (at McKinsey) highlighted the emergence of superior '*global shapers*' – successful players exploiting competitive strengths to reshape their global industries.[3] Calori et al.[4] further examined four 'mixed' industries,[5] neither clearly global nor just domestic, and identified additionally (based on interviews with executives) four types of *worldwide players* and four types of more conservative *international challengers*.

The latter '*international challengers*' included *country-centred players* (for whom international sales were almost just *the icing on the cake*); *geographical niche players; opportunistic international challengers;* and *continental players. Geographic niche players* targeted homogeneous groups of countries, based on geographical and/or cultural proximity; whilst *opportunistic international challengers* displayed no such systematic pattern. These companies targeted significant market shares, market by market. *Continental players*, though, sought dominance at a continental level, akin to regional strategies previously discussed. Calori's four '*global players*' included *global luxury niche players; worldwide specialists*; *quasi-global players*; and *transnational restructurers*. All displayed wide geographical scope, but only *quasi-global players* and *transnational restructurers* prioritised market share as opposed to mere breadth of market coverage. *Transnational restructurers* typically held a portfolio of brands, covering different segments of their sector, and relied heavily on mergers and acquisitions, often subsequently restructuring, rationalising, and reorganising.

To Calori's eight, we added McKinsey's *global shaper* classification, where strategies were innovation-based, reshaping whole sectors, making them benchmarks for other firms. As shown in Table 5.1, all nine international

Table 5.1 International strategic configurations criteria

	Country-centred players	*Geographic niche players*	*Opportunistic international challengers*	*Continental leaders*	*Global luxury niche players*	*World-wide specialists*	*Quasi-global players*	*Transnational restructurers*	*Global shapers*
Geographic scope	Home country, Gain market share	Set of countries forming a homogeneous territory. Gain market share	Home country and a few key countries. Market share or market coverage	All key countries in a continent. Gain market share	All key countries	All key countries. Wide coverage	All key countries. Gain market share	All key countries. Wide coverage and market share	All key countries, wide coverage
Segment scope	Narrow	Relatively narrow	Few segments	Relatively large	Narrow, high priced segments	Narrow segment	Narrow, but concerns mass market	Large, most business segments	Narrow, but concerns mass market
FDI policy/ entry mode	Variable	Mainly organic growth	Variable	Mainly organic growth	Licensing and franchising	Franchising	Mainly organic growth	Most entry modes, frequent M&A	Organic or franchising
Standardisation	Homogeneous	Homogeneous	Variable	Relatively homogeneous	Homogeneous	Homogeneous	Homogeneous	Heterogeneous	Heavy standardisation
International integration of value chain activities	Depending on sector. Domestic focus	Depending on sector. Global sourcing	Variable	Global sourcing	Often manufacturer controlled. Production in home country	Often vertical integration	Global supply chain management.	Global sourcing, vertical integration	Global supply chain management

Source: Calori, R. et al., *The Dynamics of International Competition*, Sage, London, 2000.

configurations have been classified according to five theoretical discriminant dimensions: (1) geographical scope of the firm; (2) segment scope; (3) foreign direct investment (FDI) policy; (4) extent of international standardisation; and (5) level of integration of activities across borders.

To explain how our '*configurations performance analysis*' (CPA) can be utilised to determine strategic recommendations, this chapter first applies this approach to the retailing sector. Internationalising more slowly, such service sectors often lack global concentration metrics and are challenging to analyse. We first present a classic CPA analysis based on our 2002 study, setting out this sector's context, our methods, and pulling out strategic implications for just one company, Norway's top retailer Varner Gruppen. We then review key subsequent changes and lessons. Appendix B applies CPA to the world's top family firms, peer-matched against non-family firms, highlighting surprising differences that distinguish family firms. In subsequent chapters, we re-apply updated CPA to a more extensive range of sectors, focusing on major global oligopolists, and providing a comparative database for other CPA users.

GLOBALISATION IN RETAILING

Some international context is essential before applying CPA. Historically, from the earliest traders to the Hudson Bay Company, retailing had been virtually the first business activity to internationalise. Sears and JCPenny had both moved internationally by the 1950s. Retailers were nevertheless relative latecomers to more fully fledged globalisation or genuine international integration. Of the 27 industry segments represented in the Templeton Global Performance Index 2000, retail ranked only 21st.[6] In 1995, only 56 of the top 100 global retailers operated outside their home market, and only five of those generated more than 50 percent of their sales in foreign markets.[7] Between 1996 and 1998, though, the number of retailers on the *Fortune* 500 increased from 46 to 56. The top 100 global retailers had increased their market share to about 20%.[8] Retailing had been galvanised by change.[9] The toy retailer FAO Schwarz had followed Kmart into bankruptcy; following a spate of domestic deals, Kingfisher had also gained control of France's Castorama in do-it-yourself (DIY); and Walmart had just gained control of Seiyu in Japan and Asda in the United Kingdom (UK).

Retailing lags in respect to some internationalisation traits: you can't export shop buildings. However, retailers can deploy FDI, arguably a more potent weapon for MNCs than trade, and several globalisation forces have proved similar to those experienced by manufacturers.[10] Such forces have included saturation within the home market, compounded by economic downturns, legislation blocking expansion, shareholder pressures for growth, high operating costs, opportunities as overseas markets open up, and even an element of the 'me-too syndrome'. Even more so than manufacturers, retailers depend on being physically present wherever they are doing business. This necessitates FDI and having to handle very distinctive structural and cultural differences across borders. Performance in local markets has proved highly sensitive to variations in consumer tastes, buying patterns, and segmentation, all of which hamper global sourcing.[11]

Retailing is segmented: value-chains, consumer behaviour, and geographical barriers are distinctive in groceries, for example, and for different clothing, furnishings, and DIY habits. Grocery retailing (aside from mail order) was more concentrated: the 12 largest in Europe already held 32% of the total European market by 1999.[12] Many grocers turned to mergers and acquisitions (M&A). By contrast, clothing remained more fragmented, with independents taking over 30% of the market: the top ten companies' combined market shares (CR10) in Germany, UK, France, and Italy were still under 25% in 1997.[13] Moves and countermoves have, though, led to increased concentration, beginning locally, then nationally, and regionally, and ultimately more globally, as happened earlier in manufacturing and consumer sectors.

METHODOLOGY

Given the international dominance already noted of the top 60 retailers, we first categorised and analysed the performance of the 64 most internationally significant retail companies, for which we could obtain data[14]: 19 being American, 4 Asian, 16 British, and 25 other European.

These companies were categorised according to the theoretical discriminating dimensions used by Calori et al. (as in Table 5.1, taking each of the five rows in turn), using data from an extensive range of industry reports, academic articles, and websites.[15] We examined the number of countries in which the company had retail operations, the extent of their overseas operations, and the percentage of revenues collected from foreign operations, these being the main determinants of geographical scope (row 1).[16] The segment scope of the firm was rated according to the number of retail formats in a company's total store portfolio and the breadth of the product range within one format (row 2). FDI policies were distinguished according to choice of entry mode and companies' preferences for market share in each country market as compared to market coverage (row 3). Neither levels of standardisation nor international integration of value chain activities (in the final two rows) proved sufficiently discriminating to be useful.[17] Key performance ratios, examined primarily from DataStream databases, were return on capital employed (RoCE), pre-tax profit margin, and revenue growth for 1996–2000, year-by-year, and averaged overall.[18]

We investigated our new CPA framework and its applicability, from the standpoint of a typical retail company. Varner Gruppen ranked just outside our list of top 100 global retailers. As the Norwegian market leader, it was not particularly advantaged in terms of its country base. Scale economies, moreover, were more limited in retail, particularly in clothing, the company's chosen sector. We drew on direct interviews (taped and transcribed) with the managing director, the operating director, and the area manager of Varner Baltja.[19] They covered the company's history of internationalisation, strategies, future plans, and opinions on industry globalisation. 'Triangulation' entailed complementary secondary data from annual reports and news articles.

INDUSTRY ANALYSIS: APPLYING THE CPA STRATEGIC FRAMEWORK

Some companies' international strategy categorisations are shown in Table 5.2. All categories proved reasonably applicable, although we found only three *worldwide specialists* and three *opportunistic international challengers. Global luxury niche* players were unique to clothing, whilst 'transnational restructurers' only occurred among multi-format grocery players. 'Country-centred' players were most numerous (25% of the sample), followed by 'geographical niche', and 'quasi-global' players (each around 15%).

Like Calori, we noted some country effect. Half of United States (US), roughly a third of the UK, and a quarter of Asian companies were 'country-centred', compared with just 4% for continental Europe. Supported by their huge home market, several US firms achieved *quasi-global* positions by exploiting standardised 'category killer' concepts. None of the *global shapers*, but all three *worldwide specialists* were from the UK. Four out of five 'transnational restructurers' were continental European, perhaps exploiting political and economic unification through cross-border integration and restructuring.

Some companies exhibited characteristics from more than one category. Metro and Groupe Andrè, for example, utilised a range of retail formats across different sectors. Similarly, Home Depot was a *geographical niche* player in terms of having a presence in only five geographically and culturally proximate foreign markets, but its innovative strategy has had great influence on the actions of other retailers in the DIY sector worldwide, as suggested for *global shapers'* circumstances, so that categorisations were not always static.

Some companies sometimes adapted their international scope and strategies, so categorisations were not always static. Marks & Spencer and Tesco were defined as continental leaders for the period studied. Tesco attempted more global strategies in Central Europe, Asia, and the USA, but like M&S, then become more country-centred. Some subjectivity of categorisation suggests care with any interpretation; but as a tool of analysis, CPA proved quite practical.

Table 5.2 Categorisation of 64 companies in the retail industry in 2000

	Country-centred players	*Geographic niche players*	*Opportunistic international challengers*	*Continental leaders*	*Global luxury niche players*	*World-wide specialists*	*Quasi-global players*	*Transnational restructurers*	*Global shapers*
Clothing sector	Next, River Island, Oasis	Cortefiel, Varner Gruppen		C&A, M&S[a]	Mulberry, Jaeger, Escada, Burberry, Donna Karan	Tie Rack, Laura Ashley	The Gap, H&M		Zara, Benetton, Mango, Kookai
Food sector	Kroger, Albertsons, Publix Supermarkets, Sommerfield, Asda, Jusco, Great A&P, Spar	Leclerc, Sainsbury, Rewe, Safeway[a]	Kmart	Aldi, Jardine Matheson, Tesco			Casino, Ito Yokado[a]	Ahold, Carrefour, Wal-Mart[a]	
Other sectors	CVS, Walgreens, Lowe's, Best Buy, Target	GIB Group, Karstadt, Kingfisher, Sears Roebuck	Boots, Costco	Vendex, Pinault Printemps	Body Shop		Office Depot, Otto Versand, Toys R Us, Mitsukoshi,[a] Groupe Andre	Tengelmann, Metro	IKEA, Home Depot

a Safeway refers to the US company. Japanese companies such as Mitsukoshi and Ito Yokado have a presence in, respectively, seven and six countries, but do not generally use their own names outside Japan. Asda is treated as separate from Walmart during the study, although it has subsequently become part of Walmart's distinctive strategy. M&S has retrenched internationally subsequent to the period covered by the study.

PERFORMANCE ANALYSIS

Statistical modelling through multiple regression analysis was used as a more reliable way to handle multiple variables acting simultaneously and establishing robust relationships, though it delivers explanations only up to a point (in this case, just 31% of the story). Performance relationships are not always simple or continuous. Averaged statistics are also important, as they provide an explanatory feel for what really matters and what doesn't; but they don't address combination effects. Practical managers and readers should also appreciate untarnished 'hard data' on single, specific, readily comprehensible issues, more readily updated and comparable in terms of their own data. Also sub-sectors within the retailing industry have reached different levels of growth, saturation, and concentration: sub-sector analyses of RoCE, revenue growth, and profit margin corresponded well to Kalish's life cycle theory of retail formats (Figure 5.1).

There was also some country effect. Sales growth for US and European companies over this 5-year period averaged around 10% compared to just 3% in Asia. US RoCEs averaged 15%, compared with 20% in the UK and Europe, with the exception of Germany at 10%; and Asian RoCEs averaged 8%.

Size mattered. We examined profits data for the year 2000 for the 56 companies banded into 7 groups of 8, ranked in terms of sales revenue. The top two groups (16 companies) extracted 67% of total aggregated profits; but profit margins for the smallest group at 8% were twice as high. Analysing RoCE/ sales graphs for grocery and clothing sectors separately, suggested a 'U'-shaped relationship in both sectors. Scale advantages appeared higher in groceries:

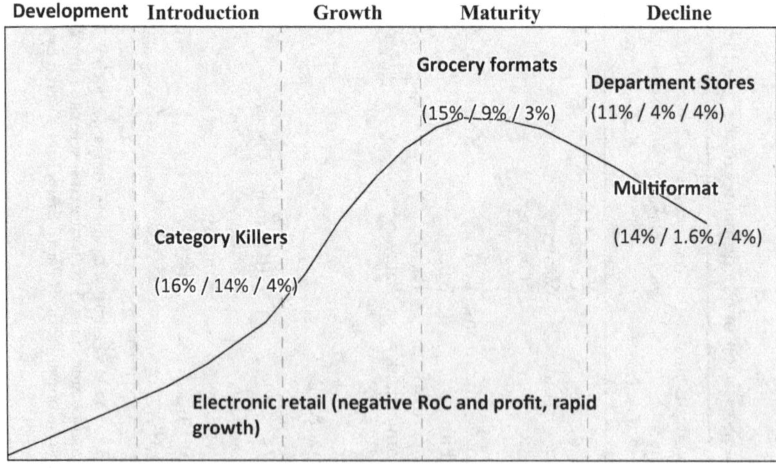

Figure 5.1 Retail life cycle of different retail formats: RoCE, revenue growth, and profit margins, 1996–2000. RoCE, revenue growth, and profit margin shown, respectively, in brackets. (Reproduced from Carr, C. and Leknes, H., *Long Rang. Plann.*, 37, 29–49, 2004. With permission.)

some very small firms made good RoCEs, but levels plummeted at around $10 billion, before gradually rising to a peak of about 20% at $30 billion sales, after which they flattened off. Relatively more very small firms made high RoCEs in clothing. The same high peak came in at a little over $2 billion sales (at RoCEs of about 35%), but there again seemed to be a 'stuck-in-the-middle' position at around $1 billion.

Armed with this basic understanding of other performance influences, we then examined the impact of international configuration choices. As shown in Figures 5.2A, 5.2B, and 5.2C, we did not find that performance improved continuously from the country-centred strategies through to the most global strategies: revenue growth began high, fell off at the regional stage, then improved markedly for more global strategies – giving a U-shaped curve. RoCEs displayed a similar, slightly less consistent pattern. At one extreme, *country-centred* players were very profitable, achieving quite good sales growth. *Continental leaders* performed worst on sales growth, essentially ceding market share, though with slightly above average RoCE. *Worldwide specialists* and *global luxury niche* players were the next poorest on sales growth, but ranked lowest on RoCE: as though strategically 'stuck-in-the-middle'. *Global shapers*, at the other extreme, grew fastest and achieved the highest RoCEs, earning profit margins of twice the average. *Quasi-global* players also enjoyed good margins and RoCEs. *Transnational restructurers* were found exclusively in the lower margin grocery sector, but their volume strategies still achieved reasonable RoCEs. Figure 5.3 suggests an even more profound U-shaped sales performance trend in clothing.

Statistical modelling through multiple regression analysis

Deploying multi-linear regression analysis, as summarised in Table 5.3, surprisingly showed that, neither size nor, more pertinently, relative market share recorded any correlation with return on capital (RoCE) even at a 10% level.[20] The most significant variable determining profitability was simply the choice of sub-sector: Clothing emerged as almost 19% more profitable in this period (other things being equal). Next in terms of significance, proved to be international strategy types: regression analysis yielded the following 'rule-of-thumb' equation explaining the RoCE% profitability:

$$\begin{aligned}\text{RoCE}\,(\%) = 17.7 &+ (18.7,\ \text{if in the clothing sector}) \\ &- (32.0,\ \text{if a worldwide specialist}) \\ &- (24.2,\ \text{if a global luxury niche player}) \\ &- (8.4,\ \text{if a geographic niche player}) - (6.6,\ \text{if quasi-global}).\end{aligned}$$

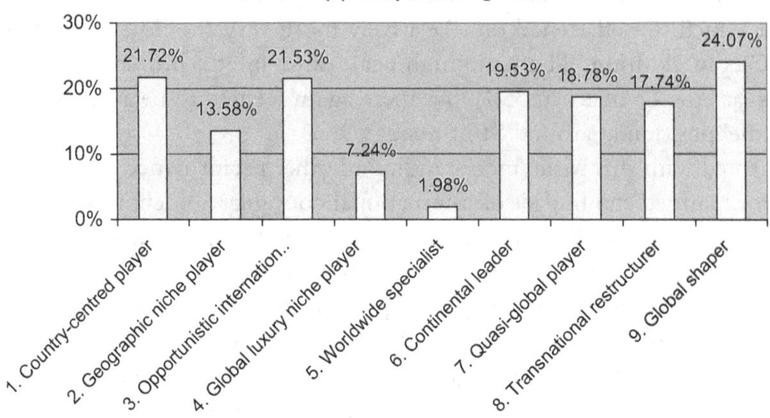

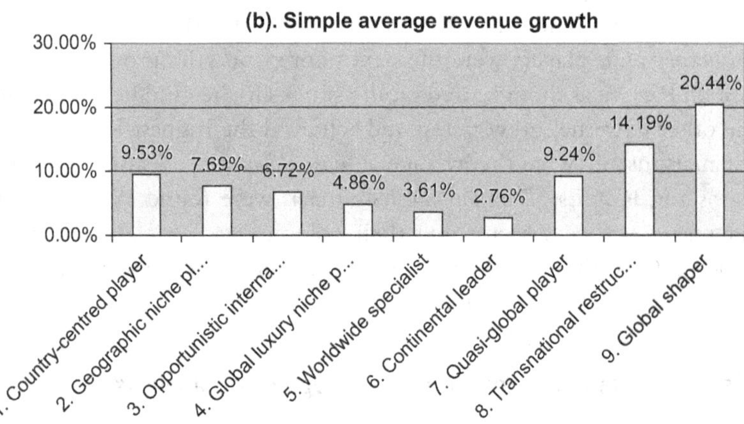

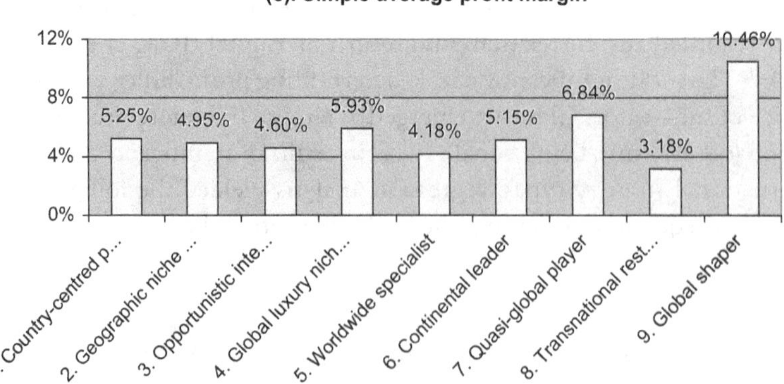

Figure 5.2 Retail configurations' average RoCE, revenue growth, and profit margins, 1996–2000. (Reproduced from Carr, C. and Leknes, H., *Long Rang. Plann.*, 37, 29–49, 2004. With permission.)

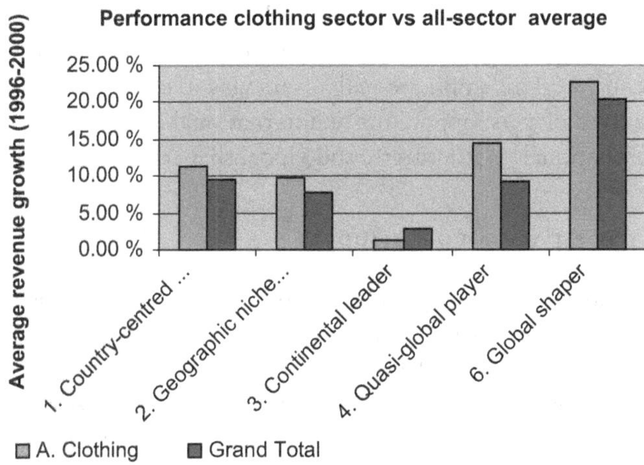

Figure 5.3 Performance of the clothing sector, by configuration, compared to retail sector average, 1996–2000. RoCE, revenue growth, and profit margin shown, respectively, in brackets. (Reproduced from Carr, C. and Leknes, H., *Long Rang. Plann.*, 37, 29–49, 2004. With permission.)

Table 5.3 Multi-linear regression analysis. All variables against return on capital employed (RoCE) 1996–2000 for 53 retailers (all sectors)

Variables correlated with RoC (Results from forward multiple regression analysis: R squared 0.310; std error 12.66)	*Coefficient (unstandardised)*	*Standard Error*	*Standardised coefficients Beta*	*Significance level*	t *score*
Sector A (Clothing)	18.7	2.1	0.59	0.000[a]	9.05
Type 5 (Worldwide specialist)	−32.0	3.8	−0.49	0.000[a]	−8.35
Type 4 (Global luxury niche)	−24.2	3.2	−0.47	0.000[a]	−7.50
Type 2 (Geographic niche)	−8.4	2.3	−2.0	0.000[a]	−3.70
Type 7 (Quasi-global)	−6.6	2.3	−0.16	0.004[b]	−2.90
Constant	17.7	1.1		0.000[a]	15.9

Source: Carr, C. and Leknes, H., *Long Rang. Plann.*, 37, 29–49, 2004. With permission.

Note: RoCE, revenue growth, and profit margin shown, respectively, in brackets.
a denotes significance at a 0.1% level;
b denotes significance at a 0.5% level.

The regression R squared was 0.31, which is not unusually low, as company performances are notoriously difficult to model; but this means that these key 'strategic' drivers identified could not explain more than 31% of performance variations: 69% was down to other factors, including operational considerations, which could justify careful benchmarking exercises.

Worldwide specialists, global luxury niche, geographic niche, and quasi-global players thus emerge as disadvantaged to the extent, respectively, 32%, 24%, 8%, and 7%. This implies equal advantages to all other configurations: country-centred players, opportunistic international challengers, continental leaders, transnational restructurers, and global shapers.

CASE STUDY OF VARNER GRUPPEN

We then considered the strategic implications of our CPA analysis for a single case company. In 2000, Varner Gruppen was a privately owned Norwegian holding company founded in 1967, incorporating six brands including Cubus, Carlings, and Bikbok, aimed at different clothing segments. As national market leader, they held a 13% market share. Revenue in 1999 was $444 million, of which foreign activities accounted for 22%. Motivated by saturation in its small domestic market, Varner Gruppen adopted a typical *geographic niche* player stance:

> Our basic motivation is expansion. Early in the nineties, we recognised that the Norwegian market would be saturated. Dressmann [their brand] could not have more than approximately 100 stores in Norway
>
> (Petter Varner, Managing Director of Varner Gruppen).

Initial international expansion was to neighbouring countries, entering Latvia in 1995, Iceland and Poland in 1996, Sweden in 1997, and Finland in 2000. Opening one new store every 12th day in the three years up to 2000, the company was among the fastest growing clothing retailers in Europe. In 2000, it had 352 shops in Norway, 10 in Latvia, 2 in Iceland, 7 in Poland, 140 in Sweden, and 10 in Finland. Varner Gruppen now aspired to market leadership in men's clothing in Germany and to continental leadership – a long-term shift in its international configuration. They recognised likely global concentration, admired bolder, more innovative strategies, and sought to benchmark from such high international standards:

> We aim to be the European market leader in men's clothing, but we need to establish operations in one country at a time, and must do Germany before we move on. This is a tough market that requires many years of work. Only a few big concepts globally will do well in the future. They are strategic and modern. [...] Large and rigid department stores and discount stores such as M&S and C&A are struggling now. [...] The development in the industry is dramatic, and the really good concepts such as Zara, Mango and the Gap are expanding rapidly
>
> (Petter Varner, Managing Director of Varner Gruppen).

International Strategic Positioning

Varner Gruppen emerged as a dynamic clothing retailer, from a less favoured country, facing typical international challenges. They asked how our analytical approach might add value in terms of strategic recommendations.

The first critical question addressed was the appropriateness of Varner Gruppen's intended strategic move towards continental leadership. Analysis based on all retailers confirmed their expectation of increased profitability, as compared with their current *geographic niche* position. Focusing on just clothing retailers, though, continental leaders have performed relatively badly. The 5-year sales growth has also been poor and undermined their explicit assumption that RoCE benefits stemmed from size or market share per se.[21]

The choice of international configuration seemed to matter more. Were the company just to remain a *geographical niche* player, regression analysis suggested this strategy might be disadvantaged to the extent of about 8% in terms of sustained RoCE levels, as compared to many other strategies including continental leadership. However, economies of scale proved particularly low in clothing. We noted C&A and M&S as the only remaining clothing retailers to have pursued continental leadership, and that both had subsequently retrenched dramatically, internationally. *Continental leaders* took on huge commitments and risk, on the presumption of questionable scale advantages, but had actually lost out in terms of *worldwide* market share. The intended option looked profitable, but our analysis cautioned against.

Retrenching either to an *opportunistic international challenger* configuration, or even more dramatically to a *country-centred* player position as M&S has done, appeared more profitable; yet regressive strategies looked vulnerable. There appeared to be a U-curve under which half-way steps to internationalisation lowered RoCEs as compared with either *country-centred* or *worldwide* strategies; but we agreed with this successful company's judgement that their future lay with more internationally progressive options.

Regression analysis highlighted the (otherwise intuitively appealing) *worldwide specialisation* option as the *least* profitable, reducing sustained RoCE by 24% (32– 8) – a decisive argument for *not* following this UK pack. The more profitable *transnational restructurer* option also seemed inappropriate. Concentration within clothing was not so far advanced that any player had yet attempted this, let alone a smaller, less internationally established, player such as Varner Gruppen; the 'fit' was also poor in terms of its current corporate structure and culture.

Global shapers, admired by the managing director, indeed performed well. Regression analysis suggested the same 8% improvement in RoCE, though (slightly less reliable) averaged statistics were outstanding for both RoCE and sales growth. However, this option entailed a radical shift in the company's attitude to entry modes and innovation; their product range was still poorly differentiated with little track record of strategic innovation likely to transform an entire 'industry structure'. The *global shaper* position also required radically extended worldwide coverage. Attempting both simultaneously was not feasible, though conceivable as a very long-term vision.

The traditional answer drawn from manufacturing experiences might have been simply to niche extremely tightly, recognising potential economies of scale, avoiding head-on competition,[22] and then to go global very pro-actively. Yet Simon's hidden champion strategy, based on global niches, was likely to prove less successful in retailing than in manufacturing. The requirement to be physically present likely required greater market dominance to reap scale economies. Tesco and M&S never achieved critical mass in the USA. In services, no benefits ensued from being hidden, brand leverage being crucial to margins. The nearest configuration equivalents, *worldwide specialists* and *global luxury niche* players, proved decisively the least profitable up to the year 2000.

Our recommendations for Varner Gruppen had to recognise its strategic context – its position as a leader from a small national market and its constraints in terms of resources and innovative competencies. The sheer scale of investments needed precluded more profitable *transnational restructurer* and *global shaper* options. We therefore recommended the *quasi-global* option as the best *immediate* path taking into account 'strategic fit'. Even this shift entailed substantial investments and risk; organisational structural changes, including greater innovation, promising only a modest improvement in profitability. Regression analysis suggested *quasi-global* retail players tended to sustain RoCEs only 1.6% higher than Varner Gruppen's current *geographical niche* configuration; but we noted that clothing companies in this category had performed particularly well (averaging 37% RoCE). Sweden's H&M appeared the most attractive model to follow, but highly demanding in terms of strategic innovation.[23]

Given that key strategic variables explained only 31% of performance variation (as implied by our regression R squared of 0.31), managers would also be interested in the remaining internal organisational part of the story, which was within their control. Benchmarking performance against top performing 'exemplars' helped determine what could be achieved through better implementation and operational improvements, as opposed to strategic repositioning. *Strategic benchmarking*, aided by analysis of strategic performance drivers, provided another fresh perspective; simplistic benchmarking against 'exemplars' in different strategic configurations could otherwise prove misleading. We confirmed excellent performances for Varner Gruppen's selected exemplars, H&M and Zara. However, their strategic configurations were different, as detailed in Table 5.4. Performance benchmarks against such exemplars (and even against clothing sector averages) highlighted some under-performance, as shown in the first part of Table 5.5. Varner Gruppen's RoCE performance was, however, about

Table 5.4 Strategic comparison of Varner Gruppen, H&M, and Zara

	Varner Gruppen	*H&M*	*Zara*
International strategy	Geographic niche player	Quasi-global player	Global shaper
Initial international expansion	1995	1964	1988
Ownership structure	Family owned and run	Quoted, but family run. 70% of shares belongs to the person family.	Family owned and run
Geographic scope	Europe, market leadership	Europe, US	All continents
Segment scope	Mass market. Narrow scope for most brands in portfolio.	Mass market. Wide scope	Mass market. Narrow scope all brands in portfolio
FDI policy	Organic growth	Organic growth	Franchise
Standardisation	Homogeneous	Homogeneous	Homogeneous
International integration	Global sourcing	Global sourcing	Vertical integration

Source: Carr, C. and Leknes, H., *Long Rang. Plann.*, 37, 29–49, 2004. With permission.

Note: RoCE, revenue growth, and profit margin shown, respectively, in brackets.

Table 5.5 Strategic benchmarking through multi-linear regression analysis

Measure	*Varner Gruppen*	*H&M*	*Zara*	*Clothing sector average*
Revenue 1999 $m	440	25,400	1850	2800
Revenue growth 1995–1999 % pa	7.3	18.4	39.0	9.6
Av margins %	6.7	14.0	9.0	8.0
Av RoCE 1995–1999 %	17.4	36.2	23.0	21.2
VG's performance variance against benchmark	–	−18.8	−5.6	−3.8
Strategic perf variance	–	−1.8	−8.5	–
Operational perf variance	–	−17.0	+2.9	–

Source: Carr, C. and Leknes, H., *Long Rang. Plann.*, 37, 29–49, 2004. With permission.

Note: RoCE, revenue growth, and profit margin shown, respectively, in brackets.

average for all *geographic niche* players, so we distinguished the proportion of benchmarked differences, explicable by configuration differences.

The latter part of Table 5.5 utilised the notion of strategic, as opposed to operational variances. Thus the 'strategic variance' of 8.4%, arising from its current configuration, more than explained its 6.35% shortfall in performance against global shapers such as Zara. However, our regression analysis warned that only 1.8% of the shortfall as against H&M would be accounted for by their choice of international strategy, as compared with H&M's *quasi-global* strategy, since these strategies also tend to be disadvantaged to the extent of 6.6%. The remaining adverse 'operational variance' of 17% suggested scope for substantial improvements, without necessarily changing its configuration. Had regression analysis produced significant coefficients, relating to relative market share, for example, this part of the strategic variance would also have been separately identified and quantified, and country variances could also have been distinguished in the same way. Similarly, had benchmarking been required against other non-clothing sector retail companies, our regression-based analysis would have first distinguished the *sectoral* strategic variance component of 18.7%. Signs were based on the same principle as in cost variances used in management accounting – variances favourable to the company being shown as positive variances.

We concluded in favour of the *quasi-global* strategic configuration that potentially yielded more marginal RoCE improvement, but merited serious consideration. Clothing retailers pursuing this option had done well: so it seemed internationally progressive and feasible. This strategy still required major resource and innovation commitments, but laid the foundations for a bolder *global shaper* strategy in the future. Either way, we recommended 'strategic benchmarking' (as illustrated) and an increased emphasis on strategic innovation, as opposed to continental market leadership; further alternatives analysed were not recommended.

SUBSEQUENT DEVELOPMENTS AND CONCLUSIONS

By 2010, top 100 retailer numbers operating in just one country halved to 20%; those operating more globally, beyond just one continent trebled to 36%, as shown in Table 5.6.[24]

By 2016, revenues were, respectively, Inditex $22.6 billion, H&M $20.8 billion, Fast Retailing $17.7 billion, and Gap $15.5 billion. Based on 6-year key averaged performance metrics, Varner Gruppen's chosen role models Inditex and H&M have become yet more global and successful, even relative to rivals, as shown in Table 5.7.

Thanks to the family's consistently aggressive stance, Varner Gruppen kept pace, trebling store numbers from 521 in 2000 to 1500 in 2016, as

Table 5.6 Geographical spread of store operations of 100 largest firms, 1996–2010

No of countries	*1996*	*1998*	*2010*
Firms in just one country	40		20
Top 100 av. % sales by foreign operations		11	27

Source: Dawson, J. and Mukoyama, M., *Global Strategies in Retailing: Asian and European Experiences*, London: Routledge, pp. 14–15, 2014. With permission.

Table 5.7 Benchmarked performance figures for global top 4s against averages for 152 retail fashion companies worldwide 2011–2016

Fashion 2016	*6y RoCE*	*6y SG% pa*	*6y RoS*	*Int Sales%*
Average	15.13	1	8.6	17
Inditex/av%	211.58	390	248.1	481
H&M/av%	296.90	229	218.3	554
FastRetail/av%	155.32	705	152.1	251
Gap/av%	308.05	−13	164.6	135
Top 5/av%	286.93	349	185.8	311
Av Top 20	28.78	4	10.9	27

Source: Analysis of data from ThomsonOneBanker.

sales climbed from $444 million to $1150 million. Its Scandinavian global niche player configuration shifted in line with its aspiration towards continental leadership. As well as bolstering international operations in other Scandinavian countries, it pressed on into Germany, Austria, and Poland. It is now present in eight countries with some 11,000 employees overall. Operating profit/sales margins for the two years 2015 and 2016 averaged 6%. We were sceptical as to whether continental leadership would be enough, but pro-active internationalisation (on which we totally concur), even faster than for other top 100 retailers, has so far paid off for Varner.

As of 30 August 2019, market capitalisations of Inditex, H&M, and Fast Retail predominated at, respectively, $96 billion, $28 billion, and $62 billion. From modest beginnings, Inditex's founder Mr Ortega's global strategy has increased his worth to some $83 billion, ranking him the third richest man in the world.[25] Not only are relative performance fundamentals strong, but, certainly from a stock market perspective, global strategies scoop the pool of all retail fashion profit expectations over the coming years. Any strategy guru still advocating national or even regional strategies over global strategies would appear to have scant regard for the stock market; anyone disinvesting from these more global retail clothing stocks over the last 20 years would have lost heavily. Our Calori CPA conducted in 2000, if anything, understated global trends and challenges posed by these strategically innovative and globally pro-active new winners. The capital intensive, geographical store development of these three successful players are shown in Table 5.8.

With a focused niche, Varner was perhaps more akin to large players like Primark at the lower price end. Established in Dublin in 1969, Primark bought Littlewoods in 2005 for £409 million, retaining 40 of their 119 stores. Only in 2006 did it move outside the United Kingdom, entering Spain. In 2016, it had some 334 stores, nearly half overseas in Spain, Germany, Netherlands, France, Portugal, Austria, Belgium, Italy, and the USA into which it entered in 2015: it employed 68,000, generating revenues of £5347 million ($6900 million).

Table 5.8 Store numbers by country, 1987–2016 Inditex vs H&M and Uniqlo

Store Numbers Inditex					*HM Stores*					*Uniqlo Stores*		
Year	**1987**	**1999**	**2011**	**2016**	**Year**	**1980**	**1990**	**1999**	**2011**	**Year**	**2013**	**2015**
Europe					**Europe**					**Europe**		
Spain	57	603	1925	1926	Spain				132	Spain		
Portugal		97	332	341	Portugal				23	Portugal		
France		59	241	288	France			11	168	France	4	8
Greece		17	160	160	Greece				22	Greece		
Belgium		20	74	75	Belgium			33	66	Belgium		
Sweden		6	11	20	Sweden	81	102	124	173	Sweden		
Malta		2	12	11	Malta					Malta		
Cyprus		5	32	35	Cyprus					Cyprus		
Norway		1	5	5	Norway	15	36	55	104	Norway		
Grt. Britain		3	90	103	Grt. Britain	6	16	34	213	Grt. Britain	10	10
Turkey		3	114	191	Turkey				8	Turkey		
Germany		2	73	131	Germany	2	28	167	394	Germany	0	1
Netherlands		2	27	59	Netherlands		13	32	118	Netherlands		
Poland		2	117	272	Poland				89	Poland		
Italy			287	355	Italy				87	Italy		
Austria			15	29	Austria			33	66	Austria		
Ireland			22	23	Ireland				15	Ireland		
Andorra			8	8	Andorra					Andorra		
Denmark			2	4	Denmark	14	26	45	90	Denmark		
Czech Rep			16	20	Czech Rep				24	Czech Rep		
Iceland			2	2	Iceland					Iceland		
Russia			207	485	Russia				19	Russia	4	5
Switzerland			16	32	Switzerland	6	28	41	80	Switzerland		

(*Continued*)

Table 5.8 (Continued)

Store Numbers Inditex					*HM Stores*					*Uniqlo Stores*		
Year	**1987**	**1999**	**2011**	**2016**	**Year**	**1980**	**1990**	**1999**	**2011**	**Year**	**2013**	**2015**
Europe					**Europe**					**Europe**		
Lithuania			16	22	Lithuania					Lithuania		
Slovenia			16	16	Slovenia				12	Slovenia		
Finland			4	4	Finland			12	49	Finland		
Hungary			20	40	Hungary				20	Hungary		
Luxembourg			3	4	Luxembourg			4	10	Luxembourg		
Serbia			14	14	Serbia					Serbia		
Romania			51	108	Romania				11	Romania		
Slovakia			6	11	Slovakia				10	Slovakia		
Monaco			1	1	Monaco					Monaco		
Latvia			11	13	Latvia					Latvia		
Estonia			5	7	Estonia					Estonia		
Croatia			28	32	Croatia				6	Croatia		
Montenegro			5	5	Montenegro					Montenegro		
Ukraine			24	53	Ukraine					Ukraine		
Bulgaria			22	33	Bulgaria					Bulgaria		
Azerbaijan				9	Azerbaijan					Azerbaijan		
Kazakhstan				25	Kazakhstan					Kazakhstan		
Armenia				11	Armenia					Armenia		
Bosnia				9	Bosnia					Bosnia		
Georgia				12	Georgia					Georgia		
Macedonia				5	Macedonia					Macedonia		
Slovenia				16	Slovenia					Slovenia		
Albania				5	Albania					Albania		
Sub-total	57	822	4014	5030	**Sub-total**	124	249	613	2347	**Sub-total**	18	24

(*Continued*)

Table 5.8 (Continued)

Store Numbers Inditex					*HM Stores*					*Uniqlo Stores*		
Year	**1987**	**1999**	**2011**	**2016**	**Year**	**1980**	**1990**	**1999**	**2011**	**Year**	**2013**	**2015**
Americas					**Americas**					**Americas**		
USA		6	49	71	USA				233	USA	17	39
Mexico		29	208	338	Mexico					Mexico		
Argentina		8	9	10	Argentina					Argentina		
Venezuela		3	25	25	Venezuela					Venezuela		
Brazil		3	30	69	Brazil					Brazil		
Chile		2	7	11	Chile					Chile		
Uruguay		2	2	3	Uruguay					Uruguay		
Canada		1	19	33	Canada				58	Canada		
El Salvador			4	7	El Salvador					El Salvador		
Panama			2	8	Panama					Panama		
Costa Rica			3	10	Costa Rica					Costa Rica		
Puerto Rico			1	4	Puerto Rico					Puerto Rico		
Dom. Rep.			4	12	Dom. Rep.					Dom. Rep.		
Columbia			22	43	Columbia					Columbia		
Guatemala			8	14	Guatemala					Guatemala		
Honduras			2	10	Honduras					Honduras		
Peru				4	Peru					Peru		
Ecuador				10	Ecuador					Ecuador		
Sub-total	0	54	395	682	**Sub-total**				291	**Sub-total**	17	39

(*Continued*)

Table 5.8 *(Continued)*

Store Numbers Inditex					*HM Stores*		*Uniqlo Stores*		
Year	**1987**	**1999**	**2011**	**2016**	**Year**	**2011**	**Year**	**2013**	**2015**
Middle East/Asia					**Middle East/Asia**		**Middle East/Asia**		
Israel		22	41	57	Israel		Israel		
UAE		3	53	66	UAE		UAE		
Saud Arabia		3	109	155	Saud Arabia		Saud Arabia		
Lebanon		3	35	40	Lebanon		Lebanon		
Kuwait		2	22	25	Kuwait		Kuwait		
Bahrain		1	10	10	Bahrain		Bahrain		
Qatar			14	15	Qatar		Qatar		
Jordan			13	15	Jordan		Jordan		
Morocco			11	23	Morocco		Morocco		
Oman			4	5	Oman		Oman		
Egypt			14	29	Egypt		Egypt		
Tunisia			2	11	Tunisia		Tunisia		
Syria			7	0	Syria		Syria		
Algeria				3	Algeria		Algeria		
Sub-total	0	34	335	454	**Sub-total**	0	**Sub-total**	0	0

(Continued)

Table 5.8 (Continued)

Store Numbers Inditex					*HM Stores*					*Uniqlo Stores*		
Asia					**Asia**					**Asia**		
Japan		5	63	145	Japan				15	Japan	857	842
China		0	143	566	China				82	China	270	364
India			4	17	India					India		
Singapore			18	22	Singapore				1	Singapore	13	22
Indonesia			16	46	Indonesia					Indonesia	2	6
Thailand			9	22	Thailand					Thailand	13	21
Philippines			8	19	Philippines					Philippines	10	22
Malaysia			13	20	Malaysia					Malaysia	12	24
S. Korea			29	67	S. Korea				6	S. Korea	115	139
Taiwan				16	Taiwan					Taiwan	42	51
Sub-total	0	5	303	940	**Sub-total**				104	**Sub-total**	1368	1569
Australia				17	Australia					Australia	0	4
South Africa				7	South Africa					South Africa		
Year	1987	1999	2011	2016	**Year**	1980	1990	1999	2011	**Year**	2013	2105
Total	57	915	5047	7013	***Total***	124	249	613	2742	***Total***	1403	1636

Source: Annual reports.

Supported by its parent, Associated British Foods, it has already moved beyond Europe, as was suggested by CPA.

Porter argues that global winners are not disadvantaged by vigorous domestic rivals, spurring them on.[26] National monopoly power little facilitates global leadership. Inditex's Spanish rival, Mango, constituted another highly formidable international role model. In 1999, Mango had only 463 stores. By 2009, its revenues were $1680 million (78% from foreign markets), supported by 8600 people and 1400 shops in over 100 countries.[27] Forty percent of its garments and accessories were made in China. Some 60% of stores were franchised. By 2010, Mango was reinforcing and consolidating positions in ten European countries and opening shops in Russia, South Korea, India, and especially China, where it was aiming for 59 outlets. 2015 revenues increased to $2600 million, though profits plunged from $120 million in 2014 to only $4.5 million after heavy investments. Between 2013 and 2017, Mango invested $680 million on innovations, including over 170 megastores worldwide and its own cheaper new product lines to counter Primark.

Fast Retailing's Uniqlo success has reflected its focus on higher technology segments entailing new materials, notably with fleece jackets. Established in 1984 with a niche in affordable basic casual wear, its brand position is as '*the world's only Life Wear brand – everyday clothes for a better life – high quality, fashionable, affordable and comfortable*'. By 2015, it had become the fourth largest fashion retailer in the world, with over 1550 shops, its strength being in Japan and Asia. Global supply chains and innovation have proved vital to such niches. '*We have already established R&D centres in Tokyo, New York and Shanghai. Now are looking to promote fully-fledged product development in Paris, London and Los Angeles as well as opening additional R&D centres in these three cities*'.[28]

By contrast, players such as Gap and Next were conservative internationally. Gap, skewed so heavily to the USA and Britain, has grown only slowly, following turnaround crises and poorer financial results. Next's revenues, supported by 540 stores in the United Kingdom and Eire, likewise grew slowly from $4.1 billion in 2013 to $4.7 billion in 2017. It operated 86, mainly franchised, stores in 33 countries internationally, but only generated $72 million of which $58 million came from franchised stores.[29] Between 2015 and 30th July 2017, its share price more than halved. Concerns included 'the freshness of its designs and rivals' increasing ability to match its competitive online delivery times': and a 'predicted drop in three-month sales [compared with Zara's 8%–9% rise], after a 3% drop in the previous quarter'.[30]

M&S's British-orientated, internationally opportunistic strategy (especially in the USA), like Tesco's, culminated in almost total international retrenchment. More impressive internationally has been Britain's SuperGroup. Like Uniqlo, it niched into a 'global lifestyle brand' exploiting an 'athleisure' trend.[31] Revenues grew 27% to $1.1 billion in 2017, with over half coming from 60 countries outside the United Kingdom. Its Superdry brand became increasingly popular across Europe and Asia. In the previous year, they opened seven stores in North America and were already breaking even there. Global niching, based on innovative technology and branding, has proved a more viable international option for modest-sized players.

Segmentation analysis confirmed clothing as by far the most profitably retail segment and Varner Gruppen's predisposition against diversification. Competitive advantages favoured European retailers, who performed far better than those in Japan and slightly better than those in the USA. Experience from, say, cars, corroborated further the importance of meeting world class operational benchmarks.[32] Strategic positioning, sector, scale, and country effects accounted for little more than 30% of the explanatory story behind performance. Managers needed to place proportionate attention on remaining operational gaps versus world class role brands and efficiencies, demonstrated by Zara, H&M, and Uniqlo. The methods of 'strategic variance analysis' (illustrated in Table 5.5) could also prove useful to others.

Overall, with hindsight, bold innovative global strategies by Inditex H&M, Fast Fashion (and even Mango) have won out decisively – despite this being a service sector, so unconducive to exports that players were forced to commit almost totally to FDI. This could lead to clothing retailer numbers decreasing at some point. Gap only narrowly escaped insolvency. We still suspect *global shapers, quasi-global* players, and *international restructurers* will improve relatively, as compared with the *country-centred* and regional strategies. Future winners seem likely to be companies with global ambition, commitment to long-term investment, strong corporate culture, a flexible and innovative organisation, and some unique yet transferable concept. *Quasi-global* retailers have not yet proven as profitable as *global shapers*, or even *continental leaders*, but already such strategies have proven a little more profitable than Varner Gruppen's current *geographical niche* position. Varner Gruppen's determined strategy of taking it beyond Scandinavia has paid off.

CPA thus appears to be a robust approach, yielding insightful strategic analysis, and complementing earlier frameworks discussed.

NOTES

1 We acknowledge copyright permission from Long Range Planning for kindly allowing us to reproduce figures and tables published earlier: Carr, C. and Leknes, H. (2004). 'Globalisation and strategic choice: Configurations in retailing', *Long Range Planning*, 37, pp. 29–49.

2 Levitt, T (1965). 'Exploit the product life cycle', *Harvard Business Review*, 2, pp. 45–56; Boston Consulting Group (1975). *Strategy Alternatives for the British Motor Cycle Industry*. London: HMSO; Schoeffler, S., Buzzel, R.D. and Heany, D.F. (1974). 'Impact of strategic planning on profit performance', *Harvard Business Review*, 52, pp. 137–145; Haspeslaugh, P. (1982). 'Portfolio planning: Uses and limits', *Harvard Business Review*, 60 (3), pp. 70–80; Porter, M.E. (1980). *Competitive Strategy: Techniques for Analysing Industries and Competitors*. New York: Free Press; Porter, M. E. (1990). *Competitive Advantage of Nations*. London: Macmillan;

Carr, C. (1993). 'Global, national and resource-based strategies: An examination of strategic choice and performance in the vehicle components industry', *Strategic Management Journal*, 14, pp. 551–568; Moore, K. and Mason, P. (1999). 'Does a global strategy pay off?' *FT Mastering Global Business*, pp. 65, London: Pitman; Simon, H. (1996). 'You don't have to be a German to be a "hidden champion"', *Business Strategy Review*, 7 (2), pp. 1–13; Baden Fuller, C. and Stopford, J.M. (1991). 'Globalization frustrated: The case of white goods', *Strategic Management Journal*, 12, pp. 493–507; and Ghemawat, P. and Ghadar, F. (2000). 'The dubious logic of global mega-mergers', *Harvard Business Review*, July–August, pp. 65–72.

3 Bryan, L., Fraser, J., Oppenheim, J. and Rall, W. (1999). *Race for the World: Strategies to Build a Great Global Firm*. Cambridge, MA: Harvard Business School Press. (See also Morrison, A.J., Ricks, D., Roth, K. (1991). 'A taxonomy of business level strategies in global industries', *Strategic Management Journal*, 13, pp. 399–418.

4 Calori, R., Atamer, T. and Nunes, P. (2000). *The Dynamics of International Competition*. London: Sage.

5 'Mixed' here refers to the degree of internationalisation. An industry is defined as 'mixed' if the ratio of exports to national production is between 10% and 50% (Laurencin 1988). Calori et al. (2000). Ibid. show that such industries tend to be characterised by the coexistence of global, multi-domestic, and mixed segments, allowing for the co-existence of both international and local competitors.

6 Gestrin, M.V. et al. (2000). *Templeton Global Performance Index 2000*. Oxford: Templeton College. According to Templeton, only 26% of retailers' assets are in foreign markets, compared with their average of 36%, or 78% for say tobacco.

7 Sternquist, B. (1998). *International Retailing*. London: Fairchild Publications.

8 Carr, M., Hostrop, A., and O'Connor, D. (1998). 'The new era of global retailing', *Journal of Business Strategy*, May–June, 19, pp. 11–15.

9 *The Economist*, 18 January 2003, pp. 61–62, 'Retailing: When you can't sell the goods, sell the shop'.

10 Bartlett, C.A. (1986). 'Building and managing the transnational: The new organizational challenge'. In Porter, M.E., (ed.), *Competition in Global Industries*. Cambridge, MA: Harvard Business School Press, pp. 367–401; Prahalad, C.K. and Doz, Y.L. (1987). *The Multinational Mission: Balancing Local Demands and Global Vision*. New York: The Free Press; Bartlett, C.A. and Ghoshal, S. (1989). *Managing Across Borders: The Transnational Solution*. Cambridge, MA: Harvard Business School Press; Yip, G.S. (1992). *Total Global Strategy*. Englewood Cliffs, NJ: Prentice Hall.

11 Barth, K., Karch, N., McLaughling, K., and Shi, C.S. (1996). 'Global retailing: Tempting trouble?' *The McKinsey Quarterly*, Winter, pp. 117–119.

12 European Grocery Retailing (2001). While these 12 leaders together hold 66% market share in France, the Italian market is less concentrated, and their share here is only 9%.

13 Kalish, I. (2000). *European Retailing 2010*. Global Retail Intelligence System.

14 Names and categorisations of companies are shown in Table 5.2. Information was obtained on sector, country of origin, foreign countries entered, revenue, and performance measures. Companies were selected primarily from Coopers and Lybrand's list of the '*Top 100 Global Retailers*', after excluding 51 that proved to be virtually domestic on closer inspection, and 7 other private companies, with restricted access to information. To this sample of 42 were added a further 22, gleaned from the FT500 (June 2000), the '*Templeton Global Performance Index 2000*', retailing and clothing sector reports.

15 Web sites: www.biz.yahoo.com, www.bodyshop.com, www.bsos.umd.edu/psyc/hanges/globe, www.costco.com, www.donnakaran.com, www.dressmann.com, www.economist.com, www.escada.com, www.forbes.com, www.fortune.com, www.ft.com, www.gap.com, www.homedepot.com, www.hoovers.com, www.ideabeat.com, www.inditex.com, www.lowes.com, www.mango.es, www.next.com, www.pricewaterhousecoopers.com, and www.walmart.com

16 The size of the relevant domestic market and of the company can each result in some bias, so that the international efforts of small firms from small domestic markets tend to be overestimated. As well as comparing ratios, we take some account of absolute levels of international activity.

17 Most retailers attempted to standardise the retail format whilst remaining sensitive to unavoidable customisation to local differences in implementation; this dimension is also hard to measure and compare. Similarly, international integration of value chain activities emerged as relatively less important as a discriminator, as retail internationalisation appeared to be market focussed rather than asset focussed. The process involved iteration between theoretical categorisations and international assessments, and some judgements.

18 We also used websites particularly for private companies. With a sample of only 64 companies, the number of companies in a strategic category can be as small as 3–4, which reduces the validity of the results. Domestic and cross-border mergers caused problems when comparing pre-merger and post-merger figures, creating some inconsistencies.

19 Interviews with managing director of Varner Gruppen 4 January 2001, operating director of Dressmann 29 August 2001, and area manager of Varner Baltja 14 September 2001.

20 Statistically, the absence of any correlation with theoretically derived *continuous* variables may have reduced any R squared representing the degree of explanation offered by remaining dummy variables. Effectively, the predictions from the model were no more than the averaged values based on data analysed, but they did handle combination effects. We allowed clothing to be identified as a specific sector variable and took this into account by forward multiple regression analysis. We finally performed multiple regression against average sales growth performances over the five years, though on a reduced data set. Country effect emerged as a significant variable (though only at the 5% level), with companies from countries other than Germany and Japan growing relatively faster.

21 Sheth, J. and Sisodia, R. (2002). *The Rule of Three: Surviving and Thriving in Competitive Markets*. Free Press, New York argued though that, apart from minor niche positions, the case for market leadership was stronger than ever; on the other, Miniter, R. (2002). *The Myth of Market Share: Why Market Share is the Fool's Gold of Business*. London: Nicholas Brearley fiercely contended the opposite supported by studies by Windermere Consultants. See also: Woo, C.Y. and Cooper, A.C. (1982). 'The surprising case for low market share', *Harvard Business Review*, 60 (6), pp. 106–114; Woo, C.Y. (1984). 'Market share leadership – Not always so good', *Harvard Business Review*, 62 (1), pp. 50–56; Bourantas, D. and Mandes, Y. (1987). 'Does market share lead to profitability?', *Long Range Planning*, 20, pp. 102–108; Jacobson, R. (1988) 'Distinguishing among theories of the market share effect', *Journal of Marketing*, 52, 68–80.

22 Yoffie, D.B. and Kwak, M. (2001). *Judo Strategy: Turning Your Competitors' Strengths to Your Advantage*. Cambridge, MA: Harvard Business School Press.

23 For details, see Sains, A. (2002). 'Hip H&M', *Business Week*, 11 November, pp. 37–42.

24 UK clothing suppliers themselves still confound expectations of dramatic internationalisation, with 69% of international trade concentrated within the single European trading block, although their global outsourcing shows signs of taking off. See, Jones, R.M. (2002). *The Apparel Industry*. Oxford: Blackwell, p. 145.

25 Shah, O. (2017). 'Inside the secret world of Zara'. *Sunday Times*, 30 July 2017.B, p. 5. Total sales rose 14%, or 8%–9% on a like-for-like basis, in the first quarter of 2017, outstripping most retail rivals. As Shah concluded: 'his 1975 principles still work'.

26 Porter, M.E. (1990). *The Competitive Advantage of Nations*. London: Macmillan.

27 Salerno, H. and Zaragoza, A.G. (2011). *The Mango Story*. London: LID, pp. 68–69.

28 Tadashi Yanni, T. (2015). *Pioneering a New Industry, Fast Retailing*, http://www.fastretailing.com/eng/about/message/ (accessed 4 July 2015).

29 Next 2017 annual report.
30 Shah, O. (2017). 'Next hit again'. *Sunday Times*, 30 July 2017.B, p.2.
31 Rovnick, N. (2017). 'SuperGroup sales growth defies gloom on high street'. *Financial Times*, 4 July, p. 20.
32 Womack, J.P. and Jones, D.T. (2003). *Lean Thinking: Banish Waste and Create Wealth in Your Corporation*. London: Simon and Schuster.

6

GLOBAL CONFIGURATIONS OF FORTUNE TOP 500s AND OUTCOMES

Chris Carr with Qianli Ma

To utilise fully configurations performance analysis (CPA), we need more comprehensive benchmarking data for all major sectors. To achieve this, we applied CPA, deploying all nine Calori/McKinsey internationalisation types, to global top 500 companies in 2006 (with Thomson) and again five years later in 2011. This takes further Rugman's top 500 company sales splits by region by analysing their international strategic orientations and performance outcomes using both consecutive 5-year periods: i.e., 10 years overall.

Creating such a database proved no mean task. Even a CPA for a single sector is highly demanding, as illustrated in the previous chapter. To cover most major sectors and global top 500 companies, we had to build up 'meta' studies from an extended series of individual sector CPA studies. Following my first retailing CPA study (with Leknes), these studies were carried out over ten subsequent years under my supervision at Edinburgh, together with two further studies, supervised cooperatively by Dr Rehan Al Haq at Birmingham University.

We covered many representative major sectors, targeting up to 100 top global players in each sector: Birmingham, for example, covered the top 100 global banks and the top 100 global insurance companies. Other configurations studies carried out at Edinburgh further included 21 sectors (summarised earlier on p. xxv). This afforded not fully complete, but comparable coverage to Rugman's 2001 analysis of the global top 500. Other sectors subsequently covered through CPA at Edinburgh include domestic appliances, discussed in Chapter 11, highlighting also the impact of the role of emerging market champions.

GLOBAL 500: SHIFTING INTERNATIONAL CONFIGURATIONS 2006–2011

There were 257 of the top global 500 companies that were able to be classified in terms of the nine Calori-based CPA configurations. Seventy-five percent of our sample were from the USA or China. Figure 6.1 shows %s of these top companies in each configuration and changes between 2006 and 2011.

Patterns in 2011 were similar to 2006. By 2011, *transnational restructurers* had increased most proportionately, becoming the most common configuration. They represented 23% of these global top 500 companies, this figure having increased by 6% as compared to 2006. *Quasi-global* players at 16% have replaced *opportunistic international challengers* (down a little at 15%) as the second most numerous. *Global shapers* accounted for 14% (down 2%). More companies adopted *global luxury niche, continental leader,* and *worldwide specialist* configurations; whilst *country-centred* players decreased most, dropping 5%, and reflecting internationalisation. *Worldwide specialists* and *geographic luxury niche* players both increased to 5%. Geographic niche players were least numerous (down 0.5%).

GLOBAL 500 INTERNATIONAL CONFIGURATIONS AND PERFORMANCE

Five-year averaged Return on Capital Employed (RoCE) for all configuration types are shown in Figure 6.2. Average RoCEs have increased slightly to just over 8% in the second 5-year period. As in our earlier study of retailers

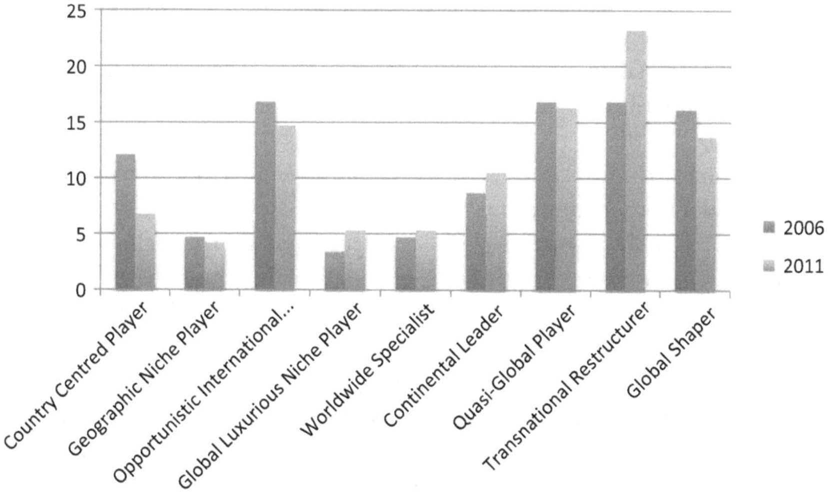

Figure 6.1 Global top 500 international configurations %s numerically, 2006 and 2011.

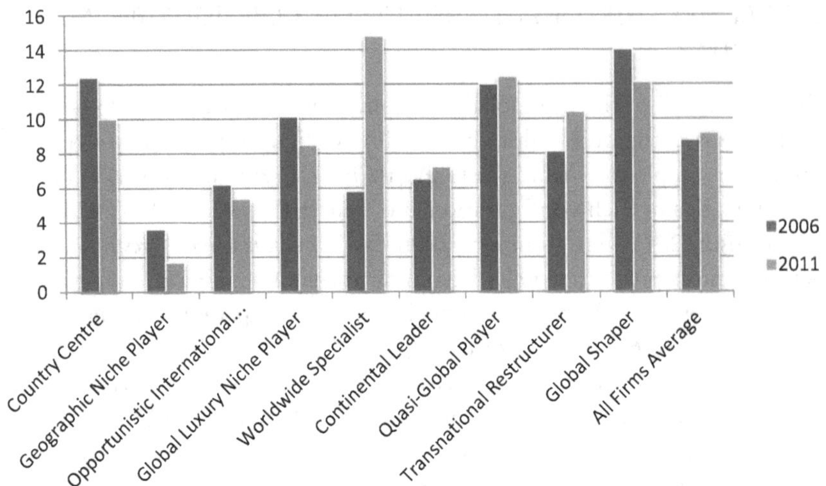

Figure 6.2 Global top 500 international configurations: average 5-year RoCEs to 2006 and 2011.

in Chapter 5 *country-centred* and *global shaper* players, at polar extremes internationally, performed notably well in both 5-year periods. Any U-curve effect (as found earlier in retailing) was, though, less pronounced and consistent for global 500 companies. *Worldwide specialists*, uncommon and unprofitable among retailers, were more common among global 500s and achieved the highest RoCEs in the last five years. Like *global shapers, quasi-global* players have proved relatively profitable. *Global luxury niche* players, though now more numerous, have fallen slightly in terms of RoCE. *Continental leaders*, also now more numerous, achieved increased profitability (in contrast to retailers earlier).

Geographical niche players' RoCEs fell, however, becoming worst overall. As companies gained more internationalisation experience, they appear to have shifted to more ambitious global configurations, thereby achieving better 5-year RoCEs. More conservative international configurations have performed less well. *Country-centred* players' and *opportunistic international challengers*' RoCEs (though still good) declined slightly.

Five-year sales growth, shown in Figure 6.3, again improved in the later period. *Continental leaders*, closely followed by *global luxury niche* players (perhaps benefitting from emerging markets), grew fastest 2006 and 2011 and also between 2001 and 2011. *Worldwide specialists* also grew rapidly, though less so in the earlier period. Otherwise, more aggressive global configurations like *transnational restructurers, quasi-global* players, and especially *global shapers*

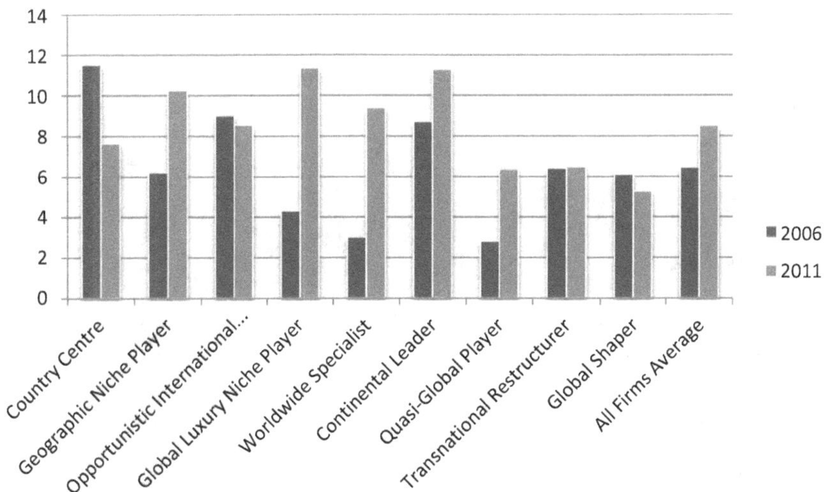

Figure 6.3 Global top 500 international configurations: average 5-year sales growths to 2006 and 2011.

saw sales grow more slowly than all types of more conservative *international challengers. Opportunistic international challengers* displayed consistently high sales growth in both periods. Geographical niche players grew even faster, though less so than in the previous period; whilst *country-centred* players also performed well, though slowing. Overall, *worldwide specialists* have now emerged as most successful in terms of both profitability and also sales growth, though this was not the case earlier; *global luxury niche* players also performed on both; continental leaders have recently gained market share, but at the expense of lower than average RoCEs; other *worldwide* players have achieved higher RoCEs, but at the expense of market share.

Figure 6.4 shows 5-year total investor returns (TIRs) for all configurations. Average returns overall have fallen slightly. On this basis, we observed rather different performance patterns, perhaps reflecting base-year biases.

Geographic niche players performed best in terms of shareholder TIRs in both periods. Global luxury niche players (an increasingly numerous group) were next best, improving in the second period. Next came continental leaders followed closely by quasi-global players. *Transnational restructurers* (the most numerous configuration) performed below average especially in the 5-years to 2011. *Worldwide specialists* (increasingly numerous) have improved on TIRs. *Country-centred* players (now less numerous) have declined on TIRs. *Opportunistic international challengers* declined, exhibiting the worst TIRs.

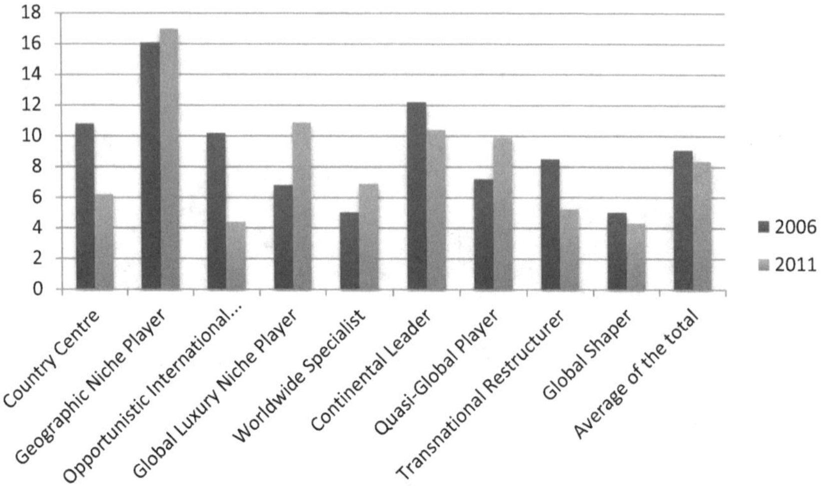

Figure 6.4 Global top 500 international configurations: average 5-year total investor returns to 2006 and 2011.

GLOBAL 500 INTERNATIONAL CONFIGURATION RoCE PERFORMANCES BY SECTOR

As shown in Figure 6.5, worldwide player (WP) configurations (being the last five categories shown) achieved the best RoCEs overall during this period (worldwide technology specialists performing best and geographical niche players worst). However, some sectors (as shown in Table 6.1) were less consistent

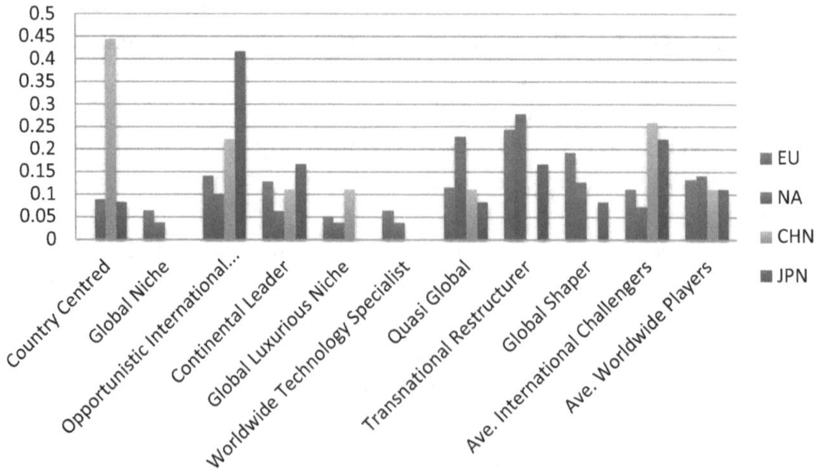

Figure 6.5 Global top 500 configurations: %s numerically by regions. Sequence order: European Union, then North America, then China, and then Japan, but no European Union in country-centred.

Table 6.1 Global 500 configurations' average 2007–2011 RoCEs by sector

Sector / *RoCE*	*CC*	*GN*	*OIC*	*CL*	*GLN*	*WTS*	*QG*	*TR*	*GS*	*Ave*
Cars/Parts	–	–	3.7	7.4	5.5	7.6	14	4.8	6.7	6.3
Banks	7.8	3.9	4.2	2.0	–	–	2.8	3.0	3.6	4.0
Capital Goods	–	–	–	–	–	7.7	10	7.1	24.6	10
Consumer Durables	–	–	–	–	5.8	–	–	–	–	5.8
Commer. & Prof. Serv	–	–	–	–	14.1	–	11	–	–	13
Div. Financial	–	–	–	–	–	–	–	4.1	4.4	4.2
Energy	–	–	–	–	–	–	–	–	15.9	16
Food Retailing	8.5	5.1	10.9	11	–	–	4.8	11	–	9.1
Food, Bev. & Tobacco	13	–	–	6.3	–	–	15.4	10.1	14.9	13
Household, Pers. Prdts	–	–	–	–	–	–	44	22	17.7	23
Insurance	–	2.6	11.5		–	–	8.7	4.6	8.1	8.0
Materials	–	–	–	11	16	8.0	24	–	–	14
Media	–	–	–	–	–	–	–	−10	–	−10
Pharma, Biotech	–	–	21	13.1	17.3	–	25.9	11.3	23.6	17.1
Retail	17.3	−13.8	–	–	–	–	18.4	–	–	11.8
Semiconductors	–	–	–	–	–	–	15.1	–	–	15
S'Ware Services		0.1	−2.0			36.1	27.7	30.7	14.4	22.4
Telecom Services	9.3	–	4.6	3.4	–	–	4.9	6.5	3.2	6.0
Tech Hardware			−1.0			−6.7	15		6.6	7.4
Transport		10	4.3	11	2.0		−1.2	6.5		5.5
Utilities				2.9						2.9

with this broad picture. In diversified financials, food & retailing, household & personal products, materials, pharmaceuticals & biotechnology, and technology hardware, worldwide players included best, but also worst RoCE performances. Only in one sector, software and services, did all worldwide players consistently achieve higher RoCEs as compared to international challengers. Worldwide technology specialist (WTS) players actually performed worst in materials and technology hardware sectors. Quasi-global shaper (QG) players performed exceptionally well (again as compared with sector averages) in household & personal products, materials, retail, pharmaceuticals/biotechnology, and technology hardware sectors. More regionally orientated configurations excelled in just a few sectors including banks, telecommunications services, insurance, and transportation.

For banks and telecommunication services, this may be because most players were *country-centred* (CC) and come from large attractive domestic markets such as the USA, Britain, and China. Chinese financial players tend to be monopolistic, benefiting from government protection and subsidies (Stowell 2010). However, for the insurance sector, *opportunistic international challengers* performed best; slightly greater internationalisation may be because many have been market followers, driven by rapidly growing customer numbers from emerging economies (Blomstermo and Sharma 2003).

Software proved particularly consistent, with our overall results highlighting worldwide technology specialists as most profitable during this recent period. Insurance, retail, and food retailing outcomes were particularly consistent, with our overall results highlighting geographical niche players as the least profitable configuration. Materials and technology hardware by contrast were notably inconsistent, in that worldwide technology specialists were certainly not the most profitable; and transport was notably inconsistent, in that geographical niche players were not the least profitable. Performance patterns in other sectors appeared more heterogeneous.

> Overall, more worldwide configurations have performed best in terms of RoCEs in most sectors. Opportunistic international challengers, though, performed best in insurance, and country-centred players in banks and telecommunication services.

GLOBAL 500 CONFIGURATION SALES GROWTH SECTOR PERFORMANCES

Figure 6.3 earlier indicated *global luxury niche* (GLN) and *continental leaders* (CLs) players as the fastest growing configurations, overall, in the five years to 2011; and *global shapers* (GSs) and *quasi-global shaper* (QG) players as the slowest.

Table 6.2 shows that in terms of sectors favouring more conservative *international challenger* approaches, CC players grew fastest in retail; and CLs grew in food & retailing, materials, food beverage & tobacco, pharmaceuticals & biotechnology, and in transport (where *global niche players* also grew rapidly). *Opportunistic international challengers* (OICs) grew fastest in insurance.

In terms of sectors favouring more aggressive *worldwide* orientations, however, GSs grew fastest in car and parts, capital goods, and technology hardware sectors. *Transnational restructurers* (TRs) grew fastest in banks, diversified financials, and telecommunications services. QGs grew fastest in commercial & professional services, household & personal products, and semiconductors. In materials, *global luxury niche* players grew fastest, in contrast to more general patterns.

Overall, Table 6.3 indicated *geographical niche* (GN) players delivering the highest TIR in both the 5-year period up to 2006 and also up to 2011; and GSs the worst in both 5- and 10-year periods up to 2011. In terms of more conservative *international challenger (IC)* orientations, *opportunistic international challengers* (OICs) performed best in insurance, where they were also particularly numerous; *geographical niche* (GN) players did well in banks and commercial & professional services; *continental leaders* did best in food & retail and in food, beverage, and tobacco, where CC players also did well. Otherwise, *worldwide players* tended to win out. *Quasi-global shapers* (QGs) performed

Table 6.2 Global 500 configurations' sector average 5-year sales growth to 2011

Sector Sales Grth	*CC*	*GN*	*OIC*	*CL*	*GLN*	*WTS*	*QG*	*TR*	*GS*	*Ave*
Cars & Parts	**–**	**–**	**3.9**	**2.7**	**5.0**	**0.8**	**5.8**	**2.9**	**9.6**	**4.0**
Banks	**8.7**	**9.6**	**11.6**	**5.4**	**–**	**–**	**8.5**	**14.0**	**7.4**	**8.9**
Capital Goods	**–**	**–**	**–**	**–**	**–**	**7.3**	**10.1**	**3.3**	**24.6**	**6.5**
Consumer Durables	**–**	**–**	**–**	**–**	**4.8**	**–**	**–**	**–**	**–**	**4.8**
Com. & Prof. Services	–	21.0	–	–	28.9	–	33.6	–	–	28.1
Diversified Financials	–	–	–	–	–	–	–	8.9	5.5	8.0
Energy	–	–	–	–	–	–	–	–	3.4	3.4
Food & Retailing	5.7	0.1	11.6	13.5	–	–	9.2	5.3	–	7.0
Food, Bev. & Tobacco	–3	–	–	5.5	–	–	−0.8	3.8	3.2	2.7
Household & Pers. Prd	–	–	–	–	–	–	7.8	6.6	2.9	5.7
Insurance	–	−1.8	14.9		–	–	3.0	5.0	5.9	7.1
Materials	–	–	–	14.0	−0.5	4.4	13.6	–	–	9.9
Media	–	–	–	–	–	–	–	–3.0	–	−3.0
Pharma & Biotech	–	–	−14	34.3	8.6	–	10.1	5.2	3.3	8.8
Retail	15.0	8.0	–	–	–	–	6.4	–	–	8.4
Semiconductors etc	–	–	–	–	–	–	13.1	–	–	13.1
Software & Services		12.2	−1.8			24.2	5.1	5.8	1.3	11.9
Telecomm Services	10.7	–	−0.5	−0.1	–	–	5.2	15.3	6.7	7.4
Tech Hardware			−2.5			−13	3.3		15.2	1.3
Transport		23.3	13.8	24.0	11.1		2.5	5.0		12.1
Utilities				−0.5						−0.5

Table 6.3 Global 500 configurations' average TIRs by sector 2007–2011

Sector TIR	*CC*	*GN*	*OIC*	*CL*	*GLN*	*WTS*	*QG*	*TR*	*GS*	*Ave*
Car & Parts	–	–	9.9	21.6	3.7	17.3	45.9	2.3	15.3	13.1
Banks	4.8	14.4	6.2	10.9	–	–	12.0	15.4	2.2	8.1
Capital Goods	–	–	–	–	–	1.2	64.0	20.4	7.8	14.7
Consumer Durables	–	–	–	–	17.3	–	–	–	–	17.3
Com. & Prof. Serv.	–	14.1	–	–	19.6	–	13.9	–	–	15.8
Diversified Financials	–	–	–	–	–	–	–	11.4	5.0	9.6
Energy	–	–	–	–	–	–	–	–	4.7	4.7
Food & Retailing	2.3	−1.4	4.1	7.3	--	–	N/A	0.4	–	1.9
Food, Bev. & Tobacco	11	–	–	12.5	–	–	8.1	6.5	8.4	8.6
Household & Pers. Prd	–	–	–	–	–	–	9.1	6.8	2.8	6.0
Insurance	–	−6.8	10.3		–	–	2.4	5.7	7.0	4.5
Materials	–	–	–	25.5	1.9	23.3	–	–	–	20.3
Media	–	–	–	–	–	–	–	−7.2	–	−7.2

best in car and parts and in capital goods, tripling sectorial averages, and in household and personal products. TRs performed best in banks, diversified financial services, and in media. Global shapers did well in insurance. WTS also did quite well in materials. Overall *international challengers* and particularly *opportunistic international challengers* (OICs) achieved higher TIRs;

but *worldwide* players became more numerous and better performing, with *quasi-global shapers* (QGs) and TRs doing particularly well in several sectors.

GLOBAL 500 WEIGHTED AVERAGE OVERALL SECTOR PERFORMANCES

Table 6.4 summarises sector differences in the 5-year period to 2011, showing first company numbers only for each General Industrial Classification System (GICS) sector examined. As the 190 companies were classified into 21 different sectors, samples in each were relatively low. Focusing on sectors representing over 5% of total numbers, the only two with higher percentages of more conservative and regional *international challenger* strategies were banks and telecommunication services. Sectors dominated by global strategies included food, beverage & tobacco, pharmaceuticals, biotechnology, & life science, with more than 80% of companies adopting the *worldwide player* configurations. Weighted average performances are then shown according to the formula: (2 * RoCE + SG + TIR)/4.

Table 6.4 Global 500 broad configurations' weighted average overall performances by sector

Sector (GICS)	*% of all companies*	*% of international challenger*	*% of worldwide player*	*Weighted RoCE/sales/TIR sector % scores*
Cars & Parts	5.26	30	70	7.41
Banks	18.95	66.7	33.3	6.25
Capital Goods	4.21	0	100	10.26
Consumer Durables	1.05	0	100	8.43
Commercial & Prof. Services	2.11	25	75	19.42
Diversified Financials	2.11	0	100	6.49
Energy	0.53	0	100	9.99
Food & Retailing	4.21	50	50	7.01
Food, Beverage & Tobacco	11.53	19.05	80.95	8.97
Household & Personal Products	3.68	0	100	14.60
Insurance	5.26	40	60	6.88
Materials	3.16	50	50	13.03
Media	0.53	0	100	−6.17
Pharmaceuticals & Biotechnology	7.37	14.29	85.71	10.09
Retail	2.63	40	60	14.95
Semiconductors	0.53	0	100	15.45
Software & Services	4.21	25	75	14.74
Telecommunication Services	6.84	53.85	46.15	3.51
Technology Hardware	4.21	25	75	4.47
Transportation	11.59	40.91	59.09	7.15
Utilities	0.53	100	0	3.85

On this weighted basis, the two most regional sectors performed lowest at 6.3% for banks and 3.5% for telecommunication services. By contrast, sectors with the boldest global configurations performed the best: at 9.0% for food, beverage and tobacco and 10.1 for pharmaceuticals & biotechnology. Less globalised sectors such as transportation and insurance, scored lower than the more globalised car and parts sector. This may be because many food, beverage and tobacco companies were, historically, large, sophisticated and, with international experience, able to evolve into successful worldwide players (Tonts and Siddique 2011). Pharmaceuticals players may have benefitted from favourable governmental regulation in the European Union, the long-established competitiveness of United States (US) companies and high research and development (R&D) investment (Commission, U. S. I. T. 1999), all bolstering entry barriers. More regional sectors like banks and telecommunications may have benefitted from large monopolised domestic markets, with large US and state-owned Chinese players well represented in the *Fortune* 500 list (CNN *Money Fortune* 500 list data 2011). Such *country-centred* players may still survive globalisation, but have been outperformed by bolder *worldwide* players.

> The most globalized sectors such as food, beverage and tobacco, pharmaceuticals, and biotechnology and life sciences performed best on weighted RoCE, sales, and TIR metrics; more regionally orientated sectors such as banks and telecommunication services performed worst on the same weighted basis. More globalized sectors typically achieved higher weighted performance scores than more regional ones.

GLOBAL TOP 500s AND THE INFLUENCE OF NATIONAL COUNTRY ADVANTAGES

Shares of world manufacturing have shifted from developed to now 41% for developing countries (Marsh 2012). China became the world's second largest economy in 2010, finally overtaking the USA in 2011 to become the number one (Sutter 2012). The European Union has overtaken the United States as the world's largest economic entity (Lamb 2011). So what strategy choices underlie such shifts, and do different configurations perform relatively better depending on which regions companies come from?

Table 6.5 first just ranks countries by their company numbers in Global *Fortune* 500 listings (*Money* CNN *Fortune* 500 List data 2011). The European Union ranks first at 30%, the USA second at 29%, Japan fourth at 14%, with China third and coming up fast at 15%. This conclusion must though be tempered: Thomson One Banker data are biased since 83% of companies providing its data are from Europe or North America.

Table 6.5 Ranking regions by numbers of *Fortune* Top Global 500 companies

Rank	*Region*	*No. of companies/%*
1	EU	148/30%
2	NA	143/29%
3	CHN	73/15%
4	JPN	68/14%

Source: Money CNN *Fortune* 500 List data 2011.

Figure 6.5 then analyses the configurations of all our global top 500 companies by numbers, according to which region they came from. European Union (EU) and North American (NA) companies deployed virtually all nine configurations but Chinese (CHN) and Japanese (JPN) only some, though partly due to poorer Thomson One Banker representation. Japanese and especially Chinese players reflected proportionately more cautious *international challenger* configurations, whereas bolder *global shaper* and *transnational restructurer* configurations were dominated entirely by the European Union and NA. As a newly emerged power, the Chinese companies are more regional than the developed economies. Being the first developed economy in Asia, Japan has a lower percentage of companies which adopted regional strategies than the Chinese counterpart, but companies with global strategies now dominate.

Whilst NA and EU companies were similarly quite globally orientated, there were no *country-centred* EU players, but several in NA. NA companies inclined more to *quasi-globals*, and EU firms towards *global shaper* configuration. Chinese configurations were predominantly *country-centred* or secondly OIC. After 1970 Japanese firms internationalised more aggressively (Schaeffer 2005): 42% have now adopted OIC approaches, and a few have moved on to bolder *worldwide* configurations.

> EU and NA companies have been more globalized than Asian counterparts. However, many Japanese firms have turned more aggressively to opportunistic international challenger or even worldwide configurations. Chinese players largely remain country-centred, an orientation still preferred by several NA companies.

Figure 6.6 analyses 5-year RoCE performances for these regional and international configurations. Worldwide players performed substantially better than international challengers in nearly all regions and particularly for North American and Japanese companies. The only exception was China, where the gap remained close and where country-centred configurations proved even more profitable than those from NA. NA companies

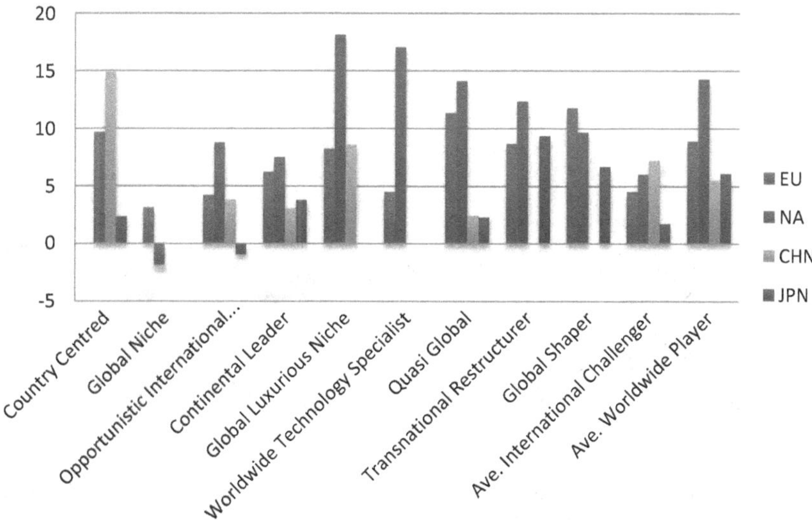

Figure 6.6 Global 500 international configurations: 5-year RoCE performances to 2011 by regions. Sequence order: European Union, then North America, then China, and then Japan, but no European Union in country-centred.

outperformed EU counterparts for all configurations except global shapers. Performances from all regions dipped for opportunistic international challengers, but improve again for quasi-global configurations. Japanese companies, and especially their more conservative international challengers, performed poorly.

> North American companies achieved higher RoCE than other regions in most configurations; but worldwide configurations, aside from those from China, have outperformed more regional approaches overall.

Figure 6.7 analyses 5-year sales growth performances for regional and international configurations. Country of origin has a marked impact. EU companies grew more slowly than NA counterparts in all except *continental leader* configurations. EU companies grew faster deploying *international challenger* configurations; for NA, there was little difference; but for Japan and China, *worldwide* configurations grew faster. NA companies grew fastest deploying *global luxury* niche or *geographic niche* configurations; the Chinese through *quasi-global* or *country-centred* configurations; and the Japanese through *global shaper* or *transnational restructurer* configurations.

> Worldwide players grew faster than regional players in all regions except the European Union. Chinese companies grew strikingly faster, especially when pursuing quasi-global and country-centred configurations.

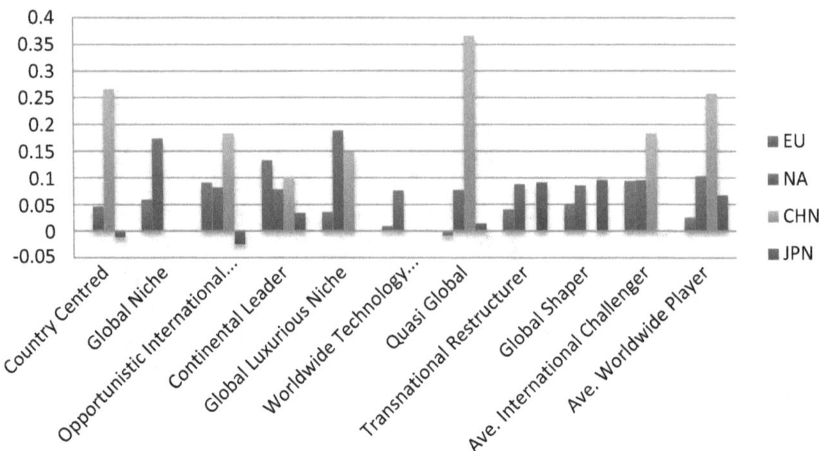

Figure 6.7 Global 500 configurations: 5-year sales growth to 2011 by regions. Sequence order: European Union, then North America, then China, and then Japan, but no European Union in country-centred.

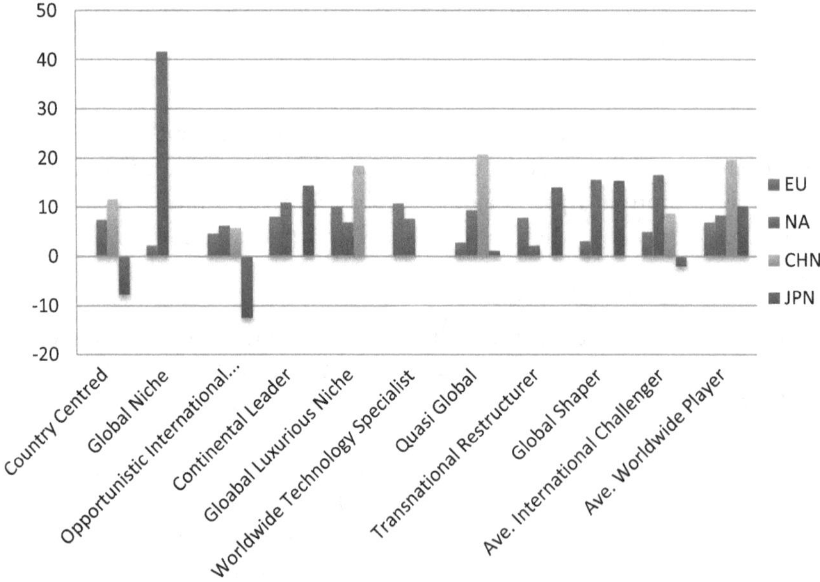

Figure 6.8 Global 500 configurations: average 5-year total investment returns to 2011 by regions. Sequence order: European Union, then North America, then China, and then Japan, but no European Union in country-centred.

Figure 6.8 analyses 5-year TIR performances. Country of origin proved important: Chinese companies performing best, followed by North Americans. *Worldwide* configurations achieved higher than *international challengers* from all regions except North America, where geographical niche players (though not numerous) performed most strongly.

Japan's more regional *international challengers* performed worst, whilst their *worldwide* players did better. EU players also performed better pursuing more *worldwide* configurations. *Country-centred* configurations performed less well, especially in Japan.

> Worldwide players achieved higher average TIRs relative to international challengers in all regions, except North America; Japan's international challengers, and especially their country-centred and opportunistic players, performed worst.

Looking at configurations by regions overall, North American and European Union companies exhibited similar patterns, with worldwide strategies predominating more regional international challenger configurations. The Chinese, as important latecomers, still have high percentages of companies pursuing the most regional country-centred configurations. Japan's country-centred players have progressed on to opportunistic international challengers, which made up about half our sample here. As countries have industrialised, the trend has been towards more global configurations.

EU companies have most frequently opted for the global shaper configuration, which achieved good 5-year RoCEs, but less good sales growth and TIRs. NA firms most frequently opted for the transnational restructurer option, but achieved their best performances (on all three metrics) through more specialised *worldwide technology specialist* and *global luxury niche* configurations. Chinese firms most frequently opted for *country-centred* configurations, which also generated the best RoCE returns. Japanese firms, by contrast, opted more frequently for the *opportunistic international challenger* configuration, which led, though, to extremely poor results on all performance metrics; their best results coming from the more worldwide *transnational restructurer* configuration. Again, the contrast between Japan and China seems to reflect respective stages in terms of industrialisation and globalisation: with many firms beginning country-centred, then moving on to opportunistic international challenger or geographical niche configurations, and with some Japanese companies now already having successfully transformed into a much bolder worldwide player, leading to improved performances. The success of most EU and NA companies turning to more worldwide configurations lends weight to this conclusion.

GLOBAL TOP 500s' CONFIGURATIONS PERFORMANCE ANALYSIS CONCLUSIONS

Figures 6.2–6.4 provided averaged performance scores for all international configurations for both consecutive 5-year periods, and Table 6.6 integrates results from all performance metrics for the most recent five-year period 2007–2011.

Table 6.6 Global 500 configurations' 5-year performances to 2011 summarised

	Numbers of companies/%	*5-year Ave. RoCE*	*5-year Ave. Sales Growth%*	*5-year Ave. TIR %*
CC*	13 (6.8%)	9.90	7.6	6.2
GN	8 (4.2%)	1.69	10.2	17.0
OIC	28 (14.7%)	5.36	8.6	4.4
CL	20 (10.5%)	7.21	11.3	10.4
GLN	10 (5.3%)	8.47	11.4	10.9
WTS	10 (5.3%)	14.78	9.4	6.9
QG	31 (16.3%)	12.42	6.4	9.9
TR	44 (23.2%)	10.39	6.5	7.4
GS	26 (13.7%)	12.10	5.3	8.4

Note: GN, geographic niche; OIC, opportunistic international challenger.

More national and regional *international challenger* configurations, representing just the first four configurations (CC, GN, OIC, & CL), made up 36%; *worldwide* players, representing more globally ambitious orientations made up 64%. Performance relationships may change over time; but this paints a far more globally orientated picture of today's global top 500s, than merely looking at geographical sales splits. Nevertheless, overall, more *worldwide* configurations achieved higher RoCEs, indeed in both 5-year periods. This was true in most sectors, but, as we've shown, they do vary. *Opportunistic international challengers*, for example, performed best in insurance and *country-centred* players in banks and telecommunication services.

In terms of long-term sales growth (being a proxy for global market share shifts), the picture is more mixed. The country of origin had marked effects. Chinese companies grew strikingly faster, though they grew fastest pursuing *quasi-global* at one extreme or *country-centred* configurations at the other extreme. *Worldwide* players grew relatively faster overall in all regions, except the European Union, and they also achieved relatively higher average TIRs in all regions, except North America. Japan's *international challengers*, and especially their *country-centred* and *opportunistic international challengers*, performed worst in terms of total investor returns.

Overall, EU and NA companies have been more globally orientated than their Asian counterparts. Japanese top firms, though, have shifted to *opportunistic international challenger* and even *worldwide* configurations. Chinese players (and indeed several NA firms) remain largely *country centred*. North American companies achieved higher RoCE than other regions in most configurations; but *worldwide* configurations, aside from those from China, have typically outperformed more regional approaches. Nevertheless, sector differences shown in Tables 6.1–6.4 remain appreciable. It therefore makes sense to benchmark against other top players from one of these broad 21 GICS-based sectors analysed.

As illustrated by Van Gruppen's strategic analysis in the case of retail fashion discussed in Chapter 5, such is a natural starting point for more full-blown CPA of a firm's more tightly defined sector. Appropriate configurations and orientations, in turn, determine international market entry modes. Here, there are two main options: going it alone, typically through green-field sites as illustrated by Inditex and Zara, or through international collaboration. In the next chapter, we will discuss two main options cross-border mergers and acquisitions (M&A) or strategic alliances.

Part III

GLOBAL STRATEGY CHOICES AND OUTCOME

7

GLOBAL COOPERATION

CROSS-BORDER MERGERS AND ACQUISITIONS AND STRATEGIC ALLIANCES

GLOBAL LOGIC BEHIND CROSS-BORDER MERGERS AND ACQUISITIONS AND STRATEGIC ALLIANCES: CARR'S 1ST LAW

Going global alone is time consuming, resource intensive, and calls for high impact, committed strategic investment decisions. Covering the globe organically, primarily through greenfield sites, is fine if, like Zara, you have a uniquely strong, inherently customised business model and a pre-emptive lead; but most companies are less favoured or need to move more swiftly. Working with others through cross-border mergers and acquisitions (M&A), international strategic alliances, franchising, licensing, or one-off tactical steps such as research and development (R&D) cooperative projects, leverage resources and competences even more quickly. Tactical steps for such options are documented in textbooks or specialist books.[1] Strategists, though, need a long-term evolutionary perspective, recognising the implications of those global consolidation processes already depicted. This chapter draws key implementation lessons from some of the most and least successful alliances and M&A cases of global consolidations.

Ohmae's *Triad Strategy*[2] stresses pre-emptive strategic moves, aimed at dominating all three highly developed triad regions: i.e., Europe, North America, and Japan/S. Korea. His logic, though slightly contentious, is well supported. However, as globalisation extends to multiple emerging markets (EMs), resource-constrained companies often require international strategic alliances (ISAs) to gain effective coverage.[3] With strong triad cores, North and South American ISAs can span out from United States (US) positions, Asia Pacific ISAs can span out from Japan/S. Korea, and East European, Russian, Turkish, Middle Eastern, and African ISAs from Europe. Ohmae/McKinsey offer succinct timeless advice on ISA implementation which tallies well with GKN's experiences going global, further elaborated in Chapter 13. Traditionally, stronger global players trade know-how, brands and international support in return for weaker partners' local market access, creating win-wins. Weaker national/regional players, struggling amidst global wars and fearful of the funding that huge investments require, eventually need stronger partners.

However, as discussed in Chapters 9 and 10, companies from emerging markets (EMs) are likewise shifting from national/regional positions. Aided by huge national comparative advantages (NCA), they are increasingly going global themselves. China and India are reverting towards the dominant world market shares they enjoyed in manufacturing 300 years ago. Such EM champions have distinctive strategic traits,[4] seeking know-how, brands, as well as local market entry support.[5] China's Haier (elaborated in Chapter 11) has become the global No. 1 in domestic appliances, following earlier greenfield sites (GFSs) in the USA and Europe, and M&A in the USA and Japan. India's Tata bought Jaguar/Land Rover, motivated by knowledge acquisition and global brand-building, and then supported them in India, China, and most recently in the Czech Republic where it is building a new modern factory. Such EM champions have become increasingly important. M&A deals fell back from record levels by over a fifth in the first quarter of 2016,[6] but Chinese cross-border M&A sharply increased, helping offsetting that temporary slack.

Figure 7.1 depicts the natural sequence of cooperative moves as consolidation begins domestically, but then proceeds more globally. This model was developed from my research in the late 1990s into four cases studies of Japanese companies entering the United Kingdom (UK) through local M&As and ISAs: Fujitsu/ICL Computers, Sumitomo Rubber International/Dunlop, NSK/RHP Bearings, and Honda/Rover Cars.

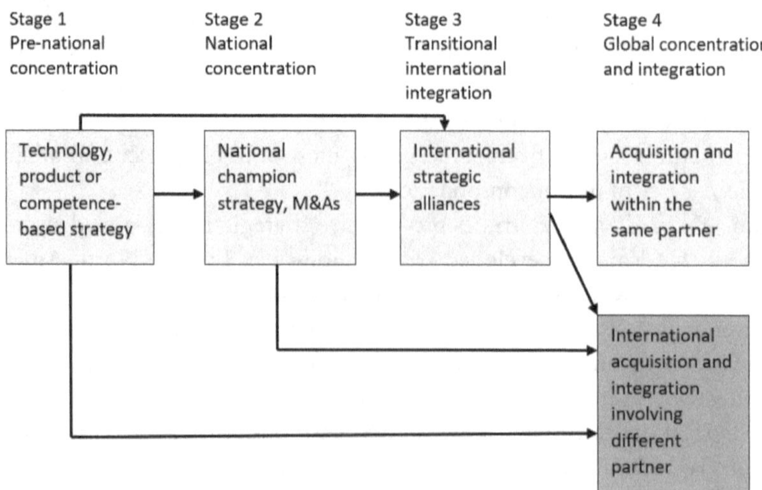

Figure 7.1 Sequential steps in domestic and global re-alignments over four stages. (Reprinted from Carr, C., *R&D Manage.*, 29, 405–421, 1999. With permission.)

At the early stage 1 of the life cycle of a new technology or market there has typically been little concentration, even domestically. Emergent new business models and technologies still compete for dominance. By stage 2 more dominant paradigms have (in evolutionary terminology) 'amplified': national leaders have emerged after riding domestic consolidation waves, sometimes aided by domestic M&A. In stage 3 scale economies begin to be exploited beyond national borders; companies hedge their commitments and international risks through joint ventures or more strategic alliances, and an ambiguous transition commences towards a more global process of consolidation. Finally, at stage 4, the economic balance tips in favour of more committed global moves, sometimes involving ISAs or international acquisitions (IAs). Global moves, countermoves and deals translate into more clear-cut global consolidation processes. Significant players from advanced countries fall in numbers. Weaker, national and regional players exit or succumb to global consolidators. Stage 2 should be evident in domestic concentration metrics and stages 3 and 4 in should be evident in global concentration ratio (GCR)4s and Herfindahls.

This four-phase process is driven by scale economies, as Adam Smith's division of labour goes beyond national and regional boundaries. Companies also rightly want to take their specialist competences global, securing maximum returns on huge capital costs incurred. As Smith illustrated, scale economies from geographically larger, de-regulated markets can dramatically increase productivity (400-fold in the case of pins). This makes sense both for companies and nations seeking enhanced wealth. Marx argued that the logic of such scale advantages would drive towards global monopolies, though, as we've seen Schumpeterian dynamics mitigate, these lead instead to global oligopolies and cyclical concentration patterns. There were indeed only four major companies left making pins by 1980, one in Scandinavia, one in Germany, and a couple in North America; but we still have a global oligopoly rather than outright monopoly.

In evolutionary battles scale economies are important, though survival depends even more upon robust adaptation. Market share may become a necessary, though rarely sufficient, condition for survival. Were this not so, Marx's global monopoly players could, like dinosaurs, predominate, atrophying competitive dynamics, spawning exploitation in place of longer-term efficiencies. Outside a handful of sectors, this extreme has thankfully so far proved rare.

The question arising is how far geographically will consolidation processes go? Generally, once scale economies overwhelm localisation constraints, consolidation processes do not halt at regional boundaries; and they relentlessly go global as depicted in stage 4.

Carr's 1st law therefore states that (with few exceptions):

> Consolidation processes, which have already gone national and shifted fully into the 3rd transitional stage, bypass mid-way regional boundaries and go global.

This was bad news for would-be European champions like France's Bull Computers. S&N (Europe's No. 3 brewer) was recently acquired by Heineken and Carlsberg, and Indesit (Europe's No. 3 in domestic appliances) by Whirlpool. Even Europe's No. 1 software player SAP, once hailed as the classic successful European regional champion, has gone global.

Note though, that more modest scale economies in some sectors, like groceries, have not yet overwhelmed localisation constraints. Fledgling international moves by Tesco (aside from Hungary, Thailand and Indonesia) failed. Even Walmart has had limited success. However lowest cost players, Aldi and Lidl, have sustained successful niche European positions, leveraging scale economies regionally, though both have recently committed to US entries and Lidl looks set to enter German speaking Namibia. Likewise. Low-cost airlines such as Ryanair, Southwest Airlines, and EasyJet have succeeded regionally (some even being national). Ryanair's lowest cost airline model required same day return of aircraft to home bases, limiting their geographic range to roughly 3500 km. As in discount groceries, cautious exploratory global moves are afoot, though Laker failed on North Atlantic routes. Air Asia X's and Norwegian Airways recent global moves still look vulnerable. Discounters' regional strategies have succeeded but could go global in the next decade or so as they reach stage 4 and Carr's 1st law finally impacts.

The logic of cross-border strategic alliances and acquisitions should be seen against this evolutionary competitive context. Deal making is not passive; often it is 'eat or be eaten'. In this game of musical chairs, no one wants to be left fighting for a diminishingly few final chairs. Concentration (in the original sense of the word) means that those numbers are falling. Outcomes relate little to gentle equilibrium or Walrasian rational, incremental price adjustments; and the norm, as Keynes proclaimed, is disequilibrium amidst genuine uncertainty.[7] Contending with Schumpeter's savage 'gales of creative destruction', companies want to survive. To do so, they find themselves running ever faster. Like sharks, they cannot stand still, act like complacent monopolists and they are finished.

LESS COMMITTED INTERNATIONAL ENTRY OPTIONS: LICENSING AND FRANCHISING

More tactical, licensing is perhaps the easiest, least immediately risky and sometimes the only feasible entry option for less accessible countries. Given intricate tie-ups, the Japanese drivetrain market was almost closed to GKN in the late 1980s. So recourse was taken to a license deal with Japan's NTN, allowing them to handle their home market. This afforded safe royalty streams and a partial answer to Ohmae's triad challenge, as GKN extended European operations to the USA and then rapidly established joint ventures in key emerging markets. Twenty-five years later the drawback was that, armed with that technology, NTN emerged as a top competitor with a global market share of around 12% (aided by positions in Brazil, for example) compared with GKN's at 40%. Even GKN's caste-iron patent for constant velocity joints expired after 30 years, allowing such licensees to return to challenge them.

Conversely, licensing other people's technology (as NTN did) has proved effective for entrants catching up when behind on technology, aiming at more committed global moves later. Haier has done likewise, subsequently becoming virtually the global No. 1 in domestic appliances (as further discussed in Chapter 11).

As a method of diversification, though, licensing is flimsy. In contracting, GKN licensed know-how from Ross Poultry in the late 1970s to enter the market for installing several chicken slaughterhouses in Iraq. It was not GKN's prime core competence. Ross Poultry made modest money safely. Partly because of the Iraq/Iran war, GKN contractors lost around 40% of the entire contract value, contributing to GKN's decision to exit contracting.

Truly great patents can seduce companies into treating licensing as their prime globalisation strategy. Pilkington's patented float glass process in the 1950s threw rivals like France's Saint-Gobain, overinvested in traditional plate-glass production lines, into disarray. Pilkington's new process represented a paradigm shift in terms of quality, which successfully transformed the global industry. Pilkington staked all on licenses covering worldwide markets, beginning lucratively in the USA. Powerful US and Japanese players naturally came back to bite them. More fundamentally, global licensing left them exposed; they lacked robust global competitive advantages, sustainable entry barriers, or any more comprehensive world-class business model. Patents expired. World-class rivals deployed FDI, securing scale economies in more international markets. Instead of becoming a global winner, Pilkington was acquired by Asahi Glass.

GKN's opposite, more defensible strategic perspective was to develop a rounded world-class business model, committing FDI to fully fledged global strategies integrating all fields of policy organisationally, well before patents expired. Going global the hard way, through 'assets-on-the-ground' can prove the trickiest, most resource-demanding strategy of all. Rivals from all regions come at you, salivated by the prospect of patent expiries, exploiting newer traditional technologies, as they too become available. Yet the greatest entry barrier of all is global strategy per se. Short of going to Mars, no greater scale will ever be found, aside from disrupters creating novel adjacent markets and technologies. Scale without responsiveness did not save dinosaurs; but with relentless re-focusing and adaptation, outcomes are as good as they're going to get. Not doing so can prove fatal.

Franchising can prove tactically advantageous – leveraging competences globally whilst reducing financial commitments. As part of well conceived globally integrated strategies, franchising has been effective where small business units duplicate some unique, innovative, business model such as McDonald's, supported by a global brand. Benetton's initial international success was also based on franchising. Even the Zara globally integrated model has increasingly used franchises, albeit only for marginal geographies.

International collaborative turnkey projects can constitute huge strategic investment decisions in aerospace or extraction sectors. Distinctive key success factors hinge on project management and technological skills; yet they remain tactical and depend ultimately on panoramic, integrated international strategies. Beyond this, the spectrum of more tactical options is wide: e.g. collaborative R&D, co-marketing projects, or co-supply projects.

Generally, most strategic global cooperation ultimately calls for major FDI assets on the ground to service customers, either through international strategic alliances (ISAs) or international M&As (IAs), strengthening integration and controls worldwide. FDI rose almost tenfold in the 20 years to 2011,[8] way beyond world output or trade growth rates. Each will be examined in turn, before looking at longer-term examples of hybrid cooperative global strategies, as ISAs often gradually evolve into full IAs.

GLOBAL STRATEGIC ALLIANCES

Forty years ago many such moves were purely one-off joint ventures, necessitated by local market regulations; today, as Ohmae reminded us, they need to be more strategically integrated within some global vision. Undisciplined, local production operations, in, say, India, inevitably press for opportunistic exports to other territories, undermining coherent pricing internationally. Multinational corporation (MNC)s' tactical joint ventures have typically transformed into global M&As or ISAs.

Many companies eschew ISAs in favour of global M&As, promising full control globally and (potentially) integration; but research evidence suggests that full control is no panacea. The issue as between alliances and M&A lies in the degree of control that is desirable. The right balance depends on sector and firm traits, and circumstances such as turnarounds, but is less obvious than it seems. Daussauge and Garrette's desk-based research found that greater control resulted in poorer performances; whereas almost 75% of successful outcomes were associated with lesser control.[9] In GKN's case, early alliances typically aimed at just 40% equity control, enough to secure international market indiscipline, whilst still securing regulatory compliances and highly motivated local partners.

MNCs adopt different views. Yet based on my research globally, other successful Japanese players, for example, endorsed GKN's stance. One had post-audited nearly a thousand ISAs and IAs. Their findings could be laid out on a simple two by two chart. On the horizontal, they depicted the degree of

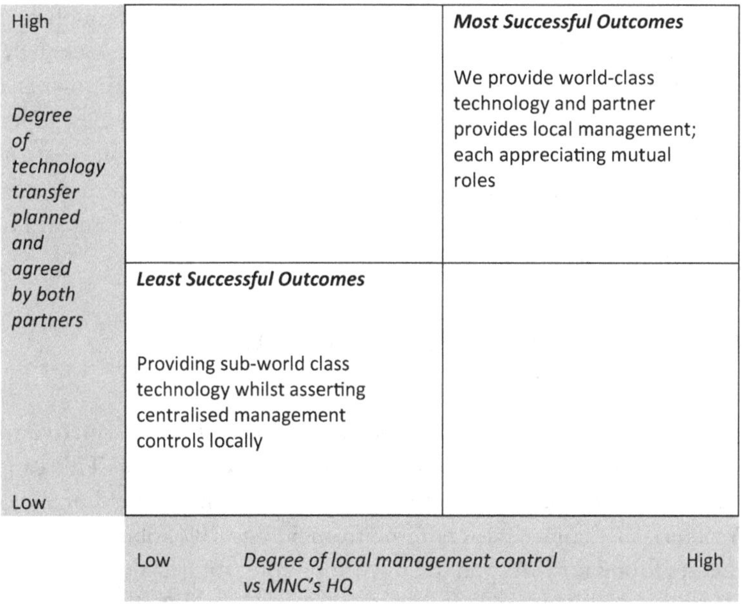

Degree of technology transfer planned and agreed by both partners		
High		***Most Successful Outcomes*** We provide world-class technology and partner provides local management; each appreciating mutual roles
Low	***Least Successful Outcomes*** Providing sub-world class technology whilst asserting centralised management controls locally	
	Low *Degree of local management control vs MNC's HQ*	High

Figure 7.2 Japanese multi-national's cross-border M&A and strategic alliance performance outcomes.

management control that they had aimed for; the other showed the degree of technology transfer involved, as shown in Figure 7.2.

Other boxes generated mixed outcomes. Cross-border M&As, ISAs, and JVs were shown alongside with results proving surprisingly consistent. A temptation (depicted on the y axis) is to go in with second best technology, as implied by traditional international product life cycle theory. This mitigates risks of top technologies being copied or cannibalised by partners/potential rivals. International strategic alliances only last on average around eight years. The counter argument is that, if you can't trust each other, then look for another partner. Conversely, the x axis depicts the temptation to press for total MNC management control, implicitly critical of local practices, versus the need to recognise local differences and to motivate local employees.

Outcomes from this Japanese MNC's thousand or so cooperations demonstrated that total domination and control indeed proved no panacea. The problem (as Daimler likewise found with Chrysler) was trying to run local businesses they couldn't fully understand. More often, success ultimately depended on being wise enough to insist on utilising the very best technologies, whilst also trusting partners' local management expertise. As GKN found, you cannot allow a local partner's aspirations to destroy integrated global marketing plans; but maintaining motivations otherwise has proved crucial.

In respect to ISAs, McKinsey's Kenichi Ohmae advises thorough preparation contractually, minimising misunderstandings, but then to lock such legal contracts in a filing cabinet, just throwing away the keys.[10] Micro-managing fails because of the pace of highly uncertain international developments; what matters is preserving and building relationships based on trust. As the chief executive officer (CEO) of a top aerospace company put it to me: 'If I can't look my opposite number in the eye and trust him, it's simple: I'm just not going to do it [the joint venture]'.

CARR'S ACID TESTS FOR SUSTAINED STRATEGIC ALLIANCES AND M&A

The danger with perceiving ISAs and IAs as two utterly distinctive modes is that we lose sight of any dynamic evolutionary perspective. This can happen. Academics are incentivised to become experts in one field or the other. M&A experts cite failure rates ranging from 50% to 70%, oblivious to similar failure rates found for ISAs and to failure rates for going-it-alone players who, all too often, get swept away by consolidators. Company mindsets are vulnerable to earlier 'psychological conditioning', having been burnt by bad outcomes into 'never again!' responses for one mode or another. Predispositions vary understandably by sector, but also by country: US executive preferences appear skewed to M&A. Some reflect the latest 'flavour of the month' or incoming CEOs' prior experiences and inclinations.

I had to present to the finance director (in charge also of strategy) and other executives at a major pharmaceutical company five years ago, only to be told that M&A or global consolidation issues were out of court, since this was not their pitch to the city, nor were major strategic alliance options being pushed. Yet, only a little while earlier, their major strategic investments had focused around cross-border M&A. Thanks to a dynamic incoming CEO, and the finance director's departure, their strategic approach changed a little later, leaving them well prepared for the welter of M&A consolidation moves which have hit the sector. As of December 2019, their shares have performed excellently.

Companies learn through experiences. Germany's Webasto has been superb at deploying ISAs for entering several markets in sunroofs.[11] With world-class technology, they enjoyed deep original equipment manufacturer customer relationships. They then partnered with an M&A-orientated UK player to enter the United Kingdom. Initial 3-year financial results were so poor that the UK partner's board wanted to withdraw from the original equipment manufacturer and to retreat to the higher-margin aftermarket. ISA executives were derided as 'jam tomorrow boys'. The CEOs, however, trusted each other. Webasto's German CEO pointed to multiple prior ISA experiences elsewhere, reassuringly: '*We're not impressed either, but just trust us and you'll make money like there's no tomorrow*'.

Eighteen months later, the customer breakthrough finally came, and volumes took off, delivering huge returns. Sadly the UK partner's more usual M&A approach later floundered. Its price earnings ratio dipped, stalling further M&A and precipitating bankruptcy as financial institutions withheld support. Webasto's ISA approach proved far more robust.

Likewise Cisco's huge experience of technology-based ISAs allowed it to beat odds cited against ISA outcomes.[12] Its Italtel ISA exemplified classic win-wins in the context of global consolidations. Italtel offered desirable packet-switching technology and entry support into Italy; and Cisco had the funds and competence to help take their technology further, worldwide.

Similarly General Electric's (GE) IAs beat adverse odds that are frequently cited. Stewart Sinclair, as their UK CEO, indeed cited these risk figures from academics (including Michael Porter) and consultants (including BCG and McKinsey), before concluding that 'only strategically sound, flawlessly executed' deals delivered results. GKN executives' dictums concurred: '*you have to do the right things, right*'. Outcomes depend on the elements of any system, so you need sound strategic and strong implementation skills. It's not one or the other.

GE's M&A under Jack Welch delivered the highest market capitalisation performance of any company during the twentieth century. Only two large companies successively performed above average during successive 5-year windows from roughly 1918 to 1990: GE and Kodak. Kodak, though, failed to keep up with global rivals Canon (in digital cameras) and Fuji (in films) and filed for bankruptcy and GE's Immelt could not sustain such shareholder value creation under harsher conditions post 9/11. Under Jack Welch, GE was recognised as the most admired company anywhere. Welch's global rule was (aside from financial services) to achieve top 3 global positions in all chosen sectors, including quality and technology benchmarks. (Stewart Sinclair confirmed this still applied more recently.) For example, Welch traded GE's strong USA position in televisions for France's Phillip's healthcare European, allowing both to move towards global dominance in prioritised arenas. His RCA acquisition and divestments were similarly predicated and successful. Welch's (DMAIC) M&A integration processes were also notably systematic and thorough.

CARR'S 2ND LAW RELATING TO INTERNATIONAL STRATEGIC ALLIANCES AND M&A

These examples highlight lessons applicable to ISAs and M&As, alike, as consolidation processes become progressively more global. Companies today are savvy regarding marketing aims and financial due diligence. IMD Country Competitiveness reports survey annually 40 key attractiveness metrics for over 40 countries: they are neatly quantified and attuned to MNC parenting perspectives.

Finance directors no longer condone M&As without proper due diligence. The USA, for example, allows triple damages where motives can be impugned, because black holes in the accounts of acquired companies can be catastrophic financially as well as to reputation. BP's oil spillages were lambasted as deplorable British management, earning devastating fines and reputation damage although local responsibility would likely have been in the hands of the USA operation they had acquired earlier. Manage such M&As in an overly hands-off manner (respecting more local cultural management differences), or fail to spot such risks in your financial due diligence, and executives land themselves in trouble.

Even Tidjane Thiam, Prudential's brilliant CEO, admitted to mismanaging their AIA M&A, saying '*but it's not every day a company gets to make a $32bn M&A like this!*' The write-off of M&A fees was enormous but he was at least addressing crucial, albeit uncertain global strategic issues. Prudential had regrettably little experience of ISAs or Asia, so it was to his credit that they pulled out decisively, learning from the process. Contrast Goodwin's failure to pull out of ABN AMRO, though pre-emptions (due to inadequately considered partnership deals already struck with Santander and others) probably tied his hands.

Such issues are familiar to most executives, but what they also need is a more evolutionary global strategic perspective. Many treat M&As or ISAs as one-offs and so become vulnerable to fragile, politicised processes and shallower analyses. It's tempting to join bandwagons all favouring say IAs at one moment, blanking them out the next (as we saw in my pharmaceutical case) when cyclical trade, FDI, and M&A trends turn down. Powerful, consistent business models needed to go global, also have implications for ISAs and IAs. Zara, for example, has consequently only deployed international JVs, infrequently and reluctantly, and IAs only for diversification moves. Global strategies and strategic investments take decades to implement, so a coherent, longer term perspective is essential.

In 1999 I proposed two more global, evolutionary-orientated acid tests, Carr's 2nd law, covering both ISAs and M&As. MBA and Master's students taught subsequently have struggled to find counterexamples, though no social science theories prove as robust as the physical sciences – or strategy academics would be billionaires.

The logic of globalisation is to tap the whole world market, maximising scale economies. This implies a world-class business model and technology. As David Harding from Bain's Global M&A practice put it in *Financial News*: '*The gold standard of M&A is a repeatable model. Doing M&A half-way may feel good but it doesn't generate results*'. But this needs diffusing and maximum presence globally, through FDI commitments not merely via trade unless the latter conditions are incredibly conducive or your scale advantages exceptionally overwhelming. Any lesser commitments, on either dimension, invite rivals.

This leads to Carr's 2nd law represented by two acid tests applicable to strategic investment decisions (SIDs), whether ISAs or M&As:

1. Does the SID genuinely contribute to a process under which some world-class business model or technology becomes disseminated effectively worldwide?
2. Does the SID further effective geographical support, as required by key customers worldwide, providing the degree of local asset support needed?

Where these acid tests are not addressed, as has happened with many domestic M&As and opportunistic international SIDs, do not expect these strategic initiatives to be sustained. Remember ISAs are anyway vulnerable, given average lives of only around eight years. Beating the odds for M&A is just as hard. If you can't pass these tests I'd not bet on you.

INTERNATIONAL M&As (IAs) AND THE PROBLEM OF SCOPE

Failing Carr's 2nd law and associated acid tests often comes down to a problem of scope. Going global is so demanding in resource terms as to create trade-off dilemmas relating to scope choices as depicted in Figure 7.3.

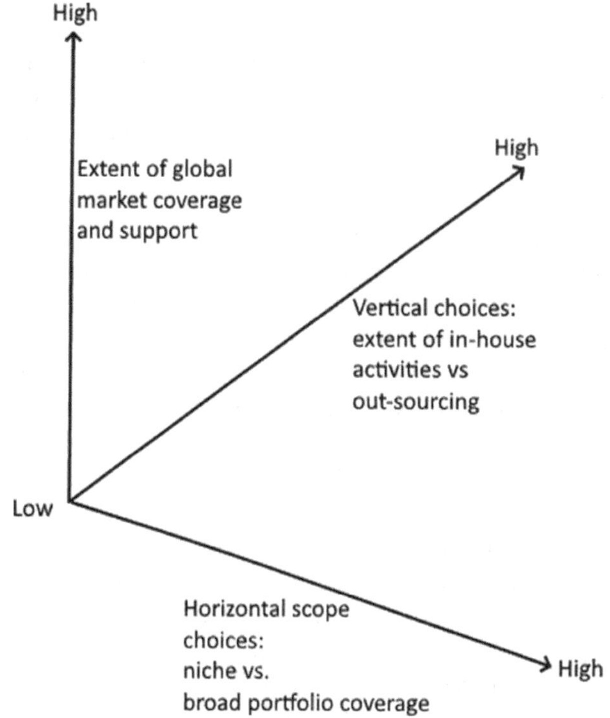

Figure 7.3 Global vs scope choices addressing global consolidation trends.

On the horizontal axis, you must decide how far you should maintain a broader product portfolio. Do you become a niche player, focused on the highly specific needs of a tight group of customers, as examined in the next chapter? Or do you go for a wide set of related services or products (as we saw was sometimes needed for global winners in spirits)? Or do you risk veering into conglomerate diversification? Do you stay within the value chain or how far should you take global outsourcing? Resource-constrained companies rarely survive global consolidation processes, adopting wider definitions on both these horizontal axes. For most, going global requires focus. The problem with stretching scope is that even powerful, normally astute players often wildly underestimate subtler differences in adjacent markets or geographies.

PROCESS PROBLEMS

Process problems further compound global M&A challenges.[13] It is not that easy finding natural M&A matches, and companies are apt to resort to opportunistic approaches, poorly linked to any more systematic, pro-active formal strategic reviews. Merchant banks or consulting companies may spot IA opportunities, but the need for secrecy can leave little time for sufficiently thorough analysis if caught on the hop. Massive problems from overstretching scope all too easily become underplayed and somewhat loose scale advantages exaggerated. Big decisions and egos easily destroy due diligence processes and more thorough-going global strategic thinking. RBS's takeover of ABN AMRO is a good example as Fred Goodwin vied with a rival bid from Barclays. CEOs get where they are from being big hitters, but egocentrics tend to behave like rival elephants in the jungle.

SIDs then tend to crystallise prematurely, relegating formal procedures to rubber stamping. Internal politics come down one way or the other, well before any formal decision reviews. In theory, finance directors, strategic planners, and ultimately boards should protect against this, but once political momentum has built up, all know their careers depend on 'listening to the mood music'. It takes an extremely brave executive to stand out against a CEO's intimated preferred decision. And in the absence of protective corporate cultures, braver (or rasher) executives may have been culled or marginalised long ago. Processes involving outside parties may be even more constrained. Once RBS was in alliance with Santander, legal pre-emptions may have compelled Goodwin to proceed with his ABN AMRO acquisition, even had final checks and balances led to deep concerns. The crucial decision may well have been the partnership agreement.

During my worldwide SID research, I probed a major German company as to the reasons for their own failed SID. The strategic planner responded without hesitation by asking if I'd ever seen the British Steel video, based on Granada TV's eye-on-the-wall investment decision investigations.

British Steel's new steel facility site had to be cold-commissioned and mothballed, as this additional capacity proved unwarranted. London Business School's accompanying teaching note highlighted the key lesson – notably just how prematurely the real decision had crystallised due to internal political momentum and lobbying. The roles played by strategic planners, and even their forthright finance director opposing the decision at board level, were emasculated. The executive chairman had unfortunately responded to early lobbying publicising his preference: '*either we do this or we will be out of the new technology and I thought we wanted to get on and make some steel*'. From that point on, their decision processes degenerated into rubber stamping, their formal processes effectively shredded, including a long-winded board level formal strategic review. Having confirmed my familiarity with this unique strategic decision teaching package, the German strategic planner continued: '*Well, that's exactly what has just happened with our strategic investment!*' He then spelt out just how much they too had lost.

SCOPE STRETCHES LEADING TO POOR KNOWLEDGE OF NEW BUSINESSES: THE CASE OF MARCONI

Scope stretches into activities you don't fully understand, in combination with such process problems, can prove lethal. Marconi, for example, under Ian Simpson diversified into a rapidly emerging telecommunications market through an opportunistic M&A. Simpson, formerly a BAe director and CEO of Rover cars (during BAe's period of ownership), became CEO of Marconi. He naturally approached former colleagues as to whether they would partner on this. The answer was no. This was outside his experience; telecommunications was a business sector he just did not know. However, a straightforward deal was possible. BAe received Marconi's military electronics business with good synergies for them. Simpson received around £7 billion, more than enough to fund his telecom M&A.

Marconi generously provided some 30 target M&As for MBAs at Manchester Business School to analyse. The problem was not, however, individual due diligences case by case, but their overall strategy. Without more related competences and parenting advantages, this was little more than a portfolio investment gamble. They possessed neither the skills of world classic conglomerates, such as Berkshire Hathaway; nor the parenting advantages likely to recover shareholder value after paying premiums, normally running between 40% and 45% on M&As. Most of these M&As were domestic. By consolidating a still fragmented emerging industry nationally, they hoped for scale economies and promising market prospects. Yet in following an overhyped M&A trend in an overhyped sector, with inadequate knowledge of the new business area, they were vulnerable: neither CEO, nor Mayo, finance director, had experience of telecoms.

Telecoms was already moving into Figure 8.1's stage 3. Marconi's growing UK presence never translated into market domination even nationally; nor could they expect to pre-dominate rivals already moving internationally. Carr's 1st law would have cautioned that even European domination would have been insufficient. The strategy failed both Carr's 2nd law acid tests. They did not have a world-class business model or technology that could have brought greater value to these M&A targets. Secondly, they lacked the capability to help take these technologies and target companies globally. Regardless of financial due diligences, Marconi's strategy was vulnerable on both counts.

For a little while, favourable conditions buoyed them up, but as Warren Buffet at Berkshire Hathaway cautioned: '*It's only when the tide goes out that you discover who's been bathing without swimsuits*'. The tide did go out. Market growth slowed and profit margins fell. Having purchased M&A targets in bull markets, even sensible policies and divestments would have risked flashing up big losses, destroying stock market confidence. Such are the dangers of M&As stretching scope beyond what you really know well.

We should not dismiss such issues as purely academic. At Marconi, Simpson's team inherited Weinstock's lifetime achievement, not only great positions in aero/electronics, but also the most prudently garnered cash reserves and balance sheet in UK engineering. With Marconi bankrupted by such foolishness, thousands, who (like Weinstock) had given their working lives to building up this enterprise, saw their jobs and pensions almost totally destroyed. One project manager, his pension cut to ribbons, struggled thereafter, taking a decade to establish himself as an electrician. Such personal stories must have been repeated a thousand-fold. CEOs' scepticism about pure academics is understandable; but to ignore lessons gleaned is inexcusable, and they need to engage beyond safe yes-men.

More positively, HSBC's highly successful acquisition of Midland Bank, as discussed with strategic planners in Hong Kong some years ago, would have passed both acid tests, and its tactical timing was excellent. It didn't need to guess. After working closely with Midland for some 10 years, it knew that business's genuine value, and that stock exchange values were way below fundamentals. Analyst pronouncements about synergies were perhaps public relations sideshows. What mattered was were they, or were they not, right to flout convention and to take their banking segment global? They believed they had a world-class business model that Midland could be successfully integrated within that global strategy, and they knew the business. That, I was told, was what you really needed to know. Both that global strategy and certainly the Midland international acquisition were extremely successful. To be fair to RBS and Goodwin, they too did a superb job integrating National Westminster successfully. Sometimes, though, success itself breeds overconfidence; and even the best executive teams somehow forget their basics.

To summarise, unless your business is exceptionally domestic, do NOT do major strategic M&A without considering Carr's 1st and 2nd laws' two simple acid tests. Do not stretch your scope into business sectors you don't know, unless you are a world-class conglomerate/portfolio investor on a par with Warren Buffet. If you do, can you really evidence any better logic than Marconi's? Is your executive team better than BMW's (as with Rover), Daimler's (as with Chrysler), or HSBC's (as with its HSI acquisition in the US sub-prime market)? In all three cases, genuinely world-class executive teams lost every single cent on their international M&A. CEOs rightly take pride in their implementation competences, but analysis and learning matters too. As one executive commented: '*You have to do the right things, right*'.

BMW/ROVER, DAIMLER/CHRYSLER CROSS-BORDER M&A STRATEGY PITFALLS

The car industry is one of the most advanced in terms of handling globalisation and associated cross-border cooperation issues. It is also one of the most instructive, from disastrous IAs, like Daimler/Chrysler, to positive lessons from ISAs such as Renault Nissan.

BMW/Rover

Few companies come close to BMW in terms of the quality of its executive teams. But at the time of their Rover acquisition in 1994, such understandable self-confidence contributed to one their worst ever strategic investment decisions. Their experience of managing assets outside Germany was then largely confined to their modest USA entry: their experience of cross-border M&As (or major ISAs) was almost nil. Again, their prime problem was scope, and they had little knowledge of Rover's mid-market which they were buying into. It is a good example of why not to ignore Carr's two acid tests.

No matter how good your business model, consultants will someday highlight issues of scale, offering seductive opportunities purportedly as the solution to global consolidation processes. Scale is a primary issue, but the prize of size, for its own sake, is a siren call beckoning you towards the rocks. Like Odysseus, CEOs may need tying to their masts, lest egos and emotions overwhelm them. Similar strategic pitches were made to BMW and Daimler: both fell, hook, line and sinker. Triggers were the same: size is crucial, others are moving, so hadn't you better follow suit? Wrong. If size were a panacea, dinosaurs would still be roaming the earth; following herds was not how your company became great.

What was true was that, by 1994, the car industry was well into stage 3. The tipping point had been reached; nothing would now stop concentration processes from ultimately proceeding to stage 4. In both cases, the false argument was that their business models would be rendered uncompetitive unless they could get to certain (indeed arbitrary) levels of car outputs expressed numerically. World class competitiveness is not enhanced through strategic investment decisions, flouting the underlying logic behind global consolidations.

Acquiring Rover was purportedly going to step up BMW in terms of total car output levels, gaining scale economies, and countering moves by rival premium players. BMW, a world-class brand supported by world-class technology, was already extending its reach across Europe and beginning to extend its bridgehead in the USA. Rover's attractions lay in their heritage of great names and brands. Not all agreed. John Bacchus, who had headed Rover's strategic alliance with Honda from 1978 to 1990, professed himself puzzled by BMW's CEO drooling over legacy names like Wolsey: '*You know most of us [in Britain] tend to think about them in terms of socks*'.

BMW's due diligence missed nothing technologically. Land Rover was lambasted on quality and appalling fuel efficiency. Undeterred, they thought, wow, if Rover's brands can survive with such lousy technology, just imagine what they could do with BMW's support. Not an unreasonable starting point for acquisitions in the same line of business, but BMW's market was high-end, and very different to Rover's mid-end. With less patience for bean counters, BMW's financial due diligence was poor, if not naïve. Fortunately, there were no blatant black holes in Rover's balance sheet, as easily arise on IAs. Honda was not run by bean counters either, but even they recognised successive hockey stick profitability forecasts from Rover, having worked closely with them for 12 years, and that the single year of profits probably reflected BAe employees' being incentivised to buy Rover cars in the run-up to disposal. Rover's successful ISA with Honda had delivered astonishing improvements in quality and performance; but part of Honda's reason for having just turned down full ownership of Rover was their far more sceptical financial assessment.

Strategically, BMW failed both our acid tests. Geographically, how could BMW help take Rover global, when, as yet, it was scarcely global itself? FDI in the USA was incipient and almost non-existent in Asia or elsewhere. Its brand strategy was so crucial, they could never countenance brand dilution by sharing showrooms with Rover. In international distribution terms, it offered Rover geographically almost nothing. Brand dilution fears likewise stymied attempts at technological integration, or anything akin to VW's excellent integrated platform strategy so beneficial at SEAT and Skoda. High-end strategies, favouring top-of-the-range components such as ZF transmissions, just did not hit price breaks needed for mid-end cars. Components represented over 50% of value-added, so such choices mounted up. Unsurprisingly, self-confident, technically proficient BMW executives in Germany veered to what they knew best. Tensions due to different corporate and national cultures were inevitable, but again, BMW's cross-cultural experiences and skills, at this stage, would have been limited. 'Your way will be our way' approaches to cross-border M&As tend not to work.

Success breeds overconfident closed mind-sets. Having studied Rover-Honda's highly successful ISA over the years, I immediately wrote to BMW's strategic planner from Witten-Herdecke University, my base as a visiting professor, offering to travel to Munich. The response was that he had no objections to my continuing to interview executives at Rover in Britain, but no interest in learning anything from me regarding the Rover/Honda ISA. This was a pity since John Bacchus, Rover's director of that alliance from 1978 onwards, recalled how their first five years were wasted, because of cross-cultural problems and attitudes inimical to learning. And this was in a highly successful alliance with Honda, which was an extremely proficient and internationally experienced company.

Yet as Winston Churchill reminded colleagues: *'However beautiful the strategy you should occasionally look at the results'*. On top of some £5 billion paid for Rover, another £1.7 billion was invested before BMW cut its losses. Aside from Mini operations, their return amounted to a nominal £10 note. The handover was marked by a civic ceremony, also attended by a Birmingham local councillor and his dog. Sadly, the wind blew at the critical moment, and that final £10 note flew off and was snapped up by the dog, who promptly ran off with it. *The Sun* newspaper's headline the next morning was 'Rover gets the £10'. A dramatic reminder: get these issues wrong and you risk losing literally everything. Never underestimate the dangers of overstretching scope and entering business fields you don't really understand, and do not ignore Carr's two acid tests when addressing global consolidation processes.

Daimler/Chrysler

Let's now consider Daimler/Chrysler, at the time the largest M&A in industrial history. Billed as a 'merger of equals' and a 'marriage made in heaven', these proved misnomers. Since 2000, less than 10% of M&As have actually been structured as 'mergers'.[14] Without rare leadership, even 'mergers' become de facto acquisitions. One or the other side prevails. Egos, internal politics, and the law of the jungle prevail in ensuing power battles. PR-spewed misnomers are dangerous legally, but also in building up false expectations. Thwarted expectations holed the Daimler/Chrysler merger below the water line, by undermining cooperative trusting relationships crucial to success.

Arguably both sides *should* have respected each other as equals. Daimler was the world-class, premium car player, and its CEO Schrempp was a battle-hardened world-class turnaround act. His executives, like BMW's, were technologically first rate. Yet Chrysler's executives were likewise champions, albeit from a different arena. They had come back from virtual bankruptcy to creating, single-handedly, the 4WD revolution, taking on and beating the world's then largest car companies, Ford and GM. Chrysler made annual profits of $2.6 million; Daimler, with vaster revenues, made $1.6 million. Chrysler executives had no need of Schrempp's turnaround skills; they expected that respect due to equal champions. They knew their unique market and America intimately: an environment un-akin to top-end cars, or to European conditions more familiar to Daimler.

But in terms of power, the two sides were not equal. Chrysler's CEO was looking for an 'out'. He admitted that he had spent no more than a few minutes on this, the biggest strategic decision that Chrysler had ever taken. Chrysler shareholders could take safe good money and run too. Addressing CEO succession mattered too. Schrempp's global vision was pertinent; his track record superb; and undermining an assertive incoming CEO might have jeopardised direction and integration. Chrysler's executives, though, would have seen things differently. When the pilot's the only person on the plane with an all-too-visible parachute, anyone would be mad not to worry. Politically, they were potentially neutered.

Consider the inevitable subsequent dynamics: Schrempp was a passionate advocate of the fast GE-style acquisition integration approach. Some 50 German integration teams pre-planned thoroughly, prior to all meetings with Chrysler executives; whilst '*in Auburn Hills, no-one even had a game plan*' for any such meetings or integration. As Bob Eaton took a backseat, Stallkamp, the next Chrysler chief, stood up for his team. Schrempp complained to Eaton, who felt duty-bound to support him. Stallkamp was fired. Holden took over, and the same happened to him. The operations director, Poore, was left as the final person fully understanding how to run such a unique business. Schrempp assumed he could, as in Germany, be flattered into playing the key vacant role. But with the US team undermined and demoralised, Poore did not want to accept this. After over 30 years of '*busting my ass*' in tough factory conditions, compensated by US bonuses (unlike in Europe) running into millions of dollars, he just laughed, walked out and others followed. Internal political victories proved pyrrhic: Chrysler profits plunged into losses. Schrempp lamely lamented: '*I thought I was buying a team of champions*'; they had all just laid down and allowed themselves to be walked all over. Now he could only send over his own right-hand man, who finally had to run a business he could never have fully understood. Daimler lost every Deutsche Mark invested: not the best outcome, for the biggest industrial merger up to this point ever undertaken.

Overstretched scope, not knowing the business and integration processes, and undermined by cross-cultural clashes, all destroyed Chrysler's performance and Daimler's investment. Consider our two acid tests: geographically bringing together two fine European and American companies was promising, but only if Daimler's car sales thereby increased in the USA or Chrysler's in Europe. But they didn't. Daimler's technology and business model from the top-end proved untransferable to Chrysler's mid-range, fast-moving market and any integration failed. Akin to BMW's acquisition of Rover, this M&A failed both acid tests. Stupendous investments damaged focus and returned nothing, aside from BMW's Mini which they redesigned themselves.

M&A examples entailing scope stretches failing acid tests

Table 7.1 summarises further cases where acid test criteria appear breached. Wise executive teams and investors learn from history, siding with William Faulkner: '*The past is never dead. It is not even past*'. Scope stretches may leave you utterly exposed as competition inevitably intensifies. We should counter desperado claims that 'this time it's different' with Mark Twain's famous rebuttal: '*History may not repeat itself, but it does at least rhyme*'.

Success chances are greater when scope stretches are modest; when related moves complete portfolio products or services valued by customers; when you understand how to manage global consolidation processes better than your partners; and when you have credible knowledge of their business, but still greater respect for what they know and you do not. The logic may then be to ride the wave of global consolidation. But being a great global consolidator takes consolidation skills too. Those inexperienced at cross-border M&As need to think twice. Prudential's CEO rightly conceded that £38 billion Asian M&As were things '*you don't do every day*' and pulled them out, undaunted by substantial M&A charges. RBS must regret it didn't do the same in respect to ABN AMRO.

RENAULT NISSAN'S MORE SUCCESSFUL INTERNATIONAL STRATEGIC ALLIANCE APPROACH

Scope stretches can prove less problematic on ISAs inherently entailing less control and integration. As we've seen, total control is no panacea. Shareholder value can be created by cooperation aimed at more limited mutual goals, whilst still contributing to visions passing our two acid tests. More focused

Table 7.1 M&A example entailing scope stretches and failing acid tests

Acquirer	*Acquired*	*Details*	*Scope stretch*	*Acid tests*	*Outcome*
Microsoft	Nokia	$8bn, 2014	S'ware/telecoms	Fails both	96% written off in 2015
Google	Motorola	$12.5b, 2012	Search/telecoms	Fails both	Sold for 23%
HP	Autonomy	$11bn, 2011	Web services, IT & software	Fails both & due diligence	79% written off after 1 yr
News Corp	My Space	$0.58b, 2011	Media/social network	Fails both	Sold for 6%
Daimler	Chrysler	$36bn, 1998	Top to med end	Fails both!	Sold. Lost all
BMW	Rover	£1.7bn, 1994	Top to med end	Fails both	Sold 2000. Lost all!
HSBC	HSI		Into sub-prime.	Fails both	Sold. Lost all!
Marconi	Multiple		Defence/telecoms	Fails both	Bankrupted
AOL	TimeWarner	$164bn, 2001	Internet/cable news content	Fails both	60% write off in 2002. Share price fall of 91%
Facebook	WhatsApp	$19bn, 2014	Social network/messaging	Depends on integration	Jury out
HBOS	Bank of Scotland	£28bn, 2001	Building society/banks	Fails both	2008 HBOS bankrupted
RBS	ABN AMRO	£49bn, 2007	Banking stretch	Fails both	Bankrupted
Disney	Pixar	$7.4bn, 2006	Some stretch	Depends on integration	Jury out
Quaker Oats	Snapple	$1.9bn, 1994	Cereals/trendy soft drinks	Some stretch. National roll-out dropped	Sold 1997 for 16% ($0.3bn)
Sears	Kmart	2005	Retailers	Domestic. Broad scope. E.g., auto serv.	2012/13 $2.5bn divestments.
Glencore	Xstrata	$65bn, 2013	Commodities trading/mining	From trading to mining	2013 $8.8bn write-downs
Nestle		2013	Weaker lower – end brands	Need to tighten scope	CEO: 'agony!'
Vivendi	MP3 and Mexican mobile deals		Communications & media/ Internet & mobile phones	CEO mistake: 'not core to communications'	Lost E3bn on these two deals

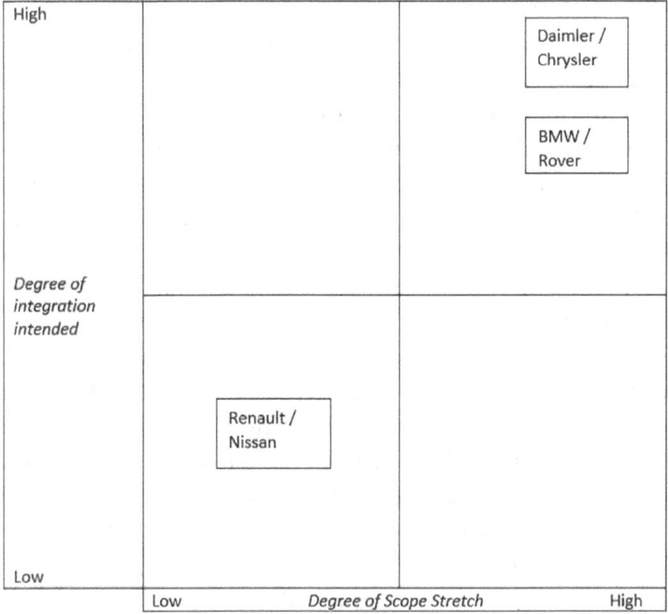

Figure 7.4 Scope stretches vs degree of intended integration.

agreements and controls are needed. Figure 7.4 considers the degree of integration intended vs the degree of scope stretch.

In contrast to BMW/Rover and Daimler/Chrysler, Renault Nissan has been one of the most successful ISAs ever undertaken. In terms of longevity, it rivals Rover Honda's successful ISA from 1978 to 1990, though it has yet to match BSH (Bosch/Siemens' ISA in domestic appliances) begun in 1965, or SNECMA's ISA in aero engines. At BSH, two German companies successfully combined forces entering international top-end markets. SNECMA's entailed French and US partners, though less extensive operations worldwide. Rover Honda's successful ISA was focused on Britain and Europe, but ended when the British government and BAe shareholders sold Rover to BMW. Fiat's approach to its Chrysler full acquisition was partly modelled upon the Renault Nissan example of how to engage in cross-border cooperation most effectively: indeed, in 2019, Fiat Chrysler has further merged with France's PSA.

As in many ISAs, the Renault Nissan strategic aims were initially highly focused and specific. Nissan was in a desperate turnaround situation. For 10 years, successive management teams had come and gone, destroying credibility and turnaround hopes. They failed to make profits or inroads against Toyota and debt spiralled to unsustainable levels. They lacked funds to develop crucial new models and faced likely bankruptcy. Survival was conditional upon cooperation. Carlos Ghosn's early briefings to his tiny

Renault ISA team were explicit: '*Our purpose is simply to make Nissan profitable and then to return home*'. Just two French directors accompanied him, one from finance and one from procurement. And Nissan executives' opening words at the first meeting? '*Please show us how to make profits*'. The agreement gave Renault 40% of Nissan's equity (offset by a minor 10% cross-holding giving 10% of Renault equity to Nissan). To judge this ISA's performance, just take 40% of Nissan's current market capitalisation ($41.6 billion as of 9.11.2017) – that's a $16.6 billion return as compared with 10% of Renault's current market capitalisation ($30.2 billion) or $3.0 billion plus modest resources contributed.

Strategic gains ensued, following Nissan's turnaround. By 2015, France produced just 1.4 million cars compared with the USA 4 million, Japan 8 million, and China 21 million.[15] Addressing global, not merely French or Japanese markets, Renault Nissan, in 2014, held 8.5% global market share, only slightly behind Toyota, VW and GM, each at about 10%. Both partners are certainly more credible following global consolidation than if each had remained dependent on their local bases.

Initial know-how transfer was confined to Renault's turnaround expertise. Aims were simple: restore profitability, targeting 4.5% return on sales, whilst halving the debt millstone. '*And if we fail, we return home*'. Their mission was solely to support Nissan's re-emergence, '*awakening a sleeping giant*', not to try to dominate meetings. The philosophy reiterated to French executives prior to meetings was mutual respect: '*One step taken together is better than two steps, with one partner using the other as merely a stepping-stone*'. In contrast to Daimler's teams, Ghosn used Japanese cross-functional teams to achieve all early objectives. Top French executives were backstops, simply vetoing any cross-functional team's decisions unlikely to hit key financial, procurement or other policy targets vital to restoring profitability. Japanese teams decided which and how many plants would be closed, though French finance executives disallowed choices inconsistent with return on sales targets. Ghosn proclaimed: '*As of today you buy components predominately from Japan, as of tomorrow we buy worldwide*', shattering Japan's keiretsu traditions and regionally orientated suppliers, but implementation was by Japanese cross-functional teams.

With the right cross-cultural approach and tone, early low hanging fruit achievements galvanised motivation and further advance. The ISA, like many genuinely successful relationships, evolved, deepening knowledge transfers and synergies. Geographically they now span the globe. Scope has gradually been stretched, though nowhere near as far as for BMW/Rover or Daimler/Chrysler. Given a relatively hands-off approach, eschewing total integration initially, this proved less of a problem. Renault Nissan passed my two acid tests.

EVOLUTIONARY PATTERNS AND CONCLUSIONS

Most companies are pragmatic. Disliking academic debates, they risk becoming either too gung-ho (as in RBS's ABN AMRO acquisition) or unduly reactive. Even excellent ISAs such as Rover Honda or ICL Fujitsu were driven by stark necessity. They simply could no longer fund new generations of products or services needed to match more global competitors. Globalisation spawns a spectrum of opportunities from licensing and franchising, to riskier, more demanding ISAs, and cross-border M&A; but opportunism is extraordinarily dangerous. These often represent the biggest investments (or SIDs) ever undertaken. M&As have proved hard enough domestically; internationally, the tendency has been to lose every last cent.

Cross-border M&As and ISAs need to address global consolidation processes discussed and acid tests. As Adam Smith's division of labour finally goes global, strategies must address this logic. Global positions call for FDI commitments not just trade: ISAs and IAs, like GFSs, provide crucial assets on the ground; wars are not won without deeper engagements.

After developing in home regions, subsequent strategies are depicted in Figure 7.1's four phase consolidation model. GKN Drivechain began with FDI asset positions in Italy, France, and Germany from the late 1960s, and then used GFSs and licensing for triad positions in the USA and Japan by the early 1980s. ISAs predominated in emerging markets during the 3rd transitional stage from the late 1980s onwards. But in the new millennium, galvanised by global rivalry in stage 4, most ISAs have transitioned to full acquisition, to achieve full integration and oligopolistic surpluses arising.

Carlsberg and Heineken correctly anticipated further global consolidation as beer moved into stage 4, so together acquired and broke up S&N, Carlsberg's former IJV partner in Russia. Carlsberg gained ownership and control of Russia's leading beer player Baltika. However disloyal and gruelling to S&N, Heineken and Carlsberg's strategic logic was well founded. Within months, Ambev had taken over the world's largest beer company, Anheuser Busch, and about a year later, this merged company took over SAB Global No 2. ISAs thus sometimes evolve into fully integrated IAs later in these games of musical chairs, though not always with the same partner. Executives in transitional sectors need to be careful to see the wood for the trees.

Evolutionary processes are not always smooth and linear, so we need to keep an eye on all three major market entry modes. In 2011, I invited my Moscow State University Graduate School of Business students to assess what entry option GKN might then need for entry into Russia if it was going to support Ford's new St. Petersburg plant: ISA, IA, or GFS? One student countered that he was negotiating a GFS on behalf of the Russian government. That made absolute sense. We'd come full circle, once again supporting

Ford with a GFS just as our team had done from the USA in 1979/1980. Ford would have wanted maximum customer support and quality insurance in an uncertain environment. Even compared with Columbia, Russia merits caution; M&As or even ISAs might well be risky.

Global strategists require more breadth than 'siloed' economists, often specialised in either trade or FDI theory, with limited knowledge of GFS, ISAs,[16] and IA market entry alternatives. They require understanding of global oligopolies, concentration processes, plays, and counter-plays, but also the flexibility to adapt sensibly from one option to another. A business model may be so strong as to favour go-it-alone strategies at one moment, but still need ISAs or IAs the next. We need that four-stage evolutionary perspective and my two acid tests. Finally, country contexts are *not* the same worldwide.[17] Just try implementing even well conceived global ISAs or IAs without deep understanding of differences in national and corporate cultures![18] Executive teams don't come much better than BMW's or Daimler's so, unless your executives are superhuman, recollect their lessons or expect dismal outcomes.

NOTES

1 See for example: Hill, C. (2016). *International Business*. Boston, MA: Cengage; Moeller, S. and Brady, Y. (2014). *Intelligent M&A. Navigating the Mergers and Acquisitions Minefield*. Chichester: Wiley; Morosini, P. and Steger, U. (2004). *Managing Complex Mergers: Real World Lessons in Implementing Successful Cross-Cultural M&As*. London: FT Prentice Hall; Lees, S. (2003). *Global Acquisitions*. Basingstoke: Palgrave Macmillan; Echavarria, M. (2016). *Enabling Collaboration. Achieving Success Through Strategic Alliances and Partnerships*. London: LID; De Man, A.-P. (2013). *Alliances. An Executive Guide to Designing Successful Strategic Partnerships*. Chichester: Wiley; Steinhilber, S. (2008). *Strategic Alliances. Three Ways to Make Them Work*. Cambridge, MA: Harvard Business Press.

2 Ohmae, K. (1985). *Triad Power: The Coming Shape of Global Competition*. New York: Free Press; Ohmae, K. (2001). *The Invisible Continent: Four Strategic Imperatives for the New Economy*. London: Nicholas Brealey.

3 Ohmae, K. (1989). 'The global logic of strategic alliances', *Harvard Business Review*, LXVII (2), 143–154.

4 Chattopadhyay, A. and Batra, R. (2012). *The New Emerging Market Multinationals. Four Strategies for Disrupting Markets and Building Brands*. New York: McGraw-Hill (see p. 7 for an excellent summary of strategy traits and p. 104 for their consequence cross-border M&A motivations); Yip, G. (2016). *China's Strategic Advantage*. Chichester: Wiley.

5 Porter, M.E. (1990). *Competitive Advantage of Nations*. London: Macmillan Press; Marsh, P. (2012). *The New Industrial Revolution: Consumer, Globalization and the End of Mass Production*. New Haven: Yale University Press; Chattopadhyay, A. and Batra, R. (2012). *The New Emerging Market Multinationals: Four Strategies for Disrupting Markets and Building Brands*. New York: McGraw-Hill.

6 *Financial Times* 24 June 2016. p. 30.

7 Genuine uncertainty is distinguished from more quantifiable risks, which can be proximated through assigning rough probabilities. See John Kay's (2017). *Long and Short of It*. London: Profile Books or Frank Knight's seminar work from the 1960s.

8 Hubbard (2013: 7).

9 Dussauge, P. and Garrette, B. (1999). *Cooperative Strategy: Competing Successfully Through Strategic Alliances.* Chichester: Wiley.
10 Ohmae, K. (1989). Ibid., pp. 143–154.
11 For further details see: Carr, C., Bayliss, B. and Tomkins, C. (1994). *Strategic Investment Decisions.* Avebury Press, Chapter 5, pp. 197–218.
12 Lendrum, A. (2004). *The Strategic Partnering Pocketbook: Building Strategic Partnerships and Alliances.* Sydney: McGraw Hill.
13 For an account of why such process problems arise see Simikin, 'M&As: the problem is the process', *Harvard Business Review.*
14 Moeller, S. and Brady, Y. (2014). *Intelligent M&A: Navigating the Mergers and Acquisitions Minefield.* Chichester: Wiley, p. 9.
15 *The Economist* (2018 Edition), *Pocket World in Figures*, p. 77.
16 It is beyond the scope of this chapter to do justice to a wealth of excellent books on ISAs, differentiating their unique associated management issues, key success factors versus common pitfalls. But see particularly: Echavarria, M. (2016). Ibid.; De Man, A.-P. (2013). Ibid.; Steinhilber, S. (2008). Ibid.; with good examples such as Cisco; Brockstedt, E. and Carr, C. (2005). 'Collaborative R&D alliances in the pharmaceutical industry', *Innovation: Management, Policy and Practice*, 7 (3).
17 See also: Harris, S. and Carr, C. (2008). 'National cultural values and the purpose of business', *International Business Review*, 17, 103–117; Carr, C. (2006). 'Russian strategic investment decision practices compared with those of Great Briton, Germany, the United States and Japan: Diversity, convergence and short-termism', *International Studies, Management and Organization*, 36 (3), 82–110; Carr, C., Pudelko, M. and Henley, J. (2006). 'Globalization and its effects on international strategy and cross-cultural management', *International Studies, Management and Organization*, 36 (3), 3–8; Carr, C. and Pudelko, M. (2006). 'Convergence of national practices in strategy, finance and HRM between the USA, Japan and Germany', *International Journal of Cross Cultural Management*, 6 (1), 75–100. Carr, C., Pudelko, M., Fink, G. and Hinges, P. (2006). 'The convergence concept in cross-cultural management research', *International Journal of Cross Cultural Management*, 6 (1), 15–18; Carr, C. (2005). 'Are German, Japanese and Anglo-Saxon strategic styles still divergent?', *Journal of Management Studies*, 42 (6), 1155–1188.
18 For books summarising key lessons for successful M&As, see particularly Moeller and Brady Ibid.; Morosi and Steger Ibid.; Lees, S. (2003). *Global Acquisitions.* Basingstoke: Palgrave Macmillan (particularly p. 171).

8

GLOBAL FOCUS AND NICHE STRATEGIES

LESSONS FROM GERMAN AND BRITISH WINNERS

Alessa Witt and Chris Carr

GLOBAL NICHE OLIGOPOLIES

The extensiveness of global oligopolies and the power of large players, throughout most sectors, is just the tip of the iceberg. It is tempting to downplay oligopolies as just 'big company' concerns: smaller companies matter too. Yet below big company oligopolies lurk more numerous global niche oligopolies. Many are further down the value chain: every car company, for example, depends on thousands of parts suppliers. They too have been transforming globally, consolidating and spawning yet more numerous global niche players and winners.

Such niche strategies emerge from our global winners model Figure 3.7 developed in Chapter 3. As sectors globalise creating dominant global winners, the logical counter strategies can only be cooperation (discussed in Chapter 7), exit/retrenchment, or to re-focus if necessary and to become (global) niche winners.

A natural symbiosis occurs between these two types of global oligopolies. As in the natural world, smaller or medium-sized species cohabit and survive alongside larger species. Figure 7.3 showed how large corporations have often had to focus within the value chain, through global outsourcing, to survive global consolidation processes. Such outsourcing creates global opportunities for pro-active suppliers. Medium-sized players tend to avoid head-on rivalry against larger more powerful players, just as hyenas rarely pick fights with lions. They prefer 'under-the-radar' positionings, complementing larger companies' offerings, or picking up smaller, more customised niches affording lesser scale advantages to larger players.

Business-to-business customers have, themselves, become more demanding, because they too are fighting global rivals. A supplier interviewed in

Spain, as early as 1999, recounted General Motors' quotation request to supply their factory in Asia. Though they already had a factory in Asia, they were warned to price-in the requirement for another plant somewhat nearer to GM's Asian factory. Trade is not enough; even light-weight suppliers require heavy-weight FDI.

Smaller companies niche even more tightly, but often struggle to offer sufficient international service support, and so become vulnerable. In 1998, turning round Nissan, Carlos Ghosn declared: '*To date we have purchased locally; as of today, we buy globally*'. Less globally pro-active suppliers, unable to respond overnight, risked being culled or being scooped up by bigger faster fish – blissfully unaware of what was coming until, suddenly, it was all too late.

Less resourced, small and medium-sized enterprises (SMEs) are sometimes assumed less likely to globalise; but often the opposite has happened. Many automotive parts suppliers had to become more, not less, global than their upstream customers. Securing critical mass required extensive portfolios of European, American, and Asian customers, each demanding geographical support for all their dispersed operations. Any semi-global bias from customers from one region was countered by opposite biases from those from other regions. Suppliers became even more global. Thanks to the internet and social media, many small and medium-sized enterprises have been '*born global*' – just as foals had to evolve to run with herds from the moment of birth.

In consequence, many niche players moved globally faster than better known larger companies, spawning yet more numerous global niche oligopolies. Eschewing head-on competition with larger players, global niche winners still had to pre-empt scale economies in more narrowly defined market segments. They too recognised the rule of three, whereby top three players dominated global profit pools. Jack Welch's dictum, that large players like GE had to achieve top three global market positions, proved equally applicable to many small and medium-sized enterprises operating in niche markets.

Two biases perhaps blinded us from seeing this. Business schools and researchers preferenced large sectors and company cases; niche widgets were less visible or exciting. Secondly, more extensively researched Anglo/American settings tend to favour larger companies rather than 'mid-caps'. In contrast, Hermann Simon's research on German's '*Hidden Champions*' has proven exceptionally insightful.[1] These were defined as low-profile firms, achieving either top three global market share positions or number one European (or regional) positions, in niched sectors, whilst having revenues below $5 billion. Whilst America and Britain had relatively fewer global niche champions of this type, Simon identified eight key success factors and found evidence of their applicability in several other countries.[2]

Three issues arise. Whilst American large companies, from Microsoft, Apple, Alphabet, Amazon to Boeing etc., dominate in several sectors, Europe's German players win out too: not only their big names like VW, Mercedes, and BMW, but also their suppliers (like Bosch), and in myriads of global niche markets frequently dominated by German family-owned Mittelstand firms. Indeed, Witt uncovered a substantial overlap between Simon's success factors and traits, independently identified, for Germany's far more numerous Mittelstand firms, most of whom operated more domestically.[3] So how do we know these are key success factors per se and not just a description of German companies generally? Secondly, how can we then be sure that even genuine German success traits would work effectively in more typical markets, such as in the USA or Britain? Such contexts do not enjoy Germany's unique form of capitalism or such relative protection from short-termist stock-market pressures. Thirdly, whilst there is a growing body of evidence for the greater defendability of top three market share positions,[4] there is no such theoretical or empirical support for regional top market positions, also included by Simon. Acclaimed regional champions have usually disappeared.

Our research therefore focused solely on global niche champions (GNCs) defined as that subset of global hidden champions (GHCs) who have achieved top 3 global (not regional) market positions. We covered 15 successful German GNC cases and 15 similarly successful British GNCs. This introduced comparative and critical perspectives, countering the danger of picking up solely traits associated with German's unique Mittelstand institutional and cultural context. It rendered our analysis pertinent to mid-sized companies from other countries. Guarding against 'survivor bias', we focussed on the subset of global winners, which had already survived at least 80 years (adopting Collins and Porras' Built-to-Last criteria).

This chapter investigates such German and British (typically mid-cap) global niche oligopolists, their success outcomes, their underlying strategies, competitive advantages, global orientations, and international entry strategies.[5]

GLOBAL NICHE CHAMPIONS' KEY SUCCESS FACTORS

What was surprising was how closely British, as well as German GNCs, conformed to Simon's *hidden champion*'s business success model (Figure 8.1).[6] We scored all our 30 GNCs for conformity or deviations from this model on a scale of 1 for perfect conformity and 7 for disagreement, through mainly chief executive officer (CEO) interviews discussing all eight aspects. Our averaged score was 1.68, not so far off that perfect 1, though

Figure 8.1 The HC model. (From Simon, H., *Hidden Champions of the 21st Century*, Heidelberg, Springer Verlag, 2009. Re-printed with permission.)

some GNCs deviated more (reflected in a standard deviation of 0.92). As one German executive commented:

> This model is very good. I could immediately identify myself with the model. Leadership with ambitious goals, these are exactly characteristics that we have here. There is a very high conformity between our firm and these characteristics.

British GNCs deviated just a touch more, averaging 1.75. Comments on global leadership, innovation, and closeness-to-customers mirrored those from Germany, aside from down-playing Simon's 'decentralization' and 'depth' traits.

We uncovered two further common GNC traits. These occurred in both countries and should be included in a more complete GNC success model. Four GNCs, in both Germany and Britain, stressed the critical importance of brand-building. Simon's concept of '*hiddenness*' proved less universally applicable to genuine global winners. This reinforced our decision to rename genuinely global GHCs as GNCs. Seven GNCs from Germany and three from Britain, also stressed 'visions and values':

> Part of the reason why we are growing as fast as we are is because my team loves what they do. They absolutely want to change the world and you'll see it at any of our company sites they all wear the company logo and they are

> proud. You could say that pride, fun, and emotional commitment is important otherwise you will not be successful. British GNC executive.
>
> The bottom line is that you need courage, and you have to seize a chance and be open to take a risk where necessary. These risks have to be calculable and justifiable with the company's strategy and ideology... If I look back on our history, I do see a lot of calculable risks that we took but we had a CEO from a construction business that believed in us. So, I guess different factors had to come together but we always stuck to our values. Mainly our CEO had a vision and a goal that he wanted to achieve and that convinced the customers and partners. German GNC executive.

These visions and values were often formally documented (particularly in Germany) emphasising three key themes: innovation (13 cases), customers (11), and employees (8).

So, what should typically medium-sized firms, confronted with global niche opportunities and likely oligopolies, do? Simon's validated, just slightly amended version of Figure 8.1 proved remarkably robust for German family-owned Mittelstand firms and even public companies from Britain. Becoming a GNC top 3 global niche champion, required leadership and leaders willing to commit pro-actively to a global vision of what was going to be needed. Regional strategies were insufficient. As we will see later, this commitment encompassed not just trade, but foreign direct investment (FDI), an issue unexplored by Simon.

It also took determined, sustained focus, recognised as crucial by British (as well as German) GNCs. German Global Hidden Champion CEOs interviewed 20 years earlier, in the 1990s, emphasised this distinction, but noted the rarity of this trait among British counterparts with whom they had dealings. Eisenwerk Bruhl, for example, contrasted the 25-year consistency of their own strategic focus on hard-to-manufacture, aluminium cast, engine heads, with British castings companies. Led by accountants keen to recover high fixed costs, their British rivals just could not say no, taking on almost any type of castings. Eisenwerk Bruhl correctly anticipated '*a blood-bath*' for such unfocused players. This happened, decimating market capitalisations of even top British rivals. '*It was like waiting for rotten apples to fall off the tree*'. Britain being a more open market, when the time came, they just acquired two of the most appropriate companies cheaply. '*It was obvious. We didn't have to spend five minutes in the Boardroom on these [FDI] decisions*'. What was less obvious was their strategic decision to focus so decisively fully two decades earlier, and their subsequent, relentless, consistent commitment.

Another German GNC example from the same period, discussed in Chapter 7, reiterated this point in respect to focus, their British ISA partner having been by contrast a looser conglomerate. Notwithstanding their successful relationship, they parted company on an acquisition opportunity spotted by the British partner, related only in terms of vertical integration. The German CEO declined: '*You don't know this business well enough and it would only make sense if you could really invest enough to bring it up to world-class*'. The British partner went ahead on its own, but its looser conglomerate strategy culminated in bankruptcy. Quod erat demonstrandum. '*One day*', the chairman lamented, '*you are the City's blue-eyed boys; the next you are out of favour, your share price plummets and that's an end to any further M&A, and that (rather than cash flow difficulties) is really what finished us*'. Pursuing consistent or more focused strategies calls for exceptional resilience in the context of city short-termism; for German family-firms, this was far easier. Another successful German GNC CEO, also interviewed in the late 1990s, highlighted that he'd been given '*carte blanche*' by the owner to pursue his chosen strategy consistently over more than two decades.

British GNCs required exceptional resilience to match Germany's commitment in respect to world-class innovation, and commensurate strength in depth regarding skills and long-term close customer relationships and customisation. For many German players, such themes were *no-brainers*. How else could they support the world's highest wage levels? This may be why many German Mittelstand companies anyway conformed to Simon's 'success traits', in contrast to Britain, where companies often over-relied on relatively lower skills and wages. Yet even resilient British GNCs' decentralisation policies differed from those in Germany, reflecting City pressures.

Where successful GNCs, in both countries, departed from Simon's model (shown in Figure 8.1) was their shared emphasis on (global) brands and reputation, and employee values underpinning both. Such commitments ultimately paid off.

GLOBALISATION ORIENTATIONS AND SUSTAINING SUCCESS

> In today's world, it is not hard to sell a product to another country; it is much harder to sustainably serve a market. German executive.

We systematically analysed all 30 GNCs' chosen internationalisation paths, drawing on senior executives interviewed (in both countries and languages).

The easiest way to appreciate GNCs' surprisingly radical global orientations is to compare them with the most recognised, commonly taught model associated with traditional advanced country internationalisers. According to Uppsala's stage-model approach (based on Danish multinationals), such traditional internationalisers typically first enter geographically or culturally proximate overseas markets. They then gradually gain international experience and undergo considerable learning before venturing further afield. Remarkably, our analysis found not one single GNC conformed closely enough to be identified as such a traditional internationaliser.

This traditional (denoted *TRAD*) Uppsala model of the establishment chain and experiential learning is, however, the baseline against which two other well known and documented internationalisation modes have been extensively contrasted and delineated: *born globals* (BGs) and *born again globals* (BAGs). BGs are relatively new venture companies, skipping conservative internationalisation pathways, and going to the market globally virtually upon conception (as happens, for example, with many new internet companies). BAGs, on the other hand, are long-established companies, which first incubate competitive advantages whilst remaining at home. Much later, triggered by some 'critical event', they then suddenly 'take-off' globally, behaving akin to BGs.

We compared our GNCs against these three well known models, scoring all deviations systematically against each. We remained open-minded to the possibility of a fourth more '*hybrid*' orientation requiring more novel delineation. Indeed, whilst no GNCs could be classified as TRAD modes, 43% conformed closely to BG orientations (just over half of British GNCs and one third of German GNCs). Twenty percent conformed most closely to BAG orientations, but again, less so in Germany (13%) than in Britain (27%).

This still left 37% (20% in Britain, but over 50% in Germany) unclassified. These GNCs, unlike BGs or BAGs, initially internationalised in line with the TRAD Uppsala model, but then veered off in a manner akin to BAGs, prompted by some critical event. Such triggering critical events (whether for BAGs or hybrids) were different for German as compared with British companies. German BAGs and hybrids engaged in accelerated internationalisation in response to technological advances, whereas the triggers for British firms were invariably managerial and CEO changes. Such hybrids suggest new, so far unacknowledged modes of successful internationalisation, appropriate to mid-caps.

SUSTAINING SUCCESSFUL INTERNATIONALISATION PATHS IN LONGER-LIVED GNCs

To check for more sustainable lessons, GNCs were further divided into three groups of newly established GNCs, denoted GNCns, (three German and five British), medium-lived GNCms (four German and five British), and long-lived GNCls which had flourished over more than 80 years (eight German and five British). Findings are summarised in Table 8.1.

Newer GNCns deviated substantially from TRAD modes, but all complied closely with BG modes (three German and five British GNCns). German GNCns indeed fitted 'pure' BGs orientations almost perfectly, though British GNCs displayed just minor deviations. In contrast, only 56% of nine medium-longevity GNCms, four German and five British, were classifiable as BGs; 22% were BAGs, and a further 22% pursued alternative hybrid paths (mid-way between TRAD and BAG modes). For long-lived GNCls, none

Table 8.1 Internationalisation paths of GNCs

Paths	*Germany*				*Britain*				*Overall*
	GNCn (n = 3)	*GNCm (n = 4)*	*GNCl (n = 8)*	*Total (n = 15)*	*GNCn (n = 5)*	*GNCm (n = 5)*	*GNCl (n = 5)*	*Total (n = 15)*	*Total (n = 30)*
TRADs	0	0	0	**0**	0	0	0	**0**	**0**
BGs	3	2	0	**5 (33%)**	5	3	0	**8 (53%)**	**13 (43%)**
BAGs	0	1	1	**2 (13%)**	0	1	3	**4 (27%)**	**6 (20%)**
Hybrids	0	1	7	**8 (54%)**	0	1	2	**3 (20%)**	**11 (37%)**
Total	3	4	8	**15**	5	5	5	**15**	**30**

Source: Witt, A., *Global Hidden Champions: The International Paths, Entry Modes and Underlying Competitive Advantages of Germany's and Britain's Global Top Three Niche Players*, Unpublished PhD thesis, University of Edinburgh, Table 3, pp. 33–34, 2015.

Table 8.2 Evolution of global niche champions' international orientations

Establishment category	*Business formation*	*Type of internationaliser*	*GNC*
Newly established GNCns	**2007**	BGs	BritN3
	2003	BGs	BritN4
	1989	BGs	GerN2, BritN3
	1986	BGs	BritN2
	1984	BGs	BritN1
	1977	BGs	GerN1
	1973	BGs	GerN3
Medium-lived GNCms	**1967**	BGs	BritM3
	1954	BGs	BritM4
	1946	BGs	GerM3
	1941	Hybrid	BritM5
	1939	BGs	BritM2
	1937	BGs	GerM2
	1932	Hybrid, BAG	GerM1, GerM4
Long-lived GNCls	**1919**	Hybrid, BAG	GerL5, BritL4
	1908	Hybrid	GerL7
	1903	Hybrid	BritL5
	1875	Hybrid	GerL6
	1871	Hybrid	BritL2
	1865	Hybrid, BAG	GerL4, BritL3
	1852	Hybrid, BAG	GerL2, BritM2
	1849	Hybrid, BAG	GerL1, GerL8
	1838	Hybrid, BAG	GerL3, BritL1

Source: Witt, A., *Global Hidden Champions: The International Paths, Entry Modes and Underlying Competitive Advantages of Germany's and Britain's Global Top Three Niche Players*, Unpublished PhD thesis, University of Edinburgh, Table 3, pp. 33–34, 2015.

were BGs. Seventy percent had adopted hybrid internationalisation modes (the ratio being slightly higher in Germany); the remaining 30% were identified as BAG-type internationalisers.

Table 8.2 analyses evolutionary patterns and orientations over time, distinguishing newer and long-lived companies. GNCns (established after 1970) moved abroad like born globals, early and rapidly. Yet the opposite was true for more enduring GNCIs (already established before 1930): they remained essentially domestic in their early years and only later engaged in accelerated internationalisation paths akin to BAGs or hybrids. Those in between (established between 1930 and 1970) pursued mixed paths BGs, BAGs, and hybrids; 1930 to 1970 thus marked a historical change in internationalisation modes.

INTERNATIONAL PATHWAYS ACCORDING TO DIFFERENT GNC ORIENTATION MODES

> If you want to be sustainable over time then you have to be present worldwide with your own subsidiaries. German L8 executive.

All international pathways called for FDI, but market entry mode choices varied according to BG, BAG, and hybrid orientations, as shown in Tables 8.3–8.5.

Table 8.3 firstly distinguishes international pathways for just born global orientations (eight GNCns and five GNCms). All used mainly exports and sales agents:

> We only use exporting in our business. We export all of our products from our headquarters in Germany and that has worked well for the past 40 years. (German N3, BG executive).
>
> We start to serve our customers mainly through exports and then see what else evolves from that. (British N2, BG executive).

BGs worked hard developing foreign sales agent and distributor relationships, deeming these essential. German executives concurred with BritN3's executive:

> We have chosen the distributor route because that way you are already working with somebody that has the contacts and has established a distribution network in that country. In most of the other markets around the world we operate through distributors. So, expansion plans really revolve around providing better support to those distributors to make them more successful. (British N4, BG executive).

Most BGs, whether German or British, chose greenfield sites (29 out of all 32 FDIs). Just two British, and no German BGs used acquisitions:

> The market is still growing, and we are organically growing with it. We would consider growing non-organically through acquisitions. Everybody is trying to grow, and it is very difficult to grow organically and that is why people start acquiring. British M4, BG executive.

Table 8.3 Market entry modes of BGs

BGs	*Germany*					*Britain*								*Total BGs*			*Total GNCns*			*Total GNCms*		
	GerN1	*GerN2*	*GerN3*	*GerM2*	*GerM3*	*BritN1*	*BritN2*	*BritN3*	*BritN4*	*BritN5*	*BritM2*	*BritM3*	*BritM4*	*Total (n = 13)*	*Germany (n = 5)*	*Britain (n = 8)*	*Total (n = 8)*	*Germany (n = 3)*	*Britain (n = 4)*	*Total (n = 5)*	*Germany (n = 2)*	*Britain (n = 3)*
Export	+	+	+	+	+	+	+	+	+	+	+	+	+	–	–	–	–	–	–	–	–	–
SA and DIST	–	+	+	+	+	+	+	+	+	+	+	+	+	–	–	–	–	–	–	–	–	–
FDI	+	+	–	+	+	+	+	+	+	+	+	+	–	–	–	–	–	–	–	–	–	–
Business formation	1977	1989	1973	1937	1946	1984	1986	2007	2003	1989	1939	1967	1954	1973	1964	1979	1989	1980	1994	1949	1942	1953
Years in between	*3*	*1*	*1*	*3*	*2*	*9*	*3*	*0*	*5*	*0*	*9*	*6*	*4*	*4*	*2*	*5*	*3*	*2*	*3*	*5*	*3*	*6*
First int. activity	1980	1990	1974	1940	1948	1993	1989	2007	2008	1989	1948	1973	1958	1977	1966	1983		1981	1997	1953	1944	1960
Entry mode	EX	EX	EX	EX	EX	EX	EX	EX	EX	EX	EX	EX	EX	–	–	–	–	–	–	–	–	–
Years in between	*3*	*1*	–	*15*	*28*	*6*	*0*	*1*	*0*	*18*	*4*	*12*	–	*8*	*12*	*6*	*4*	*2*	*5*	*15*	*22*	*8*
First FDI	1983	1991	–	1955	1976	1999	1989	2008	2008	2007	1952	1985	–	1987	1976	1993	1998	1987	2002	1967	1966	1969
Entry mode	GFS	GFS	–	GFS	GFS	GFS	GFS	GFS	AQ	GFS	GFS	GFS	–	–	–	–	–	–	–	–	–	–
Years in between	*9*	*5*	–	*0*	*10*	*0*	*21*	*0*	*1*	*3*	*7*	*6*	–	*6*	*6*	*5*	*6*	*7*	*5*	*6*	*5*	*7*
Second FDI	1992	1996	–	1955	1986	1999	2010	2008	2009	2010	1959	1991	–	1992	1982	1998	2003	1994	2007	1973	1971	1975

(*Continued*)

Table 8.3 (Continued)

BGs	*Germany*					*Britain*								*Total BGs*			*Total GNCns*			*Total GNCms*		
	GerN1	*GerN2*	*GerN3*	*GerM2*	*GerM3*	*BritN1*	*BritN2*	*BritN3*	*BritN4*	*BritN5*	*BritM2*	*BritM3*	*BritM4*	*Total (n = 13)*	*Germany (n = 5)*	*Britain (n = 8)*	*Total (n = 8)*	*Germany (n = 3)*	*Britain (n = 4)*	*Total (n = 5)*	*Germany (n = 2)*	*Britain (n = 3)*
Entry mode	GFS	JV	–	GFS	GFS	GFS	GFS	GFS	GFS	GFS	JV	GFS	–	–	–	–	–	–	–	–	–	–
Years in between	*6*	*1*	–	*0*	*8*	*2*	–	*0*	*0*	*2*	*0*	*5*	–	*2*	*4*	*2*	*2*	*4*	*1*	*3*	*4*	*3*
Third FDI	1998	1997	–	1955	1994	2001	–	2008	2009	2012	1959	1996	–	1993	1986	1998	2004	1998	2008	1976	1975	1978
Entry mode	GFS	GFS	–	GFS	GFS	GFS	–	GFS	GFS	GFS	GFS	GFS	–	–	–	–	–	–	–	–	–	–

Source: Witt, A., *Global Hidden Champions: The International Paths, Entry Modes and Underlying Competitive Advantages of Germany's and Britain's Global Top Three Niche Players*, Unpublished PhD thesis, University of Edinburgh, Table 3, pp. 33–34, 2015.

Note: EX: Export, SA and DIST: Sales agents and distributors, First int. activity: First international activity, GFS: Greenfield site, AQ: Acquisition, JV: Joint venture.

Table 8.4 Market entry modes of BAGs

BAGs	*Germany*		*Britain*				*BAGs*			*GNCms*			*GNCls*		
	GerM4	*GerL8*	*BritM1*	*BritL1*	*BritL3*	*BritL4*	*Total (n = 6)*	*Germany (n = 2)*	*Britain (n = 4)*	*Total (n = 2)*	*Germany (n = 1)*	*Britain (n = 1)*	*Total (n = 4)*	*Germany (n = 1)*	*Britain (n = 3)*
Export	+	+	–	+	+	–	–	–	–	–	–	–	–	–	–
SA and DIST	+	+	–	+	+	–	–	–	–	–	–	–	–	–	–
FDI	+	+	+	+	+	+	–	–	–	–	–	–	–	–	–
Business formation	1968	1923	1941	1882	1915	1923	1925	1946	1915	1955	1968	1941	1911	1923	1907
Years in between	*17*	*47*	*52*	*97*	*85*	*67*	*61*	*32*	*75*	*35*	*17*	*52*	*74*	*47*	*83*
First int. activity	1985	1970	1993	1979	2000	1990	1986	1978	1991	1989	1985	1993	1985	1970	1990
Entry mode	EX	EX	AQ	EX	AQ	AQ	–	–	–	–	–	–	–	–	–
Years in between	*14*	*14*	*0*	*5*	*0*	*2*	*6*	*14*	*2*	*7*	*14*	*0*	*5*	*14*	*2*
First FDI	1999	1984	1993	1984	2000	1992	1992	1992	1992	1999	1999	1993	1990	1984	1992
Entry mode	GFS	JV	AQ	GFS	AQ	AQ	–	–	–	–	–	–	–	–	–
Years in between	*1*	*0*	*2*	*6*	*0*	*4*	*2*	*1*	*3*	*2*	*1*	*2*	*3*	*0*	*3*
Second FDI	2000	1984	1995	1990	2000	1996	1994	1992	1995	2000	2000	1995	1993	1984	1995
Entry mode	GFS	GFS	AQ	AQ	AQ	AQ	–	–	–	–	–	–	–	–	–
Years in between	*5*	*1*	–	*1*	*1*	–	*2*	*3*	*1*	*5*	*5*	–	*1*	*1*	*1*
Third FDI	2005	1985	–	1991	2001	–	*1996*	1995	1996	2005	2005	–	1992	1985	1996
Entry mode		GFS	–	JV	AQ	–	–	–	–	–	–	–	–	–	–

Source: Witt, A., *Global Hidden Champions: The International Paths, Entry Modes and Underlying Competitive Advantages of Germany's and Britain's Global Top Three Niche Players*, Unpublished PhD thesis, University of Edinburgh, Table 3, pp. 33–34, 2015.

Note: EX: Export; SA: Sales Agents; DIST: Distribution; First int. activity: First international activity; GFS: Greenfield site; AQ: Acquisition; JV: Joint venture. BritM1 and BritL4, their first internationalisation was also their first FDI entry, and the third FDI was therefore left blank.

Table 8.5 Market entry modes of hybrids

Hybrids	*Germany*								*Britain*			*Hybrids*			*GNCms*			*GNCls*		
	GerM1	*GerL1*	*GerL2*	*GerL3*	*GerL4*	*GerL5*	*GerL6*	*GerL7*	*BritM5*	*BritL2*	*BritL5*	*Total (n=11)*	*Germany (n=8)*	*Britain (n=3)*	*Total (n=2)*	*Germany (n=1)*	*Britain (n=1)*	*Total (n=8)*	*Germany (n=7)*	*Britain (n=2)*
Export	+	+	+	+	+	+	+	+	+	+	+	–	–	–	–	–	–	–	–	–
SA and DIST	+	+	+	+	+	+	+	+	+	+	+	–	–	–	–	–	–	–	–	–
FDI	+	+	+	+	+	+	+	+	–	+	+	–	–	–	–	–	–	–	–	–
Business formation	1932	1849	1852	1838	1865	1919	1875	1908	1941	1871	1903	1887	1880	1905	1937	1932	1941	1876	1872	1887
Years in between	*0*	*0*	*18*	*120*	*35*	*16*	*13*	*12*	*12*	*13*	*25*	*24*	*27*	*17*	*6*	*0*	*12*	*28*	*31*	*19*
First int. activity	1932	1849	1870	1958	1900	1935	1888	1920	1953	1884	1928	1911	1907	1922	1943	1932	1953	1904	1903	1906
Entry mode	EX	EX	EX	EX	EX	EX	EX	EX	EX	EX	EX	–	–	–	–	–	–	–	–	–
Years in between	*28*	*101*	*88*	*24*	*56*	*23*	*62*	*71*	–	*73*	*28*	*55*	*57*	*51*	*28*	*28*	–	*58*	*61*	*51*
First FDI	1960	1950	1958	1982	1956	1958	1950	1991	–	1957	1956	1962	1963	1957	1960	1960	–	1962	1964	1957
Entry mode	AQ	GFS	GFS	AQ	GFS	GFS	JV	GFS	–	AQ	GFS	–	–	–	–	–	–	–	–	–
Years in between	*10*	*10*	*24*	*8*	*0*	*9*	*27*	*9*	–	*34*	*1*	*13*	*12*	*18*	*10*	*10*	–	*14*	*12*	*18*
Second FDI	1970	1960	1982	1990	1956	1967	1977	2000	–	1991	1957	1975	1975	1974	1970	1970	–	1976	1976	1974
Entry mode	GFS	JV	GFS	GFS	GFS	GFS	AQ	GFS	–	AQ	GFS						–	–	–	–
Years in between	*24*	*35*	*5*	*0*	*1*	*0*	*10*	*2*	–	*3*	*3*	*8*	*10*	*3*	*24*	*24*	–	*7*	*8*	*3*
Third FDI	1972	1995	1987	1990	1957	1967	1987	2002	–	1994	1960	1981	1982	1977	1972	1972	–	1982	1984	1977
Entry mode	GFS	GFS	GFS	GFS	GFS	GFS	JV	GFS	–	GFS	AQ	–	–	–	–	–	–	–	–	–

Source: Witt, A., *Global Hidden Champions: The International Paths, Entry Modes and Underlying Competitive Advantages of Germany's and Britain's Global Top Three Niche Players*, Unpublished PhD thesis, University of Edinburgh, Table 3, pp. 33–34, 2015.

Note: EX: Export; SA and DIST: Sales agents and distributors; First int. activity: First international activity; GFS: Greenfield site; AQ: Acquisition, JV: Joint venture.

> We have some tactical acquisitions that have really helped us. For example, we bought one company that then suddenly gave us a big presence in China. We also have technology acquisitions. We bought one company that had a piece of technology that we really needed, and it was absolutely unique and we couldn't get it anywhere else in the world. It was such a key component in one of our products that we would just end up paying them huge amounts of royalties, so we went and bought the company. So sometimes the acquisitions added new functionalities to our products and sometimes they were things that we would have done ourselves but couldn't or didn't have the time to do ourselves and it was just cheaper to buy someone else. British M3, BG executive.

Only two BGs (one German, one British) engaged in joint ventures:

> We don't do joint ventures or anything similar, that's too adventurous for us. Partnerships just don't allow us to be as flexible as we are now. Surely, the downside of doing it all alone is that it is a lot of work. Still we stick to our company's philosophy and that's simply put; either we do it ourselves or we don't do it at all. We are now running this business in third generation and our principle is to not let anyone else in the company. It goes so far that we own every piece of land and buildings, even the ones abroad are all fully owned by us. German M3, BG executive.

Whilst BGs in both countries had largely tried to avoid strategic alliances, some were more open to future possibilities, and partnerships were often needed when moving into more challenging markets with country-specific restrictions:

> We would always prefer a joint venture to an alliance. Alliances they are just like marriages: they are great for a while but then you want to get out. They should just be renewable after 10 years where you just see if you still like each other and if not you can just walk away. British M3, BG executive.
>
> I think historically we have a model of doing it all ourselves because we are very protective when it comes to our technology but that has actually changed. Now there is so much market growth and there are people who can probably offer us a market. In those areas we would probably consider joint ventures. British N2, BG executive.
>
> We usually build our own subsidiaries abroad, but we have some partnerships too. For example, in Malaysia we don't own the business 100% because legally we are not allowed. So, a joint venture was our only option. British M3, BG executive.

On average BGs began internationalising four years after establishment dates, but German BGs moved earlier, after just two years compared with British BGs after five years. After a further eight years on average, BGs then established their first FDIs, though, here, the British moved more quickly than German BGs (at 6 years versus 12). For BGs established before 1970, this difference was even more marked at 8 years versus 22; but for those established after 1970, the position has been reversed (five years versus two for German BGs). Overall though, German BGs began exporting sooner, but were slower than British BGs in terms of committing to FDI.

Generally German and British BGs preferred organic growth and, initially, direct exports and sales intermediaries. Yet what distinguished GNCs from BGs discussed by other writers, were their subsequent rapid commitments to FDI, either through greenfield sites or acquisitions (especially for British BGs). Joint ventures were largely avoided:

> We always stay ahead and, also, invest ahead. If we see that a market offers capacity, then we go and build our facilities, but we don't go looking for a partner. We are always in advance of people's requirements and needs so we go and do it ourselves. Interviewee of BritN2, BG.

Most BAGs used similar international modes when first internationalising, including direct exports, sales agents, and local distributors as shown in Table 8.4.

> In our product-based business, we will use sales agents and distributors, because having people locally makes a huge difference. Interviewee of BritL1, BAG.

The exceptions were two British firms, the only service firms among our GNCs. They remained at home longer than other BAGs (60 years compared with 50 years), and then internationalised via acquisitions in preference to trade:

> We don't use exports because we really provide services directly in a country. Generally, we will take acquisitions and improve them and grow them and bolt on others where appropriate. We are not always aiming for full acquisitions. There are places where we have corresponding skill sets. We have joint ventures in the UK and everywhere else in the world. Interviewee of BritM1, BAG.
>
> Export doesn't apply because our business is local. It's like a coffee shop and you want to drink it where it is made. Interviewee of BritL4, BAG.

All BAGs engaged in FDI, but German companies emphasised organic growth and greenfield sites in five out of FDI six cases. By contrast, British BAGs chose acquisitions in 10 out 12 possible FDI entries:

> We grow 2/3 organic and 1/3 through acquisitions...but generally we have made some pretty small acquisitions to take on a new service or take you

> into a new country. If we are going into a new market my preference is often an acquisition because it brings you a local customer base, local knowledge and people which we can then add value to by bringing skills and know-how into that. It is faster too. Interviewee of BritL1, BAG.
>
> We produce at a quality that not many people do any more and to maintain this we prefer to move abroad alone. Our technology is used in China and India but, when we move into these markets, we prefer to do it alone. Interviewee of GerL8, BAG.
>
> We follow two types of strategies that we use in emerging and developed markets. In emerging economies, we follow a pure greenfield strategy and in our developed economies we use an acquisition strategy. We need to protect our brand and at the end of the day the companies stand for quality, responsibility, and safety so any other entry mode does not apply. In developed markets the businesses that we acquire fulfil our standards but in emerging economies we prefer to build our own facilities as there aren't much established which we could acquire. Interviewee of BritL4, BAG.

As in the case of BGs, BAGs from both countries used few joint ventures (2 out of 18 FDIs), and were similarly reluctant to engage in partnerships:

> We have used all kinds of entry modes in the past, but we have realised that the only way we can sustain our reputation is when we do it ourselves or we buy a company abroad. Sometimes we use joint ventures but increasingly we feel that that can dilute the relationship. Sometimes you have got to have local content and you have to ensure that you have a good local partner and you sometimes end up feeling like you have done 100% of the work but the partner gets 50% of the profit. So, you want to get a partner that really does add value to the process. Interviewee of BritL1, BAG.
>
> We had a joint venture in the UK, but we terminated that and instead acquired a competitor. Partnerships are difficult and we prefer to own as much as we can abroad. Interviewee of GerL8, BAG.

British BAGs remained domestically focused, on average for 75 years before internationalising compared to just 32 years for German BAGs. BAGs established between 1930 and 1970 internationalised twice as fast as those established before 1930, though German BAGs again moved faster. Once they did move, British BAGs were then far faster in committing to FDI (after 2 more years versus 14 for German companies).

Table 8.5 distinguishes and analyses internationalisation pathways for all our final hybrid GNCs (three British and eight German). All chose similar entry modes, deploying direct exports, sales agents, and local distributors, but most also using extensive FDI. Out of 30 FDI entries, 21 entailed greenfield sites, 6 acquisitions, and just 3 joint ventures. Hybrids preferred FDI commitments affording greater control.

German Hybrids preferred organic growth, opting for more greenfield sites than British equivalents (in 18 out of 24 FDI cases, versus 3 out of 6 British FDIs). British hybrids used acquisitions in three out of six FDI cases (versus 3 out of 24 German FDIs). Executives in both countries often used both greenfield sites and acquisitions:

> In terms of market entry strategies, we don't necessarily prefer to enter via subsidiaries because we also do acquisitions, so in the sense that we buy smaller players. Interviewee of GerL1, Hybrid.
>
> We go abroad alone but also through acquisitions, a mix which has proven to be very successful. Interviewee of GerL4, Hybrid.
>
> Generally, we like to move abroad alone but we also do use acquisitions. Interviewee of BritL2, Hybrid.

For hybrids, partnerships were again their least preferred FDI entry mode. Only German hybrids internationalised using joint ventures (in 3 out of 21 FDIs):

> Joint ventures are not an entry mode for us, and it is a clear strategy that we follow in our business. If you want to sustain over time, then you have to be present worldwide but not at any cost, so we deliberately prefer entering markets alone. Interviewee of GerL8, Hybrid.
>
> Maybe for others joint ventures and partnerships prove to be great ways to enter markets but that was never our strategy. We like to have a tightly controlled distribution. Interviewee of GerL5, Hybrid.
>
> We have an example in China where we set up a joint venture with one of our customers which was very successful. Also in India we entered via a joint venture because we had no knowledge about the rules and regulations and we are making good business there. We either have 50:50 joint ventures or even own majority stake like in Malaysia where it is 80:20 in our favour. Interviewee of GerL2, Hybrid.

Joint ventures were used for markets with specific restrictions; but executives from both countries were aiming ultimately to take over their partners:

> It really depends on the market. When we are convinced we can do it ourselves, we will but in case there are major cultural or institutional differences we also take a partner. In countries like China we try to find a local partner because in a Chinese network you will barely manage to set foot as a company from Germany. Interviewee of GerL6, Hybrid.
>
> Partnership is something that we consider but you always need to have an exit strategy in the back of your mind. We demand from our partners that they either have the resources, know-how or market share otherwise it's more of a burden and the partnership needs to be fair. Interviewee of GerL3, Hybrid.

> Oftentimes we partner with [a local] business because it's the law and sometimes we don't even want to own a business in that country. You cannot generalise that, but we would probably want a case of ownership where we could buy the other half. Interviewee of BritL2, Hybrid.
>
> We do use partnerships in countries like China where we have little knowledge about foreign regulations. Essential here is to have majority stake otherwise it can get messy. It is important though to have an exit strategy because from our experience partnerships have an expiry date and we often buy the other part of that joint venture when we can. Interviewee of BritL5, Hybrid.

British hybrids started internationalisation through low-commitment entry modes ten years earlier than German counterparts (after 17 years versus 27). Hybrids in both countries followed up with FDIs a little over 50 years later.

Overall, most GNCs, whether BGs, BAGs, or hybrids, began internationalising using direct exports, sales agents, and local distributors. German BGs and BAGs started internationalising earlier than their British counterparts; but the opposite was true for hybrids. In the case of enduring GNCs, British companies proved even more visionary and international. Ninety percent of German and British GNCs engaged in extensive foreign direct investments, though typically British GNCs averaged two FDIs compared with over three in Germany. Here, German GNCs preferred organic growth and greenfield sites (particularly initially), whereas British GNCs preferred acquisitions, especially in services. Relatively few (albeit slightly more in Britain) used joint ventures.

HOW KEY FACTORS FOR SUCCESS VARIED BY GLOBAL ORIENTATIONS

The overall compatibility of the HC model across all GNC international orientation modes was remarkably high, especially in Germany, though our sample needs to be seen against a wider historical and evolutionary perspective depicted in Figure 8.2.

Enduring GNCs in both countries, in all three orientations, concurred on the importance of our new traits relating to visions and values, as detailed in Table 8.6 and on the crucial importance of brands and reputation.

> We had informal values that were espoused through the leadership informally and I think that most people got them but they haven't written them down, So we decided that we would write them down and I got the upper management team together to do that and most of them were values that we already had but some of them were quite inspirational. I wanted to put it a vision that people thought about. It is an important part of keeping

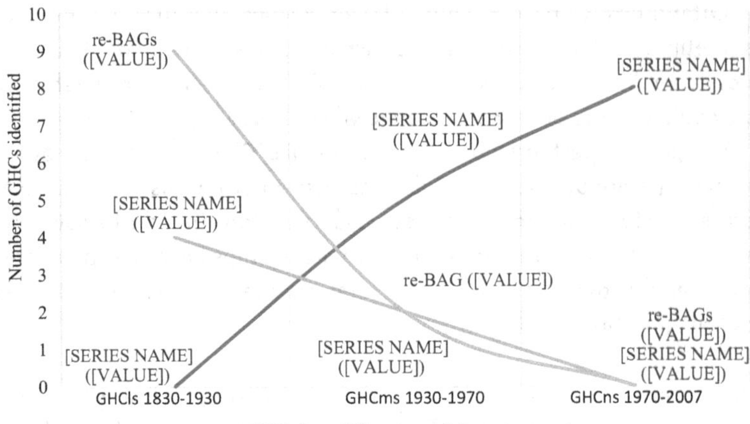

Figure 8.2 Evolution of GHC's internationalisation paths. BGs, Born Globals; BAGs, Born Again Globals; GHC suffixes n, m, and l denote new, medium- and long-establishment dates. (From Witt, A., *Global Hidden Champions: The International Paths, Entry Modes and Underlying Competitive Advantages of Germany's and Britain's Global Top Three Niche Players*, Unpublished PhD thesis, University of Edinburgh, Table 3, pp. 33–34, 2015.)

Table 8.6 'Visions and values' trait mentioned by BG, BAG, and hybrid executives

'Visions and values' Trait	*Germany (n = 15)*	*Britain (n = 15)*	*Total (n = 30)*
BGs	4	1	5
BAGs	1	1	2
Hybrids	2	1	3
Total	7	3	10

Source: Witt, A., *Global Hidden Champions: The International Paths, Entry Modes and Underlying Competitive Advantages of Germany's and Britain's Global Top Three Niche Players*, Unpublished PhD thesis, University of Edinburgh, Table 3, pp. 33–34, 2015.

your head in the competition. That's where we need to get better, and we need company values to become better and achieve that. Interviewee of BritL1, BAG.

The brand is, absolutely, essential in our business. We foster our brand continuously and try to live up to what we have built and what our brand stands for. GerL5 executive.

Charts in Figure 8.3 depict overall conformance, trait by trait, with recently established GNCns (i.e., BGs) aligned slightly more closely as compared with more enduring cases (i.e., hybrids and BAG). British BGs and BAGs diverged slightly more from the HC model; though German hybrids diverged more than British BGs.

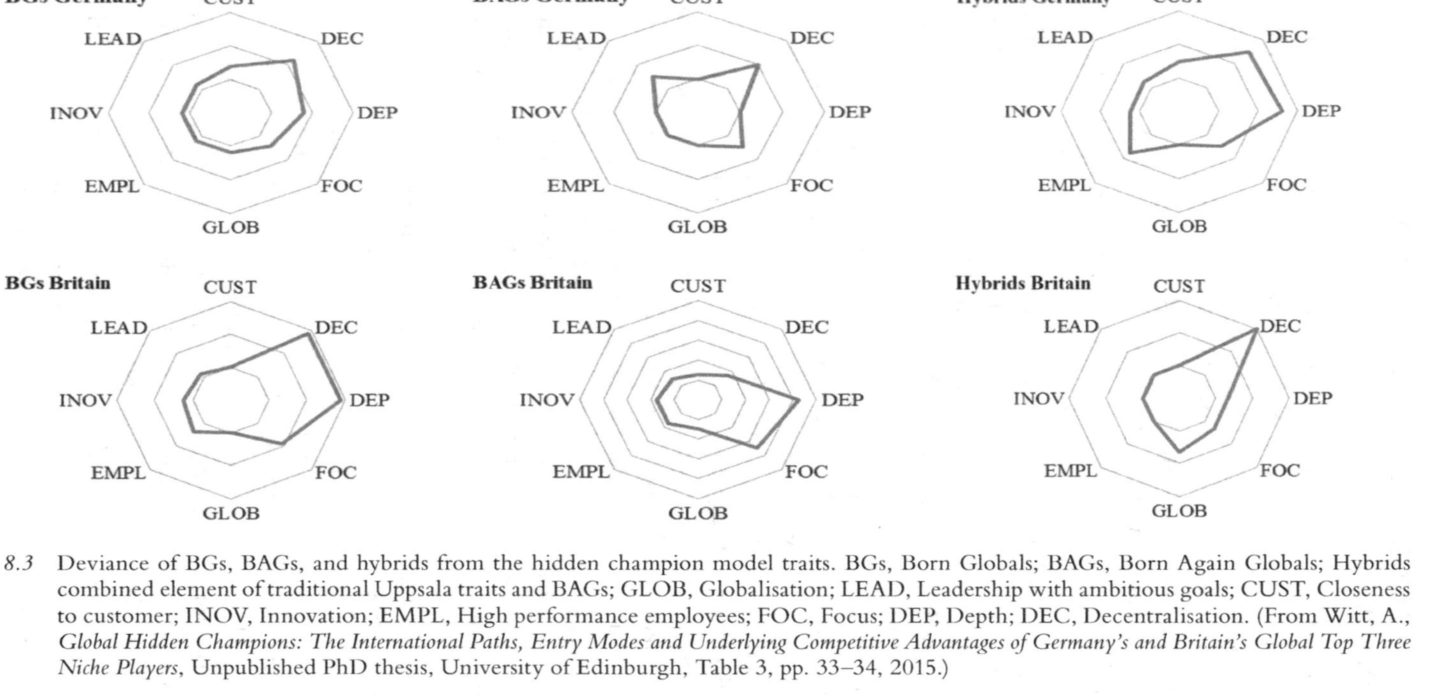

Figure 8.3 Deviance of BGs, BAGs, and hybrids from the hidden champion model traits. BGs, Born Globals; BAGs, Born Again Globals; Hybrids combined element of traditional Uppsala traits and BAGs; GLOB, Globalisation; LEAD, Leadership with ambitious goals; CUST, Closeness to customer; INOV, Innovation; EMPL, High performance employees; FOC, Focus; DEP, Depth; DEC, Decentralisation. (From Witt, A., *Global Hidden Champions: The International Paths, Entry Modes and Underlying Competitive Advantages of Germany's and Britain's Global Top Three Niche Players*, Unpublished PhD thesis, University of Edinburgh, Table 3, pp. 33–34, 2015.)

FINAL GNC MODEL RELATED TO INTERNATIONALISATION AND INNOVATION PERSPECTIVES

Table 8.7 explores the entrepreneurial and innovation dispositions of all German and British GNCs. Strategic changes, relating to such competitive advantages, did not occur by accident. Identified internationalisation paths were triggered by events. BG-style GNCs, for example, adapted to changing global circumstances (i.e., globalisation triggers) akin to BGs studied by Sapienza et al. (2006) and Zahra et al. (2006). Re-BAGs and BAGs, by contrast, adapted their strategies more in response to internal managerial changes or in response to external circumstances (such as eroding markets) and/or to historical events (notably the World War II). Critical incidents, as Bell et al. (2001) also observed, initiated strategic shifts to accelerated internationalisation. These strategic adaptions identified across BGs, BAGs, and re-BAGs were not inconsistent with broader generalisations relating to strategic fit as in our global winners model in Figure 3.7, but they appeared in response to specific factors, such as managerial changes or incidents including technological advances and product diversification moves.

For all these GNCs, as Table 8.7 details, entrepreneurship mattered. Their strategic changes, triggered by specific events, required resources, organisational routines, or what Teece (2007) termed '*dynamic capabilities*', in contrast to static '*resource-based*' perspectives. Such dynamic capabilities frameworks, though, require still further specification of traits, as delineated in Simon's *hidden champions* model and refined through our GNC analysis. We must also encapsulate scale issues related to global market leadership and international business strategies. International pathways likewise need delineating; a single false step could be onto the sort of mine which blew RBS right out of the water (Chapter 12).

GNCs avoided such debacles; instead their market positions led to a virtuous cycle, reinforcing broad orientations and economies of scale and scope advantages. Our final more complete and fully integrated GNC model, shown in Figure 8.4, modifies Teece's paradigm to include these wider issues and more historical perspectives. GNC successes could not be understood in isolation from their equally innovative international strategies. As global niche oligopolists, nested beneath larger, more visible oligopolies, GNCs' strategies have become critical success models for, typically, mid-cap players. Eschewing head-on rivalry with larger oligopolists, GNCs determined their own niches and took them global. Others, too small to compete against large oligopolists, those Goliaths of modern global business, may find that playing David takes equal understanding and commitment.

Table 8.7 Entrepreneurial orientations indicated by German and British GNCs

GNCs	*Path*	*Innovativeness*	*Proactiveness*	*Risk taking*	*Example*
GerN1	BG	Yes	Yes	Yes	*'Who doesn't have the courage to take appropriate risk won't be a winner'*. The owner started with an innovation but with limited resources and seized every chance.
GerN2	BG	Yes	Yes	Yes	Entirely new technology innovation from USA launched on EU market, followed by early FDI.
GerN3	BG	Yes	Yes	Yes	Aggressive early internationalisation pro-actively seeking new markets and distribution channels
BritN1	BG	Yes	Yes	Yes	*'If you develop something and you don't get it to work within the time frame you won't be able to sell it. Somebody else will come and take your place. So we had to move fast'*. Pro-active market seeking internationally including in Asia.
BritN2	BG	Yes	Yes	Yes	*'Today, we differentiate ourselves from the original form of our business and target a very different customer base'*. Change of focus targets on different customers and industries.
BritN3	BG	Yes	Yes	Yes	*'There is nobody that makes something equivalent that crosses so many industries. All the big players are now following what we have done'*. New technology innovation and early internationalisation.
BritN4	BG	Yes	Yes	Yes	Spin-off, followed by tight market focus and high investments into technology innovation.
BritN5	BG	Yes	Yes	Yes	*'We invest heavily in R&D, technology, and chemistry. I think our competitive edge is that we are adaptable and responsive to the market'*. Continuous investment into R&D and aggressive internationalisation in fast growing markets.
GerM1	Re-BAGs	Yes	Yes	Yes	High investments into product development. Rapidly grew business internationally after WW2. Critical incident: technological advance.
GerM2	BG	Yes	Yes	Yes	Developed market leading high-tech machine which then allowed for a rapid and early international expansion.
GerM3	BG	Yes	Yes	Yes	Through continuous R&D investments, they developed a new product line, new niche, and new customer base.
GerM4	BAG	Yes	Yes	Yes	Constant product innovation and product diversification led to international expansion, critical incident technology advancement.

(*Continued*)

Table 8.7 (Continued)

GNCs	*Path*	*Innovativeness*	*Proactiveness*	*Risk taking*	*Example*
BritM1	BAG	Yes	Yes	Yes	Strong focus of full-service provider continuously innovating its service to clients. Critical incident: management change.
BritM2	BG	Yes	Yes	Yes	*'If we see an opportunity we go for it!'* High investments in R&D, which leveraged international sales.
BritM3	BG	Yes	Yes	Yes	*'We develop a lot of ideas and products and you have to decide with which one you want to stick and then follow through. If we develop a new product that takes up to three years at least, so we can't have a short-term thinking. It's partly intuition and knowledge and that is always a risky decision'*. Costly long-term investments in R&D and continuous innovation.
BritM4	BG	Yes	Yes	Yes	Pro-active international market seeking and continuous product innovation.
BirtM5	Re-BAGs	Yes	Yes	Yes	Aggressive international expansion by new management and stronger focus on product innovation. Critical incident: management change.
GerL1	Re-BAG	Yes	Yes	Yes	Strong focus on innovation and early and pro-active market and customer seeking. Critical incident: technology advance.
GerL2	Re-BAG	Yes	Yes	Yes	Heavily invested in radical new innovations and new market niches. Critical incident: technology advance.
GerL3	Re-BAGs	Yes	Yes	Yes	*'We need to be innovative and we need to live that innovativeness in the company. So you need to take calculable risks and always bear in mind that things can go wrong. We try to avoid too risky decision because they can cause major difficulties and we had a situation before in Russia where we lost everything that we earned the years before'*. High investments in long-term R&D projects and pro-active internationalisation activity. Critical incident: technology advance.
GerL4	Re-BAGs	Yes	Yes	Yes	*'We operate entrepreneurially but with caution but surely we also take risks. We are a company with long-term visions because we need at least 10 to 12 years to develop our products. Basically, I need to know what the market wants in 10 years and know what the customer wants'*. Long-term investment into R&D projects and pro-active internationalisation. Critical incident product diversification.
GerL5	Re-BAG	Yes	Yes	Yes	High investments and pro-active opportunistic internationalising. Critical incident: technology advance.

(*Continued*)

Table 8.7 (Continued)

GNCs	*Path*	*Innovativeness*	*Proactiveness*	*Risk taking*	*Example*
GerL6	Re-BAGs	Yes	Yes	Yes	*'We are very innovative and we try to move as fast as we can to stay ahead of competition'*. High R&D investments and pro-active and fast internationalisation. Critical incident technology advance.
GerL7	Re-BAGs	Yes	Yes	Yes	*'We have the courage to take risks but we need to be able to control the risk. So if we see a project is not going well we must have the ability to stop early enough'*. Long-term investments into R&D and internationalisation. Critical incident: technology advancement.
GerL8	BAG	Yes	Yes	Yes	Risky investment into a new proto-type innovation, which then revolutionised the industry. Critical incident technology advancement.
BritL1	BAG	Yes	Yes	Yes	Seized opportunity and focused their business entirely on producing for the oil industry. Critical incident: management change.
BritL2	Re-BAGs	Yes	Yes	Yes	Focus on different innovations for different niches and pro-active internationalisation. Critical incident: management change.
BirtL3	BAG	Yes	Yes	Yes	Long-term focus, investments, and internationalisation. Critical incident: management change.
BirtL4	Re-BAGs	Yes	Yes	Yes	*'We just opportunistically came across something then we too that chance'*. Moved from manufacturing into new business niche without much prior knowledge. Critical incident: management change.
BirtL5	BAG	Yes	Yes	Yes	*'When we had our new product ready we knew it would be a success. So, we offered it where we could to everyone and everywhere'*. Risky investment into new innovation and aggressive international expansion. Critical incident management change.

Source: Witt, A., *Global Hidden Champions: The International Paths, Entry Modes and Underlying Competitive Advantages of Germany's and Britain's Global Top Three Niche Players*, Unpublished PhD thesis, University of Edinburgh, Table 3, pp. 33–34, 2015.

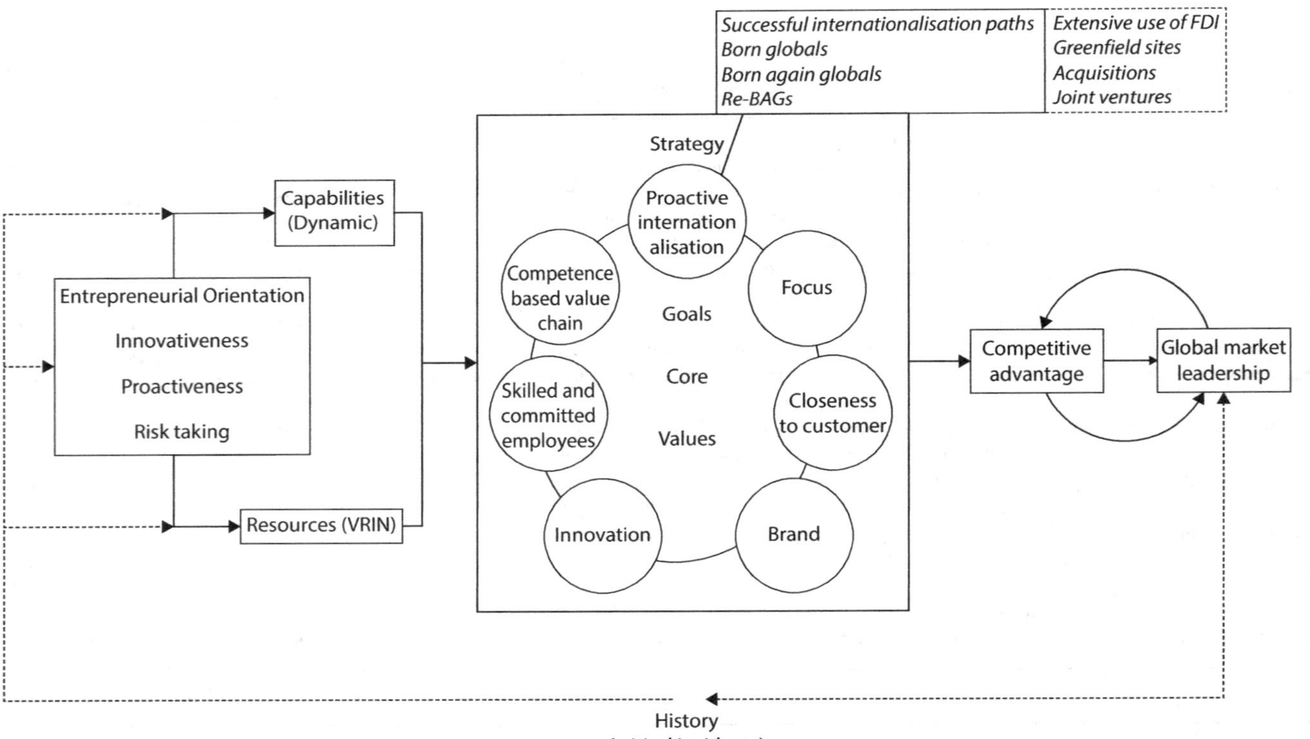

Figure 8.4 New global niche champion conceptual framework within wider schools of strategic thought.

NOTES

1 Simon, H. (2012). *Hidden Champions: Aufbruch nach Globalia*. Frankfurt: Campus Verlag; Simon, H. (2009). *Hidden Champions of the 21st Century*. Heidelberg, Germany: Springer Verlag; Simon, H. and Zatta, D. (2008). 'Growth strategies from the Hidden Champions: Lessons from Indian and international companies'. In D.-C.S. Cappallo (Ed.), *Gesundheitsmarkt in Indien* (pp. 187–204). Wiesbaden: Gabler GWV Fachverlage; Simon, H. (2007). *Hidden Champions des 21. Jahrhunderts* (2nd edition). Frankfurt am Main: Campus Verlag; Simon, H., and Lippert, S. (2007). *Hidden Champions des 21. Jahrhunderts Deutschland und Japan im Vergleich. Japanmarkt*, Frankfurt: Campus Verlag, 8–15; Simon, H. (1996a). *Hidden Champions: Lessons from 500 of the World's Best Unknown Companies*. Boston: Harvard Business School Press; Simon, H. (1996b). 'You don't have to be German to be a "Hidden Champion"'. *Business Strategy Review*, 7 (2), 1–13; Simon, H. (1992a). 'Lessons from Germany's midsize giants'. *Harvard Business Review*, 70 (2), 115–123; and Simon, H. (1992b). 'Service policies of German manufacturers: Critical factors in international competition'. *European Management Journal*, 10 (4), 404–411.

2 Witt, A. (2015). *Global Hidden Champions: The International Paths, Entry Modes and Underlying Competitive Advantages of Germany's and Britain's Global Top Three Niche Players*. Unpublished PhD thesis, University of Edinburgh. Table 3, pp. 33–34.

3 Ibid.

4 BCG. (1976). *The Rule of Three and Four* (Vol. 187). Boston: Boston Consulting Group; Henderson, B.D. (1979). *Henderson on Corporate Strategy*. Cambridge: Abt Books; Welch, J. (2002). *Jack: What I've Learned from Leading a Great Company and Great People*. London: Headline; Hannan, M.T. and Freeman, J. (1977). 'The population ecology of organizations'. *American Journal of Sociology*, 82 (5), 929–964; Porter, M.E. (1980). *Competitive Strategies: Techniques for Analysing Industries and Firms*. New York: The Free Press; Carroll, G.R. (1985). 'Concentration and specialization: Dynamics of niche width in populations of organizations'. *American Journal of Sociology*, 90 (6), 1262–1283; Sheth, J., and Sisodia, R. (2002). *The Rule of Three*. New York: The Free Press; Sheth, J., Uslay, A., and Sisodia, R. (2008). *The Globalization of Markets and the Rule of Three. Metaphors and Metamorphosis*. London: Palgrave Macmillan; Ploetner, O. (2012). *Counter Strategies in Global Markets*. New York: Palgrave Macmillan; Popescu, D.I. (2013). 'Servicing the niche market – A possible solution for the maintenance and success of the firm in the market in the context of the global economic crisis'. *Management Research and Practice*, 5 (1), 79–96.

5 For fuller details see Witt, A. (2015). Ibid.

6 Simon, H. (2009). Ibid.

Part IV

EMERGING MARKET CHAMPIONS' (EMCs') GLOBAL STRATEGIES

9

GLOBAL EMERGING MARKET CHAMPIONS

INTRODUCTION: HISTORICAL AND FUTURE EMERGING MARKET TRENDS

Long-term trends are re-establishing sectoral shares more in line with those prior to the Industrial Revolution (Table 9.1). From the 1750s to 1900, combined European and United States (US) shares of world manufacturing output rose from 23% to 86%, as the rest of the world fell back and China plunged from 33% to 6%; but by 2015 Japan had risen to 10%, as China overtook the USA and European countries fell back. By 2016 China's manufacturing output at $3.2 billion outstripped the USA ($2.1 billion), Japan ($1.0 billion), Germany ($0.72 billion), S. Korea ($0.38 billion), India ($0.34 billion), Italy ($0.27 billion), France ($0.25 billion) and the United Kingdom ($0.24 billion).[1]

On a purchasing power parity basis, the Brazil, Russia, India and China (BRIC)s' share of global gross domestic product (GDP) climbed from 18% in 2001 to over 25% in 2011, though combined GDPs of China and India were still less than half of the major G7 Organization for Economic Cooperation and Development (OECD) countries. However, Asia is expected to account for nearly 5 billion of the world's expected population in 2030 of about 8.5 billion: Standard Chartered forecasts GDPs on a purchasing power parity basis at China $64 trillion, India $46 trillion, the USA $31 trillion, with Japan and Germany ranking only 9 and 10 at $7.2 trillion and $6.9 trillion. China's share is expected to rise from 19% in 2019 to 25% by 2031, compared with India's rise from 8% to 13%, or all Asia's from 42% to 53%.

In 2019 GDP/capita productivity for emergent market (EM) countries (at current prices) was only $5400, compared with $48,600 for advanced countries: China at $10,500 and India at $2200 being far behind the USA ($65,000), Germany ($48,000), Japan ($41,000) and the United Kingdom ($42,000).

Table 9.1 Shares of world manufacturing output %s, 1750–2015

	1750	*1800*	*1900*	*1980*	*2015*
USA	0.1	1	24	23	18
Europe	23	28	62		20[a]
Japan	4	4	2	13	10
Rest of World	73	68	11		52[a]
UK		5	19	6	2
Germany		3	13	13	7
China	33		6	6	20

Sources: Kennedy, P., *The Rise and Fall of Great Powers*, Random House, New York, 1987; Balroch, P., 'International industrialisation levels from 1750 to 1980'; HIS Global Insight, 'Global manufacturing output data 1980–2010'; Marsh, P. (2012). *The New Industrial Revolution*. New Haven: Yale University Press; United Nations, *Conference on Trade and Development*, 2015.

a European estimate based just on Germany, France, Italy, United Kingdom, Spain, Poland, Switzerland, and the Netherlands.

However since 1990 Chinese figures have risen 29-fold in China and nearly six-fold in India, compared with rises of 172% in the USA, 137% in Germany, 103% in the United Kingdom and only 62% in Japan.[2]

Global multinational corporation (MNC)'s stronger management capabilities allowed them to benefit most from such trends[3] and to leverage advantages through heavy foreign direct investment (FDI) in EMs. China produced 24 million cars in 2016, compared with 5.9 million and 4.1 million, respectively, in Germany and the USA,[4] but VW's and GM's impressive entries in China kept them one step ahead. However as EM multi-nationals (EMMs) have gone global too, their strategies have severely impacted less pro-active incumbents and indeed the world economy.

IMPACT OF SHIFTING GEOGRAPHICAL TRENDS ON TOP GLOBAL PLAYERS

Weighted by sales revenues, Japan overtook both the USA and Europe (EU plus Switzerland) in 1995 in terms of its number of *Fortune* top global 500 corporates: 35% of all revenues, compared with the USA at 31% and Europe at 29%.[5] By 2005, as Japan's share fell to 14%, the USA and Europe each held 37%, but BRIC countries had advanced from about 1% to just over 4%. In July 2018, 120 top 500s were from China, compared with the USA (126), Japan (52), Germany (32), France (28), the United Kingdom (21), S. Korea (16), the Netherlands (15), Switzerland (14), and Canada (12): i.e., 436 (87%) from just ten countries. In 2017, China had only 109, other major countries including: India, Brazil, and Australia (each with 7 top 500s), Spain (9), Taiwan (6), Russia (4), and Singapore and Sweden (both 3).

Numbers of global top MNCs have been influenced by changing national competitiveness factors. These are charted annually by the World Economic Forum, based on 12 key metric clusters. The 2018–2019 rankings (being still fairly consistent with 2008–2009 rankings) were: (1) USA, (2) Singapore, (3) Germany, (4) Switzerland, (5) Japan, (6) the Netherlands, (7) Hong Kong, (8) United Kingdom, (9) Sweden, and (10) Denmark, with China ranked at 28th (compared with 30th earlier). Enjoying business and government policy conditions as conducive as the USA's, Switzerland punched above its weight with 14, compared with only 3 expected on a purchasing power parity-adjusted GDP basis. Netherlands had 15 vs 5 on par expectations; though Singapore, Sweden, Spain, and Australia were roughly on par.

SECTORAL IMPACTS OF SHIFTING NATIONAL COMPETITIVE ADVANTAGES

As global consolidation progresses, G7s inevitably cede competitive advantage in more sectors to newly industrialised countries such as South Korea, China, and India. By 2001, China had gained advantages in TV cameras, video recording, computer parts and accessories, integrated circuits, and photocopiers; India in software; South Korea in TV cameras, computer parts and accessories, air conditioning, light vessels, and video recording parts; Thailand in air vacuum pumps, motor vehicle parts, electric motors, and epoxy resins; and Indonesia in paper, men's suits, footwear, and refined copper.[6]

As Adam Smith's division of labour now happens globally, Ricardo's traditional concept of relative comparative advantage helps determine sectors G7s may still hope to dominate. Table 9.2 illustrates countries' '*revealed comparative advantage*' figures. Terms of trade and exchange rates inevitably change to ensure that no country can remain super-competitive in more than a select, diminishing number of sectors. The USA is relatively strong in sectors such as aerospace and cereals; Japan in vehicles and ship building; Germany in vehicles and pharmaceuticals; Switzerland in pharmaceuticals, scientific instruments, and watches; South Korea in ship building and electricals; Australia and India in staples; China in knitted apparel and electricals; and Russia in mineral fuels and cereals. Such trends typically impact high global concentration ratio (GCR4) sectors first; less globalised sectors, especially local and public services, may remain isolated far longer. More tightly segmented analyses may also be necessary.

Table 9.2 Indexes of revealed comparative advantages (RCAs) for selected products in 2018

Sector	*USA*	*Japan*	*UK*	*Swiss*	*Germany*	*Australia*	*China*	*India*	*Russia*	*South Korea*
Cereals	2.19	0.00	0.16	0.00	0.21	3.38	0.06	4.12	4.07	0.00
Beverages	0.82	0.18	3.36	1.00	0.68	1.54	0.15	0.18	0.17	0.23
Min. fuels	0.90	0.13	0.72	0.06	0.16	2.70	0.15	1.12	4.13	0.61
Pharma.	0.97	0.24	2.04	8.00	2.08	0.38	0.12	1.41	0.04	0.19
Vehicles	0.99	2.66	1.44	0.13	2.21	0.08	0.38	0.71	0.09	1.26
Ships	0.84	2.61	0.44	0.00	0.86	0.31	1.51	1.65	0.26	5.13
Electricals	0.74	1.03	0.40	0.31	0.73	0.01	1.85	0.24	0.09	2.16
Sci. equip	1.70	1.76	1.24	1.75	1.60	0.38	0.91	0.29	0.13	1.45
Watches	0.35	0.47	0.80	25.8	0.45	0.15	0.70	0.12	0	0.03
Apparel	0.14	0.03	0.64	0.25	0.56	0.00	2.37	1.82	0.04	0.13

Source: International Trade Center (ITC). For comparison with 2013 figures calculated from the same ITC source for the first eight countries shown, see Grant, R.M., *Contemporary Strategy Analysis*, Wiley, Chichester, 2019, p. 274 and for this text's excellent discussion.

Note: Country X's revealed comparative advantage here is Country X's share of world exports in that product/Country X's share of world exports in all products.

DRIVERS OF NATIONAL COMPETITIVE ADVANTAGE

Traditional Ricardian analysis focused on country factor endowments, such as natural resource advantages and wage levels. These can still become overriding in more labour intense sectors or where resources are scarce. China is now ceding business to Vietnam and other countries with even lower labour costs.

Porter's model concurred, but identified three further key issues effecting national comparative advantage (NCA).[7] Countries encouraging domestic monopolists paradoxically often lose out. National champions may generate better margins for a time, but, lacking exposure to global best practices, risk complacency, and often succumb once global rivalry sets in with a vengeance. To win at the Olympics, it can help to match yourself against strong home rivals. Vigorous local rivalry (rather than excessive monopoly power) contributes to NCA. Secondly, in many sectors, final assemblers represent only a modest proportion of value-added: so powerful clusters of related, supporting industries, such as Toyota City or Silicon Valley (either upstream or downstream) also prove important. Finally, as Nokia found in Finland in mobile phones, relatively more demanding customers at home may also raise your game: this can stand you in good stead once global customers everywhere demand similarly exacting standards.

Though empirically well documented, Porter's data for mobile phones have become outdated; but Nokia's subsequent demise in mobile phones also highlights a lacuna in his model. As Nokia globalised, Finland (unsurprisingly) decreased to under 1% of Nokia's revenues. Our global winners model, shown in Figure 3.7, highlighted four phases. NCA may be important during earlier stages of internationalisation, but inevitably becomes less strategically significant as MNCs fully globalise and become geographically rootless. As a strategist, Porter surprisingly downplays the importance of companies' global strategies. There was perhaps a time when we could look at the issue of national comparative advantage at a more macro-country level, paying less attention to individual players. Today, though, global players are so large, relative to the size of countries, that the performance of their global strategies can no longer be ignored. Nokia subsequently lost out to Apple, Samsung from the USA and South Korea, then to rising EM champions from China, destroying Nokia's and Finland's positions in mobile phones. Any semblance of Finland's NCAs has gone. To understand what is happening at the country level, Porter's diamond framework requires amending, as posited in Figure 3.8 and discussed in Chapter 3, and applied in Figures 9.1 and 9.2, placing key firms' global strategies firmly at the heart of matters.

British companies like Rover lost out in cars mainly because of inadequate global strategies. Porter's drivers (in the two outer rings) capture some elements of this sorry story. Simply merging Britain's national players, thereby *reducing* local rivalry, did not work. British customers were relatively less demanding, but this didn't help. Britain's failure hinged largely, however, on the Rover's virtual strategic collapse in 1978, avoided by sensibly switching to a defensive cross-border strategic alliance with Honda. BMW's cross-border acquisition of Rover failed our strategic acid tests (as discussed in Chapter 8), sealing the fate of Britain's volume cars.

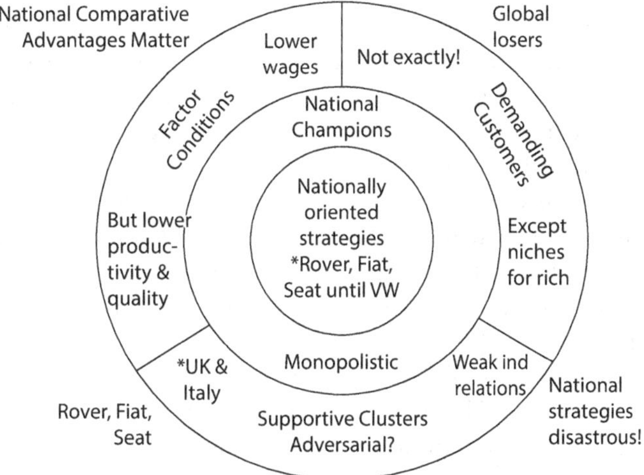

Figure 9.1 National comparative advantages, former losers in the global car industry.

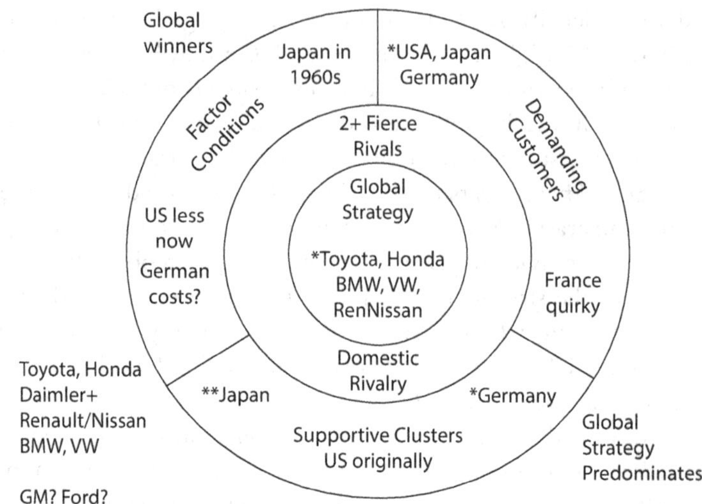

Figure 9.2 National comparative advantages, global car industry winners.

National champion strategies failed in other countries too. Spain's SEAT was saved from bankruptcy only by switching to a well conceived strategic alliance with VW, and then by VW's platform-based acquisition, which passed our acid tests with flying colours. The Czech Republic's Skoda was formerly the butt of jokes. Acquired and well integrated by VW, it has proved formidable. Nationally monopolistic and weak internationally, Fiat prior to Marchionne was almost bankrupt. Italian vehicle car production in 2013 was down to under 0.4 million. By 2016, Italy had dropped out of the top 20, whilst China's car production had climbed to 24 million.[8] In 2019, Fiat's future depended on its global megamerger with Chrysler, and on whether it can imitate Renault's alliance success with Nissan, as opposed to Daimler's more catastrophic M&A approach. In the wake of Marchionne's death, everything depends on whether Fiat Chrysler's merger with PSA can achieve sufficient integration to bolster their now more powerful global position.

Positive 'diamond' drivers shown in Figure 9.2's outer circles contributed to Japan's and Germany's competitive successes; but, more important, have been the coherent global strategies of Toyota, Honda, VW, and BMW. Japan and Germany produced 7.5 million and 5.5 million vehicles in 2016, compared with the USA down to 4.1 million. GM's demise (like Nokia's) reflected inadequate responses to such global contenders; conversely, its subsequent turnaround reflects its successful joint venture in China. The industry's future now hinges upon the Chinese market, where VW's joint venture likewise enhances its competitive position. Former monopolistic domestic conditions in India sapped NCA to the point of dependency upon 1958 licensed technology. Yet following Suzuki's hugely successful strategic alliance at

Maruti (now a full M&A), and counterstrategies by Tata (for example, acquiring Jaguar/Land Rover), India's NCA has been transformed, driven by globally orientated strategies.

As global consolidation proceeds and as global oligopoly players gradually predominate in most nations, NCAs and key players' global strategies require to be assessed together. As NCAs shift further favouring emerging markets, this calls for deeper understanding of key EMM's global strategies.

EARLY EMERGING MARKET MULTI-NATIONAL STRATEGIES COMING FROM BEHIND

Strong companies from emerging markets may deploy global strategies and orientations, analysed, so far, mainly from an incumbent advanced country perspective; but strategic 'mirroring' – the assumption that rivals, from asymmetric positions, will mirror your own strategic thinking, attitudes, and values – may likely prove naïve.[9] Even Toyota[10] recognised the foolishness of going head-to-head with mighty US incumbents, GM and Ford, earlier on. By avoiding me-too strategies and developing distinctive *Toyota principles*, they laid more robust foundations for later global supremacy.

Japan's Ministry for International Trade and Industry,[11] in those early days, aided Japanese car companies by initially eschewing US-advocated open trade and FDI policies. Static equilibrium economics perspectives discouraged Japan's focus on capital-intensive sectors; yet from a longer-term dynamic perspective, sectors such as cars crucially offered higher value-added and growth. Europeans in commercial aircraft similarly invoked 'strategic trade theory' to support Airbus' challenge to Boeing. They concurred with the USA on the desirability of free open international markets in the longer term. Yet, they too essentially argued: if we allow US car companies immediate unfettered trade and FDI access, this would destroy our embryonic industry and allow Boeing undesirably high global monopoly power. Breathing space for new entrants had to be allowed, after which open trade and FDI was fair and reasonable. Such geopolitical deals ultimately led to conditions, ripe for more acceptable global oligopoly plays and counter plays. Today, emerging countries such as China are already world trade organisation (WTO) members and world tariffs are much lower. Yet their perspective is as dynamic and long-term as Japan's, so strategic trade theory may still be reinvoked, particularly with post-Trump America reverting to mercantilism.

Dawar and Frost's (1999) framework[12] encapsulated more defensive stances earlier advocated for EM players to counter aggressive advanced country MNCs. For more heterogenous products or services customerised to the home market, emerging market *defenders* (like Goupe Bimbo, the Mexican Bread manufacturer, or Shanghai Jaheva, the Chinese cosmetics manufacturer) initially niched tightly and defensively at home, avoiding head-on competition with foreign MNCs. Where globalisation was already more advanced, other *dodgers* types (such as the Russian PC manufacturer Vist Group) opted for joint ventures with these MNCs, focusing on complementary stages of the value chain. Where technology was more easily transferable, a further *extenders* option entailed extending competences to similar products and services at home. This route was used by Jollibee [Fast] Foods in the Philippines, Televisa o Mexico in media, and by India's Asian Paints. A final route taken by *contenders* (such as Indonesia's Indah Kiat Pulp) was to take their products or services abroad to culturally similar markets, allowing them to compete more aggressively with foreign MNCs. This route was initially taken also by Mexico's Cemex in cement, though Cemex later adopted a more fully fledged FDI-based global strategy.

NEW EMERGING MARKET GLOBAL CHAMPIONS

Emerging Market Multinationals (EMMs) have clearly moved on. EMMs, such as Gazprom, Sinopec, Petrobras, and Pemex, have emerged as global champions, controlling 41% of all cross-border investment.[13] In 2018, 25% of *Fortune*'s Top Global 500 firms were Chinese.

INSEAD researchers identified four main types, based on 39 well chosen EMM cases.[14] In the short term, several focused on customers in other EMs similar to their own, either through leveraging their own unique capabilities, knowledge of low-income customers, or through niche customerisation (aided by 'frugal' innovations). Examples of the former included Asian Paints, Aramex, and Savola Foods; of the latter, Dabur, Marico, Mavi, and Mitac. Others (such as Chigo, Infosys, Mahindra Tractors, Midea, and Temsa) painstakingly focused on dissimilar developed markets through cost leadership, lower wages, scale or innovative business models, or, alternatively, on creating global brands. This could either be innovation-led, as at Haier, HTC, or LG, or M&A orientated, as at Apollo Tyres, Arcelik, Lenovo, or Tata. McKinsey further identified five success factors associated with new Asian EMMs:

1. Aggressive reinvestment aided by dividend payout rates typically just under half developed market companies, growing fixed assets at 12% per annum vs 7%.
2. Agile decision making, thanks to more concentrated ownership levels.
3. More active resource reallocation – 42% of their capital being turned over a seven year time period, as compared with 35% for US companies.
4. Focusing more on the needs of fast growing emerging market middle classes.
5. Accelerating innovation, with patent filings growing three times faster than for advanced countries.

McKinsey's exemplars have become demonstrably more global and innovative. Supported by a huge Indian research and development (R&D) centre, China's Huawei ranked as the fifth most innovative company worldwide. With overseas revenues up from 4% in 2000 to 67% in 2012, my field interviews from 1996 corroborated their pro-active early global strategy.[15] McKinsey's second example, India's Bharat Forge, rated as the second largest forge in the world. Following M&A in Germany, Sweden, the USA, and China, it has plants across India, Europe, the USA, and China. Again, my factory tours and interviews with their top executives in 2011 corroborated their remarkably pro-active innovation and global stances.

Guillen and Garcia-Canal identified several leading EMM global players, analysed in Table 9.3, and their key success factors: catering to tight *niches*, whilst then *scaling to win* and *acquiring smart* in several instances. Such findings complement INSEAD and McKinsey success frameworks, though all three success models must be viewed in relation to sectors' global consolidation stages. In aerospace, Embraer's successful global niche strategy, mirrored that of virtual global duopolists, only to be acquired by Boeing in 2019; equally, Modelo was finally acquired by AB-Inbev in 2012, its US operations then being hived off to Constellation Brands a year later. Infosys and Widpro,

Table 9.3 Successful global EMMs

Global #	*Country*	*Company*	*Sector*	*Company*	*Sector*
No 1s	Argentina	Arcor	Candy		
	Brazil	JBS	Meat processing	Embraer[a]	Regional jets
		Braskem	Sugarcane-bioplastics	Cosam	Biofuels
	Mexico	Bimbo	Bread and bakeries	Cemex	Ready-mix concrete
	Russia	Gazprom	Energy exc. oil		
	S. Korea	Samsung[a]	Consumer electronics		
No 2s	Taiwan	Acer			
No 3s	Argentina	Teneris	Seamless tubes		
	Brazil	Vale[a]	Mining		
No 4s	Dubai	DP World	Port operators		
No 5s	India	Infosys	Information services	Widpro[a]	Outsourcing services
Niche	Brazil	Natura Cosmeticos	Ecological cosmetics		
	Mexico	Modelo	Beer		

Source: Analysis of data from Guillen and Garcia-Canal, *Emerging Markets Rule: Growth Strategies of the New Global Giants*, McGraw-Hill, New York, 2013:3 (Analysed).

a Also visited and interviewed at headquarters by me in Brazil (2012), S. Korea (1995), and India (2011). Embraer was, however, acquired by Boeing in January 2019; and Modelo by AB-Inbev in June 2012, with US operations sold to Constellation Brands a year later.

discussed in Chapter 10, and DP World are not quite global leaders; and in less globally concentrated sectors, EMMs such as Arcor may so far have niched more regionally.

Other examples of EM global challengers would include Russia's Lukoil, with $144 billion revenues in 2014; Malaysia's Petronas ($79 billion); Turkey's Koc Holdings ($36 billion); Thailand's Charoen Pokphand ($12 billion); Mexico's Alpha ($17 billion); South Africa's Sasol ($11 billion); Indonesia's Goden Agri-Resources ($8 billion); or Philippines' Jollibee ($2 billion).[16]

NOTES

1 *The Economist* (2019). *Pocket World in Figures*, p. 45.
2 Analysis of figures from IMF Data Mapper, GDP/capital, current prices.
3 Bloom, N. et al. (2012). 'Management practices across firms and countries', *Academy of Management Perspectives*, February, pp. 12–33. Based on quantified comparisons between 5441 domestic and 2482 foreign multi-nationals. See particularly figure on p. 23.
4 *The Economist* (2016). *Pocket World in Figures*, p. 73.
5 Stewart, B.J. and Morrison, A.J. (2010). 'The globe: A cautionary tale for emerging market giants', *Harvard Business Review*, 88, p. 101.
6 Lasserre, P. and Schutte, H. (2006: 42). *Strategies for Asia Pacific*. New York: Palgrave Macmillan.
7 Porter, M.E. (1990). *National Competitive Advantage*. London: Macmillan; Porter, M.E. (1990: 77). 'The competitive advantage of nations', *Harvard Business Review*, March–April, pp. 73–93.
8 *The Economist* (2019). *Pocket World in Figures*. London.
9 Shirreff, R. (2016). *2017: War with Russia. An Urgent Warning from Senior Military Command*. London: Coronet, Hodder & Stoughton.
10 Interviewed in Tokyo in 1983 and 1995.
11 Interviewed in 1983, though by then their policies emphasised open trade.
12 Dawar, N. and Frost, T. (1999). 'Survival strategies for local players competing with giants', *Harvard Business Review*, 77 (2), pp. 119–129.
13 Guillen, M.F. and Ontiveros, E. (2012). *Global Turning Points*. New York: Cambridge University Press. See Guillen, M.F. and Garcia-Canal, E. (2013). *Emerging Markets Rule: Growth Strategies of the New Global Giants*. New York: McGraw-Hill, p. 3 for tabulated global leaders by sector.
14 Chattopadhyay, A. and Bartra, R. (2012). *The New Emerging Market Multinationals: Four Strategies for Disrupting Markets and Building Brands*. New York: McGraw-Hill.
15 I interviewed Huawei regarding its approach to global strategy and strategic investment decisions when lecturing at Shenzhen University in 1996. They were extraordinarily sensitive, disallowing tape recordings; but their pro-active interest in global strategy was refreshing. Half-way through the interview, they realised that I had comparable strategic investment decisions data for UK, USA, German, and Japanese MNCs. In contrast to many Russian companies, almost indifferent to internationalisation issues, I was wheeled in to lecture on comparative strategic investment decisions to their board that same lunchtime! Having disallowed all my tape recordings, they now requested: '*Could my lecture be videoed for training purposes?*' Safeguarding confidentiality, I merely confirm their early pro-active determined global disposition.
16 Several of these have high % of foreign revenues and presence in several countries as detailed in Lasserre, P. (2018). *Global Strategic Management*. London: Palgrave, p. 42.

10

CHINESE, INDIAN, RUSSIAN, AND BRAZILIAN GLOBAL CHAMPIONS

LATIN AMERICAN EMERGING MARKET MULTINATIONALS' GLOBAL STRATEGIES

My 2012 field research endorsed Guillen and Garcia-Canal's elaborated example of Brazil's Embraer's global niching.[1] Canada's Bombardier was first in the late 1980s to attack Boeing/Airbus' duopoly, by focusing on small regional jets with just 50 seats. Embraer followed with 50- and 37-seater models. Once, like China's Haier, state-owned, it too was strong operationally. It had halved assembly times, improved supply logistics and response times, and been nimbler than rivals as commuter airlines switched from turboprops to jets. As customers extended to major carriers worldwide, its market share climbed. Assembly and service networks were established in Europe, the USA, and also China supported by an equity joint venture (JV) with China's AVIC.[2] AVIC, Russia's Sukhoi, and Mitsubishi were all trying to enter, but Embraer was highly innovative, pioneering ethanol-based jets. Its pro-active global niche strategy mirrored those of German and British companies, discussed in Chapter 8, whilst exploiting Brazil's emerging market national competitive advantages (NCAs) to offset the difficulty of coming from behind technologically. Boeing, nevertheless, acquired Embraer in January 2019.

What is surprising, though, is how several Latin American emerging market multinationals (EMMs) have managed to transform sectors, previously considered internationally fragmented, becoming essentially *quasi-global shapers*. Argentina's Arcor, for example, was a tiny family start-up in 1951. Exports began in the 1960s and foreign direct investment (FDI), distribution and production, in the mid-1970s. Their slogan is '*From a candy, Arcor made the world*'. By 2011, aside from exports to 120 countries, they operated 40 plants in Argentina, Brazil, Chile, Peru, and Mexico.[3] Simultaneously, their scope has extended both vertically and in product range terms, becoming more than private-label distributors. Their story was a determined, international, pro-active bid for scale, complemented by a growing reputation for efficiency, quality, and reliability, and FDI in addition to trade: '*When we saw an opening, we were prepared to compete head to head with the multinationals*'.[4]

Economists traditionally viewed cement as internationally fragmented: drivers, such as manufacturing scale or technological opportunities were low, whilst, on the other hand, localisation pressures were high, not least in terms of transport, storage, and distribution costs. Taking an international trade perspective, American economists confidently placed cement in their least global boxes, appropriate only for national strategy orientations. Yet Mexico's Cemex emerged as a global consolidator, less by trade (recognising such impediments), but by turning instead to FDI. It first nurtured a highly efficient business model originally in the fast growing Mexican market, supported by low wages and good access to American markets. Strong cash-flows and scale economies (including purchasing) facilitated mergers and acquisitions (M&A) in addition to rapid inorganic growth.

Guillen and Garcia-Canal's example of Mexico's Bimbo in bread is similarly instructive. Bread too was traditionally regarded as a classic sector exhibiting low manufacturing scale economies, fragmentation, and negligible international trade. High transport/storage costs and short shelf-lives led to bread being frequently baked within a locus typically under 50 miles. At the low end of the market, sliced bread allowed greater scale economies, but still limited loci of operations. The United States leader Sara Lee pioneered mass production, distribution, and marketing, gleaning some scale economies as revenues climbed to $17 billion by 2001. Yet national leadership strategies in mature markets proved no panacea; its margins failed to offset its capital intensity and, after over-diversifying, it finally re-trenched to core areas, shedding nearly three quarters of its workforce. Having lost direction, its results proved unacceptable, dictating exit.

The buyer, by contrast, was Bimbo, founded in Mexico City in 1945 by a Spanish immigrant, who started with nothing but a small cake shop. With family members, 39 employees, and five delivery vehicles, they sold four types of bread. They expanded throughout Mexico in the 1960s and throughout Latin America in the 1970s and 1980s. Exports to the United States were followed by distribution deals with Sara Lee and by a dozen US mergers and acquisitions (M&A) from 1996 onwards.[5] In China, they focused on bread-based snacks. The global bread market is worth over $400 billion[6] and Bimbo focuses on health-conscious consumers, eliminating transfats from all offerings worldwide. As a family firm, they have provided a more long-term, hands-on and globally committed managerial model. By 2011, they produced, distributed, and marketed '*global and local bread products using 100 efficient local plants, tens of thousands of trucks, and over one million points of sale in 18 countries*'.[7] Their portfolio extended to 150 local brands. As the son of the founder clarified: '*We travel around the globe looking closely at all practices in baking plants. We can compare everywhere, and we can detect a good number of opportunities to raise productivity*'.[8] Mopping up Sara Lee brought more iconic brands, further consolidating their position as the world's largest bread company. Supported by FDI, Bimbo remains a highly locally-adapted global transnational in a market offering robust long-term prospects.

INDIAN EMMs IN EMERGING NEW SECTORS: IT SERVICES

Guillan and Garcia-Canal's two Indian examples, Infosys and Wipro,[9] are both drawn from information technology (IT) outsourcing services. Like many recent German hidden champions (discussed in Chapter 8), both were almost 'born global', taking off as customers everywhere sought solutions to Y2K computer bug-bears. Though not quite global top 3s, such EMMs benefitted from India's NCAs. Only Tata Consultancy Services (TCSs) ranked among global top ten IT service firms in 2014 (at No 6). Top Indian IT firms earned revenues of $146 billion in 2015 ($98 billion being from abroad), increasing their share of a global market valued at $1.3 trillion in 2014.[10] Their share of global offshoring IT-Business Process Outsourcing was about 55%; of offshored engineering, research and development (R&D) and product development about 22%; with IT contributing almost 10% of India's Gross Domestic Product (GDP).[11] Mastek, only India's global top 20 player, created the IT backbone for Britain's National Health Service.[12]

This newborn industry, in 1981, provided ideal conditions for globally pro-active Indian start-ups. The 24/7 servicing of advanced country clients' needs could be accommodated in English, handled at low cost, as time-shifting facilitated overnight maintenance/customerised services. Foreign multi-nationals set up global servicing centres in India during the 2000s, benefitting from low wages and well educated professionals, and contributed further infrastructure and training. Geographical barriers almost evaporated:

> Our industry has been global from day one because when we all began in the IT industry, there was no Indian IT industry and thus there was no competition. But we knew we had a great human capital advantage and that the fulfillment of that advantage had to be global. For people like us, going global was not a choice...To improve our ability to connect with Infosys customers, we have to get geographically closer to them. This will require a much more local presence and much more diversity than we currently have.
>
> Nandan Nilekani, Infosys' Co-founder, 2008.[13]

By 2008, Infosys were a $4 billion company, with 98% of revenue from international clients – over 60% from North America and 26% from Europe. Infosys invested in engineering talent, typically deploying six months training, '*learning how to get technical jobs done more efficiently*'.[14] In 2012–2013, they received almost 3.8 million applications for 37,000 vacancies, and provided 1.4 million persons days of training.[15] This facilitated upscaling waves of improving technologies and a *global delivery model*:

> The customer gets better value for money because, in a typical project, only about 20–25% of the effort is added near the customer in the development world, and 75–80% of the value is added from countries like India where the cost of software development is lower.[16]

TCS and Wipro each had only 1.7% global market shares, compared with IBM at 13%.[17] TCS ranked No 1 in India, compared with Infosys and Wipro at 4th and 5th, and had an even greater network of 19 global innovation labs located in India, the USA, and the United Kingdom, focused on software engineering and verticals such as insurance and telecommunications.[18] Based on my interviews with Wipro strategic planners in Bangalore in 2006 and 2011,[19] I would endorse its combination of global niching with innovation orientation. All three top Indian EMMs are well niched and globally supported.

INDIAN EMMs IN MATURE GLOBAL SECTORS

Since 2000, around two-thirds of Indian FDI has been directed upmarket to highly developed countries such as the USA, the United Kingdom, and Germany, using both greenfield sites (GFSs) and M&A.[20] During 2004–2009, some 90 Indian companies invested in 127 greenfield projects in the USA. Tata Motors, visited and interviewed in 2011, deployed cross-borders M&A such as Daewoo trucks and Land Rover/Jaguar. Mahindra & Mahindra, Piramal, Godrej, Tata Tea, Indian Hotels, Tata Chemicals, TCS, and Apollo Tyres[21] likewise used M&A extensively. Such players became adept at taking over foreign companies, supporting them in India, but also genuinely helping to take them into other emerging markets.[22] Tata Tea extended Tetley's brand to China, where neither company was previously present, and to Southern Asia and the Middle East. Apollo Tyres extended Dunlop's brand into Africa. Asian Paints acquired SCIB Chemicals in Egypt in 2000, extending operations throughout the Middle East. At a more regional level, Godrej upgraded and internationalised Kinky and Rapidol. Tata has helped Land Rover/Jaguar in China as well as India.

In 1976, Lakshmi Mittal, for example, was sent to turnaround operations at his family's steel acquisition in Indonesia. As his CFO, Aditya Mittal explained: '*It's simple and strong management. First you have to diagnose what is the real issue, and then you have to make sure that the management team and company is completely focused on resolving that critical issue*'. In Indonesia and later in Trinidad & Tobago (1989), Mexico (1992), and Kazakhstan (1995), Mittal demonstrated skills dealing with daunting governments, acquiring, and turning around rundown plants. Leveraging funds and cross-border M&A competences, Mittal followed suit in advanced countries, Canada (1994), the USA (1998), and France (1998), adding further EM acquisitions in Romania, Algeria, the Czech Republic, Poland, Bosnia, Macedonia, the Ukraine, and China between 2000 and 2005.[23] Having invested boldly during downturns, Mittal emerged strong enough as markets resurged to drive through the $23 billion hostile acquisition of Arcelor, the world's 2nd largest steel company. ArcelorMittal was bigger than the next three combined.[24]

As late as 2000, steelmaking had been a textbook '*very fragmented industry: the world's top 5 producers accounted for only 14% of production. Companies such as Nucor in the US, Thyssen-Krupp in Germany as well as Mittal and Tata responded by buying up weaker players internationally. By 2009, the top 5 producers accounted for 20% of world production. New steel giant ArcelorMittal alone accounted for about 10% of world production*'.[25] In 2006, Tata Steel acquired steelmaker Corus, itself resulting from an earlier British-Dutch $7.6 billion merger. Essar Steel of India invested almost $2 billion in a greenfield integrated steel plant during 2008–2012. Steel has been a classic case of EMMs consolidating formerly fragmented industries. Based on tonnage, the global concentration ratio (CR4) rose from 11% in 1995 to 20% in 2007 and the global CR10 from 21% to 30%.[26] The next largest players in 2007 were Japan's Nippon Steel and JFE Holdings, S. Korea's Posco, China's Baosteel, then India's Tata/Corus. Led by Severstal and Evraz, Russia became the second largest steel exporting country in 2009.[27] China's share of world steel capacity accelerated to over 40% in 2009, as they became the 4th largest steel exporter.

EMM strategies can, though, prove risky; India's Suzlon Energy, in 2013, the world's 5th largest turbine supplier, however, went bankrupt in 2019, despite its global strategy.[28] In July 2019, Sanjeev Gupta's Liberty Steel completed its E740 million acquisition of ArcelorMittal's European assets, its largest deal since it began buying up distressed steel assets in 2015, turning them into one of the largest steelmakers globally: '*These businesses move us up the scale to being a proper [fully vertically integrated] global contender*'.[29]

HOW INDIA'S EMM BHARAT FORGE CONSOLIDATED FORGINGS AND HOW WE IN BRITAIN LOST OUT

Even richer, as a canary-in-the-cage dire cautionary tale for Western companies facing internationally fragmented sectors, has been the case of Bharat Forge. Established in 1961, it exploited India's liberalisation from 1991. By 2007, it operated ten plants in six countries and was already global No 2 in forgings.[30] When I visited India's Bharat Forge in Pune in 2011, their chief executive officer (CEO) Baba Kalyani's first question to me was pointedly personal: '*How did you guys [in Britain, at GKN Forgings] blow it?*'

Kalyani knew of my engineering experience at GKN Forgings between 1974 and 1978, when we had held 45% of the United Kingdom (UK) market. I'd lived with that history, my colleague Reg Shelley having supplied board directors with performance statistics since 1945, and Peter Jarrett, our strategic planner, having retained strategic plans going back years. Our archives recounted events since Garrington's acquisition in 1919.[31] My doctoral research on forgings in the 1980s,[32] followed up in the 1990s, had taken me to top US and Japanese rivals, and twice to Germany's Peddinghaus, prior to its takeover by Bharat Forge. To convey Bharat Forge's lessons, I must share first our advanced country incumbent perspective.

GKN Forgings (GKNF) had eight major forging plants in 1974, Garrington's at over 2000 people being our largest and the site of our headquarters. Reg Shelley recalled CEO Ray Brooke's charisma during the 1950s and 1960s, driving ahead with volume lines and huge modern presses in support of Britain's then fast growing car and truck industries. Our highly automated B5 production line became a world showpiece, much photographed by Japanese rivals delving into its secrets. Aside from us, forgings were fragmented. There were over 100 smaller forgers in Britain alone, and this seemed set to continue. Our hammers and presses were labour intensive, yielding modest scale economies. As in most UK forges visited, piecework afforded incentives for tough manual work in hot, noisy conditions, akin to Dante's *Inferno*. We wore earplugs, doing fry-ups on red hot forgings during breaks. Tom Brown, coming from operations, recalled heavy drinking, even sleeping on night shifts, seven canteens different levels of staff on single sites, an obsession with '*tons-out-the-gate*', frequently caving in on relentless labour disputes, inducing ostrich attitudes.[33] Our large process and product development (P&PD) department was strong on applied engineering, but spread thinly over eight factories, including hundreds of forges and presses. We struggled to impact on productivity.

By the 1970s, we were no longer world class. P&PD was no substitute for greater operational commitment, evidenced in all three Japanese forges visited in 1983. Jarrett admitted that our impressive strategic and technological plans often disguised wishful thinking. They included big investment budgets, lending credence to financial turnaround strategies, projecting unrealistic productivity improvements. By contrast, the 'strategic plan' of our Japanese rival comprised an old fashioned engineering drawing, subdivided into multiple boxes. These began simply with market share targets, then yield and productivity targets; yet so prolific and detailed that pertinent targets were set down next to every hammer and press, such that progress was visibly monitored. Teams wore yellow military style uniforms. Driven by positive non-negotiable values and 'quality circles', they took pride in daily drills, recording progress, as yield rates and productivity rose, and as tool change times (crucial to just-in-time) fell relentlessly. Operationally, they were outstanding.

Sadly, we failed to recognise looming international threats. Responding to P&PD's new processes, the superintendent of our flagship B5 line reportedly pronounced: *I've only ten years to go before retirement and nobody's putting new processes onto my lines'*. Our trade union warned that if our P&PD membership fell by just one more, our work would be blocked in every single GKNF factory. Top GKNF management urged compliance and was uninspiring. After one rare visit, our chairman told our Chief Engineer Ron Dawson: '*You know the most interesting thing I've seen today is the colour of your shirt*'. His message went down like a lead balloon.[34] The outcome of technological complacency[35] was horrendous. I've never heard any manager or union representative take responsibility, but every single job was ultimately lost at GKN Forgings, painfully, decade by decade.[36] More top-level independent and often dramatic corroboration is provided by a former experienced GKN director, Tom Brown, who overlapped with me at GKN Forgings.[37]

Economics seemingly favoured international fragmentation, the UK export ratio being under 3%. Lowish value, heavy, bulky products like forgings rendered trade difficult; so Jarrett scrupulously examined the FDI alternative where GKN was highly proficient. Yet, since World War II only one major new forge had been opened in Europe (in Scandinavia) and break-even projections appeared impossible. From some economic perspectives an alternative might simply have been to continue to dominate a seemingly local national market; but a dominant national strategy proved doomed. The total UK forgings market fell from 662,000 tonnes in 1965 to 222,000 in 1983.[38] At the top end, GKNF was hit by German competitors exhibiting excellent technology and operational performances; elsewhere, rivalry was fierce from smaller home players, desperate for business. The GKN head office was not unreasonably short term: GKNF returns on capital were unpublishably low over virtually two decades. In 1978, as I boarded their helicopter, I caught the GKN Chairman Barry Heath and his personnel director's first words: '*The last of the Mohicans!*' They already knew their only option was to exit, through an ironically named *Phoenix* joint venture with British Steel. All forging plants were ultimately closed.

Part of our problem was that Britain no longer enjoyed relative comparative advantage (RCA) in forgings; this mattered despite low globalisation drivers regarding trade. When we debated this, my fellow engineer, Collin Patton, said persuasively that forgings were an appalling environment, but someone had to do it.[39] But we were wrong. I should have recalled Ricardo's theories and RCA metrics. We wrongly imagined that low trade rendered foreign competition and globalisation unimportant. My colleagues counselled me just to focus on becoming a great development engineer and all would be fine. Tragically, this was not the case: all 10,000 former colleagues from all eight factories, ultimately lost their jobs. In principle, we could have escaped demise at home by going global with FDI (in place of trade), just as we did successfully in constant velocity (CV) joints; but without relative comparative advantage, the economics did not stack up. In another fragmented sector, GKN's entire fasteners division disappeared even earlier; trade being easier, they had already been hit harder and more directly by cheaper Far Eastern rivals.[40]

Nor was it just us. Britain's entire manufacturing base has fallen steadily from 22% of Britain's GDP to 8% in 2019. US trends were similar; 40 years ago US Steel made headline news; today they are scarcely noticed.

EMMs like Bharat Forge encountered the same trade barriers as we did. However, the crucial difference was that now India really does have relative competitive advantage, and (as will be discussed), it really has exhibited a formidable, innovative business model and a determined global strategy, supported by FDI commitments. Such EMMs are now putting their tanks firmly on our lawns, whether that be Europe, America, Asia, or elsewhere. Even in more fragmented sectors, board directors had better scrutinise their sector's RCA metrics. Where sector RCAs are under 1, why would they anticipate future outcomes better than in forgings, where our legacy assets had formerly been so formidable?

Bharat Forge's global strategy perspective

I had not heard of Bharat Forge when I was working for GKNF or doing my doctoral analysis of forgings in the early 1980s. Forgings still appeared fragmented, though British forgers were ceding competitiveness to German, US, and Japanese rivals.[41] German family-owned Peddinghaus Forgings remained upmarket technologically and flourishing in 1992 when re-visited. My BRIC (Brazil, Russia, India and China) country research began only in the 1990s, but by the end of the decade, even Peddinghaus had been taken over by Bharat Forge. So how could an such an EMM overtake British and Germany forgers?

India's wage rates were far lower,[42] but Bharat Forge, visited in 2011,[43] had shared GKN Forgings' strategic and technological dilemmas. As a highly educated, trained engineer, CEO Kalyani likewise pondered whether CAD/CAM (computer aided design/computer aided manufacture) advances could ever render fully automated forging lines? These processes were scarcely amenable, so they undertook a bold experiment. For just one plant, they plumbed for total CAD/CAM-based automation. Production operators were almost totally replaced by engineers, recruited for design and development expertise, combined with superb programming skills. They programmed design and press tool changes directly: a risky bet on high technology IT programming skills, in contrast to GKNF's operational culture lauding those '*qualified by experience*' and timid leadership in the face of industrial relations difficulties.

Kalyani's pilot plant experiment worked out so well that most operators and setters were taken out. The model was then determinedly duplicated throughout their group. In 1987, their workforce was 85% blue collar; by 2000, it was 85% white collar with over 700 engineers.[44] Advanced technology and automation stepped up quality and reliability, so they could target top original equipment manufacturers and, for the first time, globally.[45]

India's low-cost, large emerging market base was advantageous for exports, but developing such a world-class business model becomes more crucial, drawing on FDI to go global. Their European market entry was facilitated by acquiring Germany's Peddinghaus, providing yet further high technology, ripe for exploiting even more globally (thus passing our two acid tests).[46] By 2008, Bharat Forge held 45% of the domestic Indian market[47] and had emerged as No 2 globally following further M&A in Sweden, the USA, and China.

Thus GKN Forgings' earlier problems were not entirely due to logistical barriers or inherent global fragmentation. GKNF's eminence 100 years earlier had been regalvanised during the years of Ray Brookes' charismatic leadership. With Britain's RCA relentlessly turning against us, we sadly could no longer demonstrate that world-class business model, which might (in contrast to our CV joints) have allowed us to go global. Bharat Forge, as an EMM, seized that global opportunity. As CEO Baba Kalyani put it very early on '*Confidence is essential to globalization...and it grows with every success*'.[48] His opening remark was astute, we in Britain had indeed '*blown it*'.

A NOTE ON RUSSIAN EMMs IN MATURE GLOBAL SECTORS

Neither of Guillen and Garcia-Canal's Russian examples, Sukhoi or Gazprom were elaborated. My interviews with two major resource-based Russian companies at director-level in 2010 and 2011 are constrained by confidentiality (as at Huawei, Embraer, and Samsung). What can, though, be emphasised about these two Russian global champions was their globality. They point blank contradicted stereotypes relating to Russian culture in relation to GLOBE's cross-cultural scores (based essentially on Hofstede's classifications). Such stereotypes did slightly apply to the dozen or so Russian small and medium sized enterprises. I had interviewed earlier in 1998. Yet such Russian EMMs, being so global, were untypical of more local companies. As one director put it: '*You have to remember that our [conglomerate] group was formed expressly to take over* [traditional] *companies, to smash those former Soviet cultures and to add value by putting in modern, more professional management. We are not the same as the Russian stereotypes you have here* [referring to GLOBE-based data]'.

When I played down their likely interest in my more financially based Chartered Institute of Management Accountants (CIMA) research project, a finance director countered: '*Do you know how many hundred CIMA accountants we employ in this group? Of course we are interested in this research*'. Another EMM pointed out that their finance director resided and worked in London, to be close to the stock exchange and city institutions. Without playing down institutional, political, and ethical differences in emerging markets, Russian EMMs armed with huge funds, playing on international financial markets, have partially converged on global oligopolistic orientations common to advanced country multinational corporations (MNCs). They too have become highly pro-active in respect to both trade and FDI, whether through greenfield site investments or cross-border M&A, and the management issues they face in EMs such as Africa come over as remarkably similar.

LESSONS FROM LEADING CHINESE EMERGING MARKET MULTINATIONALS

Even more important is the perspective of new leading Chinese EMMs, accounting for 113 *Fortune* Global 500 companies (based on top revenues) in 2010, compared with 44 in 2005. By 2013, they held three of the top four slots. China's economic growth averaged 10.2% p.a. 2003–2013, compared with 1.7% for the USA.[49] Its GDP growth still averaged almost 9% p.a. between 2008 and 2013, dwarfing triad regions, though recently falling back to 6% p.a.

China's rise reflected Deng Xiaoping's 1978 new economic development and open door policies, as they recognised their need for structural change and Western technology and investment. After Mao, Xiaoping bravely proclaimed, '*To get rich is glorious*'. With the return of Hong Kong and Macao in 1997 and 1999, China joined the World Trade Organization in 2001. FDI from foreign multi-nationals, though initially more through joint ventures, has aided training, technology, and unprecedented economic growth. Conversely, by 2003 Chinese companies had already invested $33 billion in some 7500 companies in over 160 countries.[50] In the first quarter of 2016 China accounted for $101 billion of $682 billion of worldwide cross-border M&As.[51]

As Chinese FDI outflows doubled between 2008 and 2012, the focus initially was on underdeveloped countries, 66% being concentrated on energy and metals.[52] However, Chinese MNC motivations have radically shifted from cost/efficiency and have become more market and knowledge driven.[53] Between 2007 and 2012, many Chinese M&A and investment strategies increasingly targeted top-end technology/innovation.[54] By 2014, China ranked second only to the USA in terms of venture capital investment at $15.5 billion (compared to $52 billion in the USA), ahead of Europe at $10 billion.[55] By 2014, they ranked number three globally on overall investments, with two thirds now going into services.[56]

Yip and McKern depict several examples of Chinese players becoming more innovative and pro-active more globally. Garnering cash surpluses from

China's large market, Geeley acquired Volvo, Dongfeng Motors has taken a 14% stake in Peugeot Citroen, and Lenovo has moved on to acquiring Motorola Mobility.[57] Manufacturers, like Goodbaby, global No. 1 in strollers and baby carriers, have moved on to acquiring world-class technology and brands. Its first overseas acquisitions in 2014 included CYBEX (a leading Germany child safety brand) and Eventflo in the USA. They now have design and technical centres in China, Europe, the USA, and Japan, so as to adapt to local markets.[58] Yip and McKern draw out five new traits associated with successful Chinese players: bold experimentation identifying and creating innovative opportunities; creative adaptation focusing on the needs of local markets (as for example, Hsu Fu Chi in confectionery); designing simple products for specifically targeted needs; and developing mixed teams and strong global leaders.[59]

Some powerful Chinese companies such as Huawei have still prioritised organic growth, investing heavily globally through GFSs. Their new CEO Eric Xu proclaimed in 2016 that '*the consolidation in the industry will be conducive to competition*', but Huawei itself '*will not go for large scale mergers or acquisitions*'. He noted that they would continue acquiring small companies with technology and teams boosting their own capabilities: '*That is what we have been doing over the last couple of years.*'[60] By 2013, China had gained dominant shares of several industrial sectors: mobile phones (71%); electrolytic aluminium (65%); iron (59%); flat glass (50%); construction equipment (43%); shipbuilding (41%); fertiliser (35%); autos (25%), and televisions 25%.[61]

Encountering increasing domestic competition in China, advanced country MNCs have countered by acquiring, where possible, strong rivals. Gillette's Duracell, for example, ceded Chinese market share to Chinese low-cost players during the 1990s. By 2002, its local market share had fallen to 6.5% compared to Nanfu at over 50%. Duracell then acquired Nanfu in 2003.[62] Procter and Gamble, Unilever, and Henkel likewise acquired 13 major Chinese FMCG (fast moving consumer goods) and chemical companies. Such M&As allowed advanced country MNCs to gain 80% of shampoo conditioners, 70% of lifts, 68% of passenger cars, 65% of colour cathode ray tubes, and 90% of program controlled telephone exchange markets in China.[63]

Chinese champions like Lenovo and Haier have, however, likewise countered with M&As in advanced country markets.[64] In 2016, Chinese international M&As surged, expanding into roughly 160 countries. China's $101 billion of $682 billion of worldwide cross-border M&As eclipsed its previous record for the whole of 2015, just in the first quarter of 2016.[65] This was in spite of a 14% decline worldwide overall and of a 57% decline in Chinese domestic M&As. Announced deals reached $119 billion in the first five months of 2016. Their negotiating sophistication, credibility, and aggression has increased, partly aided by Chinese funding support including now the private sector as well as the government. Up to June 2016, 13 Chinese companies made a total of $78 billion of unsolicited offers for overseas targets (compared with a record 17 in 2015) according to Dealogic. Domestic appliance manufacturer Midea, for example, made an unsolicited $5 billion takeover offer for German robotics company Kuka AG having gradually build up its stake since August 2015.[66]

Chinese EMMs like Geeley, which acquired Volvo in 2010 for E1.3 billion, have respected acquirees' know-how, allowing such targets considerable free rein. It invested $11 billion in new models, supporting Volvo with an R&D centre in Shanghai and plant in Chengdu, from which it will also be exporting to the USA.[67] In November 2016, Swedish production of Volvo's smaller 40-series moved to the new joint Geely/Volvo Luqiao factory, with the luxury S90 now planned to follow later. In the last three years, Volvo's sales have tripled as China has become its largest single-country market. Volvo and Geeley Lynk models '*are sharing the development of intensive components...that we can do without jeopardising the identities of the two cars*'.[68] R&D facilities are also shared. Geeley's M&As disseminate Volvo's technological innovations globally, so potentially pass Chapter 8's acid tests.

Many Chinese EMMs are now exploiting FDI and cross-border M&As, in addition to exports, as they bid for stronger global positions. In 2010, China's FDI into the USA was about $4.5 billion, compared with $13 billion from the USA into China; in 2015, China's investment into the USA at just over $15 billion for the first time outstripped the USA's into China, still at virtually the same level of $13 billion.[69] Post-Trump, this looks likely to be curtailed. European regulators are likewise showing signs of resistance, particularly Germany.

Fosun and other Chinese insurers have '*adopted their own versions of the so-called Berkshire Hathaway model for growth, in which premiums from the insurance business fuel new investments*'.[70] Whilst retrenching by cutting $6 billion in overseas assets in steel and mining, they are redoubling investments abroad in global financial, health, and tourism. In July/August 2016, they spent $1.4 billion acquiring four companies on three continents: Gland Pharma, China's largest healthcare M&A in India; Brazilian fund manager Rio Bravo Investments; Wolverhampton Wanderers Football Club; and a stake in Banco Comercial Português. Earlier leisure holdings include France's Club Med and Canada's Cirque du Soleil.

Even modest equity moves, such as Taiking Insurance's 13.5% stake and board position in Sotheby's, may signal fundamental global shifts. '*Sotheby's and Christie's thought they would move in and run Chinese auction houses. Now the Chinese are big players in Hong Kong, New York and London – the biter has been bit...The investment in Sotheby's is a statement of Chinese "soft power" and part of a strategy to transform and educate the wider population. The Chinese government is recognising the importance of culture in driving the economy; there are plans to build 1,200 museums in the next five years. China is also on a buy spree, which ranges from football clubs to Sotheby's, and is all part of building a bridgehead to the rest of the world'.*[71] Auction sales in China rose 17% to $2.3bn in the first half of 2016: and the Chinese share of world art purchases is now 35%, compared with USA at 27% and Britain at 21%. Chen Dongsheng's seat on Sotheby's board would give him *'a greater insight into what kinds of valuable assets – art, wine, classic cars, gems, and jewellery – can be developed next of the Chinese market'.*[72]

In terms of access into Europe, Ernst and Young ranked the United Kingdom as China's most popular M&A target, based on deal values, followed by France and Germany.[73] China is also now the United Kingdom's 4th largest trade partner after Germany, the USA, and the Netherlands. Correspondingly, China's greenfield FDI into the United Kingdom between January 2010 and September 2016 was almost $13 billion[74]: Between January 2012 and June 2016, there were 91 such M&As into the United Kingdom, with deal values almost quadrupling. These cross-border M&As split 44% property, 28% consumer, 8% financial, 7% oil and gas, 5% healthcare, 4% industrial, and 1% technology.[75]

President Xi Jinping's visit to Britain yielded some $40 billion deals. Confirmation of the Hinkley Point nuclear project maintains impetus, including several new joint ventures. Financial services seem set to benefit. Like US and Japanese MNCs, the Chinese are concerned lest Brexit sever European market access. Yet with an exchange rate down to $1.2 as of 29.8.2019, long-term Chinese investors are likely buy up strategic assets cheaply. As with India's Tata/Jaguar & Land Rover, aims may include taking UK acquirees global.

Our research into the largest 121 recent Chinese cross-border M&As worldwide suggests that their strategic aims are changing. Thirty-six percent of these were primarily motivated worldwide by market drivers vs 43% by resource seeking motives (mainly aimed at technologies) and 21% by efficiency seeking.[76] Surprisingly, these M&As appear to be paying off.

Studies of advanced country M&As have often cited failure rates as high as 50%–70%. Whilst Jarrel et al. (1988) and Healy et al. (1992)[77] claimed positive results immediately following M&As, Bruner (2002)'s more extensive analysis of 44 M&A studies found that acquirers exhibited negative returns. Sharma and Ho (2002) and Bouwman et al. (2009) similarly found that over half of their companies samples lost money during the first three years. Cross-border M&A studies are less conclusive, but Moeller and Schlingemann (2005) found combined company results tended to be worse compared with their pre-merger performances.

Outcomes in relation to domestic Chinese M&A have perhaps been more positive. Whilst Zhu and Wang (2002) study of 67 Chinese domestic M&As in 1998 suggested declines in Returns on Equity (RoE) and Returns on Assets (RoA), Bhabra and Huang (2013)'s study of 137 deals between 1997 and 2007 found that public Chinese firms earned significantly positive accounting returns around the event announcements. 433 earlier cross-border M&As for

58 emerging market companies yielded negative accounting ratio outcomes (Aybar and Ficici 2009), and Chen and Young (2010) found similar results for 39 Chinese cross-border M&As. However, more recently, Ning et al. (2014)'s study of 335 cross-border M&A between 1991 and 2010, and Tao and Liu (2016) found positive outcomes. Zhu and Moeller (2016)'s study was limited to UK targets, but was similarly positive aside from the financial sector. Our more recent global study distinguishes results by sector and also by international orientations, and likewise broadly confirms positive outcomes.

NOTES

1 Guillen, M. and Garcia-Canal, E. (2013). *Emerging Markets Rule: Growth Strategies of the New Global Giants.* New York: McGraw-Hill, pp. 29–35.
2 AVIC executives instructed in global strategy by author in Edinburgh, 12 September 2012.
3 Guillen, M. and Garcia-Canal, E. (2013). Ibid., pp. 75–79 and p. 79 for this quote and figures.
4 Ibid., p. 78. Source: www.fundinguniverse.com/company-histories (accessed 7 March 2012).
5 Ibid.
6 Ibid., pp. 22–29.
7 Ibid., p. 24, based on their 2011 interview with Pablo Elizondo Huerta, deputy CEO.
8 '*Group Bimbo*', Harvard Business School Case Study 9-707-521, p. 13.
9 For a more detailed case study of Wipro's inception and transformation see: Hamm, S. (2007). *Bangalore Tiger: How Indian Tech Upstart Wipro is Rewriting the Rules of Global Competition.* New York: McGraw-Hill, pp. 31–44.
10 Jain, V.K. (2017). *Global Strategy: Competing in the Connected Economy.* London: Routledge, pp. 258–268, drawing on Gartner and NASSCOM, IT-BPM Sector in India, February 2015. IT services were defined to include business process outsourcing and engineering and R&D.
11 Ibid., pp. 258 & 261.
12 Ibid., p. 261.
13 Kumar, N. (2009). *India's Global Powerhouses: How They Are Taking On the World.* Boston: Harvard Business Press, pp. 65–66 & 70–71.
14 Guillen, M. and Garcia-Canal, E. (2013). Ibid., p. 38, based on their 2012 interview with S.D. Shibulal, CEO, Infosys.
15 Jain, V.K. (2017). Ibid., pp. 263–264. TCS likewise spent about 6% of its earnings on training, providing at least 14 days of training p.a. to employees.
16 Berger, R., Dutta, S., Raffel, T. and Samuels, G. (2008). *Innovating at the To: How Global CEOs Drive Innovation for Growth and Profit.* New York: Palgrave Macmillan, p. 174.
17 Guillen, M. and Garcia-Canal, E. (2013). Ibid., p. 35 puts the global IT services market at $300 billion, IBM's revenues at $40 billion with TCS and Wipro each at one-eighth, so at $5 billion.
18 Jain, V.K. (2017). Ibid., pp. 263 & 265.
19 Wipro strategic planners visited and interviewed in Bangalore in 2006 and 2011.
20 Jain, V.K. (2017). Ibid., p. 28.
21 Visited and interviewed at top level in Delhi in 2011.
22 See Chattopadhyay, A. and Bartra, R. (2012). *The New Emerging Market Multinationals: Four Strategies for Disrupting Markets and Building Brands.* New York: McGraw-Hill.
23 Kumar, N. (2009). Ibid., pp. 53–64.
24 Ibid., p. 273.

25 Johnson, G., Whittington, R. and Scholes, K. (2011, 9th Edition). *Exploring Strategy*. Harlow: FT Prentice Hall, p. 56.
26 Ibid., p. 61 as analysed. Original data source: Metal Bulletin/IISA (International Iron and Steel Institute) and IISI, Laplace Conseil Analysis.
27 Visited and interviewed at Director level in 2011.
28 Ibid., pp. 220–222.
29 *Financial Times*, 2 July 2019, p. 13, 'Gupta's Liberty Steel seals E740m deal for ArcelorMittal's European Assets'.
30 Kumar, N. (2009). ibid., p. 84.
31 Jones, E. (1990). *A History of GKN Volume 2: The Growth of a Business, 1918–45*. Basingstoke: Macmillan, pp. 8, 9, 207, 209 re: original acquisition; pp. 217–220, 229–230, 287, 369–370. See also Lorenz, A. (2009). *GKN: The Making of a Business 1759–2009*. Chichester: Wiley, pp. 237–280 re: Phoenix exit strategy.
32 For this detailed international strategic analysis of the forgings industry, see Carr, C. (1990). *Britain's Competitiveness: The Management of the Vehicle Components Industry*. London: Routledge, pp. 119–148.
33 See Brown, T. (2017). *Tragedy & Challenge: An Inside View of UK Engineering's Decline and the Challenge of the Brexit Economy*. Matador, particularly pp. 16–36 for an excellent, detailed accounts of GKN Forgings here, and of his other experiences in top roles at GKN and other engineering companies.
34 GKN Forgings chairman later in 1977 summoned me to his office. '*I'm afraid I have to meet you he said, you're flying off with GKN's Chairman tomorrow. And he might ask me about you!*' I appreciated his interest in my career. '*Get into sales for at least two years. Sooner or later you've got to be able to sell yourself in this company and there's no better experience*'. Shortly afterwards, I switched from GKNF's P&PD to GKN Contractors and joined the international project management team taking CV Joints global.
35 My newly developed, fast-change cropping machine never made it into production either.
36 Engineers, far better than me, went too; only our brilliant disruptive powder metallurgists were transferred to fight another day.
37 Brown, T. (2017). Ibid.
38 Source: National Association of Drop Forgers and Stampers. *Economics and Statistical Reviews* – Successive editions.
39 This was what we felt our role was: '*To go out into industry with fire in our bellies*', as Mike Sharman our charismatic Cambridge Advanced Course in Production Methods and Management course director would proclaim. I wanted to be the first graduate in both engineering and economics literally, creatively forged in industry, naively convinced that academic economists would value real-world engagement.
40 For an authoritative account of the demise of GKN Fasteners see former GKN director, David Spurrell's PhD, also Warwick Business School, 1984.
41 Carr, C.H. (1990). Ibid., based on my earlier 1985 Warwick Business School PhD thesis.
42 Indian automotive component manufacturers' relatively lower labour costs and overheads have resulted in a 20%–30% cost advantage over their US counterparts. Source: Case study by Ramachandran and Mukherji, *Forging Leadership*.
43 Confidentiality precludes disclosure of any commercially sensitive data. However, Bharat Forge's strategy has been well documented in 'Bharat Forge: Bringing Chapter Four', pp. 83–94. I therefore acknowledge this contribution and integrate my own perspective from working with GKN Forgings and my visits to forging companies worldwide.
44 Kumar, N. (2009). Ibid., p. 87.
45 For a summary of the Bharat Forge's more detailed strategic and operational changes, again see: Nirmalya Kumar's (2009). Ibid., pp. 87–88.
46 For a summary of Bharat Forge's approach to the merger with Carl Dan Peddinghaus, again see: Nirmalya Kumar's (2009). Ibid., Table 4.1, p. 91.

47 Ibid., p. 94.
48 Ibid., p. 83.
49 The Economist (2016). *Pocket World in Figures*. London.
50 Chong, F. (2005). 'New brand of expansion, the Weekend Inquirer', *The Weekend Australian*, 16–17 April, p. 20.
51 *Financial Times*, 31 March 2016, 'China groups seal record trove of M&A deals. Buyers behind $101bn of takeovers in first quarter'.
52 Yip, G.S. and McKerm, B. (2016). *China's Next Strategic Advantage: From Imitation to Innovation*. Cambridge, MA: MIT Press.
53 Ibid., p. 124. Based on interviews with 52 MNCs with Chinese R&D operations in China.
54 Ibid., p. 66: e.g., Huawei, Haier, ZTE, Tencent, Lenovo, Alibaba, BY, Yuwell, Fosun Pharma. See also pp. 20–21 for evidence of their increasing technological achievements.
55 Ernst & Young, 2014, though Europe had twice as many deals numerically, India came next at $5.2 billion with about a third as many deals as China.
56 Ibid., p. 18.
57 Yip, G.S. and McKern, B. (2016). Ibid., p. 18.
58 Ibid., p. 19.
59 Ibid., p. 234.
60 *Mobile World Live*, 11 April 2016 at Shenzen Conf. 'Huawei chief rules out bumper M&A'.
61 Source: Liu, H. (2017, 2nd Edition). *Chinese Business: Landscape and Strategies*. London: Routledge, p. 193.
62 Ibid., p. 202.
63 Ibid.
64 Liu, H. (2017, 2nd Edition). *Chinese Business: Landscape and Strategies*. London: Routledge, pp. 170–174.
65 *Financial Times*, 31 March 2016, ibid.
66 Wu, K. (2016). 'Chinese Companies: The New Uninvited Guests in M&A', *Wall Street Journal*, 6 June.
67 Haour, G. and Von Zedtwitz, M. (2016). *Created in China: How China is Becoming a Global Innovator.* London: Bloomsbury, p. 63.
68 Shepherd, C. (2016). 'Volvo tightens Geely ties with shared production line in China', *Financial Times*, 3 November, p. 15.
69 *Financial Times*, 18 November 2016, p. 14. 'No free lunch. US and China foreign direct investment flows'. Source: Dealogic.
70 Weinland, D. (2016). 'Fosun keeps up its global buying spree', *Financial Times*, 8 August, p. 18.
71 O'Neill, S. and Negargar, D. (2016). 'Stake in Sotheby's heralds a cultural revolution', *Times*, 3 August, p. 3.
72 Ibid., citing Marion Maneker, commenting in *Art Market Monitor.*
73 Ernst and Young (2014).
74 These greenfield investments included $6.1 billion property, $2.4 billion alternative renewable energy, $1.2 billion hotels/tourism, $0.7 billion coal/oil/gas, $0.6 billion telecommunications, $0.6 billion financial services, $0.4 billion auto, $0.2 billion consumer products, $0.15 billion transportation. Reference 'Golden era of China ties gives way to more prosaic praise', *Financial Times*, 11 November 2016, p. 3. Source: fDi Markets.
75 Zhu, L. and Moeller, S. (2016). An analysis of short-term performance of UK cross-border mergers and acquisitions by Chinese listed companies. Working paper, London: Cass Business School.
76 Wang, L., Carr, C. and Liu, L. (2016). Chinese cross-border mergers and acquisitions: their recent motivations, geographical impact, and performances. *7th International*

Research Meeting in Business and Management, 11–12 July, Nice. Interestingly, these Chinese M&As had achieved almost twice the returns on equity in Europe and Asia, as in the USA.

77 Jarrel, G., Brickley, J. and Natter, J. (1988). 'The market for corporate control: The empirical evidence since 1980', *Journal of Economic Perspectives*, 2 (2), pp. 49–68; Healy, P.M., Palepu, K.G. and Ruback, R.S. (1992). 'Does corporate performance improve after merger?' *Journal of Financial Economics*, 31 (1), pp. 137–155.

11

GLOBAL INCUMBENTS VS EMERGING MARKET MULTINATIONALS

THE CASE OF DOMESTIC APPLIANCES

Chris Carr and Ling Liu

INTRODUCTION

When the appropriateness of global versus national or more regional strategies[1] is being discussed, domestic appliances (DAs) are often cited as a bellwether sector: it is neither clearly global nor indeed domestic. Technology levels offer potential for international trade and foreign direct investment (FDI); yet high localisation pressures have been used by sceptics to suggest that more global strategies may have been overhyped and unwarranted.

DAs was indeed the first sector used to illustrate the principles of *Competitive Strategy*, Porter's 1980 classic text, which drew on Hunt's seminal 1972 Harvard PhD putting forward the concept of 'strategic groups', entirely based on an analysis of the DAs sector. Prior to Hunt, economists struggles to understand any sustained, superior profitability hinged on Bain (1955)'s concept of entry barriers.[2] Some sectors could sustain superior profit margins if, and only if, scale economies or technology barriers etc. could ward off Adam Smith's potential entrants, threatening to commoditise the sector, relegating profitability to normal levels commensurate with the cost of capital.

But Hunt went further. He showed that even within the same DAs sector, profitability differences could endure between 'strategic groups' of companies all pursuing broadly similar strategies. We might find that one strategic group, all relatively national (as opposed to localised) and all offering relatively broad product portfolios, consistently outperformed norms and other groups of companies even within the *same* DAs sector. His explanation was that mobility barriers, mirroring Bain's entry barriers (and for the same reasons), existed between different 'strategic groups' of firms. Though only briefly acknowledged by Porter, this became one of the planks of competitive strategy and of our understanding of more oligopolistic competition.

Strikingly, however, nearly 50 years ago Hunt's thesis felt no need to conduct his oligopolistic examination in anything other than a purely domestic USA context. He made no reference to international markets or competitors; nor did Porter in 1980, not even in his chapter on global strategy. This is perhaps understandable because, back in 1965, the five United States (US) top players controlled some 80% of the entire world DAs market. Emerging countries had yet to emerge as major markets, so that the world market was largely skewed towards the USA and, to a lesser extent, Europe: even European rivals paled by comparison with top US companies. Rugman's 20:20:20 criteria for global players would, incidentally, have been inappropriate, unless normalised, since the world market was anything but evenly distributed. Hunt's study provides, though, a good starting point for a valuable 50-year longitudinal examination of this most fascinating albeit controversial bellwether sector. Hunt's research data imply that even by 1965, the global concentration ratio 4 (GCR4) had already touched 80%, the same level reached by the car sector by the 1930s.

In 1991, the London Business School published a controversial study of the DAs sector in the *Strategic Management Journal*, striking down the straw man of global strategy in an article entitled 'Globalisation Frustrated' which argued that even in such a seemingly global sector, most successful strategies were merely national (or at best possibly regional) in orientation.[3] The study was based on just five years of performance figures, lacked data beyond Europe, and was based on Stopford and Wells (1972)' loose criteria for 'global strategy': i.e., any company with 'overseas plants in several countries', as distinct from mere 'exporters'. In 2007 Ghemawat likewise used performance analysis of the DAs sector to advance his arguments for regional rather than global strategies.[4] Ghemawat deployed 2002–2004 performance data, arguing that the two international leaders, Whirlpool and Electrolux, had lost money in contrast to more profitable regional companies like (predominantly North American) Maytag. He conceded global seller concentration had increased, but warned that: '*Even when global seller concentration increases are observed, the consolidation strategies which underpin them may be mistaken*'.

However, fundamental shifts have since taken place in international markets and competition. Therefore, if this is such a significant bellwether sector, it makes sense to update and integrate all this earlier analysis, together with up-to-date global concentration, geographical sales dispersions, and configurations performance analysis (CPA). How much has changed? Have recent conditions favoured national, regional, or more global strategies or international variants as identified by CPA? Is Ghemawat right that global megamergers prove mistaken and fail to pay-off? Can we demonstrate the strategic implications for major players? As in Chapter 5, we illustrate the implications of such applied analysis by taking practical examples of major world players, specifically Electrolux, Bosch Siemens (BSH), and Indesit from Europe, Whirlpool and GE Appliances from the USA, and Haier from China.

METHODS

In re-evaluating this controversial bellwether sector, holding one key control variable (the sector) constant, we deployed our integrated, more extensive analytical techniques and metrics, set against a more longitudinal 50-year perspective. We used four measurements on performance: survival, market shares and changes, globally and in all major regions, then return on capital employed (RoCE) and sales growth rates, as used in previous studies of internationalisation and performance.

From an evolutionary perspective, firm survival per se is an important tool of analysis, requiring only the dates of entry and exit, and reducing the risk of survival bias. We analysed global market shares and consolidation indices (including concentration ratios and Herfindahl indices used by Ghemawat 2007) in the sector between 1955 and 2008. We used 5- and 10-year averaged return on capital and sales growth rates, allowing 20 years of subsequent data to be compared against Baden Fuller and Stopford (1991)'s earlier findings. Data on consolidation trend of domestic appliances were obtained from academic and secondary research on the sector including *Euromonitor* and company annual reports. Performance, benchmarking, and international sales and asset dispersions were based on Thomson One Banker. We tracked global and all major regional market shares of 40 worldwide players with global market share above 0.1% in 2008. Sales and profit performances were analysed for the top 17 players, for four 5-year windows between 1987 and 2006.

Most difficult and time-consuming was establishing the firms' international strategy classifications. Other theorists have deployed inconsistent global strategy classifications:

1. London Business School's criteria, as described in Baden Fuller and Stopford (1991) distinguishes national players, manufacturing only at home, and selling over 90% of their output locally; exporters producing only at home, but exporting over 30% of their output; and global players, manufacturing and selling in several countries.
2. Rugman (2005)'s criteria defines global players as having over 20% of sales in each of three continents; bi-regional as over 20% in two; home-regional players with over 50% in their home region; and host-orientated players with over 50% of sales in a region other than their own.[5]

3. Hunger (2003)'s criteria (also adopted by Ghemawat 2007) denote broadly described international competitive orientations: Global (GLOB), Global Aspirants (GL ASP), Strong Regional (ST REG), Strong Local (ST LOC), and Domestic Niche (DOM).

To gain a deeper perspective on strategic issues internationally, from the viewpoint of both advanced country and emerging country players, field research was carried out on two major players, Bosch Siemens in Europe and Haier in China between 2001 and 2003. Research in Germany entailed interviews with their head of global strategy. Interviews were conducted with several top-level executives at Haier, who prefer not to be identified individually. Some follow-up interviews with the senior overseas executives were undertaken in October 2009. Data availability was confined to 40 companies with global market share above 0.1%, but we conducted analysis of the top 17 companies and excluded small players with global market shares less than 0.5%. Finally, we updated our analysis through desk research, reassessing companies' latest strategic moves and outcomes.

FINDINGS

Figure 11.1 and Table 11.1 present historical trends of consolidation of the domestic appliance industry in major markets. In the United States, the number of manufacturers fell from 250 in the 1950s to 15 in the 1980s, the market being dominated by a few players like Whirlpool, Electrolux, and GE. Similar consolidation followed in Europe and China. In Europe, Baden Fuller and Stopford (1991)'s British '*national winner*' Hotpoint was acquired

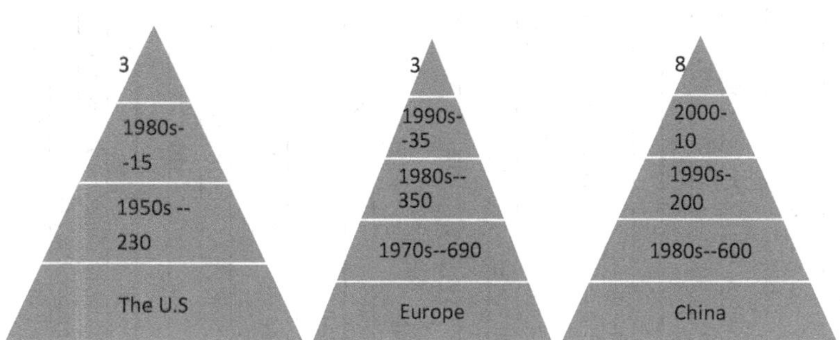

Figure 11.1 Historical trend of consolidation in domestic appliances in the US, Europe, and China. (From Liu, L., *China's Industrial Policies and the Global Business Revolution: The Case of the Domestic Appliance Industry*, Routledge, London, 2005.)

Table 11.1 Global M&A and consolidations trends in domestic appliances, 1960–2008

1955–1960	*1960–1965*	*1965–1970*	*1970–1975*	*1975–1980*	*1980–1985*	*1985–1990*	*1990–1995*	*1995–2000*	*2000–2008*
KitchenAid/Roper/RCA/Seeger/Aspera (I)/Ingis (Ca)						Whirlpool	Whirlpool		Whirlpool
Kelvinator (In)/Vitromatic SA (M)									
Naricissus (Ch)/Brasmotor (Br)/Multibras (Br)									
Philips					Philips		Whirlpool		
Iberna/Bauknecht									
Hardwick Stove (Schwittay and Administration)/Jenn-Air (Schwittay and Administration)					Maytag	Maytag		Maytag	
Magic Chef (Schwittay and Administration)/Hoover (Doukas and Lang)									
Amana (Schwittay and Administration)						Raytheon			
Polar SA (P)									
Witter/BBC/ Zanker/ Linde	AEG-Linde-BBC				Electrolux		Electrolux		
Becchi/Triplex/Castor		Zanussi							
Tappan (Schwittay and Administration)/Therma/Husqvarna/ Tricity (Doukas and Lang)				Electrolux					
AlpenInox/Domar/Thorn_EMI/Design & Man (Schwittay and Administration)/ Alfatec/White C.I (Schwittay and Administration)						Electrolux			
Refrigeracao Parana (2nd largest in Brazil)/Email Ltd (No 1 in Australia)/Voltas (In)									
Siemens/Bosch		BSH	BSH						BSH
Pitsos S.A				BSH	BSH	BSH			
Neff									
Continental (Brazil)/Refrigeracao Parana SA (B)/Yangzi (C)									
BSH pro Elektrikli Gerec (T)									
Ufesa (S)/*Eval (Tu)*/Masco Corp (Schwittay and Administration)								BSH	

(Continued)

Table 11.1 (Continued)

1955–1960	*1960–1965*	*1965–1970*	*1970–1975*	*1975–1980*	*1980–1985*	*1985–1990*	*1990–1995*	*1995–2000*	*2000–2008*
TI group (Doukas and Lang)						GEC Hotpoint	GE	GE	GE
Creda UK/*Modosa (V)/Godrej & Boyce (In, 40% JV)/Mabe (48% JV)/DAKO SA (Br)/Philacor (Phi)*									
Honeywell									
Merloni/Smeg/Scholtes/Colston UK					Merloni	Merloni			Indesit
Philco/Indesit									
GED UK									
Zerowatt/Pargest/Magic Chef						Zerowatt	Candy		Candy
Iberna/Candy/Gasfire					Candy				
Us.d. Rosieres (F)						Candy			
LEC Ref UK									
Hoover UK									
Hotchkis-Brandt Thompson_Houston		Thomson-Brandt			Thomson			EL.FI Brandt	Moulinex Brandt
De Duetruch (Fr)/Cristal (Is)								EL.FI	
Samet/San Giirgio (I)					Ocean	ocean			
Satam Brandt/Filiberti/Costan/Bonnet									
Blomberg (G)/Elektra Bregenz (Gaur and Kumar)/Arctic Russia									Arcelik
Volmo (In)/Arno (Br)									Group SEB

Source: Liu, L., *China's Industrial Policies and the Global Business Revolution: The Case of the Domestic Appliance Industry*, Routledge, London, 2005.

by Indesit: indeed all their major national players have either disappeared or would now be classified as global players. Bosch Siemens, once reliant on exports, currently has production facilities in major world markets and would now be classified as global.

Table 11.1 shows the longer-term consolidation in terms of key mergers and acquisitions (M&A). Of Wheelen and Hunger (1995)'s six top domestic appliance companies identified, Maytag, Raytheon, and White Consolidated have since exited or been absorbed; leaving two flourishing survivors Whirlpool and Electrolux, plus GE Appliances, which has since been acquired by Haier. Raytheon and White Consolidated displayed below average return on sales and return on assets until exiting. Maytag, the largest regional US player remained highly profitable until being acquired by Whirlpool in 2006.

Table 11.2 presents split of sales activities of major domestic appliance players by geography and activity. Based on 2001 data, Rugman (2005) classified Electrolux as the only non-home-regional; even Whirlpool, the global number 1, being classified as home-regional. By 2008, Electrolux's sales spread was 26% in Europe, 40% in America, and 34% in the rest of the world – almost the ideal split in line with the relative value of different regional markets though, absurdly, it had to be classified as merely bi-regional. Whirlpool, having exactly 20% of its sales in Europe, also shows greater global presence.

Hunger (2003)'s international criteria labels companies as GLOB, GL ASP, ST REG, ST LOC, and DOM. Using his own classifications, our sample in Table 11.2 splits: 17.5% GLOB, 17.5% GL ASP, 53% ST REG, 6% ST LOC, and 6% DOM. These are shown in the final column of Table 11.3 and split: 12% global (vs 17.5% earlier); 59% global aspirants (vs 17.5% earlier); 23% strong regional (vs 53% earlier); 6% strong local (as before); with no domestic niche players (vs 6% earlier). Overall, companies were far more globally orientated strategically as compared with Baden Fuller and Stopford (1991)'s 1980s findings.

The top four, Whirlpool, Electrolux, Bosch Siemens (BSH), and LG, all held substantial shares not only globally, but also in seven major world regions, far more so than in 2001. This indicates the companies' geographical spread and impact in terms of oligopolistic market power. Global CR4 between 2001 and 2008 increased modestly from 28% to 29%. The CR8 (including new Korean and Chinese players) rose more substantially from 40% to 44%, implying that Western incumbents have ceded share to Asian entrants. Regional CR4s have similarly increased, surpassing 40% with the single exception of Asia Pacific.

Table 11.2 Top global domestic appliance firms' regional sales %s 1988–2008 and diversification levels

Company		*Region*					*Non-home country %*	*Domestic appliances %*
		North AM	*Latin AM*	*Europe*	*Asia Pacific*	*Other*		
Electrolux (GLOB)	2008	32	8	26		34	97	
	2002	44		43		13		77
	1998	35	6	53	4	3	95	72
	1988	29	2	64	4	2	84	56
Whirlpool (GLOB)	2006	61	13	20	5	2		
	2002	66	11	20	4	−1	38	100
	1996	62	0	29	5	4		
	1992	63	0	37	0	0		
	1988	95	0	5	0	0		
Av. Global Players	2006–2008	46	10	23		31		
	2002	55		32		14		
	1998	62	1	34	2	4		
Indesit (GL AS)	2008			92		8		41
	1998			71		29	73	37
BSH (GL AS)	2001	3	9	80	5	3	54	
	2005						78	
Haier (GL AS)	2004						16	
	1998						3	80
GE (Diversified)	2005	56	5	25	11	4		
	2003	65	4	18	10	3	40	5
	1999						71	
Samsung (Diversified)	2007	18		27	46	9	86	
	2006	21		26	46	7		
LG (Diversif.)	2007	19		15	60	6	64	30
	2003						51	32
Matsushita (Diversified)	2008	14		13	73	0	50	
	2004	18		14	68	0	53	20
	2002	21		12	67	0	53	
	1998	18		12	70	0	51	
Toshiba (Diversified)	2008						51	
	1994	12		7	79	2	31	10
	1992	11		7	79	3	30	10
Sharp (Diversified)	2007	18		17	12	6	51	7
	2003	14		15	12	9	49	8
	1999	22		10	13	3	47	9
Av. Diversified players	2007–2008	19		19	39	61		
	2003							16

Source: Company's annual reports (various years); *Euromonitor International* – Statistics 2009, GlDatabase. Large kitchen appliances include refrigeration appliances, home laundry appliances, dishwashers, large cooking appliances, and microwaves.

Table 11.3 Top global domestic appliance firms' 5- and 10-year RoCEs and sales growth (SG), 1987–2006

	5 year average		*5 year average*		*5 year average*		*5 year average*		*Previous 10 year average*		*10 year average*		*t*						
	RoCE	*SG*	*RoCE*	*SG*	*RoCE*	*SG*	*RoCE*	*SG*	*RoCE*	*SG*	*RoCE*	*SG*	*LBS (1991)*	*Rugman*	*Hunger*	*LBS*	*Rugman*	*Calori et al*	*Updated*
	1987–1991	*1987–1991*	*1992–1996*	*1992–1996*	*1997–2001*	*1997–2001*	*2002–2006*	*2002–2006*	*1987–1996*	*1987–1996*	*1997–2006*	*1997–2006*	*Pre 1990*	*2001*	*Pre-2003*	*Update*	*Updated*	*Types*	*Hunger*
Whirlpool	7.22	11.81	4.72	3.37	6.06	5.03	16.08	11.99	5.97	7.59	11.07	8.51	GLOB	REG	GLOB	GLOB	BI-REG	GL SH	GLOB
Electrolux AB	6.42	3.59	6.91	7.03	7.46	7.96	5.76	5.36	6.67	5.31	6.61	6.66	GLOB	BI-REG	GLOB	GLOB	BI-REG	TR NAT R	GLOB
BSH					7.57	1.59	4.01	73.01			5.79	37.30	EXP	REG	GL ASP	GLOB	REG	QU GL	GL ASP
LG Electronics			7.78	15.40	14.33	21.30	14.23	10.58			14.28	15.94	NAT	REG	GL ASP	GLOB	BI-REG	QU GL	GL ASP
Haier					0.00	0.00	20.38	8.03			10.19	4.02	NAT	REG	GL ASP	GLOB	REG	QU GL	GL ASP
Indesit	5.96	16.94	8.43	16.46	8.51	11.39	9.33	6.75	7.19	16.70	8.92	9.07	NAT	REG	ST REG	GLOB	REG	QU GL	GL ASP
Samsung Elec.	9.92	33.42	11.20	17.64	11.12	3.33	12.32	−4.69	10.56	25.53	11.72	−0.68	EXP	REG	ST REG	GLOB	BI-REG	QU GL	GL ASP
Matsushita Elec.					14.32	−3.92	21.24	2.68			17.78	−0.62	NAT	REG	ST REG	GLOB	REG	QU GL	GL ASP
Arcelik			33.12	92.40	27.92	52.78	14.76	28.10			21.34	40.44	NAT	REG	ST REG	GLOB	REG	QU GL	GL ASP
Sharp Elec.	5.68	6.24	3.66	2.86			5.64	14.03	4.67	4.55			NAT	REG	ST REG	GLOB	REG	QU GL	GL ASP
Miele & Cie								5.58					NAT	REG	ST REG	GLOB	REG	QU GL	GL ASP
Sanyo	2.82	5.39	1.72	3.35			14.00	4.59	2.27	4.37			EXP	REG	ST REG	GLOB	REG	QU GL	GL ASP
GE Appliances	11.19	7.14	7.73	9.63	0.00	0.00	−3.33	11.21	9.47	8.38	−1.67	5.61	NAT	REG	GLOB	GLOB	BI-REG	CONT	ST REG
Rinnai	7.76	6.64	6.26	3.17					7.01	4.91			EXP	REG	ST LOC	GLOB	REG	CONT	ST REG
Toshiba DEA	6.09	7.38	2.38	2.92	3.11	−1.25	1.39	5.37	4.23	5.15	2.25	2.06	EXP	REG	ST REG	GLOB	REG	CONT	ST REG
Hitachi	5.14	9.88	2.28	1.88					3.71	5.88			EXP	REG	ST REG	GLOB	REG	CONT	ST REG
GD Midea							20.83	28.38					NAT	REG	DOM	EXP	REG	CONT	ST LOC
Averaged Performances by Classifications																			
LBS GLOB AV	6.82	7.70	5.82	5.20	6.76	6.50	10.92	8.68	6.32	6.45	8.84	7.59	[t] LBS (1991): GLOB denotes Global Players; EXP, exporters; NAT, national.						
LBS EXP AV	6.35	12.54	4.77	5.79	7.27	1.22	7.93	19.57	5.56	9.17	6.59	12.89	Rugman (2005): BI-REG, bi-regional; REG, home-regional;						
LBS NAT AV	7.61	10.11	12.15	27.35	10.85	13.59	12.89	12.82	7.11	9.88	11.81	12.41	Hunger (2003): GL ASP, global aspirants; ST REG, strong regional; Hunger (2003): ST LOC, strong local; DOM, domestic & niche;						
BI-REG (RUGMAN)	7.22	11.81	4.72	3.37	6.06	5.03	16.08	11.99	5.97	7.59	11.07	8.51	Calori et al.: GL SH, global shapers; QU GL, quasi global;						
REG (RUGMAN)	6.86	11.65	8.12	15.37	9.29	9.03	11.61	14.69	6.12	9.23	10.17	12.16	Calori et al.: TR NAT, transnational restructures; CONT, continental.						

(Continued)

Table 11.3 (Continued)

	5 year average		*5 year average*		*5 year average*		*5 year average*		*Previous 10 year average*		*10 year average*		*t*						
	RoCE	*SG*	*RoCE*	*SG*	*RoCE*	*SG*	*RoCE*	*SG*	*RoCE*	*SG*	*RoCE*	*SG*	*LBS (1991)*	*Rugman*	*Hunger*	*LBS*	*Rugman*	*Calori et al*	*Updated*
	1987–1991	*1987–1991*	*1992–1996*	*1992–1996*	*1997–2001*	*1997–2001*	*2002–2006*	*2002–2006*	*1987–1996*	*1987–1996*	*1997–2006*	*1997–2006*	*Pre 1990*	*2001*	*Pre-2003*	*Update*	*Updated*	*Types*	*Hunger*
GLOB (HUNGER)	8.28	7.51	6.47	6.68	4.51	4.33	6.17	9.52	7.37	7.09	5.34	6.93		**NB:** Haier used RoA for earlier 5 yr period;					
GL ASP			7.78	15.40	7.30	7.63	12.87	30.54			10.09	19.09		GD Midea and Sharp used operating profit/sales;					
ST LOC	7.76	6.64	6.26	3.17					7.01	4.91				Toshiba DEA division results for only 8 not 10 years.					
ST REG	5.93	13.21	8.97	19.64	13.00	12.47	11.24	7.80	5.44	10.36	12.40	10.05							
DOM							20.83	28.38											
Updated Classifications Averaged Performances																			
LBS EXP NOW							20.83	28.38											
LBS GLOB NOW	6.82	10.84	8.02	14.68	9.13	8.93	10.45	13.04	6.18	8.84	9.84	11.66							
BI-REG (RUGMAN)	8.69	13.99	7.68	10.61	7.76	7.52	9.01	6.89	8.17	11.70	8.40	7.21							
REG (RUGMAN)	5.57	8.75	8.27	17.58	10.24	10.10	12.40	17.65	4.85	6.93	11.05	15.38							
GL SH (CALORI)	7.22	11.81	4.72	3.37	6.06	5.03	16.08	11.99	5.97	7.59	11.07	8.51							
TR NAT RE	6.42	3.59	6.91	7.03	7.46	7.96	5.76	5.36	6.67	5.31	6.61	6.66							
QU GL	6.10	15.50	10.99	24.68	11.97	12.35	12.88	14.87	6.17	12.79	12.86	15.07							
CONT	7.54	7.76	4.67	4.40	1.56	−0.63	6.30	14.99	6.11	6.08	0.29	3.83							
GLOB (HUNGER)	6.82	7.70	5.82	5.20	6.76	6.50	10.92	8.68	6.32	6.45	8.84	7.59							
GL ASP	6.10	15.50	10.99	24.68	11.97	12.35	12.88	14.87	6.17	12.79	12.86	15.07							
ST REG	7.54	7.76	4.67	4.40	1.56	−0.63	−0.97	8.29	6.11	6.08	0.29	3.83							
ST LOC							20.83	28.38											

Source: Thomson One Banker and Company Accounts. Domestic appliance divisional figures, whenever possible, otherwise corporate figures, particularly 1987–1996.

LEADING DOMESTIC APPLIANCE COMPANIES AND PERFORMANCE 1987–2006

Financial performance

Table 11.3 presents leading company's 5-and 10-year average RoCE and sales growth (SG) during 1987 and 2006. Baden Fuller and Stopford (1991) noted better financial performances among national players within Europe in the late 1980s, but Table 11.3 suggests that this situation completely changed. Their large European players investigated just prior to 1990 split with 53% national players, 35% exporters, and 12% global players. By contrast, 17 large companies worldwide split 94% global, 6% exporters, with no survivors any longer classifiable as merely national.

Based on Rugman (2005)'s original classifications, bi-regional (BI-REG) players have been slightly more profitable over the last 20 years, at the expense of slower sales' growth. Updating his classifications suggests that regional players, previously less profitable, have become more profitable than BI-REG whilst growing twice as quickly.

Based on our updated Hunger classifications, Table 11.3's 10-year analysis of leading firms' performances shows that global aspirants performed best on RoCE and sales growth during the ten years 1997–2006. Global players were the next best performers, again on both counts, with strong regional players trailing substantially behind. During the previous ten years 1987–1996, performance differences between groups were small: global players were slightly more profitable than global aspirants, in turn, slightly ahead of strong regional players. Global aspirants, however, were substantially ahead on sales growth. Whirlpool and Electrolux both remained below average in terms of profitability, yet it is they who have survived to 2019 having led that process of industrial consolidation. Achieving slightly higher profitability ultimately afforded little protection to Maytag or to Hotpoint, identified earlier as a British winner by Baden Fuller and Stopford. More pro-active international and global strategies seem to have finally paid off.

STRATEGIC IMPLICATIONS

How far, though, does such CPA and global concentration analysis matter strategically? Consider the situation for Indesit, formerly No 3 in Europe: would its regional strategy prove enough, or did it need a global strategy?[6]

From a national or regional perspective, Indesit had been highly successful over 30 years. Between 2004 and 2006, prior to the world financial crisis, Indesit averaged a return on sales of 10% vs 2% for Electrolux, the European No. 1, and 3% for Whirlpool, the world No. 1[7]; averaged return on assets was 12% vs 3% for Electrolux and 4% for Whirlpool; averaged sales growth was 2% p.a., vs –7% for Electrolux, though much lower than Whirlpool's 18% p.a.

(boosted by M&A). But sales had risen 20-fold over the previous 20 years: it was one of three major survivors from around 100 European players in 1975 when it had been established.

In response to industry consolidation, Indesit had evolved successfully through three phases. Between 1975 and 1984 Indesit's growth strategy was purely organic: a pro-active, high volume, good quality, lowest-cost orientated strategy, akin to Ford's Model T a century ago, entailing heavy investment in new product development and well focused factories. Its industrial relations were relatively good. Its entrepreneurial style always pushing forwards, from just cookers to a full line of domestic appliances, akin to GM's when it first overtook Ford. Internationally, it grew through exports targeting markets opportunistically within Europe, being configured as a Calori *opportunistic international challenger.*

Through 1985–1995, it still grew vigorously organically, but half its sales growth now came from acquisitions. In 1987, it acquired Merloni Progetti and also Indesit, a reverse take-over enabling them to take over this bigger name. In 1989, they acquired France's Scholtes. Indesit's relatively more efficient inventory management – under 40 days vs 66 days at Electrolux – brought value to acquirees following rationalisation, integration, and internal benchmarking. As Chandler found in his diversification studies, such new strategies struggled initially due to product and country tensions affecting subsidiaries, until Indesit gradually learned to overcome the challenges posed.

Through 1995 and 2005, Indesit's pan-European strategy extended to Russia with the acquisition of Stinol in 2000 and of Hotpoint, the United Kingdom (UK)'s leading player, which doubled Indesit's size with a single stroke. Such scale uplifts and Chinese parts procurement massively increased their negotiating power in purchasing. By now they were configured as a *continental leader,* or in Rugman terms a fully fledged European *regional* player.

But, faced with global consolidation, was this enough? Should they have moved on to more ambitious *worldwide player* configurations, as perhaps *worldwide technology specialists* (like LG and Samsung from S. Korea), or as *worldwide transnational restructurers* (like Electrolux), or attempted to transform the industry by become a *quasi-global shaper* (like Whirlpool, then the world No 1), or driven hard for the global lowest cost position (as Turkey's Arcelik or Chinese rivals), or raised their global branding game in line with *global luxury niche* players like BSH at the top of the market? Such orientation choices would profoundly affect trade, FDI options (GFS, ISAs, M&A), and geographies prioritised.

CPA analysis (illustrated in Chapter 5), as updated, helps, but global competitor analysis must also consider the threat posed by China's emerging market multi-national (EMM), Haier. Thirty years earlier, Zhang Ruimin had regalvanised a defunct refrigerator factory, motivated by Ford-style scale, entrepreneurial zeal, and efficiency, then extended, too, to full-line domestic appliance ranges, gaining 18% share of the huge Chinese market.[8] Ruimin, too, added value at the group-level, exploiting platforms to maintain focus and scale, and through a flat organisational structure, akin to Jack Welch's style and approach at GE. Benefiting from scale and wages a twentieth of those in the West, Haier formalised its strategy for going global in 1997.

Ruimin's '*three-thirds*' goal was no timid Rugman/Ghemawat regional strategy; production in China for China would ultimately fall to only a third of sales; exports from China would make up another third; and the final third would come from FDI – goods produced and sold overseas, putting assets on the ground. Nor was this mere trade dumping exploiting cheap Chinese labour; gross profit margins averaged 12% for 2003–2005, surpassing Western rivals. FDI immediately targeted the USA, building US factories and paying US wages. Through 1993–2005, Haier's sales grew 21-fold. By 2005, Haier's US market shares were 26% for compact refrigerators, 50% for wine coolers, and 17% for window air conditioners. European sales rose to 17% of group revenues by 2004, spurred by an Italian refrigerator plant acquired in 2001. India's entry in 1999, supported by exports, a strategic alliance, $200 million investments, and an R&D centre, expanded to broad range offerings by 2004.

Indesit, though, faced formidable rivalry going beyond its European base: in the USA, against the global leader Whirlpool, GE Appliances, Haier, LG, Samsung, Hitachi, Electrolux, and Bosch Siemens; in China, even Whirlpool had failed to increase its 0.5% 2002 market share, LG's share had fallen back from 3.7% in 2002 to 2.2% in 2006, and only Bosch Siemens had increased its share (from 2.2% to 2.7%) against formidable home players; in India, where Whirlpool, LG, Samsung, and Haier were strong, Europeans had achieved little impact; in Latin America, Whirlpool, GE, Bosch Siemens, LG, and Samsung were already strong. Before even contemplating *worldwide* player configurations, Indesit would need to uplift its brands and its mere 0.25% R&D/sales ratio radically. Faced with global consolidation and EMMs, Indesit's successful European strategy was vulnerable.

SUBSEQUENT EVENTS AND STRATEGIC LESSONS

Updating further, we can elucidate strategic implications and lessons. Lacking any more global strategy, Indesit settled for a new factory in Turkey exploiting a growing market, lower labour costs, and perhaps clipping Arcelik's wings as another low-cost EMM rival; but it made little progress attacking Bosch Siemen's huge German home market or Electrolux's in Scandinavia. It held off on M&A or strategic alliances beyond Europe.

Indesit's configuration position and dilemma mirrored Scottish and Newcastle's in beer. Scottish and Newcastle had similarly outpaced former national champions (like Bass), consolidating across Western and Eastern

Europe, becoming No 3 regionally. This was still not enough to stave off take-over and break-up in 2007 by Carlsberg and Heineken, rightly anticipating rapid consolidation globally. Brazilian-based Ambev acquired the world No 1, yet globally passive, Anheuser-Busch just months later. Nothing in our CPA/concentration analysis suggests radically different globalisation patterns in domestic appliances: Haier, given its advantageous Chinese base, seemed likely to prove as catalytic in global restructuring in DAs as Brazil's EMM Ambev was in beer.

GE Appliances, down to the global No. 7 graveyard position, compared with its parent policy of top three positions, looked vulnerable too[9]; but it was Electrolux which put in the first bid. Table 11.4 shows subsequent 2007–2011 performance outcomes for most major world players. Europe's No 1, Electrolux, reclassified as a transnational restructurer in 2006, is interesting. Prior to this, its configuration as a continental leader had proved no more profitable than those in retailing observed in Chapter 5. Yet, even in Rugman terms, Electrolux was now an almost perfectly spread global player, hugely experienced in cross-border M&A and restructuring. Its recent 5-year averaged RoCE improved markedly to almost 10%, vying with Whirlpool. With over four times Indesit's revenues, Electrolux's R&D ratio of 2% was only slightly behind Whirlpool's, and its brands were well recognised. Electrolux's problem has been negative investor return and sales growth; like Indesit, it has ceded global market share. In September 2014, Electrolux's American-born chief executive officer announced its largest ever $3.3 billion bid for GE Appliances, explaining to the *Financial Times*:

> The opportunity to get the century-old GE business and its brands which include Hotpoint was too good to be missed...Electrolux saw the chance to introduce GE appliances in other countries as it currently generates about 90% of its sales from North America. The Swedish group has in the past decade shifted its production radically away from high cost countries such

Table 11.4 Top global domestic appliance firm performance benchmarks 2007–2011

Company		*Sales $bn 2011*	*RoCE%*	*Sales Growth*	*TIR*	*R&D% 2011*	*Cap'X% 2011*
Whirlpool	USA	18	9.9	0.6	−8	3.1	3.3
Electrolux	SWE	16	9.7	−0.4	−1	2.1	3.1
Midea	CHINA	15	14.5	36	38	na	4.1
Haier	CHINA	12	12.0	30	16	na	2.2
Arcelik	TURKEY	4.5	10.7	3.9	3	0.8	4.3
Indesit	ITALY	3.7	na	−2.7	−19	na	na
Wuxi LS	CHINA	1.7	10.8	21	29	na	2.0

Source: Analysis of Thomson One Banker data.

Note: RoCE, sales growth, and total investor returns (TIR) are 5-year averages, other figures are 2011.

as Germany to lower-cost emerging markets. Mr McLoughlin is now seeking to polish the brand's image as well as expanding into emerging markets such as Brazil and China. The GE business includes a 48% shareholding in Mabe, the Mexican appliance maker from which the US company sources about a quarter of its products... The deal reduces dependence on Europe and boosts US sales to nearly half. Investors reacted warmly sending Electrolux's shares up 5%.[10]

Wallenberg's chief executive officer added '*As the leading owner, with a long-term ownership horizon, we find Electrolux's acquisition of GE Appliances industrially attractive*'.

GE confirmed it had only abandoned attempts to sell the business in 2008 because of the financial crisis. The *Financial Times* commented: 'The deal looks a winner for Electrolux. The addition of GE's market share and distribution network gives it the punch it needs to face off with the world number one, Whirlpool. Together the two bruisers will control a fifth of the global market. Scale counts in white goods.' But this was not the end of the story.

Domestic appliances subsequent developments and conclusion

Table 11.5 shows subsequent global market share trends for the major global players between 2002 and 2016. Top US and European players, Whirlpool, Electrolux, Bosch Siemens, and General Electric, have been ceding share to Asian players (LG and Samsung from S. Korea and Panasonic from Japan), but particularly to EMMs Haier and Midea from China. Between 2002 and 2010, Haier more than tripled its share to 9.6%, though Midea (at 3.5% in 2010) grew still faster. In October 2014, Whirlpool responded by acquiring Indesit, recovering global market share ceded over the ten years to 2012. Haier's share (in retail volume terms) rose further to nearly 14% in 2016, achieving global leadership in home-laundry appliances. Selling in over 100 countries, Table 11.6 shows its impressive financial performance to 2017.

Haier's R&D at 4% of sales was supported by ten centres in key markets and some 9000 patents. By 2013, they were ranked by Boston Consulting Group (BCG) 8th worldwide among most innovative companies, rising from 20th in 2011. Their goal was to decrease low-end products from roughly 22.5% to 7.5% within 3–5 years. Having failed with bids for Maytag in 2005 and GE Appliances in late 2011, Haier acquired Sanyo's domestic appliances for $132 million, increasing its Japanese share to around 15% in refrigerators and 5% in washing machines.

Competition in the crucial Chinese market has become yet more intense. Between 2002 and 2018, Haier's share had increased from 14% to 22%, as Whirlpool fell back from 0.5% to 0.4%, and Midea's share increased 4.5-fold. *Euromonitor* reported that Midea now '*comfortably led sales in 2016, due to its*

Table 11.5 Global market shares of top domestic appliance firms, 2002–2016

	By company (% vol.)				*By brands (% vol.)*		
	2002	*2008*	*2013*	*2016*	*2002*	*2008*	*2013*
Haier	3.0	5.3	11.5	13.6	2.3	4.5	9.7
Whirlpool	10.2	11.0	8.3	11.5	5.8	5.1	4.0
Electrolux	8.2	7.6	7.2	6.8	2.0	2.9	3.3
Bosch Siemens	6.1	6.1	5.8	6.0	4.7	5.1	4.8[a]
LG	3.6	4.9	5.8	6.1	3.2	4.5	5.8
Mat./Panasonic	3.2	3.0	3.7[a]	3.3		2.9	2.9[a]
Midea	0.4	2.9	4.0	6.3	0.4	1.8	4.0
General Electric	5.5	3.7	2.7E	na	4.6	3.5	2.6[a]
Samsung	2.9	3.3	3.8[a]	5.3	4.9	3.0	3.8[a]
Indesit	na	3.6	2.8[a]	na			
Arcelik				2.3			
Hon Hai Precision				1.8			
Global CR2	18.4	18.6	19.8	25.1	10.7	10.2	15.5
Global CR4	30	30	32.8	38.2	16.3	17.1	22.1
Global CR6		36.8	38.6	42.6	50.3	24.9	23.6
Global CR10 (B + S)	43.1	51.4	55.6	63.0	25.7	31.5	38.2[a]

Sources: Data from *Euromonitor International* 2019.

Note: Bosch Siemens brand figures added for consistency over the period. Author's added global concentration calculations.

[a] 2012 figures. E: estimate.

Table 11.6 Quingdao Haier sales, ROIC, ROE, and RoS performance, 2010–2017

	2010	*2010–2013*	*2014*	*2014–2017*	*2017*
Sales $bn	*9743*		*14,422*		*20,709*
Return on invested capital av. %		17.6		21.3	
ROE av. %		32.2			
Net margin av. (RoS) %		4.0			

Source: Analysis of data from Grant, R., *Contemporary Strategy Analysis*, Wiley, respectively, p. 568 and p. 654, 2019 and 2010 editions.

comprehensive product line, strong market penetration (even in lower tier cities), and frequent new launches. Multinationals … suffered a decline in market share in 2016'.[11] Its emergence, alongside Haier, accentuates China's competitive advantages: even LG's share halved, though Germany's BSH's modest share rose to almost 3%. US anti-trust policies stymied Electrolux's bid in 2018, ironically gifting GE Appliances to Haier, as Whirlpool struggled in China. By 2018, as shown in Table 11.7, Midea's share had increased to 17%, as Western multi-nationals and even Haier fell back in the face of further formidable Chinese rivals.

Table 11.7 Market shares in China in consumer appliances, 2002–2018 (% retail volume)

Company	*2002*	*2010*	*2018*
Haier	14	22	7.1
Midea	3	14	17.0
Glanz Ent.	7	6	na
Zhuhai Gree			5.6
Joyoung			5.2
Shanghai Flyco			5.1
Zhejiang Supor			4.2
Philips China			3.9
Singfun Electric			2.0
Hisense Kelon	na	4	1.6
Panasonic	na	4	1.5
Henan Xinfeir	2	3	
BSH	2	3	
Hefei Meiling	2	2	
LG	4	2	
Whirlpool	0.5	0.4	
Others	65	40	
CR2 Concentration Ratio	21	36	24
CR4 Concentration Ratio	28	45	35
CR10 Concentration Ratio	35	60	53

Sources: ECCH; data from *Euromonitor International*, www.euromonitor.com, accessed September, 2019 and earlier.

Note: Author's added concentration calculations.

In 2018, Electrolux turnover was SEK124 billion, compared with 100 billion in 2011, selling to 150 countries with 54,000 employees. Its sales split 36% North America; 40% Europe, Middle East, and Africa; 16% South America; and 8.5% Asia Pacific. Its Return on Equity (RoE) was 18% and its Return on Net Assets (RoNA) 23%. In July 2019, Qingdao Haier's market capitalisation was $16 billion, compared with Whirlpool's $9 billion; Midea's and Electrolux's at $384 billion and $74 billion reflected diversification.

Germany's BSH, though ceding share to Asian players, has fared better than M&A-orientated Whirlpool and Electrolux. BSH was founded in the 1960s as a now exemplary cross-border strategic alliance, with these two German companies having joined forces to take on DA markets outside Germany. It is one of the world's most long-lived and indeed successful alliances formed specifically in response to global markets.

Miele is a classic top-end German niche player discussed in Chapter 8, with R&D of 5.5% of sales. A family business founded in 1899, its washing machines in 2014 sold for around £2500: even the Vatican washed everything in huge Miele commercial washing machines. It held 30% market share in its niche, but still sustained double-digit growth in North America, China,

Russia, and Australia. Sales rose from E3 billion in 2013 to E4 billion in 2018, most production remaining in eight German factories, employing 11,000 of 20,000 workers worldwide. As their chief executive officer explained it to the *Sunday Times* (16.2.2014, p. 7):

> This is the way we want it to be. You can move production to a low-cost base, but can you ensure the quality? We can react very quickly because production is very near our management and R&D. We don't have to grow too fast. We don't want to take on debt and we're family owned. That's the classic definition of Mittelstand. As a family-owned company, you can make quick decisions. You can decide to invest into a product. It's always long-term. With stock-market companies their view is a little bit different. We love what we do, we enjoy our business, we believe in the future of our business and we have been independent for four generations. You never change a winning team.

Overall, these outcomes appear, again, in line with our earlier global winners model, illustrated by the global spirits sector in Chapter 3. Haier, Whirlpool, and Electrolux have all emerged as pro-active global winners, having consolidated weaker national and regional champions, though top-end global companies in niche positions continue to flourish. Other top players have exited or been acquired. It is Chinese EMMs, who are as of 2019 setting the pace in this formerly fragmented global market. This is a cautionary tale of monumentally shifting national competitive advantages favourable to EMMs, meriting even more globally pro-active strategies by incumbents. Advanced countries appear likely to retain Ricardian relative comparative advantage in only a few sectors, where they are exceptionally advantaged. Trends may be more drawn out in even more fragmented sectors, but future EMMs should not be underestimated.

NOTES

1 This has been one of four key debates in the international business and strategy literature field (Peng, M. and Pleggenkuhle-Miles, E. (2009). 'Current debates in global strategy', *International Journal of Management Reviews*, 11, pp. 51–68.). The advocates call for proactive global strategies. (Levitt, T. (1983). 'The globalization of markets', *Harvard Business Review*, pp. 92–102; Ohmae, K. (1985). *Triad Power: The Coming Shape of Global Competition*. New York: Free Press; Schlie, E. and Yip, G. (2000). 'Regional follows global: Strategy mixes in the world automotive industry', *European Management Journal*, 18, pp. 343–354; Friedman, T. (2006). *The World Is Flat: The Globalized World in the Twenty-First Century*. London: Penguin; Sirkin, H., Hemerling, J. and Bhattacharya, A. (2008). *Globality: Competing with Everyone from Everywhere for Everything*. London: Headline Press; Van Agtmael, A. (2008). *The Emerging Markets Century. How a New Breed of World-class Companies is Overtaking the World*. London: Simon and Schuster). The sceptics advocate regional or, at most, semi-global strategies. Ghemawat, P. (2003). 'Semi-globalization and international business strategy', *Journal of International*

Business Studies, 34, pp. 138–152; Ghemawat, P. (2011). *World 3: Global Perspective and How to Achieve It*. Cambridge, MA: Harvard University Press; Rugman, A. (2005). *The Regional Multinationals: MNEs and 'Global' Strategic Management*. Cambridge: Cambridge University Press; Rugman and Collinson, 2004; Rugman, A. and Verbecke, A. (2004). 'A perspective on regional and global strategies of the multinational enterprises', *Journal of International Business Studies*, 35, pp. 3–18; Chandler, A. (1969). 'The structure of American industry in the twentieth century: Historical overview', *Business History Review, XLIII*, noted the struggles of big American companies, as early diversification strategies led to problems and declining performance, only later restored following often decades of structural adaptations and learning. As larger firms gained market share, concentration ratios increased. Scholars confirmed international diversification leading to organisation adaptations, later reversing initially negative performance outcomes (Daniels, J., Pitts, R. and Tretter, M. (1985). 'Organizing for dual strategies of product diversity and international expansion', *Strategic Management Journal*, 6, pp. 223–237; Rumelt, R. (1982). 'Diversification strategy and profitability', *Strategic Management Journal*, 3, pp. 359–369). Vernon, R. (1971). *Sovereignty at Bay: The Multinational Spread of U.S. Enterprises*. New York: Basic Books, found that in 1964 data, MNEs outperformed non-MNEs in terms of return on sales and post-tax return on total assets. Since then, however, both the extent of international diversification and the impact on performance has long been hotly contested. (Thomas, D. and Eden, L. (2004). 'What is the shape of the multinationality-performance relationship?' *Multinational Business Review*, 12, pp. 89–110; Contractor, F., Kundu, S. and Hsu, C. (2007). 'Nature of the relationship between expansion and performance: The case of emerging market firms', *Journal of World Business*, 42, pp. 401–417; and Gaur, A. and Kumar, V. (2009). 'International diversification, business group affiliation and firm performance: Evidence from India', *British Journal of Management*, 20, pp. 172–189.)

2 Bain (1956)'s study in turn dates back to Mason (1939) industrial organisational paradigm dealing with Structure – Conduct (Strategy) – Performance.

3 Baden Fuller, C. and Stopford, J. (1991). 'Globalization frustrated: The case of white goods', *Strategic Management Journal*, 12, pp. 493–507.

4 Ghemawat, P. (2003), ibid.

5 Rugman's classifications have been criticised as arbitrary, artificially reducing the proportion of 'global' players', as compared with other equally credible schema; and as lacking in any more dynamic perspective (Osegowitsch, T. and Sammartino, A. (2008). 'Re-assessing home-regionalization', *International Journal of Management Reviews*, 11, pp. 51–68.)

6 For substantiation and elaboration of Indesit's strategic position worldwide and this dilemma see Joseph Bower, 'Indesit Company: Does Global Matter', Harvard Business School, Case 9-308-071, 10 September 2008.

7 Figures in this paragraph analysed from Bower's 'Indesit Company', ibid.

8 For sources and full details, see Khanna, T., Palepu, K. and Andrews, P. 'Haier: Taking a Chinese Company Global in 2011', Harvard Business School, Case 9-712-408, 15 May 2012.

9 Sheth, J. and Sosodia, R. (2002). *The Rule of Three: Surviving and Thriving in Competitive Markets*. New York: Free Press.

10 *Financial Times*, 9 September 2014, p. 16, 'Electrolux' p. 19, 'Electrolux ready to rumble with Whirlpool after GE Deal'.

11 Euromonitor 'Midea Group leads fragmented market', www.euromonitor.com, 21 July 2017.

Part V

SUSTAINING GLOBAL SUCCESS

12

CORPORATE COLLAPSE, RETRENCHMENT, AND TURNAROUNDS IN THE CONTEXT OF GLOBAL RIVALRY

LESSONS FROM KODAK, NORTEL, GKN, AND COMPASS

Chris Carr with Anais Auriau and Patricia Ramos

HOW EVEN *GREAT* COMPANIES CAN COLLAPSE FACING GLOBAL RIVALS

All corporations discussed in this chapter were once rated among the most successful worldwide. The first three Kodak, Nortel, the Royal Bank of Scotland (RBS), like GM later, went bankrupt in the face of global challenges; Compass and GKN retrenched savagely, were turned around, and came back stronger. This chapter first examines traits associated with such *great* enduring companies; secondly, how they got into trouble; and then, thirdly, successful retrenchment and turnaround strategies.

Peters & Waterman's *excellence* model,[1] based on exceptionally performing United States (US) firms back in 1980, identified eight traits: sticking to the knitting, biases for action, being hands-on and value-driven, closeness to customers, entrepreneurship through allowing autonomy, productivity through people, hands-on and values driven, simple organisational structures with lean staff levels, and simultaneous loose-tight properties. Half of these companies soon thereafter encountered performance setbacks, leading to sharp criticisms; yet Collins and Porras's more recent studies of 18 *great* companies, sustaining performances over almost 100 years on average, drew on a remarkably similar set of US success stories.[2] Their *great* company model highlighted three key attributes:

1. Meaning in terms of passion, commitment, and integrity
2. Mind-sets in terms of the audacity to be different, though remaining accountable
3. Action-orientation, even at the expense of perfection, with well-aligned incentives.

Elsewhere, in 1997, De Geus' team from Shell, analysed 27 long-lived, *living companies*, comparable in size to themselves, and emphasised four traits: sensitivity to the environment, cohesion & identity, tolerance & decentralisation, and conservative financing methods.[3] In 2003, Stadler examined 40 European enduring multi-nationals over 100 years old, highlighting four traits from nine star performers: exploit before you explore; diversify your portfolio; remember your mistakes; and be conservative about change.

Such traits highlight basic business principles such as good stakeholder relationships, effective implementation, employee commitment, tolerance of mistakes, learning ability, and focusing core businesses. Peters & Waterman and Collins & Porras stress people relationships, but differ on 'staying close to customers'. De Geus and Stadler play up more evolutionary adaptive capabilities, including diversification and financial prudence. The lacuna, unaddressed in these US/European studies, is any requirement for global strategy.

Yet even *great* companies risk reversionary failure. Collins's (2009) *How the Mighty Fall*[4] highlighted internal reasons, through patterns of hubris born of earlier successes, arrogance, reduced willingness to learn, and neglect of core businesses:

1. Undisciplined Pursuit of More – Growth at all costs, absence of strategic decision-making, HR problems, and lack of cost discipline.
2. Denial of Risk and Peril – Non-recognition of problems, overambitious goals and high-risk decisions, continuous restructuring, and lack of dialogue within teams.
3. Grasping for Salvation – Panic, radical changes and moves, erosion of finances, confusion, and search for a charismatic leader.
4. Capitulation to Irrelevance or Death – Selling off or filing for bankruptcy.

Corporate failure has been well researched. Slatter & Lovett (1999) found three key external contributory factors – changes in market demand, competition, and adverse changes in commodity prices; but no less than ten internal causes: poor management; inadequate financial control; poor working capital management; high costs; lack of marketing efforts; overtrading; big projects; acquisitions; financial policy; and organisational inertia and confusion.[5] Argenti (1976)'s listed less quantifiable failure factors, shown in Table 12.1, flagging up managerial actions and likely failure mode patterns. Top level vulnerabilities led to bad decisions and overtrading, sapping protective controls. Hubris encouraged big project (or merger and acquisition) blunders. Financial strength faltered, spawning creative accounting and non-financial symptoms. Ships, already dangerously low in the water, became swamped by business hazards – savage competitor actions, market downturns, and disruptive technologies[6] – and once successful corporate cultures, now proved resistant to change.[7]

Recognising patterns, how is it that some great companies plunge on, whilst others do intervene, retrench, and turnaround, pre-empting crises and coming back stronger than ever?[8] Chief executives must create and maintain a 'sense of urgency' dispelling complacency.[9] Financial priorities come first, requiring first class management accounting and tough decisions to cut loss-making activities. 'Realignment' is vital to secure adequate 'bridge capital'. Recovery entails practical turnaround strategies, stage by stage,[10] which should be followed up in a final renewal stage, focussing on the impact to the organisational culture and learning, as depicted in Figure 12.1.[11]

Table 12.1 Argenti's dynamics of failure (summarised)

1. **Management** – one-man rule, non-participating board, depth of management
2. **Accountancy Information** – poor budgetary control/costing systems
3. **Change** – inadequate response to competitive, political, social (…) changes
4. **Constraints** – imposed by media, trade unions, national government
5. **Overtrading** – underestimating borrowing needs and time scales necessary
6. **The Big Project** – underestimating costs/time scales, overestimating revenues
7. **Gearing** – rapidly rising gearing leading to increased risk
8. **Normal Business Hazards** – weak response due to poor management
9. **Financial Ratios** – inflation can conceal their actual evolution
10. **Creative Accounting** – managers confused by their own poor numbers
11. **Non-financial Symptoms** – low quality and low morale of all concerned
12. **The Last Few Months** – dividends still paid out although bankruptcy is close

Source: Summarised from Argenti, J., *Corporate Collapse: The Causes and Symptoms*, McGraw Hill, New York, 1976.

Note: Developed in collaboration with respondent D.

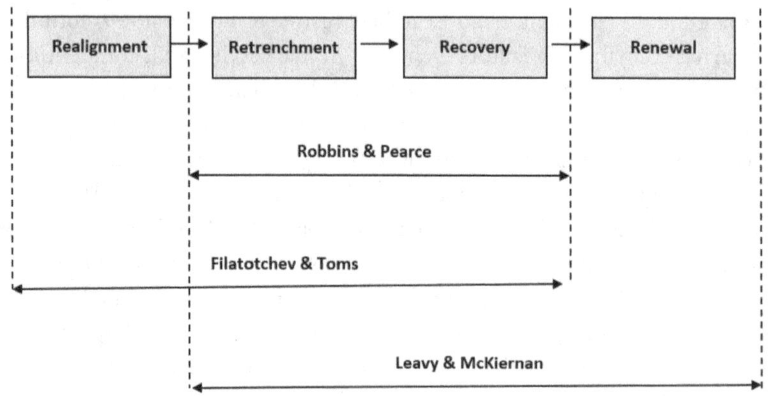

Seven Key Ingredients	Generic Turnaround Strategies
1. Crisis stabilisation	Taking control Cash management Asset reduction Short-term financing First-step cost reduction
2. Leadership	Change of CEO Change of other senior management
3. Stakeholder support	Communications
4. Strategic focus	Redefine core business Divestment and asset reduction Product-market refocusing Down-sizing Outsourcing Investment
5. Organisation change	Structural changes Key people changes Improved communications Building commitment and capabilities New terms and conditions of employment
6. Critical process improvements	Improved sales and marketing Cost reduction Quality improvements Improved responsiveness Improved information and control systems
7. Financial restructuring	Refinancing Asset reduction

Figure 12.1 Different turnaround models and generic strategies at each stage. *Note*: Integrating Slatter & Lovett (ibid).

KODAK – FROM GREAT TO COLLAPSE – LESSONS LEARNED FROM HUBRIS, BORN OF SUCCESS

Just two companies sustained above average profitability consistently throughout all five-year windows between 1918 and 1987: GE, whose stock value has halved since 2000, and Kodak, which went into bankruptcy. Thanks to incessant product innovations and efficient marketing efforts

(Gavetti et al. 2004) in the 1930s, Kodak emerged the global leader in photographic film with a world renowned brand. In 1935, Kodak responded brilliantly to the first new wave of disruption as colour film came in, by being the first company to industrialise this new advance under the name of Kodachrome. By the 1980s, Kodak ranked among the greatest global companies of the century. Yet after almost a century of uncontested domination, symptoms began to mirror Collins' hubris model: as though '*convinced to have a monopoly of divine right over the mass-market photography*' (Sauteron 2009).[12]

To gain more in-depth understanding, we used Thomson One Banker financial data to benchmark Kodak longitudinally against global rivals such as Canon and Fujifilm, questionnaires completed by current and former Kodak employees, and followed up by interviewing seven employees as in Table 12.2.

Our executives agreed, one commenting: '*Historically, if there was a competitor, Kodak would blow them away*'. And as respondents B and C put it to us: '*In practice you had employees with an extreme sense of entitlement; if people had any ideas at all about how to improve something, they expected to be compensated for it…We are Kodak. If we build it, they will buy it*'. Sauteron argued such arrogance was present at all organisational levels, with executives '*blinded by pride*', feeling that Kodak was '*unsinkable*'. The *Financial Times* (5 April 2012) evoked an entitlement culture '*among some long-serving employees who had become used to the benevolent legacy of pension, health and other benefits*'. Respondent D, a former commercialisation project manager at Kodak concurred:

> Our market share, our brand recognition, our company reputation we're so exceptional that, I believe, we just couldn't imagine losing our number one position or failure of any kind. I'm afraid that there was a certain arrogance in our company that I could especially see when we dealt with suppliers. We seemed to believe that they were lucky to be dealing with us. This belief in our inherent superiority was an unfortunate side effect of our success.

Table 12.2 Interviewees at Kodak

Respondent	*Broad responsibilities*	*Dates of employment at Kodak*	
A	First-line supervisor	1977–2012	☐
B	Plant engineering support	1980–1998	☐
C	Technician team leader	1981–1999	☒
D	Commercialisation project manager; Department manager	1973–2008	☒
E	Lead material handler	1989–2004	☐
F	Maintenance operations	1976–2004	☐
G	Laboratory technician; Process specialist	1968–1999	☒

Rochester, Kodak's base, as a 'one-company town', probably encouraged this uncritical sense of entitlement, despite looming threats. One Kodak executive felt (*Business Week* 20 October 1997) that '*Mr Fisher believed digital products would merely substitute for their analogue counterparts rather than disrupt the whole image-making process*'. Others argued, though, that '*Fisher and Carp absolutely knew that digital was coming*', and felt Kodak was '*ready for the challenge*'.[13] Far from neglecting their primary businesses, Kodak consistently invested in research and development (R&D) until 2003, leading to numerous quality and technology improvements (*Monde* 08 October 2004), though pride may have contributed to some operational complacency:

> Kodak had and has some of the best employees a company could ask for. But they did accept complacency from many and as a supervisor it was very hard to get the company to react when they needed to. They would make it very difficult to reward the high performing individuals and remove the low performers. (Respondent A)
>
> There were many lazy people at Kodak that should have been fired for lack of motivation, bad attitude, doing the absolute bare minimum they could get away with and having a huge sense of entitlement. Also, there was animosity among the hourly people against anyone in management or engineering because they felt they did not deserve to be paid more. Even though Kodak was non-union, Kodak acted as badly as any government union employees. (Respondent B)

All interviewees agreed Kodak's sheer size accumulated layers of bureaucracy, incurring costs and slowing decisions. As respondent B put it: '*A company that large at that time in history made it almost impossible to do anything quickly*'.

> Kodak was like the Government, you bought things through purchasing and most times paid three times what you could go down the street and buy for a lot less. We had so many lawyers making policies that would keep us from a lawsuit that it complicated every Human Resources practice. We had surveys and electronic training that meant nothing to the average worker. (Respondent A)
>
> At the beginning of my career, there was a lot of bureaucracy. Anything that needed to be done had to go up the chain and then over to another department. But at that time, we could afford to be slow, and the world itself was much slower. There were defined privileges for different levels of employees, and barriers were difficult to cross. (Respondent D)

By contrast, Fujifilm's lower sales and general administration/sales ratio initially allowed them to exploit a cost-leadership strategy (Figure 12.2 and Table 12.3), taking share from Kodak even in the US. '*There is no doubt that we did*

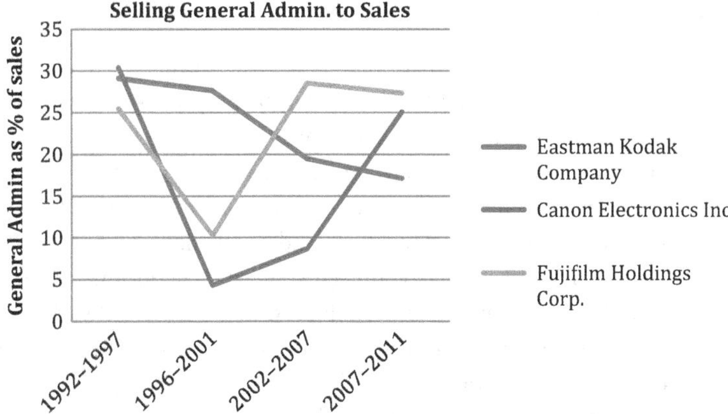

Figure 12.2 Sales, general and administrative to sales ratios: Kodak versus rivals. (From Thomson One Banker.) Note: Selling, general and administrative expenses to sales ratios for Kodak, Fuji and Canon five-year averages 1992–2011. Kodak finally highest and Fuji lowest.

Table 12.3 Fuji's low-cost value chain strategy compared to Kodak

	Activities	*Kodak* *[Differentiation strategy]*	*Fujifilm* *[Cost leadership strategy]*
Support Activities	Firm infrastructure	Important role of hierarchy, inconsistent leadership	Strong leadership by S. Komori
	Human resources management	High proportion of promotions internal; numerous layoffs	Strong corporate social responsibility; good working conditions
	Technology development	Use of many acquisitions to help move into digital; great R&D efforts.	Technology development mainly in-house
	Procurement	Dominant position with suppliers	Focus on the quality and reliability of suppliers
Primary Activities	Logistics and operations	High quality manufacturing; good distribution network	Productivity higher than Kodak
	Marketing and sales	Focus on quality, customer satisfaction and brand recognition; but lack of appropriate market research	Focus on low prices relative to Kodak's; aggressive marketing: e.g. sponsoring Olympics after Kodak withdrew
	Service	All-round service; present in all aspects of the digital imaging value-chain: e.g. kiosks, on-line sharing sites	Range of support services for customers

not see the threat of Fuji for a long time'. (respondent D). Mass commercialisation of digital cameras derived from a new disruptive technology allowed Canon to also cut costs, complementing its superiority in digital technology.

Disruptor technologies

Kodak originally succeeded through a *blue-ocean/disruptor*[14] style strategy, bringing photography to a mass market, following up pro-actively, with the new disruptive colour technology in the 1930s. This second disruption suited Kodak's business model, so massive investments shored up earlier entry barriers, sustaining outstanding profitability, as analysed in Figure 12.3.

Yet digital disruption was different in undermining Kodak's *razor-blades* business model, it brought radically altered structural economics as analysed in Figure 12.4. For a company which had sold cheap hardware, making money on consumables, profits in digital now derived from swiftly bringing new hardware and services products to a fast-changing market. Kodak was more used to searching for '*perfect products*' (*The Economist* 14 January 2012), and bringing to market new products sometimes conflicted with its own business model and film interests:

> Kodak started out as a corporation that invented a market. That's all and good, but not often repeatable. The truly successful companies use market research to determine needs and wants and market to satisfy those. (Respondent C)

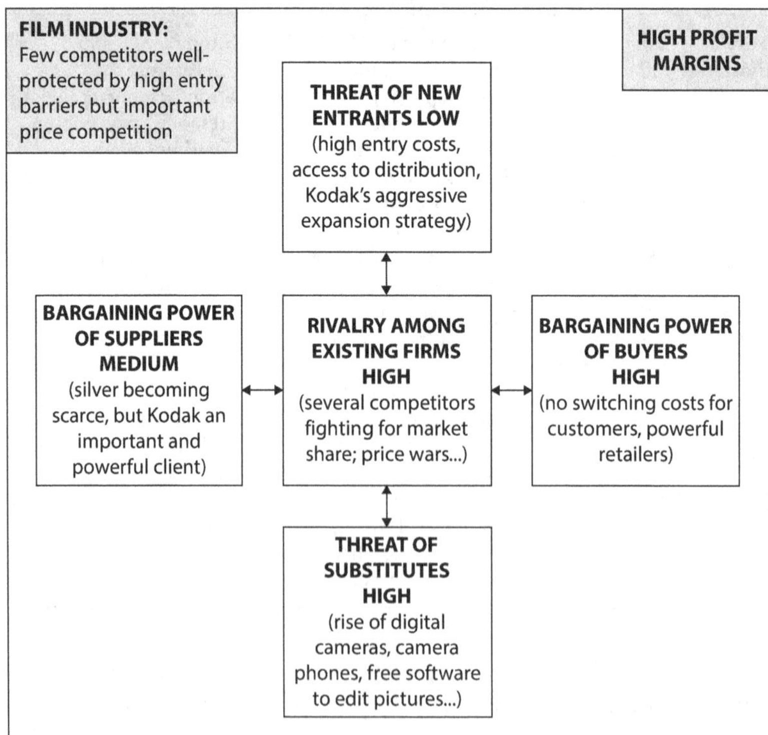

Figure 12.3 Porter's Five Forces analysis of the global photographic film industry earlier.

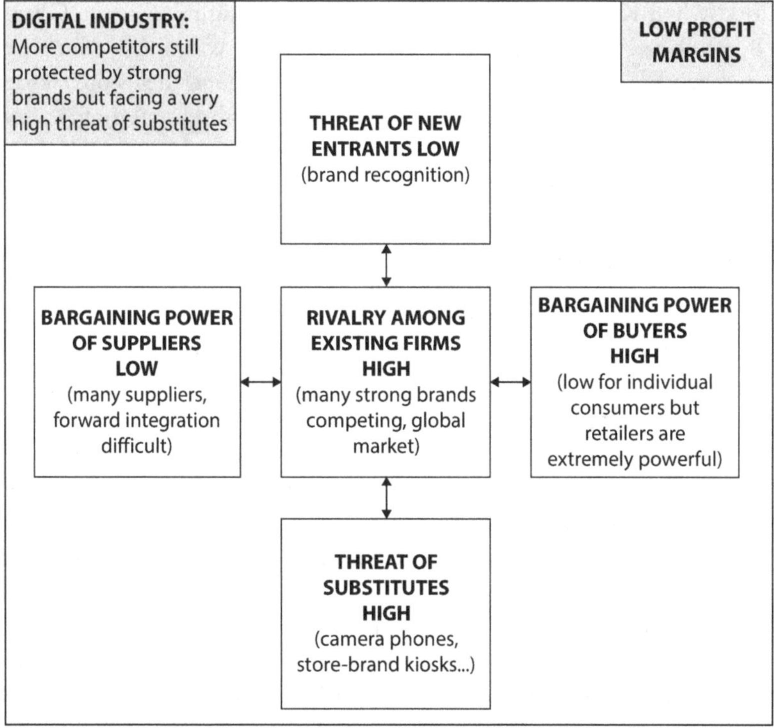

Figure 12.4 Porter's Five Forces analysis of the global digital photography industry.

> Even when they 'dipped their toes' into the digital arena, it was always with one hand hanging on to traditional. It always seemed like they were trying to use digital as a tool to sell more traditional, rather than transition to digital. (Respondent C)

Though aided by its brand name, Kodak struggled to catch up:

> The people of Kodak could not think outside the little yellow film box. Every attempt at diversifying, attempting to test the digital waters, so to speak, seemed to be 'anchored' by a need to somehow tie digital to film – an apparent refusal to migrate to new products, a refusal to even hint at eventually abandoning traditional products. (Respondent C)
>
> Another facet of this success was the incredibly high profit margins that film enjoyed. I remember being at a talk where one of our managers joked that only cocaine had a higher profit margin. This side of our success was a big factor in our timing into the digital market. Our management was addicted to that profit margin, and, I believe, unwilling to do anything that would foreshorten the length of time that we would enjoy that profit. So, in spite of the fact that we did a lot of research into digital technology, we did not want to implement it for this reason. (Respondent D)

By 2003 when Kodak abandoned film to focus on digital, Canon, Olympus and Sony were too already far ahead. The problem was not so much innovative capability, but more one of mindsets: top-level decisions wrongly assumed new markets like China would first adopt film photography, before only later shifting to digital. *Management knew what the future held; they just didn't want to believe it.* (Respondent D)

Size for the sake of size and risk denial

Collins cautioned that successful companies were apt to engage in growth strategies and '*undisciplined discontinuous leaps*' beyond core businesses, proving financially unsustainable. Kodak similarly pursued strong growth in its digital division to the point where analysts doubted their financial viability.[15] '*Gigantism was reassuring*' (Sauteron 2009, ibid.). Yet *Business Week* (20 October 1997) claimed Kodak's diversification into '*everything from drugs to copiers*' never delivered expected growth (*Business Week* 20 October 1997). *The Economist* (19 January 2012) likewise criticised Kodak's '*pricey acquisitions abandoned*' and lack of strategic focus.

Kodak suffered leadership and human resources problems. Controversies surrounded the choice of a new chief executive officer (CEO) (*Financial Times* 02 April 2012), the attitude of the board (*Business Week* 20 October 1997), and key executives resigning (*The Economist* 10 January 2002). With each CEO came a different strategy, undermining consistent leadership (*The Economist* 14 January 2012). Cost disciplines eroded (Sauteron 2009, ibid.):

> *'They acted for a long time like money was no object. Everything bought was the very best available. Nothing was reused, usually sent to the landfill or was purchased at a very low price by employees'.* (Respondent A)

Personal interests often overtook organisational needs. Employees and executives remained attached to '*time-honoured ways of doing business*' (*Financial Times* 05 April 2012) despite resulting inefficiencies: '*There were always large egos in play in every level of management and internal protectionism*'. (Respondent B)

Top executives blamed declining revenues on external factors, such as currencies, material prices, and price wars,[16] but employees interviewed blamed mismanagement:

> I don't think many of us blamed external factors at all. The main factor was lack of vision to the next big thing. [...] We were given so many new programs... Some were good, but others made no sense at all. (Respondent E)
>
> I think most employees blamed Kodak (mis)-management for the decline – but part of the problem was 100 years of no competition, and managers did not know how to market or price-adjust for competition. (Respondent C)

Kodak's historical quasi-monopoly on photography left them insensitive to market forces and encouraged recourse to ineffective costly restructurings (Lucas Jr & Goh 2009; Grant 2009). They had losses in 1997 and 2001, dashing expectations (*The Economist* 28 September 2000), and in every year between 2005 and 2010 (aside from a small profit in 2007) (Thomson One Banker analysis). Huge risks undertaken relied on ambiguous data (*Financial Times* 02 April 2012). Kodak seemed in denial: its 2000 annual report stated that '*it is a very smart time to be in the picture business*'. Communications reflected '*imperious detachment*': one senior executive joking that '*market share is not a word in the Kodak dictionary*' (*The Economist* 29 July 1999). Respondent B likewise commented: '*I would say that up until the early 90s Kodak thought it was basically immune from market forces*'.

> I don't think that the employees did not adhere to the new Kodak. The employees were willing to do anything to keep Kodak strong, their jobs depended on it. The problem was that upper management was trying to 'straighten up the chairs on the deck of the Titanic', rather than navigate around the iceberg and stop the leak. (Respondent C)

Kodak produced their first digital camera in 1975, so were not in complete denial. Yet, by trying to sustain film for so long before fully committing, they became vulnerable to a digital tsunami arriving so much faster than expected (Rick Braddock in *Financial Times* 02 April 2012). Stranded, they desperately required a turnaround.

KODAK'S FAILED TURNAROUND – LESSONS LEARNED

In 1993, George Fisher (previously CEO of Motorola) replaced Kay Whitmore as CEO. The board wanted a new direction. The first ever external appointment, Fisher, was hailed as a '*corporate saviour*' (*Business Week* 20 October 1997):

> I was working in digital media when George Fisher arrived. I was very glad to see him. I remember saying that it was pleasant to read material that had the words 'digital' and 'Kodak CEO' in the same paragraph. (Respondent D)

Fisher immediately tackled Slatter & Lovett step 1 (Figure 12.1) of *Crisis Stabilization*: short-term cash management. He slashed dividends; sold off previous acquisitions such as Sterling Drugs, the copier division, and Eastman Chemical Co., releasing $8.9 billion to pay down debts; milked the film business for cash, and reduced manufacturing costs and overheads (*Business Week* 04 August 1997 and 20 October 1997). However, in contrast to Slatter's recommended short-term financial orientation, Fisher '*invested for the long-term*' (ibid) – Boston Consulting Group (BCG) portfolio matrix style – funding digital and acquisitions (*The Economist* 23 January 2004) – a 'hybrid' strategy, with digital conceived as enhancing traditional photography.

In respect to step 2 – *Leadership*, Fisher changed a fifth of Kodak's most senior executives (*Business Week* 20 October 1997), hiring from rivals to help reinvent Kodak. Slatter stressed improving communications with external stakeholders during crises, re-securing trust. *Business Week* (20 October 1997) praised Fisher's '*remaining upbeat in public*', impressed that '*[Kodak] was about halfway through where it needs to be in the restructuring and turnaround* in 1997'; but respondent A remained sceptical:

> George Fisher wanted to take the company in different directions but the Board of Directors and stakeholders were not supporting him.

Carp also sustained these efforts, but still encountered resistance from middle managers whose traditional film business values had changed little since Whitmore's days.[17]

Strategically re-focusing proved controversial. Though divesting stagnant businesses such as microfilm and copiers was consistent with Slatter's advice for implementing product-market refocusing, this was the first time Kodak had ever re-focused and outsourced. Yet, whilst Fisher underpinned his more defined digital ambitions with heavy R&D investments (ibid), he also tried to nurture growth through analogue technology. Incrementalism, predicated on photography progressing only slowly from film to digital, was potentially flawed: entry into the digital market would not have passed Porter's value creation tests (as shown in Table 12.4).

Employees also remained sceptical and morale was damaged by 80% workforce reductions between 1993 and 2009.[18]

> Fisher started shutting down and selling everything that didn't fit the company's new image, including some profit makers. (Respondent C)

Table 12.4 Assessment of Kodak's earlier diversification based on Porter's better-off model

Porter's test for value-creation during diversification	*Did Kodak's diversification in the digital industry meet these tests?*
Attractiveness of the industry Potential for premium profits?	Unclear – the industry was attractive because of its high growth; however, its profit margins were very low compared with the film industry
Cost of entry test? Does the cost of entry capitalise all future profits?	No – Kodak invested heavily into R&D and digital products, but the digital division never achieved its profit targets
Better-off test Does the new unit gain competitive advantage from its link with the conglomerate, or vice-versa?	No – Kodak's film sales risked facing cannibalisation from digital; furthermore, the digital unit did not require the same competences and thus did not hugely benefit from its links with Kodak (except for brand reputation)

> It was with Mr. Fisher that we realized that a job at Kodak was no longer a secure job – up until that time, it was assumed that a good hard worker at Kodak would always have a job. Morale took a big downturn that day. (Respondent C)

Organisational change and process improvements

Fisher simplified Kodak's structure and management hierarchy, merging digital and consumer imaging divisions, to reduce internal conflicts and streamline decision-making processes (*Business Week* 20 October 1997). External recruitment and performance-based pay were introduced. Yet, despite several policies impacting on the company's 'cultural web' (Table 12.5), the

Table 12.5 Kodak's cultural web before and after turnaround measures

Elements of the cultural web	*Kodak before the turnaround*	*Kodak after the turnaround*
Organisational structure	• Strong hierarchy • Film and digital in separated units	• Still a strong hierarchy • Film and digital divisions merged
Stories	• A one-company town dominating the film industry worldwide • George Eastman as the visionary leader	• Kodak invented the first digital camera and can become leader in the field • Nostalgia of the old times
Control Systems	• Lack of Performance control systems • Little attention to competition and market share; emphasis on customer service	• Increased use of control matrices to assess achievements • Pay-for-performance
Rituals and Routines	• Suggestion System by which employees can submit their innovative ideas • Strong cohesion among employees and attachment to the company	• Information meetings about the digital cloud and how Kodak was involved in it • "Digital coming-out party" with new digital partners (Apple, HP...)
Power Structures	• Lay-offs mainly concern non-management people • Only insiders get to top positions	• Many managers laid off • Outsiders are now recruited for management positions
Symbols	• Corporate headquarters and manufacturing units in Rochester	• Digitalisation of the corporate logo to reflect the changes taking place
Paradigm	*Film is clearly king; Kodak revolves around media and makes money, thanks to its high-volume manufacturing of consumables (rather than equipment). The company trusts its brand and does not excel at marketing. There is little excitement around new products.*	*The company's paradigm is unclear. Film is still king, but the attention to digital is increasing and triggers excitement. Marketing is still not a strength and Kodak starts to doubt its ability to remain the dominant player.*

Note: Developed in collaboration with Respondent D.

corporate culture changed little. Fisher admitted that '*the ability to change in light of quickly changing market conditions remain[ed] a big issue for the company*' (ibid). Critics claimed that Fisher tried to introduce '*the Motorola-style of open discussion*', but failed to adapt his communication style to Kodak's. Former employees perceived inconsistencies:

> Even when they changed the CEO and the upper tier of the management systems, the other floor managers that were on hand were still there, giving the upper managers a response that we were doing great when the opposite was the truth. (Respondent F)
>
> Upper management was more worried about covering their own backside than by trying to get people more involved. (Respondent E)

In line with Slatter's 6th step, Fisher instigated process improvements, aimed at quality and cost reduction, tougher financial targets, and performance control systems for each business.[19] He improved marketing and advertising and enhanced responsiveness by drastically reducing cycle times. However, he was less successful in improving internal information systems; people tended to avoid confrontations and still inclined towards hierarchy (ibid).

Grasping for salvation, capitulation to irrelevance or death

As Collins' model suggests, there comes a point when companies finally recognise crisis, and resort to radical measures. In desperation, Kodak entered new markets such as blood tests and pharmaceuticals (*Financial Times* 31 January 2012), only to later exit having not made expected profits. Taking over in 1999, Dan Carp announced: '*the biggest turning point in Kodak's history*' – nothing short of a '*revolution*' (*The Economist* 30 December 2003). Investments in film were ended. As in Collins's model, this '*fanfare*' was initially well received – the share price rising as Kodak gained patents in digital technologies (*Financial Times* 02 April 2012) – but apparent success was short-lived. Profits and financial strength declined further, reflecting restructuring charges relating to failed new businesses such as healthcare, and its costly Advantix system unwanted by customers. R&D, Kodak's traditional strength, was cut dramatically.

As panic and confusion spread, internal disagreements arose as strategic decisions lost clarity: entries into new markets being followed by sudden exits (*Business Week* 20 October 1997). Middle managers saw little real internal transformation despite incessant top management changes (*The Economist* 28 September 2000). As stakeholders lost trust, Kodak's share price fell by two thirds between Carp's arrival in 1999 and his departure in 2005.

By the time Antonio Perez took over as CEO in 2005, there was already a sense of fatalism (Sauteron 2009, p.163). Some saw Perez as just being appointed to sell off Kodak's intellectual property rights (*Monde* 19 January 2012). Others questioned survival prospects: '*The world, it seems, is changing faster than Kodak can*' (*The Economist* 12 May 2005). By 2007, he had laid off 47,000 workers, closing factories and laboratories (*Financial Times* 02 April 2012). Diversification supported revenue growth, but profits kept on falling. Weighed down by generous pension provisions, Kodak withheld investment into growth areas (*Financial Times* 05 April 2012; *The Economist* 19 January 2012). The film business collapsed in the 2008 recession. Whilst Canon and Fuji stock prices recovered, Kodak's shares plummeted. In January 2012, they filed for Chapter 11 bankruptcy, Perez maintaining this would provide stakeholders '*a greater measure of clarity and confidence about Kodak's path forward*'. Doubts, however, persisted.

Lessons

Kodak embarked on digital when their core strengths laid elsewhere:

> I think that it turned out that George [Fisher] never did understand Kodak and its real potential, probably due to the fact that he came to us with an equipment manufacturing background. He rightly saw digital imaging as an equipment-driven technology. The trouble is that Kodak strengths lie in the media side of the ledger. We have the great material science and coating capability. We have never shown any proficiency with camera manufacturing [...] So, as well as being late to the market, we were also not playing from our strengths. It's not a surprise to me that we didn't succeed. (Respondent D)

Kodak illustrates how historically, successful, resistant corporate cultures can contribute to failure. Bureaucracy and entitlement helped trigger decline. Yet employees soon understood that Kodak's future was at risk and made strenuous efforts to improve performance. Influenced by constructivists such as Mintzberg,[20] we anticipated this as a likely critical lesson; surprisingly, we concluded it was not. Instead, our conclusions accord more closely with positivist schools. They mapped well with Collins' framework when investigated systematically. Kodak's turnaround strategy attuned poorly with Slatter's 9-point recommendations (Table 12.6). The problem was not unawareness of strategic options; but rather a failure to critique those selected in the light of their real competences as compared with global rivals:

> They kept bringing in high priced consultants and trying to take everything they said and ramming it down the throats of the workers. They started out-sourcing everything and lost the dedicated employees who would do anything for the company for contract employees that had no allegiance and would rather steal you blind. (Respondent A)

Table 12.6 Appraisal of the factors behind Kodak's failure

Factors	*Impact*	*Ranking (max 10)*
A WRONG VISION FOR KODAK Kodak goes into digital, spins-off Eastman Chemicals and health-related divisions.	Kodak exits profitable businesses to focus on imaging, where it lacks strengths compared to global rivals	**10/10**
A LACK OF STRATEGIC FOCUS AND INCONSISTENT LEADERSHIP Kodak acquires, divests, and invests without a consistent objective or vision. The company's identity changes with each CEO.	Stakeholders lose confidence in top management (both internally and externally), leading to a lack of commitment and enthusiasm.	**6/10**
TOP MANAGEMENT DENIAL AND COMPLACENCY Executives refused to acknowledge the collapse of the film business for over a decade. They had a huge confidence in their brand and in the sustainability of Kodak's success.	Kodak let its rivals engage in the new technology first and build their reputation, while it tried to sustain film for as long as possible. Complacency led to inappropriate marketing: bringing to market many unwanted products that failed to yield the expected profits.	**4/10**
A RESISTANT CORPORATE CULTURE Employees were not involved enough in the company's turnaround and new digital strategy.	This popular view of Kodak was not evidenced. Complacency arose at top level. Even with dedicated employees, Kodak could not have survived with its flawed strategy.	**1/10**

Practical lessons included: avoiding complacency and over-reliance on a strong brand; vigilant scrutiny of global rivals; making clear commitments; intellectual property portfolio management and timing; and managing the right balance between acquisitions and in-house expertise. Somehow companies must stimulate progress whilst preserving the core of their businesses (Collins & Porras 1994, ibid.). They need to remember their key strengths and stand by them, applying that competitive advantage to the right markets, rather than attempting to stay in the same market when required capabilities have changed. Kodak ultimately lacked that visionary leadership which might have pulled it back from decline. As respondent B put it: '*It would have taken that visionary strategist to pull it off*'. Not one of a succession of CEOs could stem falling profits.

The digital hurdle in the context of global rivalry proved beyond them; executives divested its most profitable businesses involving the company's key capabilities; they invested too late in a low-margin industry; lacking any overall strategic vision likely to save them, top management under George Fisher made such huge strategic mistakes that it is doubtful whether any subsequent CEOs could have thereafter reversed the situation afterwards, even had they chosen more appropriate turnaround paths. Conceivably, bankruptcy might have been staved off; but Kodak as one of the great global players of twentieth century was tragically already holed beneath the water line.

FOOL'S MATE FACING GLOBAL COMPETITION: LESSONS FROM NORTEL

As in chess, classic 'fool's mates' are surprisingly common when facing global competition. Even global winners like Kodak fell prey to hubris. Often this is linked to CEO egos – and you don't get to be a CEO without one – generally alpha-male types, desperate to prove themselves as the biggest elephants in the jungle, both internally and externally. They need robust deep-rooted visions, not public relations motherhood statements; strong disciplines and finance directors, not yes men. Otherwise, as evidenced in Argenti's insightful corporate collapse cases, no matter how successful, ego-based goals just keep getting bigger. We see no levelling out of their growth *'flight trajectories'* – no prudent reigning back – no pruning; sooner or later they'll stall and nose-dive, as happened to Ratner's. Over-confident CEOs sometimes lack experience of adverse times; human nature changes little.

Recall early global winners, the South Sea Bubble or the Hudson's Bay Company. Most incredible has been the naivety of 'financially sophisticated' onlookers and participants, and the sheer scale of disasters: Enron, Nortel, and RBS all had market capitalisations on par with nations. Egos and complexities increased with scale; absolute power could corrupt absolutely. As earlier at Enron, Nortel's mistakes were compounded by poor governance, ethics, and proper visibility.

Nortel Networks, founded in 1885 to exploit Bell's patents by making telephone equipment for the Canadian market, enjoyed a century of outstanding success. As a top global player, Nortel's valuation peaked at \$300 million, representing 36% of the Canadian stock market[21] and 15% of Canada's worldwide investments. Hubris was compounded by atrocious governance. Following an accounting scandal, CEO Frank Duns and top colleagues resigned in 2004; but even earlier, excessive short-term orientated stock options had encouraged massive, unsustainable growth between 1987 and 2000, taking them to \$30 billion revenue. It took three crises to take Nortel down: the dot.com bubble bursting in 2001; the 2004 accounting scandal; and finally the credit crunch in late 2007, as they were still struggling with turnaround measures.

Nortel should not be accused of global complacency; but their *transnational restructurer* configuration relied heavily on risky M&A. In the first three years of John Roth's leadership from 1987, Nortel acquired 14 companies for \$22 million, as he put his foot on the accelerator to *'transform Nortel from a simple telecom equipment provider into a global brand name identified with the Internet'*.

M&A just kept increasing – $30 billion in the year 2000. Debt leverage rose abruptly – rendering them vulnerable as the dot.com bubble burst – and remained dangerously high even four years later. Acquisitions such as Bay Networks ($9 billion) and Sonoma Systems ($10 billion) departed from core competences into less familiar new networks and radical outsourcing. To win business, they spent extravagantly on advertising and offered attractive loans to customers, notably $1.1 billion to Sprint Spectrum, further increasing gearing in 2001. In 2001, Frank Dunn took over from Roth to deal with consequences.

Like Argenti's overloaded supertanker, Nortel was perhaps '*too low in the water*' to survive the credit crunch wave, but, again like Kodak, they sought desperately for a turnaround. In 2005, Mike Zafirovski arrived as CEO, with a stunning turnaround track record. As Wahl 2006 commented[22]: '*If Zafirovski can't fit Nortel, probably no one can*'. His mantra was '*business made simple*', deploying a battery of techniques from his earlier career at GE, including delayering and restructuring. Again, though as at Kodak, people internally remained sceptical and cultural change was difficult:

> I don't think management was transparent in letting us know how bad Nortel's situation was. They continued to give us the perception that Nortel would turn around and everything would be okay. This went on for 10 years and countless rounds of layoffs. We were told bankruptcy was not an option, although we know now that was the plan since late 2008. Interview with Raynor, 2010.

External stakeholders were not convinced either. In June 2009, Zafirovski was grilled by a Canadian Parliament investigation committee about executive bonuses, paid whilst the company was losing money.[23] As Member of Parliament (MP) Laforest put it: '*When you share the gain you should also share the pain*', and as MP McCallum put it: '*It seems like we no longer care about the people*' (Parlvu 2009). He failed to answer a single question: so they opted to invest $13 billion in GM and Chrysler rescues instead. Financial markets likewise turned down his strategic plan, re-focusing heavy investments onto 4G 'hyper connectivity'; asked why, even Zafirovski conceded it was '*a very, very significant shift in the telecom and communications industry, so any plan that was presented at that time could have been viewed with lots of scepticism*'.[24] Asked why he'd not provided support, Industry Minister Tony Clement replied:

> Zafirovski presented a business plan which in my estimation did not meet the criteria of being commercially viable. Evidently the board of Nortel came to the same agreement because they rejected that business plan as well and they chose – not me – to go into creditor protection. (Atkin 2009)

With hindsight, scepticism was merited. Like Kodak's catch-up approach with digital cameras, this huge investment never paid off and deepened their vulnerability. As for Marconi and RBS too, the credit crunch just came as the coup de grace.

Key explanations and lessons for all these collapses can be briefly summed up:

1. Hubris – successful companies, lacking strong governance, did risk succumbing to CEO egos and totally unsustainable growth trajectories.
2. Risks were increased by huge M&A outlays in unfamiliar fields.
3. Argenti's corporate collapse scenarios were evident in sharply increased and signs of creative accounting.
4. Mistaken ambitious strategies, entailing dangerous disruptive technologies, contributed substantially to collapses.
5. Changing previously successful corporate cultures proved almost infeasible even for experienced turnaround CEOs, clearly recognising threats.
6. Good governance and robustly articulated strategies are crucial to retaining support internally and from external stakeholders, including governments.
7. Don't leave it too late or even committed turnaround actions may fail; ships ship too low in the water do risk becoming swamped by those inevitable next big waves (burst 'bubbles', credit crunches ...) albeit some years later.

SUCCESSFUL RETRENCHMENTS & TURNAROUNDS IN THE CONTEXT OF GLOBAL RIVALRY

Necessary retrenchments, staving off possibilities of collapse in the face of powerful global rivals, are more common than supposed: these capabilities have emerged as distinguishing traits for more enduring global winners.

GKN's successful turnaround in the early 1980s and re-trenchment issues in 2018

GKN's robust global winner strategy since 1759 is analysed in Chapter 13. In 1980, however, even Britain's most enduring and successful industrial conglomerates, with around 100 business units, faced potential bankruptcy. Severe macro-economic policies hiked up Britain's real (inflation-adjusted) exchange rates and demand downturns rendered swathes of British manufacturing uncompetitive, taking out over a million jobs. Several engineering companies succumbed to bankruptcy or takeovers. Losses at Rover and Ford forced them to leverage international procurement, stepping up their negotiating power, savaging suppliers. Over the next three years, component prices were frozen, despite the wholesale price index rising 44%, and top 60 UK vehicle component suppliers plunged to average return on capital employed (RoCE)s of virtually zero, compared with 16% over the previous ten years.[25] Addressing intensified rivalry and overdiversification, GKN responded ruthlessly.

Basil Woods, GKN's strategic planner, was in no doubt as to the threat of bankruptcy, but perceived their highly charismatic chairman, Sir Barry Heath, as '*not someone you could hold a highly analytical conversation with for more than five minutes*'.[26] He, and with three other top directors, led a boardroom revolution. The new top team was highly analytical and financial, but also tough and hands-on.

Fortunately, GKN was one of the few British top vehicle component companies to have already massively switched resources (sales, assets, and employees) more globally. With Rover declining fast, their customer portfolio was already predominated by US, Continental European, and Japanese original equipment manufacturers. Relatively low value-added divisions, such as screws and fasteners had been disposed of, recognising they could no longer sustain competitiveness against low cost Far East Asian rivals.[27] The drivechain division had been taken globally so successfully that it provided almost two thirds of group profit by the end of this extraordinarily difficult period. Even this, was not enough.

Management accountants assessed that over half of GKN's business units had plunged into losses. Break-even analyses and follow-ups were ruthless. Mike Bolenghi's approach to loss-making managers was: (1) Okay, you're clearly uncompetitive, so identify an investment budget and a cogent plan that will restore your international competitiveness and profitability; (2) would you really make that investment if this was your own money? (3) if you can't then convince us that you have a turnaround plan and a credible implementation track record, we will consider disposal. GKN Contractors, for whom I worked prior to my PhD, was closed. The whole forgings sub-group, where I had worked earlier, was exited via a 'phoenix' rationalisation joint venture with British Steel. Top level financial skills, and controls throughout GKN, proved resilient and the turnaround sustained.

In 2018, GKN's financial re-structuring skills were re-put to the test, following a £7.4 billion takeover bid from Melrose, who argued that more value could be released through a break-up. GKN was still making excellent RoCEs overall, but balked expectations at the end of 2017 by reporting substantial unexpected charges from its US-based aerospace parts division. Kevin Cummins, head of that division, and group CEO designate was immediately sacked, denting city confidence. GKN's share price fell to a 15-month low, wiping £600 million off GKN's market capitalisation of some £5 billion. In January 2019, Melrose's bid caught GKN napping. With only a 15-year track record, its own share price in the last two years had quadrupled (despite losses), enabling a 23% offer premium. With 80% of the offer being equity and just 20% cash, this leveraged their extraordinary (negative) price/earnings (PE) ratio and GKN's strong balance sheet. GKN responded with aggressive re-structuring, negotiating an offer of $6.1 billion for the drivechain division (roughly half group sales and profits), with another £1 billion plus plans to sell off the niche powder metallurgy business. This forced Melrose's bid up to £8.1 billion, affording huge value to GKN shareholders in return for full control. Whether Melrose can match GKN's restructuring skills has yet to be seen.

Compass's successful re-structuring and turnaround in catering services

Are services so different? Between 1994 and 2004, Compass grew even faster than Collins' *great* manufacturers, covering no less than 98 countries and becoming the global number 1 in catering/outsourcing. Success was partly fuelled by the trend worldwide towards outsourcing, as major companies recognised the need to focus within the value chain onto their real core competences. Outsourcing of such activities was negligible in 1945, but now around 50%. As their CEO Richard Cousins put it in 2014,[28] Compass, unlike most British companies from the 1980s, '*really got globalisation*'; so many engineering conglomerates like BTR,[29] where he'd served as a board director in 1984, had had excellent operations management and '*brilliant cost and budgetary controls*', but had failed to recognise this global imperative.

Yet by 2006, when Cousins was brought in as CEO, Compass' growth had slowed dramatically. Profitability had slumped. Analysts commented that yet another British company was about to go under in America. They were proved wrong, but only because Compass displayed that resilience to re-group, re-focus, and re-strengthen. Cousins exploited his tough operational management and financial skills, and global experiences from BPB. Compass' corporate portfolio was decidedly '*mixed*' – some '*really good legacy businesses*' – but some overdiversified moves had proven to be '*rubbish*'. Cousins' spent a month, travelling, listening, resisting temptations to write off prematurely many managers, who ultimately proved highly capable. But ultimately his number one priority was '*simplify, simplify and simplify again*'.

Compass re-focused onto four sectors: business and industrial with customers like Google serviced worldwide (about half of turnover), education (about 20%), healthcare and services (about 20%), and sports and leisure, including 20 top US basketball teams (about 10%). Overbold global expansion required surgical pruning, from 98 countries back to about 50. '*Barriers to entry [globally] are far higher than you might imagine* ... [though] "*a quarter of our revenue comes from global customers*"'. This entailed balanced judgments, but, finally, decisions on which countries to cut were taken '*on one day*'. There was '*no complex model*'. What mattered was getting 90% of decisions right. Attention then turned to implementation.

Unlike at Kodak, there was '*No use of consultants at all...I wouldn't even have time to read their reports. You have to have confidence in your own team...We had just three months to hit those IPO groups* [restoring financial credibility]. *Get that wrong and you'd lose support and go under…With a gun to your head it is crazy how fast you can go*'. Tougher financial disciplines were implemented using a new 'MAP' system, designed to ensure that managers (including 11,000 specially retrained) had '*nowhere to hide*': 250 different business units report through identical KPI [key performance indicator] packs. And any unflagged up deviations and '*we can break their knee-caps …we fire them*'. The company had to be obsessed with performance. '*If a manager doesn't know his numbers, he's toast*'. '*20 years ago, Compass had no KPIs and we put them in. But then it's all about consistency. Once you create a framework, you must have a simple one, you must mean it and stick to it consistency*'. But entrepreneurialism mattered too; MAP could not be pushed too far.

The turnaround plan targeted two and a half years, but then came the credit crunch. It finally took four years before they were strong enough to fund new growth investments, including four £1 billion-level M&As considered, though finally rejected. From Cousin's personal perspective, '*Three quarters of acquisitions are rubbish*'; instead £100 million went to organic investments. By May 2014, their back-to-core strategy yielded resumed growth: revenues rose to £17 billion and pre-tax margins to 7%[30] versus rivals averaging 4%–5%. They were ranked the 6th biggest employer worldwide and 28th on Financial Times Stock Exchange (FTSE) valuations (excluding public sector institutions). From a small UK-orientated company in 1973, their split had shifted to 46% in North America, a little less in Europe/Japan, with a substantial % in emerging markets. America was proving '*a great business*', and Europe and Japan were finally improving after heavy restructuring. There was £1 billion cash that was returned to shareholders in addition to a £500 million buyback scheme, dividends having risen by 10.5%. Cost reduction and people development remained obsessions. '*We stay in modest hotels and its two beers maximum. We're quite Puritanical and this gives us the authority to cut costs: we are now out of smart HQs and expense accounts*'. Compass felt strong enough to meet some resurgence in global demand: '*All our markets have exciting opportunities and, as a result, we are investing more resources around the world to deliver strong growth*'.

Richard Cousins later died suddenly; his contribution is deeply respected.

NOTES

1 Peters, T. and Waterman, R.H. (1980). *In Search of Excellence: Lessons from America's Best-Run Companies.* New York: Harper & Row.
2 Collins, J. and Porras, J.I. (1994). *Built to Last: Successful Habits of Visionary Companies.* New York: Harper Business.
3 De Geus, A. (1997). *The Living Companies – Habits for Survival in a Turbulent Business Environment.* Cambridge, MA: Harvard Business School Press.
4 Collins, J. (2009). *How the Mighty Fall – And Why Some Companies Never Give In.* London: Random House Business Press.

5 Slatter, S. and Lovett, D. (1999). *Corporate Turnaround – Managing Companies in Distress*. London: Penguin; other causes of decline included the lack of long-term strategic focus, organisational structure, internal politics, and culture. Nunes, P. and Breene, T. (2011). Reinvent your business before it's too late. *Harvard Business Review*, January–February pp. 80–87.
6 Christensen, C.M. and Bower, J.L. (1995). 'Disruptive technologies: Catching the wave', *Harvard Business Review*, 73 (1), pp. 43–53; Hamel, G. and Prahalad, C.K. (1994). *Competing for the Future*. Boston, MA: Harper Business School Press; Christensen, C.M. (2003). *The Innovator's Dilemma*. New York: Harper Business Essentials.
7 Johnson, G. and Scholes, K. (2013). *Exploring Corporate Strategy*. London: Pearson; Grinyer, P. and Spender, J.C. (1979). *Turnaround: Managerial Recipes for Strategic Success: The Rise and Fall of the Newton Chambers Group*. London: Associated Business Press, p. 203.
8 Whitney, J.O. (1987) 'Turnaround management every day', *Harvard Business Review*, 65 (5), pp. 49–55; Collins, J. (2009). ibid.
9 Kotter, J. (2008). *A Sense of Urgency*. Cambridge, MA: Harvard Business Press.
10 Slatter, S. and Lovett, D. (1999). *Corporate Turnaround – Managing Companies in Distress*. London: Penguin.
11 Filatotchev, I. and Toms, S. (2006) 'Corporate governance and financial constraints and strategic turnarounds', *Journal of Management Studies*, 43 (3), pp. 407–433; Bibeaut, D.B. (1999). *Corporate Turnaround – How Managers Turn Losers into Winners*. Washington, DC: Beard Books; Leavy, B. and McKiernan, P. (2009). *Strategic Leadership – Governance and Renewal*. New York: Palgrave.
12 Sauteron, F. (2009). *La Chute de l'Empire Kodak*. Paris: L'Hartmattan.
13 Shih, W. 'Former president of Kodak's consumer digital unit', *Financial Times*, 2 January 2012.
14 Christensen, C.M. and Bower, J.L. (1995). Ibid.; Christensen, C.M. (2003). Ibid.
15 Grant, R.M. (2009). *Contemporary Strategy Analysis*. Chichester: Wiley (7th ed.), Case No 7: Eastman Kodak, p. 609.
16 Interview of George Fisher, *Business Week* 20 October 1997 and *The Economist* 28 September 2000.
17 *Business Week*, 20 October 1997, *The Economist* 30 December 2003; Gavetti, G., Henderson, R. and Giorgi, S. (2004). *Kodak and the Digital Revolution*. Boston, Mass: Harvard Business School Case, pp. 1–19.
18 Lucas, Jr H.C. and Goh, J.M. (2009). 'Disruptive technology: How Kodak missed the digital photography revolution'. *Journal of Strategic Information Systems*, 18, pp. 46–55.
19 Gavetti, G., Henderson, R. and Giorgi, S. (2004). Ibid.
20 Mintzberg, H. (1994). *The Rise and Fall of Strategic Planning*. Englewood Cliffs, NJ: Prentice Hall International; Mintzberg, H., Ahlstrand, B. and Lampel, J. (1998) *Strategy Safari – A Guided Tour through the Wilds of Strategic Management*. New York: Free Press; Mintzberg, H., Lampel, J. and Ahlstrand, B. (2005). *Strategy Bites Back*. New York: Pearson Education.
21 CBC (2000). 'Nortel "a Canadian success story"', *Business Week* interview. CBC Digital archives 5 January, accessed 20 June 2010.
22 Wahl, A. (2006). 'Inside the new Nortel', *Canadian Business Online*, 6 November.
23 Zafirovski's executive bonus approach was in sharp contrast to Cisco's CEO John Chambers who drew a $1 million salary, but without any bonus in 2002, when the company was laying off 8500 employees.
24 Parlvu, 2009, FINA Meeting No 38, Parlvu website (on-line), 18 June.
25 See Carr, C. (1990). ibid., for this contextual and competitor analysis and for further details of GKN's strategies including turnaround steps over this period.
26 Having flown with Sir Barry Heath and Parsons, his personnel director, I can endorse this claim to charismatic leadership. The quote is from my later conversations with Basil Woods.

27 See David Spurrell's PhD 1983 thesis at Warwick Business School for a detailed top-level insider's account.
28 Richard Cousins, CEO of Compass, 'From Boffin to Baker', University of Edinburgh Business School 30 October 2014.
29 BTR, like GKN, was a major financially orientated engineering and automotive parts conglomerate. However, when then interviewed, they played down 'strategy' as often merely an excuse for failing to meet their tough double-digit RoS targets. For some years, BTR was an outstanding financial performer until being taken over by Siebe, itself later taken over and broken up. Richard Cousins learned hugely from BTR's excellent operational management and controls, but felt they were '*useless at globalization*' and so moved on to BPB. As BPB's finance director, he oversaw a tripling of profitability: he then became managing director for BPB Canada and later CEO of BPB overall. BPB was market leader in Europe, but initially sub-scale in Canada despite their strong local market share. His hands-on experience of international integration extended to some 15 countries.
30 For corroboration, see *Times* 27 November 2014. p. 63.

13

SUSTAINING GLOBAL STRATEGIES

LESSONS FROM GKN 1759–2019[1]

INTRODUCTION AND METHODOLOGY

GKN has been Britain's last great global automotive player, its number two in aero, and one of the last great corporate histories, dating back to iron and coal activities, and contributing to the Industrial Revolution's very inception. Recognition of historical studies of international business still underplays concerns relating to corporate strategy and performance.[2] We must beware of guru-style 'lessons', derived from short-term studies or cases. Two-thirds of Peters and Waterman's 43 '*excellent*' companies, based on just 5-year performances to 1980, 'slipped from the pinnacle' within the next few years.[3] Lessons, too, derive from GKN's acquisition in 2019 by Britain's private equity conglomerate Melrose.[4]

> In the world of institutions, commercial organisations are 'newcomers'... The average life expectancy of a multi-national corporation – *Fortune* 500 or its equivalent – is between 40 and 50 years and much lower for smaller entrepreneurial companies.[5]

Sweden's Stora Enso and Japan's Sumitomo both originated from copper mining, respectively, 700 and 222 years ago, but few corporations match, say, top universities, whose first-mover, institutional, and reputation advantages prove remarkably enduring.[6] Long-term perspectives are less pertinent in fast-moving sectors, like electronics or social networks; older companies, dying on the vine, cut little ice in boardrooms; but lessons can be derived from histories such as Coutts (1692), Standard Life (1825), and GKN (1759), which for centuries delivered shareholder value whilst still remaining competitive in international markets.[7]

Collins and Porras compared 18 highly successful, long-lived companies,[8] averaging almost 100 years, with 18 matched peers with less exciting shareholder value performances up to 1990. Of the successful '*visionary*' 18, Citicorp dated back 200 years, and three others over 150 years. Successful '*built to last*' (BTL) characteristics included: emphasising organisation-building rather than dramatic inventions or heroic leaders; corporate values transcending mere profit orientation; cult-like cultures; safeguarding core themes; preserving this 'core' ideology, whilst stimulating progress; home grown management (only two of the successful 18 had ever gone outside for chief executive officers, CEOs); and '*big hairy audacious goals*' (BHAGs); yet complemented by substantial experimentation, incremental learning, and never being satisfied, regardless of rivals.

Ten out of 18 of Collins and Porras *visionary* companies were Peters and Waterman's same '*excellent*' companies and all likewise (apart from Sony) American. We found little differences in the 5-year 2007–2011 performances of the two samples, though the much criticised '*excellent*' sample came out slightly ahead. Declining United States (US) performances, discussed in Chapter 9, renders such US-centricity dangerous. China may lack long-lived companies, but Europe is underrepresented.

Stadler though examined 40 European multi-nationals over 100 years old in 2003 and highlighted four traits of nine star performers: exploit before you explore; diversify your business portfolio; remember your mistakes; and be conservative about change. De Geus' study at Shell, based on 27 long-lived, similarly large companies highlighted organisational learning; sensitivity to the business environment; cohesion and identity; tolerance and decentralisation; and conservative financing methods.[9]

This chapter examines whether BTL enduring traits were reflected in GKN's far longer successful corporate history up to 2013, before finally updating in the light of its acquisition by Melrose in 2018 for £8.1 billion. It focuses on longer-term diversification and performance, recognising struggling early US, European, and Japanese diversifiers later learned to restructure and divisionalise, thus restoring successful performances[10,11] and potential city short-termism.[12]

GKN at the start of 2018 was Britain's only surviving top 50 company from 1905.[13] Of the 66 largest United Kingdom (UK) vehicle component companies affording financial information from 1970 to 1982 as examined in my PhD,[14] only GKN and one tiny forging company, Brockhouse, remained UK-owned. BBA, remained independent, though having exited automotives in 2000. Most succumbed to overseas acquisitions or disappeared altogether. BTR, for example, merged with Siebe in 1999 forming Invensys, briefly becoming Britain's largest engineering company by market value, before plummeting and being acquired by France's Schneider (*Financial Times*, 1 August 2013:1), ending its legacy of almost two centuries.[15]

My 1985 PhD thesis followed convention by subdividing these former 66 companies into groups, scrutinising for key success factors, based on performance measures of returns on capital and sales growth over three periods: 1970–1974, 1975–1979, and 1980–1982. Yet even 12 years of '*longitudinal analysis*' underplayed concentration within the UK supplier sector: this has been so intense that some earlier '*success relationships*' from 1985 no longer look robust. My earlier scepticism regarding diversification, based on poor experiences, for example, at Dunlop and RHP, now appears more questionable: BBA's aerospace services diversification and GKN's aero parts diversification have both proven successful.

Numbers depleted as dramatically throughout the USA and Western Europe, though not in Asian and emerging markets. Of 347 supplier companies in Thomson One Banker's data base in 2013, 30 came from the USA and 29 from Europe. Most came from Japan (113), South Korea (32), and the rest of Asia. Just eight came from France, four from Germany,[16] one from Italy, and one from Spain. US companies accounted for 29% of total sales; European 20%; Japan 38%; South Korea 8.5%; and Brazil, Russia, India and China (BRIC) countries collectively 4.5%.

If European long-lived companies appear under-researched, US companies (aside from financial institutions) rarely pre-date the Civil War, 150 years ago. Global concentration within Europe resulted in supply activities becoming largely confined to global multi-nationals, as happened with car assemblers. GKN, by 2013, was one of a small cadre of European multi-nationals surviving by competing globally. Its prior 5-year return on capital at 14% and its sales growth at 11% were well above sector averages, not only in Europe, but worldwide.[17] Other global successes included Europe's leading supplier, Bosch, Germany's private and secretive family company (from 1898); Krupp (from 1811); and Thyssen (from 1871) in steel[18]; though GKN's global evolution uniquely illustrates the vicissitudes and lessons of history since 1759.

Few of Higgins and Toms' successful British firms from 1950 to 1984[19] still survive. In reviewing Britain's top 50 companies by market capitalisation from 1905, only GKN (then #15) survived independently (flourishing globally) at the onset of 2018.[20] From the original 1935 Financial Times Stock Exchange (FTSE 30), just GKN, Tate & Lyle, and Rolls-Royce remained intact. Though bankrupted in 1971, Rolls-Royce was the world's 2nd largest aero-engine manufacturer. Tate & Lyle was successful globally following an impressive 150-year history. Table 13.1 shows market capitalisation performances including Lever/Unilever, the only other top player with data back to 1905. GKN's market capitalisation grew 340-fold from 1930 to 2018; Tate & Lyle 297-fold; and Unilever's 504-fold, albeit reflecting the merger of two large companies.

GKN's unique 259-year history dated back to its Dowlais iron plant and coal activities at the heart of Britain's Industrial Revolution.[21] David Lees, GKN's former chairman was also Tate & Lyle's chairman – combined

Table 13.1 Britain's top 1905 manufacturers: market capitalisations, 1905–2018

Market capitalisation £m	*1905*	*1919*	*1930*	*1948*	*4 August 2013*	*9 February 2018*
Unilever	4.0	24.3	132.0	185.6	35,308	65,000[a]
GKN	4.5	8.2	20.3	35.3	5754	6910
Tate & Lyle	Na	Na	9.3	29.8	3883	2760
Rolls-Royce	Na	Na	Na	Na	22,356	15,110

Sources: Hannah, L. (1976), *The Rise of the Corporate Economy*, Abingdon, Oxon: Routledge, pp. 102–3, 189–191; *Sunday Times* 4 August 2013. Business, p. 11.

Note

a *Financial Times* 9 February 2018. £@1.400. At 4 August 2019, market capitalisations were Unilever £132 billion, Melrose (including GKN) £8.0 billion, Tate & Lyle £3.3 billion, and Rolls-Royce £14.5 billion, *Sunday Times* 18 August 2019.

experiences of over 400 years. In February 2018, GKN held 40% of the world market in automotive drivetrain constant velocity joints and was a leading global player in aero parts.

I worked for GKN from 1974 to 1980, first in GKN's sub-group forgings, and then on the four-man project management team, building (in collaboration with UK and German subsidiaries Hardy Spicer and Uni-Cardan) GKN's drivetrain plants in the USA in 1979/1980. This emerged as the first stage in a comprehensive global strategy, and a '*crucial jump*' extending GKN's historical success (*The Economist* 2012B: 29).[22] In the four decades since, I have researched the global strategies of GKN longitudinally (including subsidiaries in the United Kingdom, France, India, China, and Brazil) and in over 150 other major automotive and automotive component companies worldwide. My 1985 PhD thesis and first book in 1990 afforded product-matched comparative analyses. Two first-class earlier archival histories by Edgar Jones covered 1759–1918 and 1918–1945,[23] whilst Andrew Lorenz's history of GKN from 1759 to 2009 likewise benefitted from excellent company access.[24]

To gain an initial performance perspective, I analysed five years of financial figures up to 2012/2013. The average unweighted five-year return on capital employed was 6% worldwide; 8% for the USA; 3% for Japan; 7% for Germany; and 13% for the United Kingdom; whilst French companies averaged losses of 26%. The average $ sales growth over the same period was 8% worldwide; 4% for the USA; 11% for Germany; 8% for the United Kingdom; 4% for France; whilst Japanese company sales fell by 2%.

This chapter explores four questions. What traits allowed just one major British automotive components company to survive amidst such global concentration? Which strategic success lessons endured? What role did GKN's historical legacy play? What prospects emerge for such sustained strategies in 2019, following its takeover by private equity conglomerate Melrose, while lacking global expertise and presence?

GKN's HISTORICALLY BASED COMPETITIVE ADVANTAGES FROM 1759 TO 1900

Iron making originated in Mesopotamian deslagging breakthroughs at the start of the Iron Age. The price fell by about 97% in the 400 years to 1000 BCE.[25] Britain's take-off in iron and steel at the start of its Industrial Revolution benefitted from inventions including Huntsman's *'crucible processes'* in Sheffield in 1742.[26]

GKN, or rather its initiating partnership and first Dowlais iron plant, was *born local* in 1759 and certainly not *'born global'*.[27] Its land lease and original aims were confined to Viscountess Windsor's estate and Merthyr Tydfil, the site of Dowlais Iron's construction. The Merthyr and Aberdare regions had been centres of iron making during the Tudor period. Competition among ironmasters still remained *'like today's professional cricketers playing on the county circuit'*.[28] Yet Merthyr Tydfil reflected a powerful *'cluster'*: as Manby noted in 1802, *'No place in the kingdom has had so rapid an increase in trade and population in the same number of years'*.[29]

John Guest, whose Dowlais plant ultimately prevailed, was the epitome of an Adam Smith-style capitalist entrepreneur. This first waterwheel-powered blast furnace flourished, right up to Guest's death in 1789, through technical expertise (supported by his partner's 1757 patent), capital accumulation, division of labour, a degree of vertical integration, increasing regional market coverage and scale, and, thereafter, through frugal savings and ploughing back profits.[30]

Iron and steel have been a microcosm of British manufacturing. Britain's share of world manufacturing rose from 1.9% in 1750 – compared with China's leading position at one full third – to 4% in 1800, to almost 20% by 1860, finally just overtaking China. *'In Britain and Ireland, manufacturing output per person rose eightfold between 1750 and 1860, four times as much as in France and Germany, and six times as much as in Italy and Russia. In China and India, manufacturing output per person fell'*.[31] Similarly in steel-making by 1850, Britain accounted for 70% of all 70,000 tonnes produced worldwide, the sector's evolution being a *'specific example of a general rule of manufacturing...the "experience" or "learning" curve'*.[32]

Scale, within the context of Britain's manufacturing competitiveness,[33] was crucial to Dowlais Ironworks, but also turned upon historical events. Pig iron also fed into canons and munitions, being encouraged by the Seven Year's War (1759–1763) and the American War of Independence (1775–1783) which increased demand for munitions and hindered imports for Swedish and Russian iron. Dowlais benefitted, making profits of nearly £2500 in 1764 on its initial investment of £4000[34]: i.e., a 62% return on investment. Dowlais further grew through early internationalisation, often in support of industrial customers similarly responding, domestically and internationally, to demands brought about by wars.[35] Its output subsequently quadrupled to 2000 tons by 1790, even though ceding market share to its two local rivals, including Cyfarthfa, the world's largest iron producer.[36]

Demand slowed during the Napoleonic Wars (1793–1815), offset by doubled tariffs pricing out iron-bar imports from Sweden and Russia.[37] It was only after changes in management and major further investments in puddling furnaces, coke technology, and especially in rolling mills and steam power, that Dowlais finally ascended to pre-eminence.[38] Scale economies were high especially in rolling mills[39]; profits, typically between 15% and 20%, were almost entirely ploughed back. By 1815, national concentration had risen such that the top 15 accounted for 53% of the coke pig iron output. Though dipping after the wars, markets recovered boosted by railways (1830–1850). Given growth and booming prices, Dowlais benefitted hugely from its (BHAG type) investments. In 1837, its output was 15% higher than Cyfarthfa's and profits surpassed £100,000.[40] Five of Dowlais's 15 blast furnaces used Neilson's more productive hot blast processes; by 1860, these constituted 95% of output, increasing productivity from 15 tons/man in 1840 to about 20 by 1866.[41]

With British ironworks companies so competitive, direct exports rose from 16% in 1815, to 45% by 1830, and 60% of total pig iron production by 1870.[42] Principal markets were America, France, and German states (though German iron masters fought back after acquiring British technology after 1843). Dowlais excelled in rails, having cooperated closely with Brunel on Britain's earliest railways.[43] It won huge export orders in Russia: indeed at around 65,000 tons of iron '*the largest contract of the kind ever made*' according to Lady Charlotte Guest, chief executive in 1852.[44] Dowlais's exports further included Italy, Holland, Germany, the USA, and Canada and exceeded the national average of 35% of total output. Lady Charlotte was the first 'Iron Lady'[45]: '*I am iron now and my life is altered into one of action, not sentiment. I am not afraid of the men. I will be their master*', she wrote on 11 July 1853, successfully facing down a strike which brought Dowlais to the brink of ruin'.[46]

Dowlais's focus on iron was 'fortunate', though risky during the seventeenth and eighteenth centuries. '*Probably no industry made so many men wealthy*'.[47] '*No other industry [was] followed on so vast a scale, or involve[d] so great expenditure of capital. Great profits [were] no doubt frequently secured, but these often coincide[d] with equally large losses*'.[48] Following 1854, £100,000 of plant investments, including a massive rolling mill taking them into higher value-added finishing operations, left Lady Charlotte '*grieving*' over the financial strains, there being '*no hope of any profit being made for a long time to come*'.[49]

Dowlais had also vertically integrated into coal, '*both as an insurance policy against potential labour difficulties and as a counterbalance to periodic depressions in the iron market*'.[50] Even so, survival next depended on massive (BHAG) investments, ploughing back profits into steel. Having earlier secured the first licence to use the Bessemer patent in 1871, her successor, William Menelaus combined both Bessemer steel converters and novel Siemens-Martin 'open hearth' furnaces, allowing special steels for ship's plates, boilers, armour, and forgings. Steel tonnage increased from 26,000 tons in 1871 to 119,000 tons in 1884. By 1884, demand for iron rails had ceased; but their new mills now turned out 5000 tons of finished steel rails a week.[51]

Dowlais's diversification strategy from iron, to coal, and steel through 1870–1890, allowed falling iron profits to be balanced by rising profits, first from coal, and then from steel, as detailed in their accounts.[52] This '*three-legged corporate strategy*' was crucial to their surviving iron's inevitable decline.

Two other constituents made up GKN: Keen and Nettlefolds merged with Guest in 1899–1902. John Nettlefold began as a small ironmonger and then purchased in 1823 a British patent to make screws with buttress heads. Profits peaked by 1846, '*which suggested that if dramatic growth were to be sustained a major initiative needed to be implemented*'.[53] In 1854, he purchased the US Sloane patent for the automated manufacture of woodscrews with gimlet points.[54] This was swiftly followed up with a (BHAG) bet-the-company, risk-capital-based investment, designed to pre-empt US rivals entering Britain.[55] Compared to cumulative profits over the 10 years to 1852 of £5186,[56] Nettlefold spent three years raising £30,000 for exclusive rights in Britain. '*In addition, he needed to build a new type of factory to ensure that a sufficient number of screw-cutting lathes could produce such economies of scale to support the increased overhead*'. The sum of £10,000 came from his brother-in-law, so that Nettlefold and Chamberlain were (like the Guests) '*a family partnership using accumulated savings and profits to fund a modern industrial enterprise*'.[57]

By 1865, they produced 90,000 gross per week – more than the entire national output for 1850. They were vertically integrated, having purchased their own wire-drawing mill, and added some 730 varieties by 1871 – such that they dominated the British fastener market '*and to a lesser extent the world-wide screw market*'.[58] Export markets included: Russia, America, Italy, Poland, Spain, France, Malta, India, New Zealand, Japan, Germany, Canada, Belgium, Switzerland, and Australia. In 1880, they acquired their major rival, the British Screw Co for £100,000 – another BHAG – following a pre-planned, protracted 10-year price war.[59]

GKN's final creator was Arthur Keen, bringing his own company the Patent Nut & Bolt Co (PNB), together with Guest and Nettlefolds & Chamberlain, in a three-way merger in 1900–1902. '*Neither an inventive engineer nor an expert on steel-making...Keen was the essence of an authoritarian businessman...with an obsessive passion for growth, whether internally generated or by acquisition...in the mould of Joseph Chamberlain or J.H. Nettlefold, Arthur Keen exhibited qualities of drive and vision...not without a trace of ruthlessness*'.[60] Partnering with his father-in-law and with Frances Watkins, an American holding a patent on a nut-making machine, Arthur Keen floated PNB as a limited liability company in

1862 with a capital of £200,000 to mass produce nuts and bolts. Its style and strategy paralleled Nettlefolds, likewise seeking to 'dominate the nut, bolt and rivet trade in the Birmingham area through a policy of price-cutting and selected take-overs' – similarly vertically integrating by taking over Cwmbran ironworks and its collieries in 1864 and 1872, and taking over and even closing down rivals such as T.F. Griffiths in 1869.[61]

Like Dowlais, they too specialised on railway customers' insatiable demands which aided internationalisation. In 1867, they too won huge Russian orders, but declined local factories offering them '*a practical monopoly of the Russian trade for fasteners*'. Most successful were colonial exports, but close economic analysis deterred empire or continental factories, or American entry, due to heavy duties of 2.5 cents per lb. Unlike Nettlefolds, they avoided head-to-head competition by licensing American machines and know-how to continental rivals.[62]

By the end of the nineteenth century, Keen had '*bought and sold patents throughout the industrialised world, [taken] over ailing competitors and sought alliances with other successful companies. Keen did not draw back from taking major risks. The PNB with its three nut and bolt works, rolling mills, ironworks at Cwmbran and collieries formed an integrated group. There was, however, a weakness…steel*'.[63] Between 1896 and 1902, he addressed this through their most audacious BHAG, the three-way merger which formed GKN.

Dowlais's family partnership came in with its newly constructed steelworks at Cardiff, and its profitable collieries in South Wales. Nettlefolds' fasteners and Keen's nuts and bolts came in too, creating 'Guest, Keen and Nettlefolds', Britain's 15th largest company in 1905 – with profits of almost £800,000. The new corporate architecture mirrored Dowlais's insistence that strategy required three strong complementary legs: GKN's '3 legs' leitmotif proved powerful enough to take them through the next century too.

GKN's TRAITS, CORPORATE AND INTERNATIONAL STRATEGIES FROM 1900 TO 1950s

Had GKN followed some fixated guru-style 'sustainable competitive advantage', the group would not have survived the twentieth century; instead the roles of CEOs and of its corporate centre evolved, adhering rather to Darwinian adaptation well matched to radically changing historical circumstances. It was one thing to ride the wave of British manufacturing success up to the end of the nineteenth century; quite another to survive the decimation of decreasingly competitive British manufacturers. Britain's share of world manufacturing peaked at 23% in 1880, but has since plunged to 3%; America's share peaked at 45% around 1950, but fell to under 20% in 2010; Japan and China's shares, by contrast, climbed back to, respectively, 12% and 20% in 2010; reversals in steel have been even more dramatic.[64]

By 1909, Britain's competitiveness was fast ebbing away: one bolt manufacturer reported, '*Our manufacturers [were] gradually being pushed out [of export markets] through low prices of German, French and American goods*'.[65] Dowlais followed Nettlefolds in seeking protection through a cartel...UK steel rail output more than halved in the decade following its peak in 1882, overtaken by America and matched by Germany.[66] World War I, though, sustained overall activities and modernisation.

In 1919, GKN acquired Cotterills, a fasteners rival and also bringing in Garrington forgings (dating back to 1830).[67] In 1920, merger with Lysaght, a group of almost comparable size, brought in galvanised steel, rolling, and trading operations (including Australia), and Sankey's wheels and automotive body parts: together doubling revenues and '*making major contributions for more than half a century*'.[68] GKN's coal output expanded to 6 million tons per annum (p.a.) with 36,000 employees by 1925, being perceived as even more significant than steel or fasteners[69]; output doubled, before being by savagely cut back by 1935. GKN shed Dowlais's steel plant and rolling operations, but expanded other steel-related businesses on the continent and in India with the acquisition of Williams in 1934. Nettlefolds with its virtual monopoly of the British woodscrew trade, reputation, and continuing dynamism internationally, held up well 'consistently contributing around 35%–40% of the group's profits during the 1920s and 1930s'.[70]

Huge (BHAG) diversification moves between the wars were crucial to surviving the Depression and fierce market vicissitudes. Tom Peacock, Keen's successor from 1920, 'was a details man rather than visionary',[71] and James Jolly, who joined him as joint Managing Director in 1934, was an austere chartered accountant. Peacock was intuitive and opportunistic. 'His great expression was, "*You have got to have the feeling in the water*"',[72] though many of his 'fruit salad' acquisitions, subsequently audited, proved not to have been profitable.[73]

> Subsidiary performances were monitored in two ways: by attendance at their board meetings and by scrutiny of their accounts...Not trained in the intricacies of engineering, or steel-making technology, Jolly wisely avoided becoming enmeshed in the production side.[74]

Yet GKN's generalist style up to World War II was open to criticism. Post-tax profits remained at £450,000 from 1902 to 1919, doubling to £860,000 with the Lysaght merger in 1920. Profits grew modestly to almost £1 million in 1930, dropped during the Depression, but stagnated at £1 million between the end of the 1930s and 1945.[75] Profitable growth returned in the 1950s, with the re-acquisition of nationalised steel plants in 1955 and with a fairly consistent return on net assets over 15%; but Peacock's final 'lean years' 1961–1963[76] were hit by strikes, stop-go economic conditions, and competition.

GKN's TRAITS, CORPORATE AND INTERNATIONAL STRATEGIES FROM 1960s TO 2012

Ray Brookes, finally CEO on Peacock's death in 1965, was by contrast, self-made, charismatic, hands-on, persuasive, shrewdly effective, with a 'devastating' mastery of details and visionary. Starting with forgings, his bold investments in higher technology, more automated production for automotive sectors, paid off. However, UK vehicle production peaked in 1964, only to halve by 1980, and the UK forgings market declined by two-thirds. With over 40% of the UK forgings market, limited international trade, and industrial relations problems, GKN could not reverse low falling profits and eventually exited forgings. GKN's steel operations were nationalised in 1969.

However, from 1953 onwards, Brookes had been battling for entry into transmissions equipment, finally landing his prey Birfield in 1967 for £28 million. Birfield brought £40 million of profitable sales, Hardy Spicer in the United Kingdom and French, Italian, and German assets including a 38% stake in Uni-Cardan. Uncharacteristically, up to this point, '*Ray Brookes had never heard of Uni-Cardan*'.[77] Nevertheless, his correct intimation to shareholders that these operations were '*complementary to the existing and increasingly international trend within GKN*' was to prove '*the greatest understatement in the history of the group*'.[78]

With Birfield came hot forgings, cold extrusions, and malleable iron castings, which could be integrated naturally into existing operations, but also transmission products such as prop shafts and patent-protected constant velocity joints (CVJs) making GKN the undisputed UK market leader.[79] Automotive parts increased to a third of GKN's overall revenue. In 1971, Brookes achieved 51% equity control in Uni-Cardan, increasing continental turnover to £81 million, compared £15 million in 1970.[80] As Trevor Holdsworth, later CEO, stated: '*Generally speaking going into automotive was the best thing we did. But the best single move we ever made was Uni-Cardan. That changed everything*'.[81] In the 12 years of Brookes' chairmanship to 1974, GKN's sales and profits both trebled, achieving record £100 million trading profits. While the United Kingdom still accounted for more than 60% of profits, GKN's international orientation was shifting. '*One thing I did do*', Brookes remarked. '*I made GKN international in spirit*'.[82]

CVJs were crucial to front-wheel drive, where demand took off as cars shifted to smaller, fuel-efficient designs. Following trebled US sales between 1970 and 1976, GKN won huge orders from Chrysler and Ford in 1978 and 1979. Corporate parenting support for ensuing globalisation was impeccable. In 1978, GKN increased its Uni-Cardan shareholding to 82%.[83] GKN's international project management team built two $100 million turnkey CVJ plants in North Carolina, USA, drawing on Hardy Spicer's executives in the United Kingdom, but also on world-class technology support from Trevor

Bonner's teams at Uni-Cardan.[84] Uni-Cardan spearheaded long-term supply agreements with Toyota, Nissan, and finally Honda in the early 1980s, though conceding license deals to NTN, Japan's major player in this field.

Such globalisation ultimately saved the company. At corporate level, GKN also joint-ventured with Brambles from Australia, building up a highly successful new services business CHEP, which achieved 80% of the UK retail pallet servicing market.[85] Yet, survival now depended also on extreme financial measures to adapt to dramatically worsened UK conditions. 'The 1980–1982 recession changed the face and shape of GKN for good'.[86] In the context of plunging UK car production, the average returns on capital employed (RoCE) of the UK's top 100 component suppliers went over the cliff: having averaged around 18% in the 1970s, average return on capital employed fell to zero during the period 1980–1982.[87] A new top team took over on 1 January 1980, led by Trevor Holdsworth, becoming chairman, Roy Roberts as MD, Basil Woods as strategy head, and David Lees as finance director – all internal appointments. Holdsworth and Lees were both chartered accountants, whilst Roberts was a 'tough, hands-on, operations man'.[88] At this point, GKN employed just over 104,000 people worldwide, and 69,000 in Britain, where it had over 70 operating subsidiaries.[89] Most reflected Peacock's earlier less-related acquisitions and were still loosely controlled in the style of other UK holding companies.[90] Around two-thirds of these business units moved into the red, demanding brutal turnaround decisions.

GKN Contractors was closed. The facility for composite leaf springs, the main new automotive development with comparable technological opportunities to CVJs, was dropped. GKN's Allied Wire and Steel was exited via Phoenix 1, a joint venture (JV) with British Steel. GKN Forgings and Brymbo Steel followed suit in 1986. The group exited fasteners. Credible, convincing executives in other areas received investment; but any doubtful cases were given short shrift, divested, or closed.[91] Efficiency was stepped up. Holdsworth later reflected on this period of quite exceptional change: '*I think we've completed, as much as anyone can ever complete anything, the total break by GKN from its 200-year history*'.[92]

By the end of 1983, GKN had halved UK and worldwide workforces to 33,600 and 54,000, respectively: £220 million being spent rationalising, closing, or selling businesses.[93] 'Driveline' components, principally CVJs, became crucial. 'In 1983, motor components – of which driveline was by far the biggest element – generated no less than 68% of GKN's trading profits'.[94] Uni-Cardan, the prime driveline contributor, was encouraged to build up 'one of the first genuinely global operations in the manufacturing world'. JV plants were built in Delhi and Shanghai, ultimately culminating in 49 international plants in 31 countries by 2006.[95] Initially usually JVs, most subsequently evolved into full acquisitions.[96] 'In 2007, Driveline division won 80% of all available new drive-shaft orders across the world, and 90% in emerging markets'.[97] Having sustained 40% of the global CVJ market and extended into all-wheel drive systems, the division represented 44% of GKN sales in the first half of 2013.

GKN developed Sankey's off-highway and defence activities, winning Ministry of Defence contracts for Warrior armoured personnel carriers in 1980, though Alvis defence was later sold off. In 2013, the renamed 'Land Systems' division provided 'technology differentiated power management solutions and systems' to agricultural, mining, and industrial machinery markets, including the aftermarket globally. Following Stromag's acquisition for £170 million, the division accounted for 13% of turnover.

Powder metallurgy, a rare instance of a new technology developed in-house[98] and ironically scaled back in the early 1980s, was also expanded. By the mid-1990s, this small division had plants in the United Kingdom and Italy and a 49% JV with India's Mahindra and Mahindra. A strategic review, under C.K. Chow, recognised further potential: '*We decided to try to be a global consolidator of this sector*'.[99] GKN duly integrated their own related sinter metal activities and, in 1997, acquired Sinters Metals Inc., for £337 million – catapulting them to twice the market share of their leading sinters rival.[100] Ten further acquisitions followed, including the largest American ferrous powdered metals supplier, Hoeganaes, for £348 million in 1998. In 2013, the division represented 12% of turnover.

In partnership with an Australian company Brambles, GKN also developed a pallet-management industrial services division, adding Cleanaway – a waste disposal business – in 1981. In 2001, this combined business was boldly spun-off, realising £3 billion of immediate value to GKN shareholders. The strategy impressed the city and re-focused GKN on engineering.

Sir David Lees, who stepped up from finance director, to become GKN's next chairman for the next 14 years, similarly saw his '*expertise as strategy and numbers*': '*I certainly believed that the group needed to focus much better and as quickly as made sense. The internationalisation was clearly very important…I was profit and cash driven. The strategic track was to do a lot of acquisitions in our core business and a lot of divestments in the non-core ones*'.[101] Having culled the group to automotive and industrial services, Lees '*was quite keen on the third leg strategy…about the limit you could achieve without conglomeration*'.[102]

From an initial stake in 1988, Westland Helicopters was acquired in 1994 finally for £440 million. For Lees, '*Westland was a great acquisition because the helicopters business made us a lot of money and we got a very good price when we sold it…But just about the most important thing was that it gave us entry into aerospace*'.[103] GKN recognised that global consolidation would ensue in aerospace, just as it had in automotive. In 2000, they engineered a 50:50 helicopter JV with Italy's Finmeccanica before later selling out for £1063 million. Crucially, helicopters afforded entry into aero parts and the chance to consolidate this still fragmented global sector.

Westland's Aerostructures business, like Uni-Cardan earlier, proved a hidden gem. It allowed GKN to germinate a vital new leg, with potential for global strategy just as earlier executed in CVJs.[104] As Lees put it, '*Kevin Smith discovered Structures and developed it...It was there, minding its own business and accounting for no more than 20% of Westland's sales and profits*'[105] – essentially a 'Cinderella'. In just four years, Smith transformed Aerospace Services into a world leader, through tightly focused, complementary acquisitions. The division grew to 29% of overall turnover in 2013 following major outsourcing deals: including $120 million for McDonnell Douglas's parts and composites plant[106]; $136 million for Airbus' wing and sub-assembly plant at Filton[107]; and £633 million for Volvo's aerospace components arm.[108] Take-over of part or all of the US-quoted Spirit AeroSystems was also seen as likely.[109]

In 1959, GKN had 76,000 employees, of whom three-quarters were in the United Kingdom[110]; in 2017, it had 59,800 worldwide, and just 5,500 in the United Kingdom. From a loose holding group of 80 business units, it had successfully transformed into four engineering divisions, each focused onto specific global customer segments and growth opportunities. Supported by operations in over 30 countries, its sales grew 36% in the five years to the year end of 2017.

LESSONS DRAWN

Jones and Khanna suggest business '*historical evidence avoids spurious labelling of some phenomenon as "new", and by so doing may challenge current explanations of their determinants*'.[111] Not one of 13 top studies of 'born globals' summarised by Rasmussen and Madsen[112] evidences comparable internationalisation to GKN's even by the 1840s. GKN's '*born local*' approach, by contrast, sustained success far longer. Even based on Rugman's controversial criteria, GKN transformed its global sales/assets/employee spread. Going global worked, contradicting Rugman's scepticism as to the desirability of global strategies.

Traditional strategy drivers, relating to scales/experience curve effects and market power, figured repeatedly throughout GKN's history and throughout the group. Yet in its early days, GKN still had to prevail over even bigger players such as Cyfarthfa in iron. Technology acquisition followed by highly applied development, rather than invention, proved critical, but only in the hands of classic entrepreneurs, totally determined upon dominating their chosen markets.

Location-based competitive advantages proved important during GKN's first 150 years to 1900. Dowlais Iron's rise was linked to the powerful local cluster around Merthyr Tydfil; whilst Nettlefold's and PNB's were linked to Birmingham's fastener/metal fabrications cluster. GKN was part and parcel of Britain's rising ascendency, as the country's share of world manufacturing rose from 1.9% in 1750 to 20% in 1860.[113] Porter's 'diamond model' of national competitive advantage[114] contributes some valuable perspective here: wages rose by 1800 to as high as anywhere, but more important was superior productivity, in turn boosted by technology and scale; supply clusters; links with crucial customers, particularly railways; further encouraged by initially vigorous home competition.

Yet Porter's '*diamond model*' doesn't fully capture historical events more directly contributing to GKN's rising fortunes particularly at Dowlais Iron. Wars fuelled demand for iron, coal, steel, and engineering products and for the products of GKN's industrial customers. Britain's dominant position in international trade and in its colonies likewise favoured GKN, its own suppliers, and its customers. All three constituent companies Guest, Keen, and Nettlefolds, each had to battle through enormous numbers of home competitors. Given Porter's earlier work on competitive strategy, his 'diamond model' surprisingly plays down the more critical role of robust, internationally competitive strategies. Effective global strategies were probably more important than broader conceptions of national competitive advantage even in the eighteenth and nineteenth centuries: they were certainly far more crucial in the twentieth and twenty-first centuries once Britain's national competitive advantages had diminished after about 1850.[115] The rise and fall of Britain's Courtaulds, the former world leader in man-made fibres, affords a cautionary tale of strategies proving less robust.[116]

In the last hundred years, Britain's former ascendency in manufacturing has reversed. Its world share fell from 20% in 1900 to 2.5% in 2010, and steel output fell to just 1.6% of China's.[117] Rover has gone. Had GKN passively relied on domestic market dominance, it would have disappeared alongside other British major automotive suppliers.[118] With just 13% of its workforce in Britain, serving foreign not domestic multinational corporations (MNCs), Britain's national competitive advantage has become almost irrelevant.[119] In 2015, Oxford economics estimated GKN contributed 42,000 jobs and $5 billion to the US economy, compared with £1.3 billion to the United Kingdom's. What mattered to GKN was sustaining effective global and corporate strategies.

Yet executing GKN's global strategies, so crucial in the face of reversals in home country competitiveness, has required unique resources and skills.[120] The issue was not just exports (where GKN would be matched by many more visible players like BAe Systems); GKN's exports were already highly developed at least 60 years, if not centuries ago. Implementing modern global strategies has been about managing foreign direct investment (FDI): i.e., the entire panoply of greenfield sites, license deals, JVs, acquisitions, their integration, and evolution worldwide. Foreign direct investment has grown far faster than even international trade, as multi-nationals have recognised its strategic significance. Few British players have mastered this; GKN had to do so repeatedly and in several activities. Rugman and Ghemawat correctly highlighted that relatively few of the world's largest companies were yet fully global,[121] but their corollary that global strategies were unnecessary is contradicted by both the experience of GKN's and its rivals. This lends support to contrarian global strategy advocates,[122] recognising geographical shifts that have occurred in recent years.[123]

In terms of scope, GKN could never have survived the nineteenth century shift to steel had it naively 'stuck to its [iron] knitting'.[124] In the nineteenth, twentieth, and even twenty-first centuries, GKN has so far only survived through astute management of typically at least three or four key 'legs' at any point in time. Collins and Porras's equivocal dictum 'Preserve the Core/Stimulate Progress' resonates, but Stadler's more explicit endorsement for diversification is more apposite. GKN's willingness to enter new fields, its determination always to be growing the next new 'leg' has proved crucial, albeit matched by equally decisive pruning. Generally, though, GKN eschewed crassly unrelated diversifications. Exceptions arose in the first half of the twentieth century, particularly with Peacock and Jolly's more intuitive 'fruit salad' acquisitions.[125] Several contributed to GKN's near undoing in the early 1980s.

This crisis marked the end of the loose holding company style, pursued by GKN along with many UK corporations up until the 1980s. Had it not changed dramatically in 1980, mirroring structural shifts of other British and European corporations,[126] even GKN risked bankruptcy.[127] This supports Chandler's thesis of divisionalisation ultimately improving performances; but undermines Higgins and Toms's counter-thesis based on UK empirical evidence only up to 1984.[128] Having finally divisionalised, GKN subsequently remained commercially successful.

Conservative financial management, balanced against these overriding corporate strategies, remained GKN's consistent hallmark: policies more consistent with de Geus's long-lived traits, than those of Collins and Porras's long-lived 'visionary companies'.[129] Draconian corporate pruning and management accounting also proved vital to survival in the early 1980s, when so many big British manufacturing names disappeared. On the other hand, periodically and repeatedly throughout GKN's history, determined top executives executed Collins and Porras' BHAGs, and these frequently proved crucial. Sustained corporate/financial strategies required never-ending, astute judgements steering between simplistic Scylla and Charybdis extremes.

CEO tenures over 254 years, analysed in Table 13.2, up to Mike Turner's appointment as chairman in 2012, averaged 13.5 years. (In January 2018 Mike Turner remained chairman, but Anne Stevens replaced Sanderson as CEO.) This is less than Collins and Porras' most successful 'visionary' BTL firms at 17.4 years, though higher than other BTL peers at 11.7 years.[130] However, taking the last 94 years since World War I, a period more comparable with Collins and Porras's sample, tenure has been much lower at 8.1 years; or as

Table 13.2 GKN's past chief executive eras, tenures, and timelines, 1759–2012

Year	*Company*	*CEO/Chairman*	*Tenure years*	*CEO style. events.*
1759	Dowlais Iron	John Guest	27	Classic entrepreneur. Low key Methodist, strong work ethic.
1786		Thomas Guest	21	As John Guest, organisation builder
1807		William Taitt	7	(Married Sarah Guest). Entrepreneur
1815		Josiah Guest	37	Classic entrepreneur, as John Guest
1852		Lady Charlotte Guest	3	Financial. Charismatic.1853 Strike
1855		GMs: GT Clark/William Meneleus '56	27	Operational organisation builder
1882		EP Martin, GM	10	Operational organisation builder
1892		Ivor Guest Lord Wimborne	8	L. Charlotte died 1895. Son, Lord Wimborne extremely hands-off.
1823	Nettlefold	John Sutton Nettlefold	37	Ironmongers. Birmingham factory 1834. Mill 1884. Entrepreneur.
1860–1874		+ Joseph (Snr) Chamberlain	18	Entrepreneur and financially orientated org' builder
1878		Joseph Nettlefold Ch	3	Entrepreneurial & deals orientated
1881		Frederick Nettlefold	10	+ Charles Steer Director
1891		Edward Nettlefold	11	Joined GKN board
1864	PNB	Arthur Keen		Dour, tough, financial org' builder,
1900	Guest Keen	Arthur Keen		M&A deals orientated.
1902	GKN	Arthur Keen	38	Created Guest, Keen & Nettlefold
1918		Bessborough, Ch	2	JH Jolly Sec/FD more influential
		Francis Keen		Edward Steer Jt MDs
1920		Edward Steer Ch	7	Seymoor Berry Dep Ch

(*Continued*)

Table 13.2 (Continued)

Year	*Company*	*CEO/Chairman*	*Tenure years*	*CEO style. events.*
1927		Seymour Berry Ch to 1928	1	Tycoon style, deal-making & organisation builder
1920		Tom Peacock, Jt MD, Dep Chairman in '33	14	Retires as Jt MD in 1941, Stays Dep Ch. Deal-making style.
1934		James Jolly, Jt MD, John & Sam Beale Non Ex Ch	13	Kenneth Keen, Jt MD from 1936 Jolly Financial & admin – orientated
1947		James Jolly, Ch	6	Financial & admin – orientated
1953		Ken Peacock, Ch	8	Intuitive, free-wheeling M&A
1965		Ray Brookes, Ch	8	Charismatic. Hands-on & effective.
1974		Barry Heath, Ch	3	Charismatic. Hands-off.
1977		Tr Holdswoth, MD, Ch	11	Hands-on strategic/financial style
1988		David Lees Ch	16	Hands-on strategic/financial style
1998		C.K. Chow, MD M. Beresford, MD		CEO, but Sir David Lees a very influential hands-on Chairman
2001				
2002		Kevin Smith, MD David Lees, Ch 16yr		CEO – big aero push, but Lees v. influential until retirement in 2004
2004		Roy Brown, Ch	8	Hands-off as compared with Lees
2012		Nigel Stein, MD/Mike Turner Ch	5	Hands-on CEO. Further aero push… Hands-off style
2012			6	Chairman as Brown
	254 years	Average tenure (of 26)	13.5	Vs. 17.4 for BTL 'visionary' sample

Source: Carr, C. and Lorenz, A., *Bus. Hist.*, 56, 5, 1–27, 2014. Reprinted by permission.

compared to 16.2 years for GKN's earlier period up to 1918. Long tenure and family ownership characterised GKN's earlier continuity and success; but in the last hundred years, GKN has conformed as a more typical Anglo-Saxon corporation, subjected to fierce stock market pressures. Anne Stevens' confirmation as full (as opposed to stand-in CEO) was likely triggered by the need to fight off Melrose's takeover bid. Recent tenures have been shorter than for 'visionary' BTL companies.

A subtler lesson, discussed in the previous chapter, is just how close even successful companies occasionally came to bankruptcy; strategic investment decisions and commitments on the global stage are so huge, that a single mistake courts corporate disaster; and hubris has proven common.[131] GKN's defences here were: its sustained financial conservatism; its downplayed, sombre, highly professional corporate culture ceding less credence to big corporate egos[132]; thorough succession-planning; and its strong strategic/financial planning – a process which, supported by a succession of CEOs especially in the last 50 years, proved remarkably robust.

The severe 1980 recession tested GKN's defences almost to destruction; but here again, home-grown management made tough financial and strategic decisions and achieved an impressive, fully sustained turnaround. These themes endorse more sombre, less charismatic top leadership themes commended by Collins and Porras, and more recently by Stadler and Dyer.[133] In 2018, Warren East admitted 111-year-old Rolls-Royce had been close to bankruptcy following his arrival as CEO in 2015. Owing to unprecedented fines, the company saw huge losses in 2016/2017. Their impressive recovery reported in 2018 owed much to his tough, financially orientated turnaround measures, akin to GKN's traditional controls, prudency, and where necessary restructuring.[134]

More positively recent research by Credit Suisse Holt lends support to Warren Buffet's dictum that high quality companies, by combining some defensible market power with distinctive internal cultures and competences, really have yielded performance persistence to a degree sometimes underestimated by the stock market. The top global performance quartile, based on their preferred cash flow return on investment measure, not only sustained 11% compared with a 6% global average over the last 60 years, but also displayed remarkable persistence between successive periods.[135] GKN matched up to these cash flow return on investment criteria.

Subsequently, taking the most recent accounts available for the years 2012–2016, GKN's returns on invested capital were consistently between 16% and 18% every year; trading margins between 8.2% and 9.2%; and free cash flow between £200 and £370 million p.a.; whilst earnings per share grew 18% and sales 36%. Since its major turnaround in the early 1980s, GKN remained consistently profitable. The dictum '*Form is temporary. Class is permanent*' still seemingly applied.

CITY SHORT-TERMISM AND EVENTS SINCE LATE 2017

In 2017, Kevin Cummings, GKN's head of US aerospace parts division, and designated successor to Nigel Stein as group CEO, was fired following £112 million of unexpected charges relating to his division. This followed an earlier October 2017 warning that profits would be £40 million less than expected. GKN's financial director, his rival for GKN's top post, had already left. GKN was exposed to top succession issues, just as underlying pre-tax profits dipped 16%, coming in below city profit expectations, and denting their reputation. GKN's share price dipped around 18%. On 17 January 2018, Hanson-style Melrose pounced opportunistically with a £7 billion hostile takeover bid, at an apparent premium of around 32%. Eighty percent of their offer though was based on Melrose paper, based on a remarkably short performance track record. Established only 15 years earlier, three-quarters of Melrose's stock market performance has come in just the recent two years 2016–2017. Melrose's prime contribution was likely predicated on radical divestments over the next three years.

GKN's defence response was to promote Anne Stevens, a former non-executive, to full CEO to take charge of a full strategic review, aimed at raising margins and to review major re-structuring/divestment options. The aim here would have be to remove 'low hanging fruit', pre-empting rapid shareholder value gains from ruthless divestments and undermining Melrose's opportunities for quick gains. ICI, Britain's largest chemical company, for example, prevented a hostile acquisition attack by Hanson by divesting its entire Zeneca pharmaceuticals business, affording shareholders immediate gains. Zeneca's divestment market value was higher than its imputed value as a going concern within ICI, allowing ICI to return immediate shareholder value, rather than affording the same opportunity for rapid wealth gains to Hanson. This subsequently allowed Zeneca to merge with Sweden's Astra, as has proved highly successful. The danger with such quick shareholder gains is that the parent group may thereby lose rejuvenation possibilities from attractive activities. Shed of higher value-added pharmaceuticals, ICI's core chemicals business ultimately succumbed to take-over from Akzo Nobel. However, in the context of city short-termism, had ICI not optimised shareholder value, it would have almost certainly have been immediately taken over and broken up by Hanson.

The Stevens review at the end of February 2018 therefore pledged to demerge aerospace and automotive businesses by mid-2019, and £340 million cash benefits to shareholders by 2020 from a three-year restructuring plan. Their niche business Powder Metallurgy, just 11% of turnover in 2016, was put up for possible sale at £1–2 billion. Discussions with the major US automotive player Dana secured the possibility of creating an even more powerful global automotive parts player and divestment. On 9 March, Dana offered to buy GKN Driveline (45% of sales and 42% of profits in 2016) for $6.1 billion

(£4.4 billion), being recommended by GKN's board in preference to Melrose. Dana offered $1.6 billion cash, $3.5 billion in shares, as well as assuming £720 million of GKN's £1 billion pension deficit as compared with just £150 million offered by Melrose.[136] A new merged automotive parts company would be formed called Dana plc, 52.8% owned by Dana shareholders and the rest by GKN shareholders. GKN was also considering major strategic moves in relation to aerospace parts, with Spirit a leading world aerospace supplier potentially interested.[137]

In such a context, Melrose's £7.4 billion bid (previously lauded by the *Times* and much of the city press) appeared low, effectively valuing remaining GKN's aero and off-road divisions at virtually zero. Why would GKN shareholders hand 40% of the upside from increased shareholder value to Melrose shareholders? On 12 March, Melrose therefore raised its bid to £8.1 billion, increasing GKN shareholders' share in any final merged company from 57% to 60%. Melrose castigated GKN's 'poor management' for a divestment of precisely the type they would be considering too. GKN's defence team, however, deserved credit for forcing up the 32% premium bid a further £1 billion, and pension fund contributions from £150 million to almost £1 billion.

City short-termism, nevertheless, was swain by Melrose's increased bid and the charms of more swash-buckling Hanson-style tycoons, such as Melrose's Peckham, Roper, and Miller. Almost 24% of GKN shares were owned by those such as hedge funds who had held shares for a short time. Roughly 20% were held by institutions and investors who also held shares in Melrose and would thus have had conflicted, somewhat short-termist interests. Hanson had never really recovered momentum after losing its hostile bid for ICI, as a result of its defensive divestment of Zeneca (the same tactic as necessarily deployed by GKN's defence team). Indeed, Hanson was itself subsequently broken up. Melrose could have faced a similar loss of momentum, its share price having quadrupled over the previous two years, despite losses in 2017. By comparison, GKN had averaged 16% return on capital employed over the previous five years and was certainly no turnaround case.

The major benefit to Melrose from such a conglomerate acquisition offering no synergies now rests on even better financial re-engineering than could have been achieved by GKN's own highly experienced management team. They will likely gain more from leveraging GKN's strong balance sheet and more conservative financial gearing, than from more ruthless pricing policies to drive up profit margins and divestments. Having criticised GKN's defence team's plans to divest driveline and powder metallurgy divisions, Melrose quickly invited bids for powder metallurgy and off-road divisions. Drivelines seem likely to follow suit. Having conceded to the British government that GKN's aero/defence division would be kept in the United Kingdom for at least five years, Melrose would though be more constrained than GKN's board, which had not ruled out selling this lucrative division to some US player such as Spirit. Initial indications of Melrose's GKN acquisition struggling were played down by Goldman Sachs highlighting that 'end markets' remained 'upbeat'[138]; but one certain gainer has been Melrose's Simon Peckham. Ranked second highest among FTSE CEO's in 2017, he '*banked £42.8m, equal to 43 times his 2016 pay*'.[139]

In paying a premium over 40%[140] for GKN in the context of negligible synergies, Melrose shareholders should remember that some 50% to 70% of acquisitions are estimated to have failed in terms of recovering shareholder value. I would further caution that the track record of tycoons in GKN's long history has proved poor. Such a conglomerate acquisition fails both acid tests elaborated in Chapter 8. Melrose brings no technology competence to GKN and has no capability globally, remotely matching GKN's. The 'Dana plc', had it been executed by the GKN team would sadly have stripped Britain of its one remaining global champion in the automotive sector. However, it would at least have potentially passed both my tough acid tests. Both these businesses were engaged with drivetrains and related activities. GKN's earlier proposed driveline divestment deal with the US company Dana would have offered genuine synergies, $235 million of estimated annual cost savings by 2020, closely related scope advantages, and creates potentially a stronger global player.

Such city pressure, exacerbated by the Melrose hostile bid, and consequent defensive moves by GKN's top management, undermined GKN's crucial three-legged corporate strategy which had sustained it for 259 years up to this point. As the *Sunday Times* argued, just before Melrose's raised bid: '*Whatever happens, GKN will be broken up...Most of GKN's owners have little interest beyond the next quarter*'.[141] Indeed, first to come out supporting Melrose was Aviva investors, owning just over 1% of GKN and 5% of Melrose[142]; they had an immediate overriding interest in favouring Melrose. At the start of the battle, investors indicated to the *Financial Times* they were seeking a level of about 450 p; though the Dana deal may have changed that view, one investor said.[143] With Melrose's bid then raised to 445 p, shareholders had to set that against GKN's board's internal valuation of 503 pence per share.

Sadly, the share of arbitrage shareholders who bought into GKN speculatively anticipating a deal may have been as high as 20%, added to some 20% with (like Aviva) shares in both companies. GKN would have had to win over almost all longer-term independent shareholders.[144] Most gruelling was that the Elliot Management hedge fund acquired 2.4% just after Melrose's bid: this proved finally decisive, allowing Melrose to win by a margin of 52% to 48%. After final undertakings on GKN's defence business, Greg Clark, business secretary, waived through Melrose's final £7.9 billion bid.[145] Melrose's final bid (plus almost £1 billion in commitments to GKN's pension fund) compares with £5.65 billion, GKN's market capitalisation the day prior to the bid, or £5.1 billion on 19 December 2017 prior to any bid anticipation. GKN's aggressive defence secured an increased offer as compared with Melrose's initial bid of £7.4 billion and a final premium somewhere between 40% and 55%. That was their board's fiduciary responsibility: they did what, in the context of city short-termism, they had to do.

At the end of October 2018, Melrose again reported poor results. Its market capitalisation dropped to £7.5 billion (now including GKN) from £11.2 billion on 26 August 2018.[146] By 6 November, even the *Times*, which had attacked GKN management whilst eulogising Melrose throughout, was headlining '*Melrose droops*' as its share price dropped to 172 p, compared with 240 p after winning its bid: '*Melrose Industries has strengthened its management team in an admission that the founding executive team has become stretched since it bought GKN*'.[147] GKN's global position so far remains intact, but whether Melrose can really match GKN's international and restructuring skills has yet to be evidenced. As of 18th of August 2019, Melrose's share price was 164 p and its market capitalisation at £8.0 billion.

GKN's two profit warnings of £40 and £130 million, together just 3% of their market capitalisation, triggered this takeover by Melrose, despite returns on capital averaging 16% over the previous five years and the most successful sustained global record of any company in Britain since 1759. As Michael Heseltine pointed out, this takeover would not have been possible in most continental European countries. GKN's mistake, with under 10% of its employees in Britain, was not to have transferred its head office and listing to say its Uni-Cardan base in Germany. Simultaneously, Anglo-Dutch Unilever, having just escaped the Kraft Heinz's takeover bid, understandably attempted to transfer its headquarters and listing to Rotterdam, Holland, but was subsequently thwarted by city interests. Likewise, Anglo-Dutch Reckitt Benckiser, beset by shareholder activists, might now be regretting they too had not made the same move much earlier. City short-termism has clearly been a factor behind the vulnerability of all three major survivors from Britain's Top 50 companies from 1905. 200-year-old De La Rue, a global champion in security printing, facing tough continental rivals such as French-Dutch Gemalto,[148] looks equally vulnerable. AstraZeneca narrowly escaped Pfizer, fully meriting political support through impressive global and market capitalisation performances by overtaking even GSK. The *Times* 2 April 2018, p. 45 reported: '*America's activists are stalking the City*', focusing on three big targets: Barclays, Whitbread, and Rolls-Royce; and in August 2019, Advent was bidding for Cobham. City short-termism has undermined Britain's sustained global winners.

CONCLUSION

Like hidden champions,[149] GKN may have passed beneath most readers' radar. Though older than Collins and Porras's BTL companies, it would not pass their US-centric[150] criteria including US CEO reputation surveys and cumulative stock returns from 1926 to 1990. GKN ranked only 165th out of 200 on Higgins and Toms's top performing British companies between 1950 and 1984,[151] reflecting difficulties in the early 1980s. Yet, up to its takeover by private equity conglomerate Melrose in 2018, almost no other large manufacturing company anywhere in the world, had grown and achieved global market positions, so consistently over 259 years. Though growth slowed, it delivered shareholder value over decades, in contrast to Melrose's market capitalisation's growth achieved mainly in just the two years 2016–2018.

Of Britain's top 50 companies a century ago, only GKN survived and flourished independently up to 2018, though Lever Bros. and Reckitt also continued as Anglo-Dutch mergers Unilever and Reckitt Benckiser. Though finally taken over by the financial conglomerate Melrose, GKN remained Britain's major independent automotive survivor following massive global restructuring[152] and a world leading supplier to the aerospace market. As an illustration of a sustained corporate-level strategy since the inception of the Industrial Revolution, its intricate, decisive Darwinian adaptations to historical evolutionary trends were almost unparalleled. Just as in literature, we can learn much from 'classics' from whichever country they come.

GKN's sustained strategy shared some, though not all, BTL traits identified by Collins and Porras.[153] Like BTL 'visionary' and Stadler's enduring companies, GKN relied less on inventions, inventors, or on exceptionally charismatic leaders; indeed 'tycoons' put GKN at risk through poorly related acquisitions. Most CEOs, like Arthur Keen, were 'organisation builders' – tough, dour, but sometimes paternalistic, they reflected protestant work ethics and values. Key technology derived from licensing and acquisitions, entailed long gestation periods, whilst GKN 'tried stuff to see what would work' (another BTL 'visionary' trait). The hard part though was application and scaling-up, ultimately upon on a global stage.

Likewise GKN's survival reflected several BTL-style BHAGs, notably its huge reorientations from iron to steel; from these and aging technologies like coal into metal fabrications; later from lower-value engineering technologies such as forgings, fasteners, and into automotive driveline components and aero fabrications; and crucially globalisation. Yet this has been balanced by an (often essential) financial conservatism, more akin to de Geus's long-lived companies,[154] than to BTL visionary 'strategic vs pure profit-driven' traits.

Like BTLs, GKN historically favoured internally promoted CEOs aided by succession planning, though less so in recent years. Parenting policies resonate with BTL-style 'preserve the core/stimulate progress' themes, emphasising relatedness, yet ever-searching to move on in more evolutionary terms. But this entailed at least three '*legs*' in terms of corporate strategy – a policy at odds with Peters and Waterman's[155] 'sticking to the knitting' – and entailing more aggressive product and technological diversification than most BTL 'visionary' companies.

Yet the critical contrast, as against BTL and Stadler's enduring companies, has been GKN's global strategy. Collins and Porras make no mention of internationalisation,[156] ravaging their examined sectors and many of America's best long-established companies, notably Kodak. Had GKN not globalised so pro-actively, it would have been long-gone, along with most other major British players.[157] As the US share of world manufacturing plunges, just as Britain's did, even the finest US companies may not survive without equally determined global strategies. General Motor's bankruptcy is one case in point. Another US icon, Anheuser-Busch's conservative, domestic orientation afforded little protection against its acquisition in 2009 by Inbev, in turn formed from a Brazilian/Belgium merger.[158]

An overarching lesson is the requirement for Darwinian evolutionary adaptability. Corporate 'theories' stress time-detached principles associated with 'sustained[159] competitive advantage'. Some emphasise market power[160]; others more resource-based advantages[161]; though none provide thorough historical examples. But as Darwin concluded, 'It is not the strongest of the species that survives, not the most intelligent that survives. It is the one that is adaptable to change'. GKN's sustained advantages resulted from adopting diametrically opposite market-versus-resource-based extremes, according to radically changing historical contexts and circumstances. Strategists should be more modest when drawing lessons from strategies – whether 'fast' or 'agile'[162] or whatever is today's buzz word – not supported by more 'robust' longitudinal studies. The value of a historical perspective here is not only in lessons afforded to business executives facing globalisation; but as a vital part of the education of business academics themselves.

GKN's themes over 260 years contain much needed longer-term corporate lessons, yet short-termist city pressures have undermined such longer-term themes. Ironically, GKN has, itself, become '*the last of the [British] Mohicans*'[163] – the last of the country's major automotive players, its third largest industrial company, and its only large company sustaining successful strategies dating back to the onset of the Industrial Revolution. The largest BAe and Rolls-Royce were not major players in 1905. Ironically, it was Germany rather than Britain which stepped in to save BAe from a recent potential French takeover. Warren East admitted Rolls-Royce was close to bankruptcy following fines, when he took over as CEO in 2011. City short-termism has likewise been a factor in the demise of Britain's other companies. In 2018, 276-year-old Whitbread was finally pressured by activist investors into partially breaking-up and selling off its coffee business.[164]

The problem shared by GKN and Whitbread is that adapting to evolutionary changes as traditional sectors mature, calls for some degree of diversification as in GKN's three-legged corporate strategy. It takes decades to enter and build up robust positions in new markets. GKN drivelines came from GKN's Birfield acquisition in the 1960s, following a ten-year campaign by CEO Ray Brookes; but taking this business global and achieving 40% global market share, took 50 years and massive resources. At GKN Forgings, our process and product development team devoted half our manpower to powder metallurgy from the early 1970s onwards. Fifty years later, just as this business achieved global competitiveness, GKN in 2018 was under huge pressure from the city to divest this, securing immediate shareholder value. GKN's aero defence parts division originated from GKN's Westland Helicopters takeover in 1985. By 2018, following several cross-border acquisitions, consolidating a previously fragmented sector, it was emerging as a potential global leader. Even conceding breaking up the group and divesting both drivelines and powder metallurgy was not enough to satisfy impatient city investors and share activists. Whitbread, pressured by Elliot Management's 6% stake, has likewise yielded to breaking itself up and divesting its newer coffee businesses faster than it wanted. Impatient city capital has rendered well-related three-legged corporate strategies almost infeasible. We must now look to continental, and particularly German and family companies analysed in Chapter 8 and Appendix B, for further exemplars of enduring success.

Looking towards future much needed[165] business histories of similarly 'robust strategies', cases like France's Saint-Gobain (1665), Italy's Beretta (1526), or Stora Enso, dating back to a Swedish copper mine over 700 years ago, could likewise prove fascinating if accessible.[166] Just as Melrose's hostile bid was being encouraged by short-term city interests and hedge funds, Swedish capitalism stepped in to protect Stora Ensa from far more serious and immediate financial difficulties. Family capitalism has been similarly protective in Germany and France. Saint-Gobain's shareholder performance was poorer than GKN's prior to its takeover by Melrose.[167] Yet, in June 2018, their CEO successfully defended their longer-term strategy based on related diversification (as at GKN), contemptuously dismissing counterarguments.

Locating in compatible countries, conducive to longer-term strategies, must now be on boardroom agendas for more enduring global strategies. Short-term financial markets, prioritising hedge funds and short-term speculative interests, no longer garnish globally enduring champions. Even GE, founded in 1878, America's and the world's most financially successful company during the twentieth century, has been progressively dismantled in the twenty-first century. Following divestments in appliances, lighting, train manufacturing, distributed power, and shrinking GE Capital, GE was planning to divest healthcare and oil services and focus on three divisions: equipment for the electricity industry, renewable energy, aero engines and other aircraft parts.[168] The last original member of the Dow Jones Industrial Average to be dropped from the index, saw its market capitalisation fall from \$580 billion in 2000 to \$70 billion on 16 August 2019, following reports of accounting irregularities far more serious than GKN's earlier.[169]

Yet, more robust, longer-lived strategy business histories, demonstrating sustained success, still constitute rare and valuable beacons. They illuminate more timeless lessons, but also throw into stark relief potential errors. They challenge superficial gurus, assumptions often taken for granted, and short-termist city commentaries. To transpose Keynes, 'Practical men, thinking themselves above theory, are almost always the slaves of some defunct strategy theorist': more sustained business histories matter to them too.

NOTES

1 I gratefully acknowledge Andrew Lorenz's contribution and copyright permission from Taylor & Francis Group and their journal *Business History* for kindly allowing us to reproduce tables and material published earlier: Carr, C. and Lorenz, A. (2014). *Business History* , 'Robust strategies: Lessons from GKN 1759–2013', 56, 5, pp. 1–27.

2 Jones, G. and Khanna, T. (2006). 'Bringing history (back) into international business', *Journal of International Business Studies*, 37, pp. 453–468; Chandler, A. (1972). *Strategy and Structure: Chapters in the History of the American Industrial Enterprise, Macmillan*, Cambridge, MA: MIT; Chandler, A.D. (1990). *Scale and Scope*, Cambridge, MA: Belknap Press.

3 Peters, T. and Waterman, R. (1982). *In Search of Excellence*. New York: Harper and Row; Pascale, R. (1990). *Managing on the Edge*. London: Penguin, pp. 16–17.

4 Cobham's leading global player in aircraft refuelling systems, founded in 1934, in August 2019, faced the same challenge of acquisition by US private equity conglomerate, Advent, source *Sunday Times*, 4 August 2019, Business, p. 7. Neither Melrose nor Advent had any prior experience relating to automotive or aerospace. Britain's other more recent aero global niche companies include Meggitt and Ultra Electronics.

5 De Geus, A. (1999). *The Living Company: Growth, Learning and Longevity in Business*, London: Nicholas Brealey, pp. 1–2. A third of the companies listed in the 1970 *Fortune* 500 list had gone by 1983 (Royal Dutch Shell Group Planning PL/1 1983) and '*in some countries, 40% of all newly created companies last less than 10 years*'. Overall, De Rooji, E. (1996). *A Brief Desk Research Study into the Life Expectancy of a Number of Countries*, Amsterdam, the Netherlands: Stratix Consulting Group concluded that the average life expectancy of firms of all sizes was just 12.5 years throughout Japan and most of Europe.

6 An eminent law firm's partner (interviewed, London 5 July 2012) originally chose to study law at Trinity Hall, a small Cambridge University college. Its reputation, he pointed out, dated back to its founding six centuries earlier to address the shortage of lawyers following the Black Death! Top 100 law firms globally netted $82 billion in revenue and $31 billion profits in 2012 (*Times*, 9 July 2012, 32–3), but few date back over a century or so.

7 Healey, E. (1992). *Coutts & Co: 1692–1992. Portrait of a Private Bank*. London: Hodder and Staughton and Moss, M. (2000). *Standard Life 1825–2000. The Building of Europe's Largest Mutual Life Company*. Edinburgh: Mainstream.

8 Collins, J. and Porras, J. (1994 and 2002). *Built to Last: Successful Habits of Visionary Companies*. New York: Harper Business. These companies were: Citigroup 1812, Proctor & Gamble 1837, Philip Morris 1847, American Express 1850, Johnson & Johnson 1886, Merck 1891, General Electric 1892, Nordstrom 1901, 3M 1902, Ford 1903, IBM 1911, Boeing 1915, Walt Disney 1923, Marriott 1927, Motorola 1928, Hewlett-Packard 1938, Sony 1945, and Walmart 1945.

9 De Geus, A. (1999). ibid. Companies include: Anglo American, Booker McConnell, British American Tobacco, Daimaru, Du Pont, East India Companies, Anthony

Gibbs, W.R. Grace, Hudson's Bay Company, IBM, Kennecott, Kodak, Kounike, 3M, Mitsubishi, Mitsui, Pilkington, Rolls-Royce, Rubber Culture, SKF, Siemens, Societe Generale, Suez Canal Company, Sumitomo, Suzuki, Unilever, and Vestey. See also O'Hara, W. (2004). *Centuries of Success: Lessons from the World's Most Enduring Family Firms*. Avon, MA: Adams Media.

10 Chandler, A. (1990). ibid.

11 Channon, D. (1990). *The Strategy and Structure of British Enterprise*. London: Macmillan; Dyas, G. and Thanheiser, H. (1976). *The Emerging European Enterprise*. London: Macmillan; Kono, T. (1984). *Strategy and Structure of Japanese Enterprises*. Chichester: Palgrave-Macmillan.

12 Kay, J. 'Finance needs trusted stewards, not toll collectors', *Financial Times*, 23 July 2012, p. 11; Lex, 'Kay review', *Financial Times* 24 July 2016, p. 16; and Oakley, D. and Burgess, J. (2012). 'No silver bullet to end City short-termism'. *Financial Times* 24 July 2012, p. 3.

13 Until 2019, GKN was the only British top 50 company from 1905 surviving independently. Lever Brothers from this same 1905 ranking, though, survives and flourishes today as part of Unilever, formed by a merger in 1930 with Margarine Unie from Holland. See Jones, G. (2005). *Renewing Unilever: Transformation and Tradition*. Oxford: Oxford University Press for an excellent pertinent business history. Lever & Co. dates back to 1884 and the Dutch side to 1872. Likewise, Reckitt from 1905 also survives and flourishes today following two mergers: the first with J.J. Colman in 1913 and the second with Benckiser from Holland in 1999 forming today's Reckitt Benckiser. Reckitt & Sons, J.J. Colman, and Benckiser date back to 1840, 1814, and 1823, respectively. See Chapman-Huston. (1929). *Sir James Reckit. A Memoir*, London: Faber and Gwyer and Reckitt, *The History of Reckitt and Sons Ltd.* These mergers complicate direct performance comparisons with GKN. Other 1905 top 50 companies have mostly been acquired by, and fully integrated into foreign multi-nationals. In automotive components, Dunlop, for example, was acquired by Sumitomo Rubber Industries, ironically Dunlop's own Japanese subsidiary in 1909.

14 Carr, C. (1990). *The Competitiveness of U.K: Vehicle Component Manufacturers*. London: Routledge.

15 Wembridge, M. 'Invensys set to join foreign legion in £3.4 bn takeover by Schneider', *Financial Times* 1 August 2013, p. 1: this article cited a senior industrials banker at Espirito Santo: '*Of course there is some emotion tied up in old names but these are global industries and you can't be parochial about it. The Board's job includes maximising shareholder value and they have realised substantial value*'. The automotive conglomerate Tomkins was likewise acquired by a Canadian consortium in 2010.

16 Data limitations, due to private companies being excluded, understate Germany.

17 GKN's share price increased some 70% over the 12 months to 1 August 2013, virtually double that of the FTSE 100, due partly to its earlier city track record and its increasing global dominance in aero parts.

18 For histories of Krupp and Thyssen, see James, H. (2012). *Krupp: A History of the Legendary German Firm*. Princeton: University of Princeton and Fear, J. (2005). *Organizing Control. August Thyssen and the Construction of German Corporate Management*. Cambridge, MA: Harvard Business School.

19 Higgins, D. and Toms, S. (2011). 'Explaining corporate success: The structure and performance of British firms, 1950–1984', *Business History*, 53, 1, pp. 85–118.

20 Imperial Tobacco (#1), Watney (#2), Coates (#3), United Alkali (#4), Vickers (#6), Guinness (#10), Whitbread (#13), Bass (#14), Dunlop (#16), John Brown (#30), and Reckitt and Sons (#41, and now part of Reckitt Benckiser) at least survive in some form as part of larger groups following mergers or acquisition. Lever Bros (#24) continues successfully as part of Unilever, an Anglo-Dutch merger, though they rank number two to P&G in most markets (Jones, G. (2005), ibid.; *The Economist* 30 June 2012, pp. 69–70) 'Consumer good. Fighting for the next billion shoppers'. Anglo-Dutch Shell originates from a merger in 1906, with the British side dating back

to the 1890s (De Geus, A. ibid., p. 3). BP was not in the UK top 50 in 1905: like Shell, it was a major global player in 2012 though both lagged well behind ExxonMobil's market capitalisation of £80 billion (*Sunday Times*, 30 September 2012, p. 3).

21 Jones, E. (1987). *A History of GKN: Volume 1. Innovation and Enterprise, 1759–1918*; Jones, E. (1990). *A History of GKN: Volume 2—The Growth of a Business. 1918–1945*; and Lorenz, A. (2009). *GKN: 1759–2009—The Making of a Company*. London: Financial Times.

22 My hands-on operations experience with GKN and technical knowledge of their international plants, and subsequent UK and international plant visits, help address the slight blind spot in our knowledge of day-to-day management practices Cooper, Y. and Lyth, P. (2009). *Business in Britain in the Twentieth Century: Decline and Renaissance*. Oxford: Oxford University. I also visited plants of major rivals, such as NTN in Japan, interviewing their president in 1983.

23 Jones, E. (1987 and 1990), ibid.

24 Lorenz, A. (2009), ibid.; Kobrak, C. and Schneider, A. (2011). 'Varieties of business history: Subjects and methods for the Twenty-first century', *Business History*, 53, 2, pp. 401–424.

25 Hunter, R. (2004). *The Value of Iron*. Rotterdam: Metal Bulletin Conference.

26 Ibid., 4.

27 Knight, G. and Cavusgil, S. (1996). 'The born global firm: A challenge to traditional internationalisation theory', *Advances in International Marketing*, 8, pp. 11–26.

28 Sources: JA3, 5&7. For full JA original archival sources, all of which are numbered as here and throughout our text, see Jones, E. (1990), ibid.

29 Source: JA18, ibid.

30 Source: JA14.

31 Marsh, P. (2012, a). *The New Industrial Revolution*. New Haven: Yale University, pp. 4–5.

32 Marsh, P. ibid., pp. 7–9.

33 Britain's competitiveness at this point reflected several factors highlighted in Porter, M. (1990). *Competitive Advantage of Nations*'s diamond model: Strong supply clusters such as Merthyr Tydfil and Sheffield, vigorous rivalry between these ironmasters, strong industrial customer sectors, and some comparative sector advantages, though not low wage costs.

34 Source: JA23.

35 Dowlais's internationalisation thus represents a departure from the traditional, Uppsala, model of direct exporting initially targeted on geographically or culturally proximate countries, though neither could it be correctly classified as '*born global*'.

36 Source: JA28.

37 Source: JA35.

38 Source: JA28.

39 Sources: JA40–41.

40 Sources: JA62&65.

41 Sources: JA267&104.

42 Source: JA105.

43 The significance of social networks and value of social capital should not be underestimated here. Ojala, J. and Luoma-aho, J. (2009). 'Stakeholder relations as social capital in early modern international trade', *Business History*, 50, 6, pp. 749–764. The Guests were friends of Brunel affording mutual help during the development of iron rails, placing them in prime position in this market both domestically and internationally, as with their huge Russian order. They were well-placed to spot the latest technology developments and potential licensing opportunities. Lady Charlotte was well connected.

44 Source: JA107.

45 Albeit the daughter of an Earl and decidedly feminine, 'She had experienced a brief romance in May 1833, just before meeting Sir John Guest, with the young Disraili,

who described her as '*very clever, [worth] £25,000 and domestic*'. She thought him '*wild, enthusiastic and very poetical*', but could not understand why a serious person would be trying to get into Parliament' (Jones, E. (1987), ibid., p. 84). Like James Jolly, Trevor Holdsworth, and Sir David Lees in the twentieth century, Lady Charlotte took over as CEO in the mid-nineteenth century, having earlier served effectively as finance director. She had held on 'iron grip' on all Dowlais Iron's accounts and finances, down to the minutest cost and profit calculations (see, e.g., ibid.: 264). Her diaries, documented in Jones (ibid.: 280), help address the gender gap in our knowledge of business history [McKinlay, A. (2011). 'Business in Britain in the twentieth century', *Business History*, 53, 7, pp. 1189–1190.]

46 Jones, E. (1987), ibid., p. 280 and Guest, C. (1847). '*Journal*, Vol XI, 24, November. Bessborough, Lady Charlotte, Schreiber, unpublished, p. 725'.
47 Jones, E. (1987), ibid., p. 302).
48 Jeans, J. (1906). *The Iron Trade of Great Britain*. London: Methuen & Co, pp. 8–9.
49 Guest, C. 1853. *Journal*, ibid., Vol. IX, 14.
50 Jones, E. (1987), ibid., p. 251.
51 Ibid., 209.
52 Ibid., 303.
53 Ibid., 137.
54 Lady Charlotte Guest similarly recognised the US technology lead here, having scrutinised the new American process of making screws by machinery in August 1839.
55 Source: JA137–9.
56 Analysis of Nettlefold's accounts in Jones, E. (1987), ibid., p. 137, based on Nettlefold, J.A. *Private Journal* 1834–1854, 30–35 and loose working papers within.
57 Ibid., 139.
58 Ibid., 146, 147, 150, and 153.
59 Ibid., 157.
60 Ibid., 165.
61 Ibid., 172 and 174.
62 Ibid., 181–185.
63 Ibid., 192–193.
64 Marsh, P. (2012, a), ibid., pp. 19 and 152.
65 Lorenz, A. (2009), ibid., p. 57.
66 Ibid.
67 I worked in GKN Forgings in their Garrington plant as a process and product development engineer from 1974 to 1978. Only briefly overlapping with Brookes, I was, however, able to research employees' experiences of his 'hands-on' charismatic management leadership style going back decades.
68 Ibid., 71.
69 Jones, E. (1990), ibid., p.73.
70 Ibid., 167.
71 Ibid., 173.
72 Lorenz, A. (2009), ibid., p. 95.
73 Author's earlier interview with GKN's strategic planning director in the late 1990s. The term '*fruit salad*' refers to several highly unrelated acquisitions undertaken at this time.
74 Jones, E. (1990), ibid., pp. 287–288.
75 Jones, E. (1987), ibid., pp.389 and 1990, ibid., p.368.
76 Lorenz, A. (2009), ibid., pp. 98 and 103.
77 Ibid., p.120.
78 Ibid.
79 Ibid., 119.
80 Ibid., 141.
81 Ibid., 142.
82 Ibid., 151.

83 Ibid., 176.
84 As project engineer on the four-man international project management team, I can attest to the level of first-class international technology transfer involved.
85 Ibid., 165.
86 Ibid., 207.
87 Carr, C. (1990), ibid., p. 199.
88 Lorenz, A. (2009), ibid., p. 193.
89 Ibid., 198.
90 For an account of other British companies following such corporate level approaches between 1950 and 1984, see Higgins, D. and Toms, S., Explaining corporate success.
91 My earlier interviews with key executives over-viewing these decisions in the late 1990s.
92 Lorenz, A. (2009), ibid., p. 249.
93 Ibid., 208.
94 Ibid., 223.
95 Ibid., 337.
96 My interviews with top executives in GKN's subsidiaries in Brazil and India, in October 2010 and January 2011.
97 Ibid., 139.
98 Almost half my process and product development colleagues at GKN Forgings worked on this new powder metallurgy process throughout the 1970s.
99 Ibid., 303.
100 Ibid., 304.
101 Ibid., 253.
102 Ibid., 257.
103 Ibid., 279.
104 Author's discussions with GKN's strategic planner in the mid-2000s.
105 Ibid., 330.
106 Ibid., 314.
107 GKN was Britain's third largest aero manufacturer after BAe and Rolls-Royce.
108 Marsh, P. 'GKN chief bullish over global economy', *Financial Times* 1 August 2012, p. 20.
109 Wembridge, M. 'GKN focus on aviation sees results take off', *Financial Times* 3 July 2013, p. 17.
110 Lorenz, A. (2009), ibid., p. 98.
111 Jones, G. and Khanna, T. (2006), ibid., p. 453.
112 Rasmussen, E. and Madsen, T. (2002). The born global concept. *Paper Presented at 28th EIBA Conference*, Athens, Greece.
113 Marsh, P. (2012a), ibid, 4–5.
114 Porter, M. (1990). *Competitive Advantage of Nations*. London: Macmillan.
115 Jones, G. (2010). *Beauty Imagined. A History of the Global Beauty Industry*, Oxford: Oxford University, illustrates similar crucial strategic adaptations to complex changing historical and competitive conditions in the case of the beauty industry.
116 Owen, G. (2010). *The Rise and Fall of Great Companies: Courtaulds and the Reshaping of the Man-Made Fibres Industry*. Oxford: Oxford University.
117 Marsh, P. (2012, a). ibid., 19 and 152.
118 Carr, C. (1993). 'Global, national and resource-based strategies', *Strategic Management Journal*, 14, pp. 551–568.
119 Porter, M. (1990), ibid.'s '*Diamond*' framework understates the rising impact of global strategies in this situation, as discussed earlier in relation to Nokia and Finland.
120 Barney, J. (1991). 'Firm resources and sustained competitive advantage', *Journal of Management*, 17, 1, pp. 99–120 and Carr, C. (1993), ibid.

121 Rugman, A. and Verbeke, A. (2004). 'A perspective on regional and global strategies of multinational enterprises', *Journal of International Business Studies*, 35, 1, pp. 3–18.; Rugman, A. (2005). *The Regional Multinationals*. Cambridge: Cambridge University Press; Ghemawat, P. (2003). 'Semiglobalisation and international business strategy', *Journal of International Business Studies*, 34, 7, pp. 138–152; Ghemawat, P. (2007). *Global Strategy in a World of Differences*, Cambridge MA: Harvard Business School; Ibid., *World 3.0.*; Ghemawat, P. and Ghadar, F. (2000). 'The dubious logic of global megamergers', *Harvard Business Review*, July–August, pp. 65–72; Ibid. (2006). 'Global integration is not equal to global concentration', *Industrial and Corporate Change*, 15, 1, pp. 595–623; Ghemawat, P. (2011). *World 3.0: Global Prosperity and How to Achieve It*, Cambridge, MA: Harvard Business School, further argue that many sectors are not globally concentrated. Their empirical data and interpretation on global concentration metrics were, however, challenged by Carr, C. and Collis, D's (2011)'s 'Should you have a global strategy', *Sloan Management Journal*, 53, 1, pp. 21–24.

122 Ohmae, K. (1990). *The Borderless World*. New York: Harper Business; Ibid., *The Invisible Continent*, London: Nicholas Brealey; Carr, C. (1990 and 1993), ibid.; Bryan et al. (1999). *Race for the World*. Cambridge, MA: Harvard Business School; Sirkin et al. (2008). *Globality*. London: Headline Press; Ploetner, O. (2012). *Counter Strategies in Global Markets*. Basingstoke: Palgrave.

123 Hout et al. (1982). *How Global Companies Win Out*. Boston, MA: Harvard Business Review, pp. 98–109. Yip, G. and Hult, G. (2012). *Total Global Strategy*. Upper Saddle River, NJ: Prentice Hall; Dicken, P. (2007). *Global Shift*. London: Sage; Nolan et al. (2007). *The Global Business Revolution*. London: Palgrave Macmillan; Carr and Collis, ibid.

124 Peters and Waterman, ibid.

125 Porter, M. (1987). 'From competitive advantage to corporate strategy', *Harvard Business Review*, 65, 3, pp. 78–93 argues that some 70% of M&A 'fail' in the sense of their being ultimately divested. GKN's 'fruit salad' acquisitions were classic examples of M&A, not passing Porter's 'better-off' tests, though I would take issue with his defining 'failed' M&A as those divested. GKN could never have evolved to its present position without intelligently combining both M&A and divestment decisions. Its entry strategy into aero components proved highly effective through initially acquiring, but then later divesting (and at a substantial profit) Westland's helicopter business.

126 Goold, M. and Campbell, A. (1987). *Strategies and Styles*. Oxford: Blackwell; Whittington, R. and Mayer, M. (2000). *The European Corporation*. Oxford: Oxford University; Colli, A. et al. (2011). 'Mapping strategy, structure and ownership and performance in European Corporations: Introduction', *Business History*, 53, 1, pp. 1–13.

127 Author's interview in the late 1980s with one of the four key directors responsible for GKN's boardroom coup at this time.

128 Chandler, A. (1972), ibid.; Higgins and Toms, ibid.

129 De Geus, ibid.; Collins and Porras, 1994, ibid.

130 Ibid., 297.

131 Collins, J. (2009). *How the Mighty Fall and Why Some Companies Never Give In*. London: Random House and Larson, M. et al. (2011). 'Strategic responses to global challenges: the case of European banking 1973–2000'. *Business History* 53, 1, pp. 40–62.

132 My experiences from 1974 onwards; Lorenz, A. (2009), ibid.; Behrens, A. (2009). *Culture and Management in the Americas*. Stanford: Stanford University, pp. 213–217, contrasts British leadership styles with those encountered in the USA and Brazil. The British style, termed the '*beaver*' style, is perceived as '*predictably industrious*',

though perhaps slightly '*inflexible, reliable, unobtrusive, and non-threatening*'; GKN's culture is likewise downplayed in comparison with US and Brazilian companies interviewed by the author.

133 Collins, J. and Porras, J. (2011) *Built to Last*, New York: Harper Press; Stadler, C. and Dyer, C. (2013). 'Why good leaders don't need charisma'. *Sloan Management Review*, 54, pp. 94–95.

134 *Financial Times* 18 January 2018. p. 16 and 2 August 2017, p. 12. The latter commentary applauded RR's renewed focus on cash, arguing the '*Turnover is vanity, profit is sanity and cash flow reality. Rarely has this adage been truer than at UK engineer Rolls-Royce*'.

135 'Numbers add strength to Buffett's law of selection', *Financial Times*, 4 August 2013, p. 20. GKN's sustained return on capital performance and its strong financial controls would almost certainly put it in this top performing quartile globally, though access to Credit Suisse Holt's unique adjustments would be necessary to confirm this.

136 *Times* 10 March 2018, p. 47. 'GKN sell-off deals blow to Melrose bid. Automotive division goes to US buyer for $6bn'.

137 *Financial Times* 28 February 2018, p. 13. 'GKN speeds split to fight takeover'.

138 *Financial Times* 15 August 2018, p. 24. 'Melrose'.

139 *Financial Times* 15 August 2018, p. 14. 'Pay for UK's leading bosses climbs 11%'. Source: report by Chartered Institute of Personnel and Development and High Pay Centre.

140 Melrose's final bid price of 465 p was 40% higher than GKN's share price on 11 January 2018, the day before its bid, though shares began climbing from 19 December 2017 from 299.5 p, so the final price was 55% above this nadir. Previous highs were 448 p on 8 June 2007, a decade earlier, or 606 p going back to 16 April 1999. GKN's earlier nadir was 72 p on 6 March 2009, so many shareholders buying more opportunely would have seen huge gains.

141 Dey, I., *Sunday Times* 11 March 2018, p. 4. 'Whatever happens, GKN will be broken up'.

142 Hipwell, D. *Times* 13 March 2018, p. 35, 'Top investor backs GKN takeover bid'.

143 Hollinger, P. *Financial Times* 12 March 2018, p. 15. 'GKN to lay out higher valuation case as Melrose looks at raising £7 bn offer'.

144 *Financial Times* 13 March 2018, p. 14. 'Industrials. Battle lines. Melrose adopts Napoleonic tactics in GKN bid'.

145 *Financial Times* 25 April 2018, p. 19. 'Melrose Industries. GKN purchase cleared'.

146 *Sunday Times* 28 October 2018 'Top 200 companies' and earlier editions.

147 *Times* 6 November 2018, p. 41. 'Melrose droops'. *Times* 6 November 2018, p. 45. 'Melrose beefs up board after £8bn takeover'.

148 *Times* 4 April 2018, p. 38. 'De La Rue to appeal over blue passports going to foreign rival'.

149 See Simon, H. (2009). *Hidden Champions of the Twenty-First Century*. Heidelberg: Springer. GKN passes Simon's criteria for *hidden champions* in all respects save one: sales have grown to around $9 billion, exceeding Simon's artificially imposed ceiling of $4 billion; but not many companies aim to keep sales down.

150 Sony is the only non-US visionary company. Established in 1945, its share price fell by three-quarters prior to 2012. Source: *Financial Times*, 1 August 2012, p. 14, 'Panasonic the hedgehog'.

151 Higgins and Toms, ibid.

152 Freyssenet, M. (2009, Ed.). *The Second Automobile Revolution*. Basingstoke: Palgrave Macmillan.

153 Ibid.

154 De Geus, A. (1999), ibid.

155 Peters and Waterman, ibid.

156 Collins, J. and Porras, J. (2011), ibid. This is a surprising omission given internationalisation studies reviewed in Glaum, M. and Osterle, M. (2007). '40 years of research on internationalisation and firm performance', *Management International Review*, 40, 3, pp. 307–350.

157 This view is corroborated by Tom Brown, a former GKN director, overlapping with me at GKN Forgings, but with deeper, more extensive top-level management experience. Aside from directing several GKN divisions at home and abroad, Tom has chaired 15 engineering companies. See Brown, T. (2017). *Tragedy & Challenge: An Inside View of UK Engineering's Decline and the Challenge of the Brexit Economy*. Matador. Tom also emphasised global focus strategies akin to German Mittelstand companies, based on successes at GKN Birfield Transmission, where he was MD, re-echoing lessons from our Chapter 8 comparing British and German global niche players.

158 Macintosh, J. (2011). *Dethroning the King: The Hostile Takeover of Anheuser-Busch. An American Icon*. Chichester: Wiley.

159 Empirical research and supporting cases seem, however, far too short-term to justify such claims. The prime argument is the theoretical idea that market power may prove more sustainable than relying on potentially imitable technological advantage; but GKN's history suggests that both are intertwined, dynamically changing substantially over time.

160 Porter, M. (2008). 'The five competitive forces that shape strategy', *Harvard Business Review*, 86, 1, pp. 78–93.

161 Barney, J. (1991). 'Firm resources and sustained competitive advantage', *Journal of Management*, 17, 1, pp. 99–120.

162 See Doz, Y. and Kosonen, M. (2008). *Fast Strategy*. Harlow: Pearson: '*If you want to be a winning company today, you have to learn a new competitive game*'. Nokia's recent falls in global market share, financial, and stock market performances suggest greater caution over their analysis on page 5, drawing lessons from its superior '*agile*' strategy, as compared with other players like Ericsson and Motorola. Nokia's 100-year history might perhaps yield other perspectives.

163 Somewhat twisting Barrie Heath, former GKN chairman's first words to his HRM director Mr Parsons, on collecting me in his helicopter in 1978. His reference to GKN Forgings sadly now reflects GKN's fate as Britain's last, major global automotive player.

164 *Times* 26 April 2018, pp. 38–39. 'Whitbread finally agrees to break up and sell the coffee'.

165 Napolitano, M. et al. (2012). 'Call for papers: Theoretical and empirical research on business longevity', *Business History*.

166 This chapter has focused on larger multi-nationals. However, Britain's oldest building group Durtnell, an SME established in 1591, sustained a similarly robust strategy. Alex Durtnell is the 13th generation to run the business. In a tough cyclical business, they have survived more downturns than most. Their former chairman, John Durtnell, attributed their longevity to tight niching in southeast England in segments least affected by downturns, such as churches, private schools, art galleries, and luxury houses; and to financial conservatism and to '*quite brutal*' employment cutbacks when necessary: Source: Bloom, J. (2012). 'How Britain's oldest house builder survived the recession', *BBC News* 26 October.

167 As of 5 July 2018, Saint Gobain's share price was E38, showing no growth in the last five years, and as compared with a recent peak of just over E52 a year ago. In 2017, its net profit margin was 4% and return on equity 8.4%, comparing unfavourably with GKN. Source FT on-line.

168 *Financial Times* 27 June 2018, p. 1. 'GE takes stride towards break-up by spinning off two big divisions'. GE will be left with less than half the revenues it had only a decade ago.

169 See Harry Markopolos's 170-p attack reported by Fortson, D. 'Did Jack Welch build his GE house on sand', *Sunday Times* 18 August 2019, Business, p. 5.

Part VI

GLOBAL CONCENTRATION, OLIGOPOLIES, AND GLOBAL CAPITALISM

14

THE POLITICAL ECONOMY OF GLOBAL OLIGOPOLIES

POLITICAL ECONOMICS HISTORICALLY

Historically, politics trumped economics. Over a millennium, violent rulers and religions, mutually endorsing each other, controlled most of the wealth. Opportunities to acquire capital largely related to land, a few jewels and transient food resources. Property belonged to feudal-style overlords; no matter that you had worked and saved over a lifetime, any surplus was subject to their whims. Wealth created largely related to the number of serfs or slaves under an overlord's control and any surplus unconsumed was generally appropriated by overlords, or temples of one form or another. Average incomes, Malthus argued, were circumscribed by the balance between natural resources and populations. In better resourced regions, populations tended to rise, albeit mitigated by wars or famines, frustrating rising living standards. Over centuries, economic growth was often zero or irrelevant. European wages rose substantially in the aftermath of the Black Plague, only to fall back as populations recovered. What seemingly mattered was appropriating and retaining more than your fair share.

Adam Smith tracked centuries of such bleak economic history even in Britain, then second only to Holland on Gross Domestic Product per capita (GDP/capita). Before that William the 1st had split England's conquered properties, half for himself, one third for the Church, and one sixth for his barons. As Europe's wealthiest landowner, the late Duke of Westminster put it, the secret of his family's commercial success was simply having been good friends with William the Conqueror, although Grosvenor Estates has now gone global. Nonetheless, in 1776, Adam Smith highlighted other far more positive drivers fundamental to the wealth of nations: geographically spreading markets and capital availability meant that incorporated companies could finally exploit scale and the division of labour, yielding extraordinary productivity gains as exemplified by pins.

Britain's fledgling market economy, notwithstanding reactionary mercantilists, flourished. Real income per capita outstripped dire Malthusian predictions. Colonialism, the Navy, and international trade (shamefully including slaves) helped too. Power mattered: the Dutch East India Company boasted the world's greatest army. But policy choices mattered too: the Bank of England itself resulted from Dutch financial innovations coming over under William the 3rd. Smith's positivism, denouncing most economists as 'Jeremiahs', was vindicated. Britain, spurred on by pioneering enterprises like GKN, became the vanguard of the Industrial Revolution: by 1815, its GDP/capita had risen to 12% higher than even Holland's. America, newly constituted in 1776, embraced market economy principles yet more fervently and on a scale later eclipsing Britain. Huge scale economies however induced industrial consolidations (such as Carnegie's in steel), provoking serious concern and anti-trust policies.

Oil: just one global oligopoly's impact on rivals and political economics

As to the implications of even a single global oligopoly, oil is hard to beat. By 1870, after just seven years in the business, Rockefeller had established Standard Oil and captured 10% of an emergent United States (US) market. Colluding secretly with key fellow refiners and railroads, he unapologetically routed and gobbled up rivals: '*This movement ...has revolutionised the way of doing business all over the world...It had to come. The day of the combination is here to stay; individualism is gone, never to return*'.[1] Its scale daunted small states and even Washington, prior to greater concerns and regulatory powers; notwithstanding Standard Oil's decreed breakup in 1911, its 'daughters' Exxon, Mobil, and Socal (later Chevron) still set prices collusively.

In 1928, chief executive officers (CEOs) of the big four global players (including also BP) met secretly at Achnacarry Castle, drawing up plans to control outputs and prices – so secret even governments remained in the dark until 1952 – rivals oblivious of their oligopoly plays were driven to the wall – with just three other major players finally falling into line.[2] So secret, yet these were the players who quietly drove geopolitical events reshaping the world up to and including World War 2 (WW2), delivering the Allies 90% of global hi-octane oil, compared with Axis powers collectively just 3%.[3] Baku region's oil alone was equivalent to three time's German production; even Hitler recognised that failing to secure this at Stalingrad could ultimately cost them the war. In the absence of naval supremacy, Japan faced similar problems in the East.

Following WW2, though the global Herfindahl concentration index for oil production fell from 0.2 to 0.05 between 1950 and 1975,[4] the global concentration ratio (GCR)4 in 1972 was high at 48% (Exxon, Shell, BP, and Texaco); the GCR7, including the remaining 'Seven Sisters' (Socal, Mobil, and Gulf) being 58%.[5] Cross-holdings among all seven[6] controlled Middle Eastern supplies; that is, until OPEC demonstrated they could play the global oligopoly game too. They doubled oil prices in 1973. GCR4 fell to 29% in 1998, fluctuating and recovering slightly to 32% in 2004. By 2008, Herfindahl, having dipped, was back to 0.05, as in 1975.[7]

This fluctuating global war scenario has been complicated by opaque state involvements, not reflected in public market research reports providing global market share data. In 2016, Saudi Arabia's Crown Prince's Initial Public Offering plans for Aramco, though, implied a market capitalisation over $2 trillion. Shell, ExxonMobil, Chevron, and BP have been among the largest companies in the world with revenues dwarfing nations; but, in turn, they are now eclipsed. In the first half of 2019, Saudi Aramco produced 13 million barrels a day, generating $47 billion net income, compared with 16 million barrels and $34 billion for all other top five combined.[8] With the planned acquisition of petrochemical giant SABIC, a 20% stake in Reliance India's refining/petrochemicals, and deals in China, Malaysia, and South Korea, Aramco is another reminder of the coming impact of global emerging market multinationals (EMMs).

What is extraordinary is how for half a century, strategists, outside those top four global oligopolists who secretly agreed the rules of the game at Achnacarry Castle in 1928, remained oblivious to moves determining their futures. Even governments remained in the dark until decades later. The power and impact of such global scale lies beyond our imaginings. Yet today's global political economy has become more complex. That original big four, though still eclipsing nations, face massive countervailing global rivalry and environmental challenges that none dare ignore. Their reputations and fundamental business models are at stake; shareholder value performances over the last eight years have been lacklustre; engaging with public opinion and policies has never been more important.

RECENT GLOBAL TRENDS AND PERSPECTIVES

Geographical surveys, 'mapping the global network revolution',[9] argued that globalisation was now 'entering a new golden age', driven by strategic ambitions, new technologies, cheap money, and global migration. World real economic growth averaged 3.4% p.a. in the 10 years to 2018 and was expected to average 3.6% per annum (p.a.) up to 2024.[10] Total exports of goods and services rose from 19% in 1980 to 26% in 2000 and 29% in 2017.[11] Foreign direct investment rose, even faster than trade, to over a third of world GDP.[12] Global services accounted for half the world's workforce, over 60% of the value of world trade, having doubled every five years.[13] Global Mergers and Acquisitions (M&A) almost tripled from $1.2 trillion in 1996 to around $3 trillion estimated for 2016,[14] despite setbacks in

North America and Europe.[15] China's cross-border M&A, almost negligible in 2007, 'skyrocketed' in 2016,[16] offsetting falls elsewhere. Global M&A resumed upward trends in 2017[17] and rose further in 2018.

Global oligopolists, hit by the 2008 downturn, have recovered. Maersk, the No. 1 global oligopoly player in container transportation, for example, has acted as lead indicator for global trade, almost all of which is transported by containers. Containers began in 1956 and revenues grew nearly every year subsequently before stalling in late 2014.[18] Global container trade resumed 4% growth p.a. in Quarter 4, 2018. Maersk's revenues plunged in 2009, recovering to $20 billion in 2016[19] and $39 billion in 2018. Their 2018 annual report commented: '*The Liner industry consolidation wave rolls again. 8 to 20 top players disappeared in the last 4 years. The [global] share of the top 5 players had increased from 45% to 64% overall, and from 53% in Long Haul*'.

For global oligopolists, growth in many nations is modest compared with Asia or, increasingly, Africa. Many nations are small even compared with faster growing cities. McKinsey expects just 20 such top cities, which are home to 75% of the world's largest companies, to generate a third of world growth by 2025.[20] Britain's GDP is below the state of California's, which is growing much faster: its population is matched by just a few large Asian cities, again growing far faster. Fewer than five nations enjoy GDPs higher than Apple's $200 billion cash holdings. BlackRock now manages a global portfolio of $4.5 trillion of assets: such footloose global financial capital could reach some $900 trillion by 2020.[21] '*Put not thy trust in princes*', nor in nations, nor even in regional institutions, for there is [limited] *help in them.*

POLITICAL TENSIONS ARISING FROM GLOBALISATION

The implicit assumption of those securing success, in arenas that are globally oligopolistic, is that their approach will prove acceptable. Extreme monopolists, whether domestically or globally, have always been subject to ferocious political criticism. Overstepping the mark endangers revolution. Marx's criticism of capitalist exploitation culminated in half the world opting for alternative state planning systems. Rival systems risked destroying each other, and indeed, the planet, through nuclear holocausts. Attitudes vary radically worldwide and change, especially among the young, displaced and disaffected. Political consensus on the merits of global markets, trade and foreign direct investment (FDI) could evaporate in the wake of a populist backlash.

Given evident global concentration and oligopoly plays, Marx's criticism of capitalism has not proved naïve. Ironically, just as Francis Fukuyama was proclaiming global capitalism's triumph,[22] Marx's prediction of increasing global concentration levels has become manifest in several sectors. Adam Smith's argument, relating to advantages from technological specialisation and division of labour, was built upon his correct presumption of huge scale economies. Yet as Marx argued, these same scale economies have tended to drive global concentration levels higher. Without offsetting mechanisms, global capitalism could incubate '*the seeds of its own self-destruction*'. Scary instabilities in the Great Depression and in 2008 inflamed political tensions. Failing to address wider societal concerns, including wealth and income distribution,[23] invites counter-movements, united under banners blindly scapegoating 'austerity' or 'globalisation'.

Footloose concentrated capital likely contributed to the 2008 economic crisis. Single corporations placed countries at financial risk. Iceland was not able to bail out Icelandic banks; Scotland could not have bailed out RBS; UBS posed similar risks to Switzerland. Knock-on effects from smaller bank collapses, such as Lehman's, highlight risks from today's potentially struggling larger players, like Deutsche Bank, yet far more integrated into the world's economic system. Financial assets worldwide are expected to rise to $900 trillion in 2020.[24]

Fortunately, we have also evidenced powerful dynamic countervailing forces. Paradoxically, it has been global oligopolistic plays and counter-plays (rather than perfectly functioning price mechanisms) that have maintained capitalism's vibrancy. It is also this same Schumpeterian dynamic, highlighted in Figure 2.4's concentration waves in sector after sector, which has boosted productivity to unprecedented levels, not least in the world's poorest regions. Extreme global monopolies, anticipated by Marx, have proved rare; the real threat has been intensifying worldwide competition.

Corporations, over-reliant on monopoly power per se, have not sustained great performances. Porter's evidence in 1990, that domestic monopoly power usually proved counter-productive,[25] is fully endorsed by our findings. In 1989, US Steel, for example, was both America's and the world's biggest steel company; by 2014, it had been overtaken by ArcelorMittal the new global leader. Anheuser-Busch was both America's and the world's biggest brewer, right up until its takeover by Ambev in 2004. Global competition has proved so tough a task master, that complacency imperilled performance and survival. Capitalism has proved ferocious '*in tooth and claw*', taking no prisoners from *anyone* considering the world owed them a living.

Advanced countries still sometimes predominate, but empire days have gone. They no longer dominate, as of right, attractive, higher value-added work, affording higher profits and wages. All top 20 airlines in 2000, for example, were US or European; by 2014, half were based in Asia, with Emirates leading in terms of passenger miles.[26] Global oligopolies have proved extraordinarily powerful, but, increasingly, incumbents have been losing out to new emerging market champions.

Much anger over '*globalisation*' derives from anguish as country legacy advantages have diminished. Complacency or poor skills risk condemning us to living standards closer in line with aspiring nations, catching up but accepting lower wages. No longer are we shielded from the consequences of questionable economic choices. Greece and Russia have suffered dreadfully, whilst alternative economic choices greatly benefitted China. Over ten years Greek real wages almost halved, whilst those in China tripled over the same period. Though recovering, Greece's real GDP in mid-2018 remained 25% lower than pre-crisis levels in 2007.[27]

World GDP still increases steadily, but China and India are reverting to positions on a par with the West, as before the Industrial Revolution. They now dominate increasingly numerous attractive, high value-added sectors. Pay asymmetries globally are evening out in favour of emerging markets (EMs). As global rivalry encompasses more sectors, this '*steady extension of contestable markets*',[28] has triggered advanced countries' '*lost decade*' of falling real wages. After inflation, United Kingdom (UK) average pay of £503 per week is £35 less than in 2008. American, Japanese, and European central banks are reporting similar unprecedented trends despite record employment levels. Populists scapegoat immigrants, but fail to explain global trends or Japan, where there have been none; blind anti-globalisation rhetoric risks regions becoming less, not more attractive to global wealth creators.

If once predominant American car giants such as GM and Chrysler (and very nearly Ford) entered bankruptcy, if regions like Detroit and Michigan degenerated into rust bowls, others have still less scope for manoeuvre. Advanced regions no longer possess powers or unique resources, once afforded to colonial empires. Everyone from everywhere now craves '*their place in the sun*' and work that is most lucrative. In economic and business terms, this is World War 3.

THE WEALTH OF NATIONS IN THE TWENTY-FIRST CENTURY

In the context of extensive globalisation and globally oligopolistic rivalry, nations benefit from two prime drivers of wealth. First, a country may have its own global winners, though that contribution is diminished by their need to disperse assets and wealth to support markets throughout the rest of the world. Conversely, countries benefit from local subsidiaries of all other global winners, as captured by the total of all inward FDIs. Though unanticipated in Adam Smith's overarching theory, both sources have become dominant sources of income in the twenty-first century.

We can now capture and analyse both sources of wealth using huge databases such as Thomson One Banker or S&P Capital IQ, supplemented with inward FDI analysis, but conceptualisation is helpful if we are to distinguish those portions of constituent elements contributing to national incomes.

Ultimately, few countries can hope to secure top 4 global winners in more than about 5% of sectors: the primary role of multinational corporations (MNCs), in turn, is efficient asset dispersion in line with global market demands, not better trade or wealth outcomes for their countries of origin.

What matters is not sales revenue, but value-added retained in the home country. Even so, a global winner only enhances domestic incomes to the extent that they exceed average value-added productivity levels. High technology jobs, such as Apple's, add greatly; McDonalds' or domestic service type jobs contribute less. Dominate the world's lowest value-added sectors and your nation becomes poor.

Global oligopolists, moreover, evolve, becoming increasingly '*footloose*' and acting like MNCs from anywhere. Pressured by global capital markets, pension and hedge funds, most have a fiduciary responsibility to maximise efficiencies and profits. Though profits appear vast and interest costs low, their discretionary scope is highly constrained. Over the last 150 years, however, the real opportunity cost of capital has not been that 1% or so p.a. available from banks or bonds, nor even their weighted average cost of capital, but the 7% p.a. safer, inflation-adjusted yields from property, reflecting rising populations and incomes. Over this same period, corporate returns averaged 6.9% (inflation-adjusted), proving riskier (as evidenced by higher variances statistically). Any discretionary scope on strategic investments is curtailed, unless and until (less productive) property returns could be reduced; but doing so globally (say through taxation, or through draconian population policies as in China) would prove politically intractable if not infeasible. Meantime, global oligopolists' wealth creation policies become increasingly homogeneous and asset geographical dispersion rates tend towards 95% or so.

As globalisation proceeds, wealth seeking nations need to gain above average shares of global oligopolists' investments, mainly from rival countries controlling most sectors. The proxy for these foreign country investments collectively is inbound FDI. However it is vital to distinguish value-added elements critically. The latter can be negligible in tax havens: Cyprus dominates nominal Russian FDI, but is largely a politically convenient postbox. FDI adds greatest value when wedded to cluster effects as in automotive supply chains. FDI from Toyota, Nissan, and Honda almost single-handedly turned around Britain's entire car production, whilst inducing FDI from global winners in a host of supply sectors; by contrast, any contribution from home players was largely down to GKN in components. Such FDI decisions will be repeated in other sectors. Higher real incomes depend increasingly on attracting and retaining investments from foreign global oligopolists, not just our own.

To envisage the future, imagine our 195 nations, as though they were all equally sized standardised nations. (China and the USA effectively representing several.) Envisage, as though equally sized and standardised, just the 173 General Industry Classification System (GICS) sectors plus just 22 global niche sectors (though certainly underreflecting those discussed in Chapter 8). Imagine perfect global integration, as each nation achieves global leaders in single sectors, plus other top 4s in just three of all 195 sectors. Each nation leads on focusing on just

2% of products and services once covered extensively at home. In 98% of sectors, their wealth is dependent on FDI from other global oligopolists.

We are only part way along this globalisation road; for sectors such as public services, it is still early days. Yet even proceeding thus far has proven strategically crucial to companies and countries displaced. By the time of my interviews in Hong Kong in the mid-1990s, most of their once thriving manufacturing sector had gone. Their factories had seemingly taken that speedy ferry from Hong Kong to China's mainland, becoming resettled in more cost competitive zones in neighbouring Shenzhen. This graphic metaphor captures outcomes in manufacturing sectors, where countries' relative comparative advantages were low.

At the end of 2009, Nokia held 39% global market share in smartphones, Porter having endorsed Finland's national competitive advantage (NCA) in the sector. But by Q2, 2019, Nokia was out, following Schumpterian *global wars*, as the GCR4 fell from 79% to 60%. Even Apple, clocking up its billionth disruptor iPhone in 2016, fell back to 10% global market share (GMS). Samsung's leading share at 23% was challenged, in turn, by Huawei (18%), Xiaomi (9%), Oppo (9%), not to mention India's start-ups like Ringing Bells' \$3.70 smartphones.[29] Notwithstanding US President Trump, Huawei's 5G revenues grew 23% in the first half of 2019.[30] As Nokia's global strategy failed, Finland experienced diminished relative comparative advantages and wealth contributions. No future visions pertaining to strategy or national wealth can ignore EMM global oligopolists, analysed in Chapters 9 through 11.

Such national wealth creation (W), can be summarised mathematically to accommodate global databases such as Thompson One Banker, or S&P Capital IQ capturing nearly 5 million public companies globally. W in country, c, is given by:

$$W = \text{Sum}\left[\text{Vi} \times (1 - \text{D}) \times (\text{Vi} - \text{Va})\right] + \text{Sum}(\text{F} \times \text{Vf}).$$

where Vi are firm i's (restricted to country c) value-addeds, calculated by taking gross profits plus all salary remunerations. For firms where these two latter figures are unavailable, Vi would have to be estimated from averaged sector figures, generated from all firms in that sector affording complete data. Di is firm i's geographical dispersion ratio outside its home country, most crudely estimated from generally available foreign sales ratios. Va is the current figure for averaged value-added productivity for all global firms: i.e., the sum of all global Vi/the sum of all employees worldwide. Li is firm i's value-added leverage %. F is the value of all inbound FDI into country, c. Vf is the leveraged value-added from FDI, though note this is an investment, not an income-based ratio: these figures can be fractional in tax-havens, but high in high value-added sectors in stronger host countries.

For those without access to such databases two messages remain clear. Value your country's own global oligopoly winners, but don't expect too many or too much from them. Secondly, maximise value from global oligopolists inbound FDIs and understand their motivations. Policy choices greatly affect wealth contributions from entire sectors: had Thatcher's government not won Toyota, Nissan, and Honda FDI's nearly 40 years ago, Britain's car and component sectors' wealth creation would have been fractional; lose them by weakening their access to European Union markets, and the converse applies. The same applies to almost all sectors. This why 'global competitiveness', surveyed annually by the World Economic Forum, and the subject of my first book, matters and is not just a zero-sum game: lose high value-added activities and incoming FDI and you really do risk becoming poorer.[31]

APPROPRIATIONS BY COUNTRIES AND PERFORMANCE OUTCOMES FOR ALL 30,000 COMPANIES

More precisely, Chapter 1 evidenced that just 632 global top 4 oligopolists appropriated some 40% of all sales and value-added across all 158 GICS sectors. Tables 14.1 and 14.2 extend this analysis to all 30,000 large companies

Table 14.1 Appropriation of sales, EBIT profit pools, salaries, gross income, employment, 2011–2016. Analysis of 30,000 companies by country of ownership

Country%	*Nos*	*Sales*	*6yr EBIT*	*IntSales*	*Employ*	*Sals*	*GrPrft*	*R&D*	*CapX*	*SGA*	*Intang*
Gl Total	100	100	100	100	100	100	100	100	100	100	100
USA	12.4	27.7	30.4	20.8	24.5	10.6	35.4	41.5	26.7	35.0	20.8
China	10.9	10.3	11.9	4.7	14.9	29.6	6.7	6.4	10.1	6.5	4.7
HK	0.7	1.3	1.6	1.4	1.7	1.2	1.4	0.3	2.3	1.1	1.4
JPN	12.0	13.4	8.5	12.8	11.0	6.5	12.4	16.8	12.1	15.1	12.8
KOR	5.9	3.7	2.7	3.9	0.2	1.8	2.9	3.9	3.4	3.3	3.9
TWN	5.2	1.9	1.2	3.4	0.8	1.7	1.1	2.6	1.3	1.1	3.4
GBR	3.1	4.6	3.0	6.5	5.3	6.5	3.9	3.0	4.6	4.6	6.5
IRE	0.2	0.6	0.5	1.2	1.0	0.4	0.8	1.5	0.3	0.8	1.2
FR	1.6	4.2	4.2	5.6	4.5	6.5	3.7	2.6	3.9	3.5	5.6
DEU	1.2	4.4	3.9	8.4	4.1	5.0	4.2	6.1	3.4	5.3	8.4
IND	6.2	2.2	2.0	1.5	3.8	2.1	1.4	0.5	2.5	0.3	1.5
CH/HK	11.6	11.6	13.5	6.1	16.6	30.8	8.1	6.8	12.5	7.7	6.1
GBR/IRE	3.3	5.2	3.5	7.6	6.3	6.9	4.7	4.4	5.0	5.4	7.6
AUSTRAL	2.2	1.4	2.0	1.2	1.0	2.0	1.2	0.2	1.4	1.1	1.2
CYM	3.5	1.5	1.5	1.1	2.8	1.1	1.8	1.9	1.6	1.5	1.1
CAN	2.3	2.2	2.3	3.0	1.9	1.9	1.9	0.4	2.8	2.2	3.0
Top 4	39.2	58.0	55.9	47.3	58.4	54.9	60.6	69.5	56.1	63.1	47.3

Source: Analysis of Thomson One Banker data.

Note: Again, as in Chapter 1, I acknowledge gratefully the contribution of Olivia Mason who helped enormously with my analysis of these Thomson One Banker data sets. Employ, employee numbers; Sals, total salaries and wages; GrPrft, Gross Profit; R&D, as % of sales; CapX, capital expenditure/sales %; SGA, sales, general & administrative costs/sales %; and Intang, intangibles/sales %.

Table 14.2 2011–2016 30,000 companies' performance outcomes by country of ownership. Returns on capital employed (RoC) and sales (RoS), sales growth (SG), and value-added proxy, being salaries (Sal) + profit (Prft)

Country%	*6yRoC*	*6yrRos*	*6yrSG%pa*	*%Sal+Prft*
Gl Total	21.3	13.2	44.7	100.0
USA	17.2	10.7	45.6	23.0
China	24.4	14.5	76.5	18.1
HK	11.3	22.4	42.4	1.3
JPN	16.4	9.2	33.4	9.4
KOR	25.9	7.8	48.2	2.4
TWN	11.9	7.6	20.4	1.4
GBR	24.7	22.3	52.8	5.2
IRE	22.2	17.8	54.1	0.6
FR	32.6	12.8	19.6	5.1
DEU	23.0	12.7	25.9	4.6
IND	25.6	11.0	29.3	1.8
CH/HK	23.6	15.0	74.5	19.4
GBR/IRE	24.6	22.0	52.9	5.8
AUSRAL	22.6	16.8	72.3	1.6
CYM	32.6	12.9	112.0	1.4
CAN	14.9	11.7	61.4	1.9
Top 4	19.5	12.4	51.0	57.7

Source: Analysis of Thomson One Banker data.

Note: Again, as in Chapter 1, I acknowledge gratefully the contribution of Olivia Mason who helped enormously with my analysis of these Thomson One Banker data sets. Employ, employee numbers; Sals, total salaries and wages; GrPrft, Gross Profit; R&D, as % of sales; CapX, capital expenditure/sales %; SGA, sales, general & administrative costs/sales %; and Intang, intangibles/sales %.

worldwide, deploying the same methodology and Thompson One Banker data, to identify appropriations and performance outcomes for major countries worldwide. Taken together salaries (Sals) and gross profits (GrPrft) are my proxies for value added (VA), in turn, prime contributors to country GDPs. Even taking all 30,000 public companies ignores the tail of private and small companies, and so overstates appropriating %s. Much of this value-added is also highly geographically dispersed through FDI. Nonetheless, their collective VA constitutes a major, and increasing, constituent of national and global incomes and GDPs.

In 2016 just four top regions, the USA, Japan, China/Hong Kong and UK/Ireland, comprised almost 40% of the world's top 30,000 companies numerically. Their companies accounted for around 60% of all sales, gross profits, employment, R&D, capital, and marketing related expenditures. Their value-added appropriations, comprising salaries and gross profit at, respectively, 55% and 61%, approached 58%. Geographical dispersion rates would be higher for Britain, Hong Kong, Ireland, and for tax havens such as the Cayman

Islands (CYM), reducing any direct VA benefit from companies headquartered there; FDI analysis is also needed. Nevertheless, global oligopolists' appropriations, countries of origins, and dispersion policies (through FDIs) are now critical determinants of wealth creation worldwide.

Over the full six years, 2011-2016, companies from these same four regions appropriated some 55% of all earnings before interest and tax (EBIT) profits. Their sales growths were slightly above averages for other countries; but their profitability ratios were slightly below. Such analyses are pertinent to global oligopolists' geographical decisions, but their commercial perspectives should at least be considered by national policymakers too.

POLITICAL CONCERNS OVER INEQUALITY, EXCESSIVE POWER, AND ANTI-TRUST

Creating wealth in companies and countries depends upon political outcomes. The challenge to leadership is capturing the hearts of those hurt, damaged, and or simply confused by shifting patterns of global rivalry. Voters may prove gullible to populist politicians, proclaiming '*F*** business*' or blindly attacking scapegoats, including '*capitalism*', '*austerity*', '*globalisation*', the European Union, other trade blocs, or immigrants. Albeit popular, this risks destructive economic wars, which could one day become real, through class wars or between competing nations, as in previous world wars.

Rising global oligopolies and concentration levels have not, despite understandable concerns, led to increased inequality *worldwide*. World Bank researchers found '*Between 2008 and 2013, the number of countries experiencing declining inequality was twice the number exhibiting widening inequality*'.[32] '*Over the 20 years from 1993 to 2013, the number of poor people [defined as subsisting on under $1.90, calculated in 2011 prices, based on purchasing power parities] fell by over 1 billion, from roughly one in three to about one in ten*'.[33] From 1988 to 2013 within-country inequality has risen only slightly in advanced economies, as compared with far greater reductions between countries: indeed, inequality between 2008 and 2013 fell in two out of three advanced countries, particularly in northern Europe.[34]

Even so, Piketty's argument[35] cannot be ignored. Between 1879 and 2015, average wealth pre-tax returns globally were 6% p.a. vs global GDP growth of 3% p.a. (Piketty's 'g').[36] In recent decades, wealth returns have been persistently above GDP growth. The wealthy have been getting wealthier. Over these 145 years, equity returns averaged just slightly below housing returns at 7% p.a. globally, though proving far more volatile; but substantially higher than bonds at 2.5% or bills at 1% p.a. For those concerned with oligopoly returns, global equity returns have proved less attractive long-term than far safer and less productive property investments. Inheritance tax rates paid by major property estates have often proved minimal,[37] so perhaps prime concerns regarding sustained inequalities in wealth, should rather relate to land

and properties. It is harder to argue that global oligopoly returns are excessive, whilst safe property returns have proved more attractive.

Piketty makes points which corporate governance systems would be unwise to ignore. Global markets do incentivise increasingly unequal pay for top performers, whose economic value is higher than ever. This is hard to avoid in a world where the record transfer fee for a single world-class football player doubled in 2017 to $220 million, and where Bruce Springsteen's life-time earnings amounted to some $2.7 billion.[38] Sir Martin Sorrell's remuneration and behaviour at WPP, which he had built up over 33 years, were criticised, forcing his resignation on 14 April 2018. WPP shares though fell 6.5% that same day, reducing shareholder value by $1.3 billion; by July he was a competitor; by the end of August 2019, market capitalisation had fallen from $20 billion to $14 billion. By losing Sorrell, shareholders lost far more than his remuneration. CEO Marchionne earned a fortune, but his sad demise hit Fiat Chrysler shareholders and employees severely. Average Financial Times Stock Exchange (FTSE) 100 CEO pay rose to £3.5 million a year in 2019, 117 times average full-time employee pay at £30K;[39] but their collective value-added rival entire nations. Such is their impact on shareholder value, CEO remuneration judgements are inherently contentious.

Even so, 84% of S&P 500 CEOs were hired internally in 2015, compared with 63% in 2005.[40] Persimmon's CEO's exceptional bonus package of around £100 million in 2017, whilst justifiable in shareholder value terms, also reflected home government housebuilding incentives and domestic oligopoly power, reflecting low rather than high international competition. The UK construction sector's productivity was only 9% higher in Q1, 2018 compared with the same period in 1997, whereas output per hour worked rose 28% for the UK economy as a whole;[41] and the quality of their homes was subsequently criticised. At 1320 times Persimmon's average wages,[42] such CEO remuneration levels appeared unwarranted and divisive. Levels of child poverty in Britain, remained at 20% between 2002 and 2016, despite the proportion where at least one parent was working rising from 48% to 66%.[43] Employees not benefitting from their own efforts risked disillusionment and, in 2019, investors were themselves rebelling.[44] Extreme excesses would be unacceptable in Germany, Scandinavia, or Japan and, in business, we depend on others and our reputations.

Yet globally, using Thomson One Banker's data on the world's top 30,000 global players' value-added figures, I found no relentless decline in the share of labour's salaries as suggested by Piketty's more macro-data-based analysis.[45] The split most disfavouring labour has occurred in former state planning nations, notably Russia and China. Appropriating state power to further broader societal aims, including equality, has ironically sometimes favoured the powerful, just as happened historically.

More fundamentally, such global commercial power must however be seen to be handled fairly and responsibly. Before drooling over prospective tax havens and playing nations off against each other, multinationals should beware the likely backlash. Societies reject dystopias. The Russian Revolution was perhaps more a response to feudalism than capitalism, but oligopolists then wisely adapted. Like Rockefeller and Carnegie, a century ago, Bill Gates and Warren Buffet honourably opted for stunning levels of philanthropy: just one project, coordinated through President George Bush, saved more lives in Africa than ever in history. Even in the teeth of Trump, '*Globally, 232 firms that are collectively worth over $6trn have committed to cutting their carbon emissions in line with the [Davos Paris] accord's goal of limiting global warming to less than 2 degrees C*'.[46] Their visions need to span beyond politicians' and sometimes even shareholders' myopic horizons.[47] Global oligopolists' wealth creation is greater than ever in history. So, what will be their legacy? Just as oligopolists wisely acceded to Smithian anti-trust policies a century ago, global oligopolists should now recognise that some measure of anti-trust must now go global too.

RECONCILING ADAM SMITH'S, SCHUMPETER'S, AND MARX'S THEORETICAL PERSPECTIVES: CARR'S UNIVERSAL FRAMEWORK AND APPLICATION IN THE CONTEXT OF OLIGOPOLIES

Smith, Schumpeter, and Marx are still recognised as '*The Great Economists*', though Yueh adds Ricardo, Marshall, Keynes and a few recent names.[48] In relation to macro-economic policies Yueh positions them along a spectrum from state- to market-orientated economists, with Marx advocating state responses and Schumpeter (as also Hayek and Milton Friedman) at the opposite pole suggesting more market-based economic policies. Smith and Ricardo (as also Marshall, Fisher, and Solow) are positioned slightly towards the state intervention side. Keynes (as also Douglas North and Joan Robinson) would be more mid-way and interventionist.

In relation to global concentration processes, Smith's and Marx's perspectives represent opposite polar extremes. Adam Smith recognised '*division of labour*' would internationalise. Trade implied sensibly extending markets geographically, contrary to mercantilists' parochial interests. Specialisation and scale economies could go global. Yet for Smith, if not for Marx, this would have still implied fragmented commodity-style global markets, where highly numerous rivals remained price-takers. GCRs would remain negligible or zero. Marx, in contrast, envisaged scale economies so huge as to drive concentration towards global monopolies, with all GCRs converging to 1.0. Both extremes have occurred, but have become rarer, less sustainable. Most sectors have evolved into global oligopolies, loose or tight, their GCRs

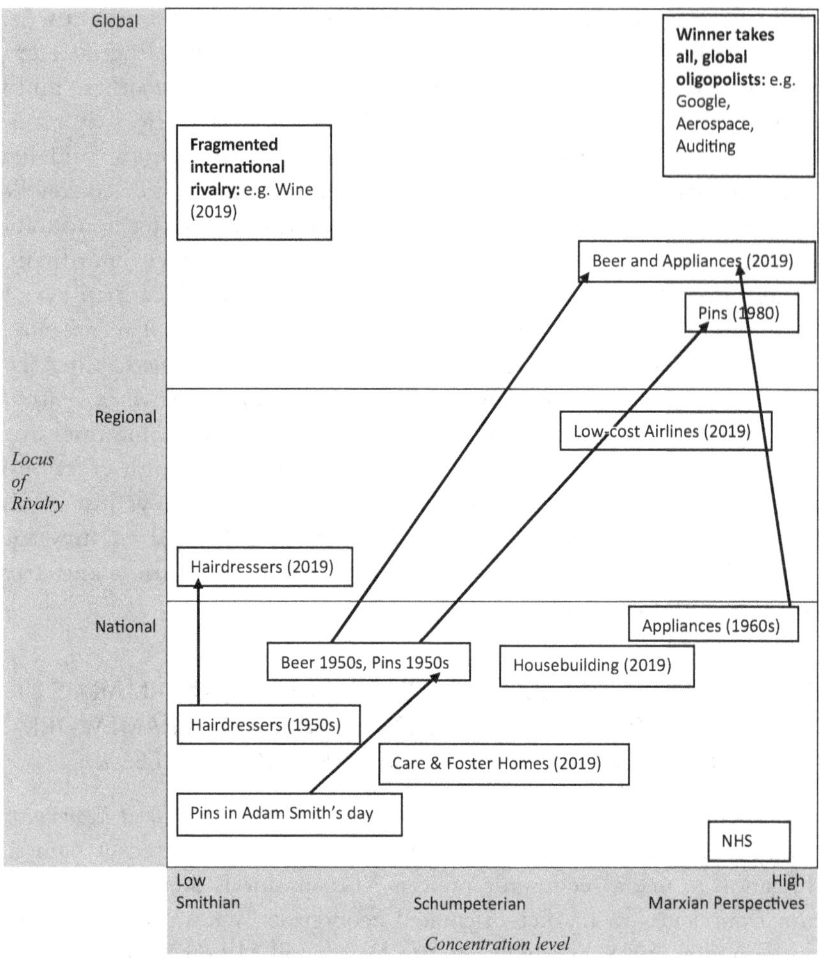

Figure 14.1 Carr's universal theory of oligopolies: Smith, Schumpeterian, and Marxist influences related to sectors' loci of rivalry and concentration ratios.

varying substantially. Mapping them, as earlier, reveals the relative pertinence of diametrically opposite theoretical poles.

Figure 14.1's overarching new theoretical perspective (as earlier discussed in Figure 2.9 in Chapter 2) allows implications to be summarised. The starting point is locus of competition. Then based on the relevant concentration ratio, we can position sectors according to GCRs, regional concentration ratios (RCRs), or national concentration ratios (NCRs). Pertinent theoretical and policy perspectives then logically reflect the sector (or cluster of sectors) being considered.

For low GCR sectors, Smith's theoretical framework rightly encourages entrepreneurs to focus their skills, exploit any division of labour, and to niche, pre-empting blinkered mercantilist-orientated rivals. Though, not naïvely; others will follow suit. Lives of riches may last no longer than that of fireflies'. Before they know it, they find themselves again struggling to deliver profits beyond their cost of capital. Like rats on treadmills, or Red Queens, they can only run ever faster, never achieving quite such stupendous fortunes or easy lives as once fondly envisaged; though savouring schadenfreude watching more foolish rats topple right off their treadmills, wondering what on earth hit them. Such pitfalls beset '*commoditised*' fragmented sectors, lacking entry barriers; eschewed by disciples of Porter's '*Five Force*' analyses, they offer less scope for oligopoly plays.

At the opposite polar extreme, in sectors displaying exceptionally high GCRs, Marx's global monopoly profit appropriations have sometimes proved feasible. Typically associated with '*winner-takes-all*' global scale economics and '*network externalities*', this has been a feasting ground for fortunes.

Imagine a sector as lying in the spectrum between these two poles – akin to some heavy globe suspended by tensioned cables. One set of cables restrain sectors, keeping them more in line with Smith's idealised fragmentation; another set of cables pull them, increasingly forcefully, towards global concentration (on the right-hand side) as envisaged by Marx. Most sectors examined have been in permanent flux, veering off-centre, to-and-fro, as suggested by Schumpeterian perspectives. Most veered towards the Marxian pole, fell short, only to revert towards the Smithian pole, as global Schumpeterian '*gales of creative destruction*' cut in.

Within a decade, for example, Nokia's 40% lucrative global market share of mobile phones was destroyed by Apple, Samsung, and Chinese smartphones. Even Apple by mid-2018 had slipped back to No. 3. Huawei the new No. 2 is ceding share to new Chinese low-cost disruptors. Far from sclerotic, these consolidation processes proved dynamic. They propagated GCR oscillation waves, pitting titans against titans. They have been relentlessly battling it out, in a lethal global game of musical chairs, running ever as chairs disappeared. To capture this GCR4s should ideally be complemented with a volatility disruption index capturing incumbent turnover rates.

Sometimes we must distinguish two related phenomena. On one axis we depict the level of concentration measured by CRs; the other concerns the locus of markets and competition. A century ago, the locus of rivalry in most sectors was predominantly national. Half a century ago, white goods and domestic appliances, as elaborated in Chapter 11, were dominated by America's top five players; but oligopolies were perceived nationally rather than globally. The US CR5 exceeded 90%, suggesting powerful oligopoly plays and super-normal profits for larger players; but American economists and competition bodies remained unconcerned over (not even published) global CR figures. International trade was just the icing on the cake. US subsidiaries in Europe operated relatively autonomously, competition being perceived country by country. For strategic and anti-trust purposes, the locus of rivalry was treated as essentially national. This would have positioned the appliance sector bottom right in Figure 14.1, reflecting a 90% US CR5. Regulators alerted to oligopolistic plays ignored global competitive arenas.[49]

As Chapter 11 showed, competition has since become so global as to invalidate more local competitive analysis. Appliances have moved up to the top right, reflecting substantial GCR4s around 32%. Whirlpool's fiercest rival is no longer the other top US players, who have all gone, but China's Haier followed by Europe's Electrolux. Adopting an antiquated US perspective, anti-trust policymakers turned down a proposed Electrolux/GE Appliances M&A which would have rebalanced global rivalry, only to accept GE Appliances takeover by Haier, further strengthening Haier as the most formidable global player today, directly threatening Whirlpool given its weak shares of today's crucial Chinese and Asian markets. From a blinkered US anti-trust perspective, these US rulings made sense; from a global anti-trust or strategic perspective, they were counter-productive and merely undermined the global competitiveness of top American and European players.

Figure 14.1's universal framework, underpinned by GCR maps, recognises such shifts in the locus of rivalry. In sectors, where trade, FDI, and international competition are negligible, this locus is national, NCRs mattering most. Where concentration ratios are almost zero, as in the pin industry in Adam Smith's day, we have fragmented, commoditised competition where players are price-takers, with negligible oligopoly power, so that classical economics applies. However, move well over to the right, and sectors potentially yield Marxian monopoly power, more exploitational profits beyond capital costs, provided they enjoy entry barriers. Government or regulators, themselves, often create such barriers, as once happened in airlines under International Air Transport Association (IATA), and as happens in services deemed essential, such as the National Health Service (NHS).

Move downwards, and on the left, we see more fragmented privatised public services, like dental services. NCRs are higher in care homes, but oligopolists such as Four Seasons may have underestimated fragmentation forces, overestimating benefits from scale, just as happened far earlier to Prelude in the US lobster fishing business. Profitability has sometimes proven low, rendering market leaders vulnerable. The leading British funeral provider, Dignity's share performance in 2019 was weak. Even leaders on major UK infrastructure public contracts, like Carillion, have failed.

Child fostering has also raised policy concerns. Demand for child fostering rose 60% in the decade to 2019, with the CR3 in England rising to 45% as private equity bought up and consolidated small independent foster care agencies, returning 20%–30% p.a. on their investments; but policies hiking up charges from councils 'held to ransom' have been criticised:[50] half these children find themselves moved every three years, and what happens if one of the big three go bust? Local oligopolies can prove as exploitational as global ones.

A final example is house building, dominated by the big four in Britain, but otherwise fragmented. Spurred by the government Right to Buy scheme, these national oligopolists have performed superbly. Not only has the leading company, Persimmon's, dividend yield averaged over 5%, but its market capitalisation almost tripled between 2011 and 2019, raising concerns about any exploitation of oligopoly power, as discussed earlier. Yet even this solid national locus of rivalry could be about to change, should modern prefabrications finally rock the sector. Japan's leading player in this field, Sekisui House, has only 5% of the Japanese market, but matches the production of Persimmon, Taylor Woodrow, and Barratt combined and has formed a joint venture (JV) to enter what it sees as a lagging market, ripe for change.[51] Such disruption could eventually shift even this national locus of rivalry to global.

From a theoretical stance, we must ask what determines dynamic shifts as between the two polar Smithian and Marxian extremes. In more market-based competition, our best model for exploring and explaining global oligopolies has proved to be Schumpeterian. New business model paradigms emerged, driven by entrepreneurs, often challenging over-powerful oligopolists. Not many years ago even taxi drivers' pitches were invaded by hire car oligopolists such as Hertz, only for both services to have been disrupted by yet more radical business models, such as Uber, not to mention Alphabet's self-driving cars. Their locus of competition in Figure 14.1 has been shifting rapidly upwards, albeit constrained by regulators, local governments and politicians. Schumpeterian disruption from innovative, increasingly global entrepreneurs, has barred local oligopolists from complacency and easy profits.

Yet, substantial scale economies can trigger dynamic sector shifts both vertically upwards and towards the right along the horizontal axis. The starting point for strategy (or policy concerns) is firstly to position sectors to which you are most exposed, their concentration metrics and mappings, just as this book has charted and tabulated in all 173 General Industry Classification System-coded sectors, recognising trends, orientations, evolutionary shifts, and performance outcomes. Figure 14.1's universal oligopoly theory posits that the relevance of Smithian, Schumpeterian, and Marxian theoretical perspectives shifts according to sectors' positioning on these two axes. National economies reflect distinctive sector mixes; but averaged positions have moved upwards and rather more the right (almost Global Force 8s).

ADDRESSING THE CHALLENGES POSED BY GLOBAL OLIGOPOLIES

Global oligopolies, so powerful and pervasive, have been underappreciated by economists. Since Adam Smith's *Wealth of Nations*, most have clung to the law of large numbers, dispensing with the necessity of '*opening the box*' relating to corporate strategies. But policy makers must now peer into '*that box*'. As discussed,

Smith's famous pin manufacturers were concentrated in the hands of just four global majors even by 1980; his presumption of large numbers no longer applies in most business sectors. Apple, Microsoft, and Amazon have all now surpassed $1 trillion market capitalisations, whilst fewer than five nations enjoy GDPs higher than Apple's $200 billion cash holdings. In the twenty-first century most of the '*wealth of nations*' has been spawned and dispersed (via foreign direct investment) by relatively few global oligopolists, many of whom did not exist at the turn of the century. Foreign investment, as discussed, increasingly determines our wealth, and, as a proportion of global GDP, it has risen from 7% in 1990 to 40% in 2019.[52]

Our analyses extended beyond just Apple and Amazon, covering no less than 30,000 of world's large companies with collective value-added on par with continents. Big data has allowed us to analyse almost entire global value streams. Over several years, appropriations by top 4 global oligopoly players averaged around 40% across all 173 GICS sectors: not just for profits but for almost all metrics including R&D, capital expenditures, sales and general administrative expenses (often reflecting branding), and intangible assets. This 40% appropriation figure further rose to nearly 60% for sectors with above average global concentration ratios. No one concerned with public policies can ignore these appropriation levels, nor the power that their scale delivers. Nor can we understand anymore the wealth of nations in the twenty-first century, without first recognising appropriated shares taken today by just top four sector players, in turn concentrating heavily (in terms of ownership) in just four top states, now including China. Such global oligopolists, rather than more numerous and lauded SMEs, have predominated wealth creation. They extend to 'hidden' global niche champions, as examined in Chapter 8 covering Germany and Britain, and increasingly to distinctive emerging market champions, examined in Chapters 9 through 11.

Most are increasingly footloose globally, whilst regulators have been constrained by regional or even national mandates. The Organisation for Economic Co-operation and Development, comprising the world's 36 richest nations, has finally responded to the internet age by publishing proposals to standardise corporate tax rules across borders. They now rightly recognise that key assets are increasingly borderless and intangible, and these too we have analysed. They have concluded, for example, that digital companies in the EU have been paying on average 8 or 9% tax on their profits in Europe, compared with 23% for traditional businesses, costing EU countries E70 billion a year in lost revenues.[53] Global cooperation is increasingly needed here, though mandates should extend to anti-trust policies.

A New Applied Political Economics, integrating Business and Global Strategy, is needed. This field should supplant that less engaged, mathematics-based economic *theory*, which somehow usurped the fine applied tradition of insightful, impactful economists such as Smith, Ricardo, Marx, Marshall,

Keynes, and Galbraith. Any such rejuvenation of applied economics must encompass an empirical understanding of today's global oligopolies and of the strategies required to create and sustain them.

This book's scope has been huge, spanning all General Industry Classification System sectors, decades, even centuries, and so many regions that inevitably much data and analysis becomes dated. It provides though the first embracing map outlining the whole world of global oligopolies, their detailed strategies, and impacts. Though imperfect, these novel frameworks and analytical techniques are readily updatable, deploying amazingly powerful data bases as illustrated. Blending these new concepts, techniques, and resources should allow us to engage more fully policy makers, executives, and our students, in addressing some of the most challenging economic and strategic issues of our age.

NOTES

1 Sampson, A. (1976). *The Seven Sisters: The Great Oil Companies & the World They Shaped*, London: Bantam, p. 30. For Rockefeller's critique of Adam Smith and a superb account of the early consolidation of the oil industry, see Chernow, R. (1998). *Titan: The Life of John D. Rockefeller, Sr*, London: Little Brown.
2 Sampson, ibid.
3 Channel 4, 24 August 2019, 9 pm. 'World War 2. The Battle for Stalingrad'.
4 Ghemawat, P. and Gadar (2000), ibid.
5 Analysis based on Samson, ibid., p. 241.
6 Ibid., p. 202, again drawing on US Congress, *Multinational Hearings*, 1952.
7 Ghemawat and Gadar (2000, ibid.)'s Herfindahl indices for oil production fell further to 0.02 in 1990. Between 1998 and 2008, my calculated His recovered from 0.04 to 0.05.
8 *The Economist*, 17 August 2019, p. 53. 'Saudi Aramco. Tap dance'.
9 Khanna, P. (2016), ibid.: pp. 38, 42, 43, 49, 51, & 57.
10 IMF Data Mapper figures averaged 2009–2018, and forecasts averaged 2019–2024.
11 World Bank, OECD National Accounts data online, accessed 28 August 2019.
12 FDI inflows in 2015 reached $380 billion in the USA and $310 billion in China (including Hong Kong); and FDI outflows $300 billion in the USA and $183 billion in China and $129 billion in Japan. Source: *The Economist* (2018). *Pocket World in Figures*. London, p. 59.
13 Khanna, P. (2016), ibid., p. 155.
14 *Financial Times*, 30 September 2016, pp. 15 and 17 'Global dealmaking hits 3-year low'.
15 *The Economist*, 1 October 2016, p. 89, which also provides analysis of geographical trends back to 2007. Cross-border M&A overall fell 110% during the first nine months of 2016.
16 *The Economist*, 1 July 2017, p. 56. Source: S&P Capital.
17 *Times*, 4 January 2018, p. 44.
18 *Financial Times*, 2 September 2016, p. 14. 'Cold comfort to rivals as Hanjin goes under'.
19 *Financial Times*, 7 November 2017, ibid.
20 McKinsey estimates more middle-weight emerging market cities will account for yet a further third of world economic growth.
21 Bain and Company cited in Khanna, P. (2016), ibid., pp. 320–321.
22 Fukuyama, F. (1992) *The End of History and the Last Man*. New York: Free Press.

23 Piketty, T. (2013). *Capital in the Twenty-First Century*. Boston: Harvard University Press.
24 Khanna, P. (2016). *Connectography: Mapping the Global Network Revolution*. London: Weidenfeld & Nicolson, pp. 42 and 320. Projections for 2020 from Bain Consultants.
25 Porter, M.E. (1990). *The Competitive Advantage of Nations*. New York: Free Press.
26 Grant, R. (2016). *Contemporary Strategy Analysis*. Chichester: Wiley, p. 315.
27 *Financial Times*, 9 August 2018, p. 6. 'Greek economic output is still 25% below 2007 levels'. Source: Thomson Reuters Datastream.
28 French, S. (2017). 'Denied a pay rise yet again? The reason may not be close to home'. *Times* 8 August, p. 39. Simon French is chief economist at stockbroker Panmure Gordon.
29 Source: *Statistica*, 2019 for global market shares Q4, 2009 and Q2, 2019. *Financial Times*, 25 July 2016, p. 15. 'Apple nears 1bn sales tally for iPhone' and ibid., p. 18 'India start-up launches $3.70 smartphone'.
30 *The Economist* 'Huawei', 3 August 2018, p. 6.
31 Oliver Kamm, *Times*, 11 October 2019. 'Forget the league table, seeking a competitive edge is a loser's game' picks up the weakness in World Economic Forum competitiveness annual league tables, that they underplay exchange rate and wage rate effects bringing overall trade exchanges back into balance. The same point was made in my first book, Carr, C. (1990). *Britain's Competitiveness: The Management of the World Vehicle Components Industry*. London: Routledge. However, as I explained this is not a zero-sum game, because the vehicle industry enormous value added depended upon both the fortunes of Britain's major players and on Britain's competitiveness from the viewpoint of Japanese and other overseas vehicle multinationals. Thirty years later we can see that it was the latter incoming FDI which transformed Britain's sector prospects. Should Britain now become less attractive, in the wake of the slight fall of its WEF index, or because of a no-deal Brexit, there will be serious consequences: Robert Lea, *Times*, 11 October 2019, p. 39. 'Nissan factory "can't survive no-deal" '.
32 Quote by Francisco Ferreira from the World Bank's poverty research centre, reported in the *Financial Times* 3 October 2016, p. 7.
33 *The Economist*, 8 October 2016, p. 75, 'How the other tenth lives'.
34 Campbell, C., Cardiff, G. and Kao, J.S. (2017). Taking on inequality. Source World Bank, cited in *Financial Times* 'How global income inequality has shifted since the crisis', 21 August 2017, p. 12.
35 Piketty, T. (2013), ibid.
36 *The Economist* 6 January 2018, p. 55. Source: National Bureau of Economic Research.
37 As Europe's wealthiest property owner, The Duke of Westminster, nevertheless paid minimal inheritance tax. The family's wealth dates to 1066. As the late Duke put it, the secret of their sustained financial success was having been good friends with William the Conqueror. In recent decades, Grosvenor Estates have gone global.
38 Krueger, A.B. (2019). Rockonomics. *A Backstage Tour of What the Music Industry Can Teach Us about Economics and Life*. New York: Currency, p. 99. Female stars like Madonna appear to have lost out, with total earnings some $1 billion less. 'Pollstar data indicates that the top 1% of artists increased their % of total revenues from 26% in 1982 to 60% in 2017' (p. 84). Young stars like Taylor Swift are now challenging big music global oligopolists, since streaming accounts for two-thirds of recorded music revenue (p. 178). As concerts revenues become an increasingly important part of stars' earnings, Swift's pioneering use of Verified Fan may also prove influential (p. 146).
39 *Sunday Times* 25 August 2019, Business, p. 3. 'Investors pile on board for pay rebellions', source: CIPD which funds the High Pay Centre.
40 *The Economist* 25 July 2016, p. 22. Source: Spencer Stuart.
41 *Financial Times* 16 August 2018, p. 4. Source: Office for National Statistics.

42 Source: *Times* 5 July 2018.
43 *Financial Times* 17 March 2017.p. 1. Source: DWD.
44 *Sunday Times* 25 August 2019, ibid.
45 Piketty, T. (2013), ibid.
46 Source: *The Economist*, 24 August 2019. 'I'm from the company and I'm here to help', pp. 14–16. See also 'What companies are for', ibid., p. 7. Consolidation having left two thirds of US industries more concentrated, American profits had risen to 8% of GDP compared with 5% in 1989; over 180 oligopolists had signed up to broader goals than shareholder value; but the priority lay with ensuring dynamic [Schumpeteerian] competition through anti-trust.
47 Ibid., but see also Meyer, C. '*Prosperity*'. Oxford: Oxford University Press.
48 Yueh, L. (2018). *The Great Economists. How Their Ideas Can Help Us Today*, London: Penguin Viking, and talk at the Edinburgh Book Festival 15 August 2018.
49 Hunt (1969), ibid.; Porter, M. (1980), ibid. A trail of eminent US economists gave evidence to successive anti-trust bodies and hearings, arguing that competition was predominantly domestic in this DAs sector. None presented global CR or Herfindahl figures or serious studies conducted globally; subsequent events have undermined their conclusions.
50 Source: *BBC Radio 4*, 27 August 2019, Today's programme, citing accounting report two years earlier, and foster care expert interviewed.
51 *Sunday Times*, 31 August 2019. 'The Japanese builder who wants prefabs sprouting up', pp. 4–5.
52 Source: OECD, cited by Simon Nixon, *Times*, 10 October 2019, p. 39. 'Is scrutiny of overseas takeovers an issue of security or protectionism?'.
53 Source: OECD, cited by *Times*, 10 October 2019, p. 27. Editorial 'Tax International'. Apple had been paying an effective corporate tax rate of less than 1% on its European profits.

15

SUMMARY OF IMPLICATIONS FOR BUSINESS

GLOBAL OLIGOPOLIES ARE UBIQUITOUS AND INCREASINGLY DETERMINE PROFITS AND VALUE-ADDED

Global oligopolies, so pervasive in practice, have largely been evaded by theorists. Since the days of Adam Smith's *Wealth of Nations*, most economists have clung to the law of large numbers. They argue, incorrectly, that they need not 'open the box', relating to the behaviour of individual corporations. Game theories, pertinent to oligopolistic behaviours as players react to each other's moves, are fun, popular, and readily comprehensible; but empirical evidence in relation to real world global oligopolies has so far proved elusive.[1] Anyone can have a theory, but, if it is not evidence-based, it is not science.

Certainly, strategists need to 'open that box'. Corporations are now so large that we must understand how they both create and appropriate wealth globally. By 1980, as discussed earlier, Adam Smith's famous pin industry was already concentrated in the hands of just four players globally, one from Scandinavia, one from Germany, and two from North America. His assumption of large numbers no longer applies in most business sectors. Apple, Microsoft, and Amazon were all each valued at over a $1 trillion as of 7 October 2019,[2] whereas fewer than five nations enjoyed a Gross Domestic Product (GDP) higher than Apple's $200 billion cash holdings.

Most are aware of a few powerful, almost 'winner-takes-all' global oligopolists such as Facebook, Apple, Amazon, Netflix, and Google. We recognise the power of their disruptive strategies to transform societies and entire sectors – though their market positions, too, face disruptions and are far more dynamic than commonly assumed. Facebook, Apple, Amazon, Netflix, and Google, however, are just the tip of an iceberg. The sheer ubiquity of such global oligopolists, even at niche levels, is astonishing. Oligopolies, once the preserve of manufacturers, then of Internet companies, have extended even to services. The most powerful, stable, and lucrative global oligopoly is now auditing and associated management consulting services: '*just four major global firms – Deloitte, PWC, Ernst and Young and KPMG – audit 97% of US public companies, all of the UK's top 100 corporations, and 80% of Japanese listed companies*'.[3]

Our analysis in Chapters 1 and 14 extended not to just 5, but to 30,000 large worldwide companies, their collective value-added on par with entire continents. From a shareholder perspective, big data provided the tools to analyse global profit pools. The top four global oligopoly players averaged around 40% of all these profits over successive multi-year periods across all 173 General Industrial Classification System (GICS) 8-digit sector codes – or around 60% for sectors with above average global concentration ratios. Ignoring such data, now that we have mapped (albeit sometimes tentatively) every single sector, would be strategically senseless. How could anyone, ignoring players appropriating such high shares and scale benefits, comprehend a subject such as competitive strategy?

Yet, we should beware overgeneralised, black and white theories. This book has mapped the highly variegated world of oligopolies, sector by sector, contouring precise global concentration levels, their trends, and associated international strategy orientations and performance outcomes. Extending vertically, as well as horizontally, they included successful 'hidden' niche champions, from Britain, but especially from Germany, in turn, reflecting distinctive, highly global, enduring strategy models. Companies ignoring such variegated global strategies not only miss profit opportunities, but they could find themselves boxed into a fast-diminishing number of more sheltered enclaves, such as the public sector or lower value-added services, only to encounter further novel global oligopolists such as Uber or Deliveroo.

WHY STRATEGY THEORIES STILL NEED TO RECOGNISE SPECIFIC SECTOR DIFFERENCES

Executives must recognise that global sector concentrations vary hugely. Universal claims that globalisation is or is not happening, betray little pertinent knowledge and strategic thinking. Several factors behind globalisation, global strategy orientations, and approaches to cross-border mergers and acquisitions (M&As) and strategic alliances are already well understood. However, global strategies do not guarantee successful outcomes, even in sectors conducive to trade, but can also prove remarkably effective in those (such as cement) least conducive. Most sectors experienced global consolidation, contradicting over-general theories espousing the supposed superiority of regional over global strategies. On the other hand, groceries and certain areas of banking, for example, have yielded relatively poor outcomes for global oligopoly players. We must, as has been shown, interpret global concentration and consolidation metrics carefully, in the light of extensive empirical data. Strategic analysis must be sector specific.

That is why global consolidation patterns require mapping. Strategists, lacking such knowledge, risk becoming narrow 'experts'. Many understand singular aspects of strategy, arising from specific disciplines such as sociology, but lack that appreciation of competition so essential to robust strategic analysis.[4] Strategy is a holistic concept, encompassing matters of corporate life or death.[5] Being a great violinist is an invaluable initial step to understanding, but does not qualify you, to conduct the orchestra. Single-track gurus can be dangerous.

Even primitive atlases and charts proved invaluable to early global explorers. This book and its maps afford some fundamental knowledge of where and to what extent global consolidation, oligopolistic moves, and countermoves are happening, and of likely outcomes. In the future, 'big data' will extend that knowledge: our maps will become yet finer-grained 'apps'.

SUMMARISING GLOBAL CONCENTRATION TRENDS BY SECTORS

Summarising concentration trends, detailed in Chapters 2 and 3, the full gamut of 173 sectors examined was inevitably biased towards sectors offering better global data. This removed, for example, locally orientated public sector services. The key measure for concentration is the global concentration ratio (GCR4), being the combined market share of the top four companies. Yet, the finding that only around 2% of sectors could be classified as 'fragmented global competition' according to sector GCR4s under 2.5%, underlines the strategic significance of global concentration for most business sectors.

'Transitional sectors' in terms of global competition, where GCR4 concentration ratios remained at or below 10%, accounted for another 13% of sectors. Here, there was still scope to debate the merits of more national or regionally orientated strategies. However, as we saw in cases like steel, moves and countermoves including cross-border megamergers occurred at levels only slightly above such thresholds. Even here, you must likely shift to foreign direct investment instead of relying on trade. 'Fragmented' and 'transitional global' sectors taken together, though, only represented about a sixth of all 173 sectors examined.

Deploying global force levels, analogous to Beaufort wind force scales, we classified 71.5% of all 173 sectors as at least force 7s – 'loose [global] oligopolies' – based on GCR4s of 40% or higher. At such levels, we often observed global oligopolistic moves, even cross-border megamergers, countermoves, and shakeouts. Examining longer-term trends for just 100 (of those 173 sectors) affording consistent classifications over time, their median had moved up GF 7.9 (virtually a 'tight global oligopoly') from global force 7.3 in 1994. Thus, in most sectors, you cannot today credibly neglect global strategic management choices arising from global concentration and oligopolistic moves and countermoves.

WHICH GLOBAL STRATEGIC ORIENTATIONS ACHIEVE BETTER PERFORMANCE OUTCOMES?

Adopting Rugman's simple geographical sales spread metrics, Chapter 4 showed that the numbers of global top 500 '*bi-regionals*' and '*global players*' had respectively doubled and trebled. Global players on average outperformed regional strategies on 5-year returns on capital employed (RoCE), sales growth, and investor returns. Most large world corporates have understandably raced to extend their geographical coverages.

More nuanced strategic implications were highlighted deploying strategic groups analysis (Chapter 3) or preferably Calori-based configurations performance analysis, based on nine subtler international orientations, sector by sector (Chapters 5, 6, and 11). Systematically charted performance outcomes unsurprisingly reflected global forces levels and varied by major regions. Overall, North American companies achieved higher 5-year RoCEs than other regions in most configurations. Worldwide orientation players (encompassing the five most global configurations), aside from those from China, have outperformed more regional approaches overall. They grew faster in terms of sales than our four more regionally orientated players in all regions, except the European Union[6]; they also achieved higher average total investor returns relative to more regional international challengers in all regions, except North America.

GLOBAL MARKET ENTRY STRATEGIES: GO-IT-ALONE GREENFIELD VS M&As & ALLIANCES

The simplest strategic recommendation for well resourced companies, from countries enjoying strong competitive advantages in internationally advanced sectors, was to go for top four oligopoly leadership positions or, failing that, to niche (Chapter 8).

Most also needed to turn to international cooperation through cross-border M&As or strategic alliances, either as aggressors, or as defenders tacitly accepting some loss of sovereignty. Chapter 7 laid out results indicating the most effective approaches to handling global consolidation when engaged in M&As or strategic alliances. By means of detailed case studies, we saw that the evolutionary global logic of either cross-border M&As or ISAs needed to address two acid tests: did they really transfer some superior business model or technology and did that partnership really aid the underlying process by which Adam Smith's division of labour could finally go global? This was the point at which global scale economies could be optimised as the most powerful final barrier against entrants struggling to match either your business model or your global scale advantage. Crucial implementation lessons are best gleaned from detailed failure and success case studies contrasted.

Our global evolutionary perspective also aided judgements, as between self-sufficient greenfield site approaches (demonstrated by Zara in Chapter 5); more minor franchising and licensing; and the two major cooperative options: cross-border strategic alliances and M&As. Aside from the increasing impact of M&As, Pankaj Ghemawat calculated in 2016 that 'America's top 1,000 public companies now derive 40% of their revenue from alliances, compared with just 1% in 1980'.[7] GKN's successful global strategy (in Chapter 13) shifted from greenfield site options (in the USA); tactical technology licences (in Japan); to typically 40% equity-based cross-border strategic alliances and finally transitioning 30 years later to full acquisitions, as best comprehended from a longer-term evolutionary perspective.

SUSTAINING WINNING GLOBAL POSITIONS

Size per se is not everything. Some mid-caps despair when they see global concentration and oligopoly plays, but it turns out that they too (through more focused niche strategies) can achieve global winning positions. Chapter 8 uncovered lessons from 30 of the most successful global mid-cap niche players, contrasting the United Kingdom with Germany, and their precise international market entry strategies. Key success factors varied, unsurprisingly, moving away from Anglo-American approaches to other highly successful modes of more patient capitalism, such as the German model. Our analysis here dissected international orientations, contrasting born global and born again globals with traditional (Uppsala) and hybrid modes, to discover those traits associated with more enduring successes (beyond 80 years or so). Our resulting success framework developed further Hermann Simon's well regarded hidden champion model. The major institutional difference here reflected family ownership and patient capital in every one of these 15 German cases; so that same issue has been addressed on a worldwide basis, in Appendix B, comparing international strategies and performance outcomes for the world's top family companies, peer-matched against public companies.

Although their effect has been more recent upon the global stage, the impact today of emerging market champions, analysed in Chapters 9 and 10, has already ratcheted up global rivalry. As we saw in Chapter 11, Haier's impact from China has been like a tsunami, shocking for large incumbents or for anyone naïvely envisaging competition as merely regional or 'semi-global' in domestic appliances – the sector so often used as the bellwether litmus test in debates regarding 'global vs regional strategies'. These cases pinpoint precisely how emerging market champions have challenged and frequently overtaken advanced country incumbents, even in sectors traditionally perceived as internationally fragmented or even local. These are merely the forerunners of what is to come.

Finally, we recognise the need for far more enduring global corporate lessons – sustainability in the literal sense of the word. As Chapter 12 showed even superb global players, soon or later, require superb global retrenchment and turnaround skills, or come crashing down through avoidable pitfalls and hubris. The time to learn is when you think you know it all. The basics here were ruthlessly dissected through graphic cases. From a far longer term, historical perspective Chapter 13 showed, what worked for GKN at the onset of Britain's Industrial Revolution from 1759 onwards, necessarily had to evolve a century later as Britain ceded ground to the USA, and then changed again as the USA in turn ceded ground to a rising Asia. Findings up to 2018 concurred with just some of the themes from today's literature on enduring companies. To last, you cannot rule out diversification, though some sort of three-legged approach has proved far more successful than unrelated moves. Nor can you rule out unfashionable traditional prudence and financial conservatism. Axiomatically, a long-term global strategy is no use if you are at risk of not surviving the next 12 months. The field of business studies is replete with stories of success, but no company is likely to survive beyond a century or so without robust financial controls capable of taking them through at least one major financial crisis. However, the lacunae in American studies, such as Collins and Porras's *Built to Last*, is that you absolutely must have some credible global strategy.

Yet the consistent theme in this book is that not even global champions are safe. Its theoretical paradigm concurs with Adam Smith's belief in the power of division of labour and of markets, writ globally not just locally. Yet if his assumptions were that true sector concentration ratios (CRs) would be zero or negligible, globally or even nationally. As Marx pointed out consolidations follow the logic of Smith's recognised scale economies. But global concentration levels have only rarely reached, let alone sustained, Marxian monopolistic predictions. What has happened and continues to happen is that global concentration ratios generally are asymptotic towards around 40%, displaying highly dynamic Schumpeterian waves as disruptors rise to challenge incumbents, only to be challenged in turn. And then next big disruptor may very well be from the next big fast growing region, not necessarily your own. Elements of Smithian, Marxian and Schumpeterian all help to make up a more universal perspective, but the pertinence and salience of each can only be determined knowing the GCR4 in your own sectors. So mapping those trends had to be a necessary starting point in comprehending these challenging issues.

One false step financially, especially in an Anglo-Saxon context characterised by hedge funds and impatient capital, also now risks immediate takeover by private equity hoping for opportunistic gains. In 2018, this is precisely what happened to GKN, leading to its acquisition by Melrose, albeit at an attractive price to shareholders. Clearly, GKN and Unilever left things too late, but pro-active (public company) global oligopolists seeking enduring success will likely be critically scrutinising their head office locations.

Those companies seen as valuable 'assets', particularly when exchange rates fall, may also soon fall prey to yet more powerful rivals (including those from emerging regions such as China) as further consolidation occurs worldwide. The latter is not necessarily negative. The top teams at both Scottish and Newcastle and at SABMiller in brewing did superb jobs for their shareholders and outcomes were not disastrous for all their employees. Great assets and employees often find themselves highly respected in globally orientated companies.

Like evolution, global consolidations are relentless and never-ending. Only by understanding these processes, and the requirements they place upon us for credible global strategic management, can we aspire to call ourselves strategists.

NOTES

1 Though, *'prisoners' dilemmas'*, of interest to game theorists, might conceivably now arise as global oligopolists invest some $160 billion in 5G.

2 Eric J. Savitz (7 October 2019). 'Amazon stock belongs in the $1trillion club with Apple and Microsoft, analyst says'. Barron's accessed online.

3 Brooks, R. (2018). *Bean Counters: The Triumph of the Accountants and How They Broke Capitalism*. London: Atlantic Books.

4 Other typical examples are specialists examining somewhat Machiavellian organisation dynamics. This is important for organisational experts, but tells you little about what you should be doing strategically. Without knowledge of global concentration and rivals, such *'strategy experts'* cannot provide credible international strategies and policies. Rather than appropriating, inappropriately, the field of strategy, they should be termed *'organisational experts'*. See also: Tourish, D. (2019). *Management Studies in Crisis: Fraud, Deception and Meaningless Research*. Cambridge: Cambridge University Press for a broader critique of this issue.

5 Often repeated claims by such strategy 'experts' that they need not know about global strategy on the grounds that all business is now global or that, conversely, the whole globalisation thing is anyway overdone, lack credibility. Such arguments betray international naivety and inadequate understanding of competitive strategy.

6 Chinese companies unsurprisingly grew strikingly faster, but particularly when pursuing *quasi-global* or (at the other end of the spectrum) *country-centred* orientations.

7 *The Economist*, 17 September 2016. *Special Report: The Rise of the Superstars* and 'A giant problem', p. 6.

Appendix A

THE PROBLEM OF MEASURING GLOBALITY

INTRODUCTION

For international business researchers, geography is paramount. Rugman's studies of Multinational (MNC)s' international and regional sales dispersions suffer from three critical problems.[1] First, his data are not normalised. You cannot compare Nokia's overseas sales ratios with those of say Motorola, without adjusting for the relative market sizes of Finland and the USA. Secondly, even the most 'perfectly spread' multi-national would involve uneven international and regional sales dispersions. Thirdly, his criteria are arbitrary. Twenty percent cut-offs have no 'logic' or basis in theory. They bear no relationship to companies' international strategic choices or to the likelihood of global shakeouts and rationalisations.

This appendix first demonstrates how to make the necessary normalising adjustments. Secondly, it provides for a spectrum of measures across the main strategic choice dimensions. The emphasis is on practical measures which can be used, as far as possible with large scale databases including, though not limited to, the Rugman and Calori approaches already discussed. Thirdly, it shows how these measures translate into meaningful international strategic configurations. Having laid out global dispersion measurement principles, this Appendix concludes by dealing with the perennial problem of measuring global concentration. The underlying hypothesis is that global strategic choices (expressed through these measures) are a function both of scale (in terms of relative global market share) and the level of global concentration in any given sector, this in turn being a function of the forces of globalisation versus those pressures for local adaptations, again as discussed earlier.

NORMALISING COMPANIES' FOREIGN SALES RATIOS

Foreign sales ratios are often expressed by the ratio of foreign sales outside a company's country of origin (FS) to its total turnover: expressed here by FSo/T.

However, if the country of origin is large as in the case of United States (US) companies, this ratio understates the real extent of their globalisation as compared with companies originating from smaller countries. Even the most perfectly spread multi-national would still need a proportion of sales in its home country, commensurate with that country's share of world output.

For example, in 2001/2002, the United State's share of world output was 21.5% compared with Italy's at 3.0%. To measure the extent to which a US company has progressed along the path towards being a 'perfectly spread' multi-national, we should compare the FSo/T ratio with just the 78.5%, which effectively represents the limiting case.[2] What we need is the company's 'normalised' (FSo/T)n, which is its nominal (FSo/T) divided by 0.785.

Similarly the 'normalised' (FSo/T)n for an Italian company would be its nominal (FSo/T) divided by 0.97. In practice, the adjustment is small for smaller countries; miniscule for say Luxembourg; but it is appreciable for large countries such as the USA, China, or Japan. The normalising adjustment would be minor for say Finland's Nokia. However, in comparing Motorola of the USA, the latter's nominal (FSo/T) effectively needs to be increased by the multiplier (1/0.785) in order to compare like with like. This may seem nit picking, but adjustments like this occur in other internationalisation metrics.

More generally, normalised foreign sales/total sales ratio, (FSo/T)n for a company located in country 'c' is given by:

$$(\mathrm{FSo}/\mathrm{T})\mathrm{n} = \frac{\mathrm{FSo}/\mathrm{T}}{1-(\mathrm{OUTPUTc}/\mathrm{OUTPUTworld})}.$$

Thus, the normalised (FS/T)n for a firm from country 1 (c1) would be MP (multiplier) times that of a firm with the same sized un-normalised FS/T from country (c2), where:

$$\mathrm{MP} = \frac{1-(\mathrm{OUTPUTc2}/\mathrm{OUPUTworld})}{1-(\mathrm{OUTPUTc1}/\mathrm{OUTPUTworld})} = \frac{1-0.03}{1-0.25} = 1.29,$$

in the case of a firm from the USA as compared with one from Italy.

Table A.1 provides country-based data supporting such adjustments though, in sector studies where market data are available, it is more correct to use country market sizes rather than output figures. The advantage of normalised (FS/T)n is that as we approach the 'perfectly spread' multi-national, this ratio tends to 1. We can form a more complete picture of a company's geographical

Table A.1 Normalisation weightings based on 2006 GDPs

GDPs at Purchasing Power Parity in 2006 ref Wikipedia $m		*Normalisation*		
		% outside	*Multiplier*	*% inside*
World	**48,144,466**			
Europe	16,335,942	66.07	1.513	33.93
EU	14,374,629	70.14	1.425	29.86
N. America	**15,375,927**	68.06	1.469	31.94
USA	13,262,074	72.45	1.380	27.55
Asia	**12,329,441**	74.39	1.344	25.61
Japan	4,367,459	90.93	1.099	9.07
S. America	2,879,544	94.02	1.063	5.98
Africa	**1,062,730**	97.79	1.022	2.21
Arab League	1,019,770	97.88	1.021	2.12
RoW	160,882	99.67	1.003	0.33
All America	18,255,471	62.08	1.610	37.92
Euro less MidEast	15,316,172	68.19	1.466	31.81
N. America + Eur		34.13	2.929	65.87
N. Am + Eur-ME		36.25	2.758	63.75
N. America + Ap		42.45	2.355	57.55
Eur + Ap		40.46	2.471	59.54
N. Am + Eur + Ap		8.52	11.733	91.48
All Am + Ap		36.47	2.741	63.53
All Am + Ap + Eur	1,223,612	2.54	39.346	97.46
N. Am + Eur + Ap-ME		10.64	9.397	89.36
Germany	2,897,032	93.98	1.064	6.02
China	2,630,113	94.54	1.057	5.46
UK	2,373,685	95.07	1.051	4.93
France	2,231,631	95.36	1.048	4.64
Italy	1,852,585	96.15	1.040	3.85
Canada	1,269,096	97.36	1.027	2.64
Spain	1,225,750	97.45	1.026	2.55
Brazil	1,067,706	97.78	1.022	2.22
Russia	979,048	97.97	1.020	2.03
S. Korea	888,267	98.15	1.018	1.85
India	886,867	98.16	1.018	1.84
Mexico	840,012	98.26	1.017	1.74
Australia	754,816	98.43	1.015	1.57
Netherlands	663,119	98.62	1.013	1.38
Belgium	663,119	98.62	1.013	1.38
Turkey	392,424	99.18	1.008	0.82
Sweden	385,293	99.20	1.008	0.80
Swiss	377,240	99.22	1.007	0.78

spread by designing further similar dispersion ratios, also asymptotic towards 1. Together, these ratios form powerful vectors more fully describing the extent to which companies are national, regional, bi-regional, tri-regional, or yet more global. Combining these ratios in turn, we can derive a more comprehensive global dispersion index.

NORMALISING COMPANIES' FOREIGN REGIONAL (OR CONTINENTAL) SALES RATIOS

The un-normalised (FS1/T) for a company's largest regions (typically a continent such as North America, Europe, Japan, etc) is here termed (FS1R1), being the foreign sales outside that first main region. Normalised (FS1R1)n is again given by:

$$\left(\mathrm{FS1R1/T}\right)\mathrm{n} = \frac{\mathrm{FS1R1/T}}{1-\left(\mathrm{OUTPUTR1/OUTPUTworld}\right)}.$$

Again, as (FS1R1/T)n tends to 1, the company tends towards the idealised split for the 'perfectly spread' multi-national. At a glance, this ratio gives an idea of how far the company is merely regional (expressed at the extreme by a score of zero) or how far it is approaching the most global tendency, at least in regard to that first regional split (expressed at the extreme by a score of 1). Regional multipliers can again be easily calculated just as for normalised foreign sales ratios, just as discussed in Section 1.

Thus, we now have two dispersal vectors (FS0C1/T)n, (F1R1/T)n providing some basic description of a company's domestic national and regional choices.

When handling a company's 2nd region (or continent), it is preferable to take FS2R2 as the total of all sales outside either the 1st or the 2nd regions. This yields another index FS2R2/T, which can be normalised to an index FS2R2, as given by:

$$\left(\mathrm{FS2R21/T}\right)\mathrm{n} = \frac{\mathrm{FS2R2/T}}{1-\left(\mathrm{OUTPUTR1}+\mathrm{OUTPUTR2}\right)/\mathrm{OUTPUTworld})}.$$

Dealing with the cumulative extent of both regions (or continents), we then have a further dispersal vector which in the extremes will be zero for the pure bi-regional company, or 1 for a company tending towards 'perfectly spread' globalised multi-national.

A company's 3rd region (or continent) can be handled likewise, but again, note it is important to treat sales outside all three regions (viewed cumulatively). Again, a result normalised index of zero would represent a pure tri-regional company, whilst an index closer to 1 would represent the 'perfectly balanced' globalised multi-national. In practice, company accounts data are often only available for a maximum of three main continents, excluding the 'rest of the world' category, which is simply a residual affording no further interesting information. Thus, it is often infeasible to go beyond the four dispersal vectors: (FS0/Tn, FS1R1/Tn, FS2R2/Tn, and FS3R3/Tn). These four vectors (each tending towards 1 for the most globalised type of company) thus immediately provide a clear description of the extent to which a company is either national, region, bi-regional, tri-regional, or even more global.

From a theoretical viewpoint, one way of combining constitute vectors is to sum the squares as follows. Let us say data are available for K regions, where the final Kth region is essentially just 'the rest of the world'. A single overall global sales dispersion index (GSDI) could in principle then be calculated for the company, where:

$$\text{GSDI} = (1/\text{K}) \times \sum (\text{FSiRi}/\text{Tn})^{\wedge}2, \text{ summing from i} = 0 \text{ to} (\text{K} - 1).$$

Clearly, there are no sales outside the final Kth region, so there is no point in summing beyond (K − 1). The reason for squaring is that it accentuates deviations from 1. The most 'perfectly spread' imaginable multi-national would have an all dispersion vectors equal to 1 and an overall GSDI of 1; a single country firm would have a GSDI of 0. A problem here though (as also happens when using un-normalised Herfindahl indices) is that this otherwise excellent theoretical overall measure is then sensitive to the number of regions being reported. Unfortunately, companies vary enormously in their reporting policies.

In practice, only just under 20% of the global top 500 companies can supply data for all of the first four vectors: even here data for the final 3rd region are often somewhat suspect, as the very last 'residual' element in practice only averages about 7.6% and depends enormously on how companies treat the first three area definitions. Many companies, for example, count the Middle East within Europe, and 'Asia Pacific' has several different definitions, and even American firms often fail to distinguish whether their data are the USA only, North America only, or North and South America. Furthermore, many companies providing regional data, then omit to give the split of overseas sales outside their own country, and this vector is arguably anyway of less relevance for a company with appreciable sales outside its first region.

There is therefore a case for keeping things simple and just taking the global sales dispersion index (2) from the first two main regions:

$$\text{GSDI}\left(2\right) = \left(1/2\right) \times \left(\left(\text{FS1R1}/\text{Tn}\right) + \text{FS2R2}/\text{Tn}\right).$$

The first geographical dispersion vector, FS0R0/Tn, is of course still useful, where available, for determining whether a company is merely national in orientation. Similarly, the third regional dispersion vector, FS3R3/Tn, is still useful (where available) for determining whether a company is fully as opposed to semi-global in orientation, but researchers handling large databases should recognise that presently something under 20% of companies allow computation even of all four dispersion vectors. Furthermore, we must be consistent in taking GSDI measures based on the same number of constituent vectors.

In terms of cut-off criteria, it would be sensible to define categories as follows:

National companies: where FSo/Tn < 20%
Regional: where FS1R1/Tn < 20%
Bi-regional: where FS1R1/Tn > 20% and FS2R2/Tn < 20%
Semi-global: where FS2R2 > 20% and < 40%
Global: where FS2R2 > 40%.

However, these cut-offs remain somewhat arbitrary, albeit no more so than those un-normalised measures proposed by Rugman.[3] We need firstly to examine patterns among leading world companies, and, secondly, to assess levels associated with typical patterns of international competition. Modest levels of sales dispersions by large powerful multi-nationals may expose weaker players in faraway places to huge competitive threats. The first question can be assessed using databases easily; the second calls for sector studies of international competitive behaviour.

THE EXAMPLE OF CANON

In 2001, the Japanese company Canon had an un-normalised FSo/T ratio of 71.5%, North and South Americas sales of 33.8%, European sales of 20.8%, leaving residual rest of the world sales at 16.9%. Canon's accounts though do not split out Asia Pacific, with most of these being included in the last category. Using the ratio of Asia Pacific Global Domestic Products (GDPs) (excluding Japan) to that for all other countries in the rest of the world, it is estimated that Canon's above 16.9% 'rest of the world' sales, splits 14.6% for non-Japan Asia Pacific and 2.3% for the final non-Europe, non-America, and non-Asia Pacific countries. Thus, Canon's Asia Pacific sales are estimated at 28.5 (Japan) + 14.6 = 43.1% Asia Pacific. Normalised vectors are then calculated as follows:

Key data: proportions of world output in terms of GDPs (based on 2006) *outside*:

Japan 0.9093; Asia Pacific 0.7439; N&S Americas 0.6208; Europe 0.6607; Asia Pacific & Americas combined 0.3647; Asia Pacific, Americas, and Europe all combined 0.0254.

$$\text{FSo/Tn} = 0.715 \times (1 - 0.9093) = 0.7863$$

$$\text{FS1R1/Tn} = (1 - 0.431)/0.7439 = 0.7649$$

$$\text{FS2R2/Tn} = (1 - 0.431 - 0.338)/0.3647 = 0.6334$$

$$\text{FS3R3/Tn} = (1 - 0.431 - 0.338 - 0.208)/0.0254 = 0.9055$$

$$GSDI = (0.7863\hat{}2 + 0.7649\hat{}2 + 0.6334\hat{}2 + 0.9055\hat{}2)/4 = 0.6061 = 61\%$$

$$GSDI(2) = (0.7649\hat{}2 + 0.6334\hat{}2)/2 = 0.5097 = 51\%$$

Canon's GSDI at 61% is in practice quite exceptionally high. Its GSDI (2) of just over 50% is also exceptionally high: its global sales dispersion vectors (0.79, 0.76, 0.63, 0.91) being relatively well balanced, though with a bias (unsurprisingly) towards Japan and its prime Asia Pacific Region. In terms of cut-offs, Canon would thus be defined as 'global' – and in fact Rugman (2006)'s criteria also lead to this same 'global' classification.

NORMALISED GLOBAL ASSET DISPERSION RATIOS

International business theory distinguishes multi-national enterprise behaviour in respect also to international asset dispersion. For example, whilst some multinational corporations (MNCs) might successfully internationalise primarily based on exports (and trade), in general, others are forced to support such international sales by international asset dispersion. Indeed, the term 'multinational' has traditionally been reserved solely for enterprises characterised by such foreign direct investment (FDI) rather than sole reliance on trade. Thus, at the other extreme from 'international strategies' based almost solely on exporting, we have 'multi-domestic' enterprises such as Unilever which historically relied much more heavily on assets located in host countries. The distinction is important for strategy behaviour and organisational structure.

Fortunately, precisely the same principles apply for foreign assets (FAs), as throughout the whole analysis already discussed for FSs. Equally fortunately, companies that do provide foreign sales data breakdowns generally do the same for foreign assets data breakdowns, so metrics can be calculating for all foreign asset dispersion vectors conveniently at the same time, providing a further set of powerful analytical tools. Again, the Foreign Asset/Total Asset (FAR1/FA) ratio for some region 'i' needs to be normalised as before:

$$(FARi/TA)n = \frac{FARi/TA}{1-(OUTPUTRi/OUTPUTworld)}.$$

We can employ the same data for 'weightings' as were applied when normalising foreign sales ratios. The entire set of asset dispersion vectors (FA0/TA, FA1/TA, FA2/TA, FA3/TA…etc) can likewise be calculated in precisely the same manner. And these dispersion vectors can be summarised in terms of a single global asset dispersion index (FADI) again in precisely the same manner:

$$GADI = (1/K) \times \sum (FAiRi/TAn)^{\wedge 2}, \text{summing from } i = 0 \text{ to } (K-1).$$

The most 'perfectly spread' imaginable multi-national would have a GADI of 1; whereas a country-based company with no overseas assets would have a GADI of 0. Data restrictions are similar, as for international sales dispersion ratios. So again, in practice, it is probably sensible to settle for:

$$\text{GADI}(2) = ((\text{FA1R1}/\text{TAn})^{\wedge 2} + (\text{FA2R2}/\text{TAn})^{\wedge 2})/2.$$

GLOBAL ASSET INTEGRATION AND GLOBAL DISPERSION AND INTEGRATION INDICES

Researchers with access to multi-nationals recognise an important theoretical distinction between looser 'multi-domestic' forms, allowing subsidiaries greater autonomy, and those more internationally integrated, where there is greater emphasis on scale economies and internationally based synergies. This suggests an additional global asset integration index (GAII) vector, based on integration measures reflecting the extent of central strategic and financial controls, knowledge transfer within the organisation, movement of people, and so on.

One problem with the GAII is that, unlike most other indices detailed in this appendix, its calculation cannot be done based on external data that are frequently available from companies' published accounts. Any calculation relies on access to companies and may reflect subjectivity where derived from executives' opinions. Where feasible, GAIIs would ideally be included within a final overall global dispersion and integration index (GDII), where:

$$\text{GDII}^{\wedge}2 = (\text{GSDI})^{\wedge}2 + (\text{GADI})^{\wedge}2 + (\text{GAII})^{\wedge}2.$$

Again, we take the sum of the squares to accentuate the impact of any indices falling well below the 'perfectly spread, perfectly integrated' global company, where each of these indices (and their constituent elements) tend towards 1. By contrast, a company with no overseas sales, no overseas assets, and thus inevitably no global asset integration would of course have a GDII equal to zero.

Where global asset integration data are not available, as in desk research studies, it may still be worthwhile calculating the simpler global dispersion index (GDI), which takes into account both sales and asset dispersion internationally, whilst necessarily then just dispensing with the final (GAII)^2 in the formula above:

$$\text{GDI}^{\wedge}2 = (\text{GSDI})^{\wedge}2 + (\text{GADI})^{\wedge}2.$$

GRAPHICAL INTERPRETATION OF GLOBAL SALES AND ASSET DISPERSION AND INTEGRATION MEASURES

Global sales dispersion measures underpin measurements along the vertical access, whilst asset dispersion and (where available) integration measures underpin measures along a horizontal axis, as shown in Figure A.1. Companies (and sectors through a process of averaging for all major players) can be positioned, providing some framework for anticipated international strategy and organisational archetypes.

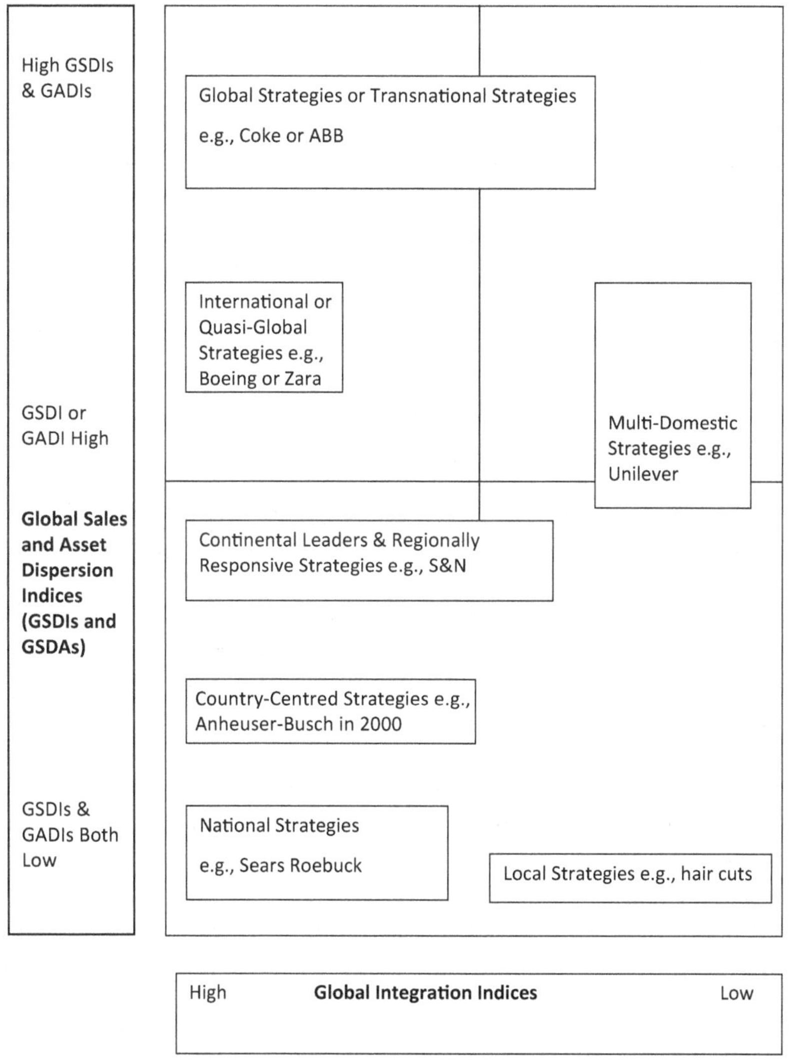

Figure A.1 Global sales and asset dispersion and integration positions.

Most globally orientated multi-nationals now recognise that relying unduly on exports, or on crassly over-standardised strategies, encounter fierce local barriers. This happens in more extreme cases of global oligopoly power such as in the aero sector and in the early days of some new strategy formula; but MNCs usually progress to '*global*' strategies deploying greater international asset dispersion and FDI, and greater integration and responsiveness.

Some MNCs, like Unilever early on, adopt more *multi-domestic* organisational forms, using low levels of exporting, relying instead on FDI. Here, global asset dispersion levels are high, relative to levels of global sales dispersions. In practice, many, like Unilever, have now evolved far closer towards *transnational* structures.[4] Pure 'international strategies' (unsupported by FDI) appear increasingly relegated to positions of quasi-monopoly or early international product life cycle stages.

These are controversial issues and should be determined by robust methodologies, scoring systematically within data constraints, such as company access. In secondary research involving large databases, it may be easier to concentrate on the global sales and asset dispersion axis, or to combine these dispersion measures with other well acknowledged strategic choice variables as discussed in this book. As *multi-domestic* and more local organisational forms decline, this shift of emphasis may become increasingly justifiable.

MEASURING FOCUS VS DIVERSITY IN TERMS OF THE SCOPE OF A FIRM'S ACTIVITIES

Geographic analysis constitutes only one dimension in terms of a company's strategic choices. If we are to analyse the latter systematically, we must also be equally systematic in measuring a company's focus in terms of the diversity of its activities. This constitutes effectively a second dimension. Measurements along both geographic dimension (using the above vectors, summarised by GDI measures) and the focus dimension enables accurate positioning in terms of the classic matrix, displaying both geographic scope and activity scope. The strategic choice matrix shown later in Figure A.2 has its antecedents in Porter (1980)'s strategic groups approach, but also provides the theoretical basis of Calori's empirically determined eight international strategy configurations.

Before presenting Figure A.2, we first require clear measurements. Similar principles apply as in determining geographical scope, and indeed (from a practical viewpoint), data can be picked up from company accounts in the same manner. Measures are simpler as there is no need to handle the first activity as in any way special, as happens with foreign sales ratios; nor is there any need to normalise ratios. The first scope dispersion index (SCDI1) vectors can be defined simply as:

$$\mathrm{SCDI}_1 = \left(\text{All sales } \textit{other than} \text{ the } 1^{\mathrm{st}} \text{main activity}\right)/\text{Total sales}$$

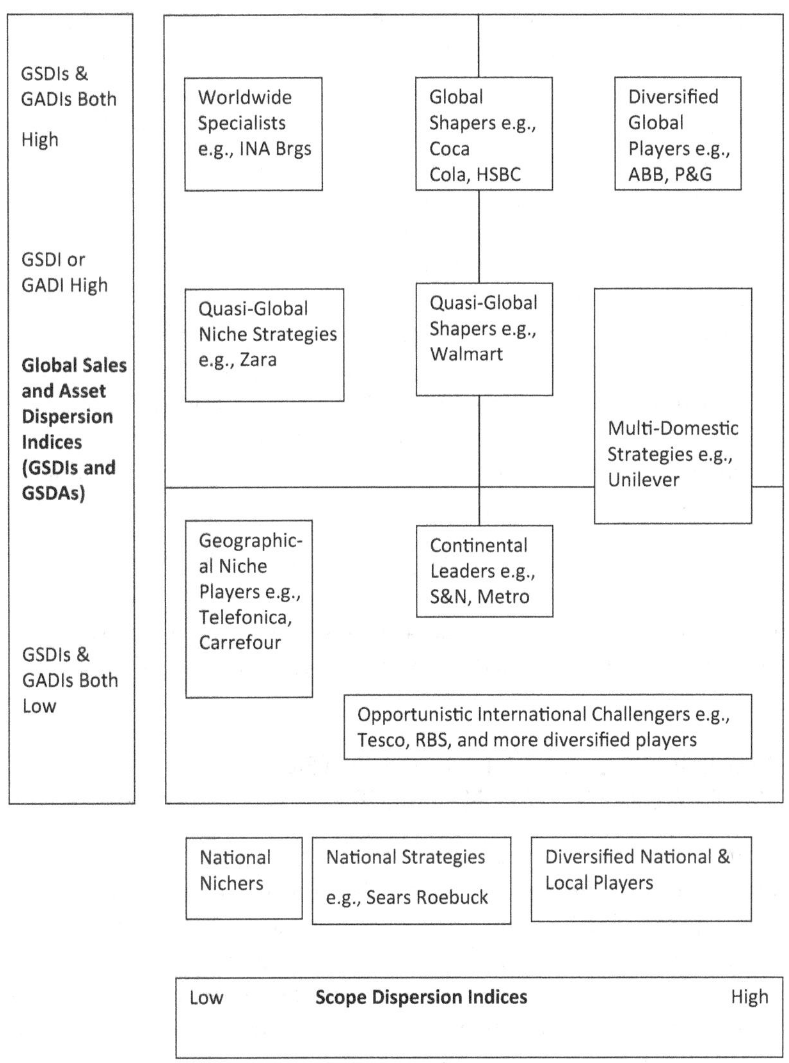

Figure A.2 Global sales and asset dispersion and scope dispersion positions.

Again $SCDI_2$ = (All sales *other than* either of the first two main activities)/Total Sales
Or SCDIi = (All sales *other than* any of the first 'i' activities)/Total Sales

Again, theoretically an overall Scope Dispersion Index (SCDI) can be defined as:

$$SCDI = (1/(L-1)) \times \sum(SCDIi)\hat{}2, \text{ summing from } i = 1 \text{ to } (L-1).$$

where L is the number of activities for which data are available. Again, clearly there is no need to calculate the final SCDL as this would be zero.

On this basis, a firm focused on just a single activity would have a scope dispersion index of zero. A firm with say four activities each of equal sales values, would have scope dispersion vectors (0.75, 0.5, 0.25) and an overall scope dispersion index of $((1/3) \times (0.75\,\hat{}\,2 + 0.5\,\hat{}\,2 + 0.25\,\hat{}\,2)) = 0.292$. Note that the SCDI does intentionally increase both with the number of activities and with the 'even-ness' of its spread of activities.

A clear problem is that again companies reporting practices are quite different, and that few go beyond reporting four or five activities. For practical purposes, many researchers will be happy to utilise simply the first SCDI (1) index, which is simply the square of the first SCDI1 measure:

The first simple scope dispersion index, $SCDI(1) = SCDI_1\hat{}2$.

Or where data are available for four activities, as in the above example, we could go to say SCDI(3) where:

$$SCDI(3) = (1/3) * (SCDI_1\hat{}2 + SCDI_2\hat{}2 + SCDI_3\hat{}2).$$

Figure A.2 below now illustrates that scope dispersion indices can be combined with sales and asset dispersion indices forming 2 × 2 strategic choice matrix boxes.

MEASURING FOCUS VS DIVERSITY IN TERMS OF VERTICAL INTEGRATION CHOICES

The third dimension in terms of a company's strategic choices is its degree of focus in terms of keeping all activities in-house vs outsourcing. Measurement here is simpler still. All we need is a single measure indicating the degree of in-house activity vs utilisation of outsourcing. Again, the antecedents for such positioning are based on Porter's strategic groups approach, vertical integration versus geographic scope being two of his classic dimensions when charting competitive groups within sectors. This is not a dimension picked up on in Calori's empirically determined international strategic configurations, but international sourcing has now reached a level where it is unwise not to measure this too. Nike and Dell's international strategies now entail highly strategic significant choices along this dimension: outsourcing to China and India, for example, has become very important.

In principle, all that is needed is one simple, single vertical integration index (VII) of value-added (VA) divided by total turnover T: VII = VA/T.

VA in turn is simply turnover less the total cost of all purchases (including both materials and services etc. bought-in). There is, however, a practical problem of measuring value-added. Whilst most company accounts now yield data on geographical and activity segments (as needed for all measures already discussed), almost no company accounts provide direct data for the value of all purchases. Nor is the problem solved by trying to go to the 'cost-of-goods sold' entries under profit and loss accounts, as this simply is the opposite side of the coin of the gross margin, a ratio sensitive to many other unrelated factors.

Recognising the practical limitations of data that are available from company accounts, we are forced to disaggregate two constituents of value-added where data frequently are available. Firstly, we have the total value of all wages and salaries, the value-added most visibly created by the company's own employees. Secondly, we can add the final pre-interest, pre-tax, profit. This is the element of value-added which effectively accrues to all parties who have either contributed to (or have a claim upon) the capital employed in the company. This figure is available in company accounts. In practical terms, we can measure our vertical integration index through the equation:

$$\mathrm{VII} = \mathrm{VA/T} = \left(\mathrm{W/T}\right) + \mathrm{PM}.$$

where W is the total wage and salaries and PM is the pre-interest, pre-tax profit margin (expressed as a proportion of turnover).

Again, in the extreme, the limiting case is given by a company that requires no outside procurement or bought-in services, where the VII becomes 1. The lower the VII, the more the company depends on outsourcing.

Sectors such as aerospace, for example, would have far lower than say forgings; but even within the same sector, international companies exercise substantially different choices. Japanese car companies such as Toyota owe a good deal of their success internationally to radically lower VII levels as compared with US car companies such as GM. Whether it is worthwhile charting 'strategic groups' on this basis depends, of course, on the extent of policy differences exhibited by rivals and on the extent to which they have become key factors for success in particular sectors. Usually this is not worthwhile, as there is a real danger of spawning so many strategic configurations as to render analysis inconclusive. Nevertheless, just as with a number of other key policy areas, it is sensible to complement analysis of key international strategies with supplementary measures highlighting related policy choices.

MEASURING THE CONTRIBUTION OF EXTERNAL COOPERATION VS ORGANIC GROWTH

The final dimension in terms of a company's strategic choices is the extent to which it relies solely on organic growth, as opposed to that generating through external 'cooperation' with other companies via joint ventures/strategic alliances, or acquisitions. The distinction is well known in the field of corporate strategy, exemplified by firms such as BMW (apart from their short-lived, ill-fated Rover acquisition) as opposed to conglomerates such as General Electric or Hanson, making heavier reliance particularly on acquisitions.

Taking the most extreme form of cooperation secured by equity control, i.e., acquisitions first. The organic growth index, OGI, would be given by:

$$\text{OGI} = 1 - (\text{Turnover generating from M\&A/Turnover}).$$

The latter may be viewed cumulatively and potentially over the entire life of the company, but in practical terms, we would normally have to stipulate some cut-off time period which would be typically over the most recent 10 years. This calculation can only generally be an estimate. Where it coincides with a new activity or a new division being formed, we can sometimes use the activity segment data afforded by company accounts to make better estimates of the contribution from acquisitions. If not, we have to use the turnover split at the time of the original deals. We then must estimate differential rates of growth for the various businesses which have come together through acquisitions. This allows some estimate of the current proportion of turnover that has accrued through acquisitions.

Mergers and acquisitions (M&A), however, are only the most extreme form of 'cooperation' with external organisations, as effectively coerced by the stock market. There are many stages of cooperation along the full spectrum of full hierarchical control through M&A at one extreme, and to more cooperative arrangements relying to a greater extent on more hands-off market relationships. At the risk of undue complexity, the only way to handle this more complete picture is to apply 'weighted' scores. Typically, weights for such different levels of cooperation would run from 1 or 2 for generally looser, more market-based arrangements such as low level license deals or franchising, up to say 6 or 8 for joint ventures or full scale international strategic alliances such as Renault Nissan, and finally to 10 for control-based acquisitions.

Thus, where data are available for cooperations other than acquisitions, we would first need to make the same calculations as for acquisitions. What percentage of sales are effectively covered by such cooperative arrangements? These then need to be weighted as just discussed. For example, the Scottish brewer S&N has an even higher proportion of current turnover (and indeed profits) coming from its 50% stake in Baltic Beverages Holdings, its Carlsberg joint venture, than from full acquisitions such as Kronenbourg. It has been fully engaged in creating BBH's business plan for the next three years,[5] but its control is far from total. Even weighting this contribution by say 0.7, this nevertheless considerably augments the contribution to S&N which comes from externally generated growth. Thus, a more overall organic growth overall index (OGOI) considering wider cooperations would be defined by:

$$\text{OGOI} = 1 - \left(\Sigma(\text{Turnovers from all cooperations} \times \text{Weighted indices})\right) / \text{Turnover}.$$

MEASURING THE CONTRIBUTION OF TECHNOLOGY AND INNOVATION

Strategic choices in respect to technology and innovation can be measured most easily in relation to technology. Typically, here we would use research and development (R&D)/Turnover ratios, which would typically be associated with strategies entailing specialisation (i.e., low scope dispersion indices) and high organic growth indices. BMW following its abandoning its Rover acquisition remains a good example. Thus, a pure technological innovation index (TII) would be defined by:

$$\text{TII} = \text{R\&D} / \text{Turnover}$$

Unlike other indices, this will typically be a figure below 10%. This index can be normalised (TIIn) to a range within 0 and 1, by dividing by the highest ratio found within the group of companies being examined, or within a wider grouping such as the global top 500. R&D/turnover ratios run from averages as high as 10%–12% in sectors such as aerospace, to averages under 6% in the case of general engineering.

In sectors such as fast-moving consumer goods, or drinks, however, innovation often focuses more on brand developments. Unless brand values and investments can be measured directly (as is possible for well known ones such as Coca Cola), the most practical measure is often simply 'sales and general administrative expenses/turnover'. A problem here is that it is hard to know how far such expenditures really constitute effective brand investments. Again, this can sometimes be estimated: goodwill provisions from brand-oriented M&A can sometimes be helpful.

Even in technologically orientated sectors, high technological innovation indices often combine naturally with high brand values. The two go hand-in-hand to such an extent that one is almost impossible without the other. BMW and Microsoft are both cases in point.

In sectors such as banking and insurance, on the other hand, innovation in information technology developments is often far more crucial, and indeed company accounts for these players rarely provide any data at all in respect to either R&D or Sales & General Administration (SGA) expenditures.

Therefore, to build up a more complete measure for innovation, it is also desirable to consider the capital expenditure/turnover ratio. By weighting such measures, according to key factors for success assessed for particular sectors, it is possible to arrive at a more overall technological innovation overall index:

$$\text{TIOI} = \sum\left(\text{R\&D/Tn}\right) \times \text{W1} + \left(\text{S\&GA/Tn}\right) \times \text{W2} + \left(\text{CE/Tn}\right) \times \text{W3}.$$

Clearly by this stage, measures are in danger of proliferating and of becoming increasingly subjective. However, there is one final index which, though yet more difficult to score, should not be ignored: the strategic innovation index (SII) is simply a score based on the degree to which a company has a demonstrably innovative business model. Examples are often the subject of classic business case studies and are easy to recognise. Dell, Southwest Airlines, Home Depot, Walmart, and Nintendo to name but a few do not measure particularly high on quantifiable ratios such as those above, but in terms of strategic innovation indices, they constitute benchmarks against which scores for other companies can be normalised. The measurement problem is compounded by the fact that such successful strategies are volume-based, so that inherently their more measurable innovation ratios are often remarkably low!

An innovation overall index (IOI) can be arrived at by weighting all innovation indices above according to key factor for success judgments for particular sectors:

$$\mathrm{IOI} = \sum \left(\mathrm{R\&D/Tn}\right) \times \mathrm{W1} + \left(\mathrm{S\&GA/Tn}\right) \times \mathrm{W2} + \left(\mathrm{CE/Tn}\right) \times \mathrm{W3} + \mathrm{SII} \times \mathrm{W4}.$$

Those accepting that strategic innovations are often of paramount importance will almost certainly apply high W4 weightings, complemented by far more modest weightings for the first three more easily quantifiable indices.

COMPREHENSIVE INTERNATIONAL STRATEGIC CHOICE VECTORS

Whether or not researchers utilise the full gambit of strategic choice vectors as defined in this paper depends on their confidence in gaining access and in handling data measures which become more numerous, complex, and subjective. These can be summarised in the form of universal strategic choice vectors as already discussed:

Universal strategic choice vectors being (GDI, SDI, VII, OGOI, IOI).

The geographical dispersion index, of great importance to international business researchers, may usually be decomposed into the following vectors:

(FS0n, FS1n, FS2n, FS3n, FA1n, FA2n, FA3n), as already defined and discussed.

Returning to our main geographical and scope dispersion matrix from Figure 2, we can see that typically most of today's highly successful international companies in practice combine policy choices. Readers will note that every company example included would score extremely high in terms of innovation overall indices though most particularly in terms of strategic innovation indices.

Certain of these other latter indices also combine naturally with particular international strategies: e.g., diversified global players unsurprisingly usually make more extensive use of external cooperation and particular M&A. Calori et al. (1999) tend to term this configuration 'worldwide restructurers'. At the other extreme, niche players often exhibit high levels of organic growth; whilst worldwide specialists usually exhibit high technological innovation indices.

The overall hypothesis is simply that the universal strategy choice vectors will be a function of relative size and the degree of globalisation in any given sector. The latter of course is changing over time. Defining and determining globalisation will be facilitated by classifying the world's top companies, particularly the *Fortune* Global 500 and top 30,000 as already begun. Such empirical investigations promise to shed light onto this overall hypothesis.

Haier's Three Third's Vector

There is, however, a novel simpler metric, which emerged from Chapter 8 examining Haier's global strategy in the domestic appliances sector. As we have seen, there are two ways of measuring a firm's commitment (thus offering potential entry deterrents to rivals) in global markets: trade and FDI. Trade is generally far easier. However, unless sectors are highly trade-conducive or competitive advantages/scale economies are exceptionally high, this will not always be economic. More typically securing double-digit market shares in overseas markets calls for 'assets on the ground' and much heavier investment commitments. The latter also entails organisational changes, such as shifting to transnational modes and substantial learning in terms of adapting to foreign markets and cultural or institutional differences.

Such FDI represents far higher levels of international commitment, and so it is (from a strategic perspective) a more crucial ultimate entry deterrent. Issues are asymmetric depending on whether a firm is from an advanced country where wages are typically high, or from an emerging country where the opposite tends to apply. For the former, FDI advantages in terms of arbitraging lower labour costs overseas; but for the latter, firms must sacrifice home market attractions and cost advantages in order to take the fight to incumbent rivals. Thus, for Emerging Market Champions, FDI represents an even higher, though often crucial, level of commitment.

Strategically, we therefore need a simple vector that expresses the level of global commitment, placing adequate emphasis on FDI as opposed to easier trade alternatives. Haier's 'three thirds goal' is highly ambitious, but offers a simpler vector through which we can express and investigate such global commitments. This goal states that:

1. One third of sales will come from production in the home region (China) serving that same domestic regional market;
2. One third of sales will come from production in the home region, serving overseas markets: i.e., through trade and exports;
3. One third of sales will come from overseas production, located in and directly supporting overseas markets: i.e., through FDI.

Such a goal is long term and highly ambitious. Even Haier, one of China's most globally orientated players, is only part way along such a journey. In 1998, it had no appreciable recorded overseas production and export trade was just 3% of revenue. By 2010, trade/exports were up to 14% and overseas production were up to 13.5% (Khanna et al. 2012: 16). This implies Haier was just over 41.25% (42% trade, 40.5% FDI) along the path to its ultimate stated goal of 33.33% home/home, 33.33% trade, and 33.33% FDI-based overseas production.

This suggests an easy novel vector of a firm's global commitment:

> Overseas sales through trade %/33.33, overseas production %/33.33.
> Or we could just take the average figure as an initial short-hand single metric.

Such metrics ideally need to be 'normalised' as we have done for foreign sales ratios or we would again hit the Luxembourg problem. It only works sensibly for Haier here because China is approaching a third of the world market. Comparable figures for European or American firms would have to take Europe and America as their bases (not of course nation states), both regions likewise approaching a third of the world market. Mathematically, we could improve this metric. But the essence is simply to capture just how far along the ultimate journey we'd be on, were we to serve global markets in accordance with their importance, balancing sensibly trade against tougher yet necessary FDI commitments.

Clearly, the ultimate path (under 'perfect globalisation') would be defined by:

Total overseas sales ratio = Global Market − Home Market/ Global Market.

Say two thirds in the case of China, though this ratio varies by market.

So that a strategic decision to commit to 50:50 on FDI vs trade yields an ultimate 3 thirds aspiration: vectors thus monitor progress along that path.

So, for firms for a smaller region with just 20% of the global market, for example:

$$\text{Total ultimate sales ration} = 80 / 100 = 80\%.$$

So same FDI vs trade strategic commitment yields an aspiration of:

20% home production for home market; 40% further home production for exports and trade; and 40% production from overseas facilities based on FDI.

Matching Haier's 2010 commitment would imply an overseas export ratio of 42% × 40% = 16.8%, with production from overseas of 40.5% × 40% = 16.2%. Or broadly 16.5% on both ratios.

MEASURING GLOBAL CONCENTRATION

If international business researchers are to relate their analyses of international strategic choices to the context of particular sectors, it is essential that they finally have some systematic method for assessing the degree of 'globalisation' in particular sectors. No one could expect the same pattern of international strategic choices in sectors such as shoe repairs or barbers as in sectors driven by far greater forces for globalisation, subject to lower pressures for local adaptation (Prahalad and Dox 1987, Bartlett and Ghoshal 1988, Yip 2001). Unfortunately, the latter frameworks, though helpful, are not easily scored. Furthermore, rapid recent internationalisation has undermined Yip (2001)'s distinctions of sectors such as cement, retail, brewing, and steel as essentially more national/local. All four sectors have since experienced radical international strategy moves, as exemplified by Cemex, Zara, SABMiller, and Mittal Steel.

One approach is to supplement such (ideally up-dated) appraisals of 'driving forces' with harder measures based on international trade and FDI data. This is feasible for many sectors, when defined at a broad two-digit Standard Industrial Classification (SIC) level, but the data are rarely available at more disaggregated three- or four-digit SIC levels often required when studying patterns of international competition. On the other hand, Ghemawat and Ghadar (2000 and 2006, ibid.) further utilise economists' favoured concentration measures highlighting different trends in global concentration in several sectors. Such measures get closer to the crux of issues relating to international competition, international strategic choices, and any ultimate question of global rationalisation. A similar approach is adopted here, though these should ideally be complemented with some further key measures.

For economists, the issue is one of sector fragmentation, albeit at the global level. For this, the best traditional measures are either the global concentration ratio indices (GCRIs), most typically the GCR4s, these being the combined market shares of the top four players in any sectors. Other variations, such as the GCRI5 used in Ghemawat and Ghadar (2006, ibid.), are possible; but GCRI4s have been favoured in studies of globalisation (Schwittay 1999), because a GCR4 level of 40% marks a level of concentration in which oligopolistic behaviour becomes likely (Scherer 1990).

GCRIs tend though to be less comprehensive than global Herfindahl indices (GHIs), the measures traditionally most favoured by economists and again utilised by Ghemawat and Ghadar (Ibid.).

$$GHI = \Sigma\,(GMSi)^{\wedge}2, \text{ summing for all 'i' participant firms worldwide.}$$

where GMSi is the global market share of the ith firm.

The Herfindahl index is the measure favoured by the US's Anti-Trust Division of Justice for determining whether a sector's level of concentration provides a prime facie case for an investigation of potentially oligopolistic behaviour (as, for example, in the case of M&A investigations). It is therefore logical to extend their criteria to analysis of more global oligopolistic behaviour, though it is possible their established cut-off criteria may need reviewing. As with other dispersion indices, the Herfindahl takes the squares of individual measures and for the same reason that we need to emphasise dispersion effects.

Adopting the same cut-off criteria as the US's Anti-Trust Division of Justice, but applying this globally, a GHI over 0.18 indicates a prima facie case of global oligopolistic behaviour. Under these conditions, we would therefore expect strategically highly significant action and reactions among companies competing between each other globally. Again, adopting criteria traditionally only used domestically, we would take a GHI under 0.1 as indicating a sector not yet concentrated globally. A GHI range between 0.1 and 0.18 would be regarded as a case of '*semi-globalisation*'.

In practice, data are rarely available for all global players, and there is less to be gained by going beyond a GHI 20, which sums the squares of global market shares for just the top 20 players. Strictly speaking, the most general GHIN, which is the abbreviated global Herfindahl for the top N players, also requires normalising. If not, the measure will vary with the sample number N, particularly if N is small. Normalising Herfindahl indices is, however, straightforward, and we can calculate the GHI normalised (GHIn) when dealing with just N participants as:

$$\text{GHIn} = \left(\text{GHIN} - 1/\text{N}\right)/\left(1 - 1/\text{N}\right).$$

As with dispersion indices discussed earlier, it is sensible to look also at the trend in such indices (again, as is done in Ghemawat and Ghadar 2006). Sectors with very low and falling GHIs would be regarded as globally fragmented, so that we would anticipate more conservative international strategies and lower levels of global sales and asset dispersions. The opposite would be anticipated for sectors exhibiting high GHI levels above 0.1 and certainly if above 0.18. On the other hand, sectors with lower, but increasing GHI levels might well be experiencing transition to more aggressive international strategies, with global sales and asset dispersions set to rise.

Finally, Schumpeter's[6] more dynamic theoretical model suggests we must also look at what is happening in terms of the number of significant players in any sector. It may be quite wrong to expect any sustained happy equilibrium in terms of global oligopolies. Schumpeter's model warns us to expect 'gales of creative destruction', brought about by innovation and technology, which would be heralded by our suggested IOIs as discussed above. This would lead us to anticipate waves of global fragmentation, as new paradigms spawn new worldwide entrants, followed by waves of global rationalisation. If so, this will be marked not merely by changing traditional economic concentration measures, but by rising and then falling numbers in terms of significant global players. It is this latter process which poses a critical threat to more passive international strategies. It is therefore advocated that we must also try to measure, simply the number of key players globally and track any change in this critical number over time.[7]

NOTES

1 Rugman, A. (2005), Ibid.
2 Should a US company's Fo/T ratio be above 71.5%, it is effectively discriminating against its home country, and there is even a case for viewing the company as having a base in whatever country represents the bulk of its turnover.
3 Rugman, A. (2005). Ibid. p. 244.
4 As advocated by Bartlett and Ghoshal (1989), Ibid.
5 Walsh, D. and Kennedy, S.H. (2007). 'S&N prepares to repel joint Carlsberg-Heineken bid', *Times* 18 October 2007, p. 50.
6 Schumpeter, J. (1947). ibid. See also Christiansen and Raynor (2003) for more recent evidence on the strategic significance of such technological disruptions in several sectors.
7 Shares of world outputs for the major continents are:
US plus Canada = 21.5 + 1.96 = 23.46; G + F + UK + IT = 4.64 + 3.27 + 3.0 = 14.14; China + Jap + Kor = 12.77 + 7.55 + 1.98 = 22.3%. Assumed Asia Pacific figure 0.25 if defined narrowly or 0.30 if defined more widely including Australasia; assumed N. American figure 0.25 or 0.28 if including all Americas north and south; assumed EU figure of 0.25 or 0.30 if all Middle East included. I.e., rest of the world figure assumed at 0.25, or 0.12 if other regions all defined more broadly. Figures below are based on 2009, though it is of course better is to use readily available updated GDPs for major countries worldwide.

Appendix B

WORLD'S TOP FAMILY FIRMS VS PUBLIC FIRM PEERS: INTERNATIONAL STRATEGY CONFIGURATIONS AND PERFORMANCE OUTCOMES

Chris Carr and Suzanne Livingston[1]

This appendix examines the international strategic choices and 'configuration orientations' of 65 of the world's top family firms, comparing them with a matched sample of non-family firms. Family firms' 'international' 'configurations' examined, proved just as worldwide and profitable as those pursued by non-family firms.

FAMILY VS NON-FAMILY FIRMS: COMPETITIVE BEHAVIOUR AND PERFORMANCE

Internationally, many family firms have enjoyed unique, recognised advantages such as remarkable long-term commitment and employee loyalty.[2] How many companies match Walmart for sheer size, or Hoshi Ryokan, or other family firms for longevity[3]? Families frequently wield power far beyond equity stakes, controlling companies such as Porsche, in turn, later acquired by VW, itself reflecting family interests. Many are notably agile, niche-focused, high-quality customer service providers.[4] They include famous brands like Benetton, Heineken, and BMW. Yet surprising little has appeared in well recognised strategy or international business journals or textbooks on family firms,[5] and still less on their global strategies or performances. Family businesses were downplayed 'inefficient anachronisms', antithetical to success in international markets.[6]

From a resource-based view (RBV) sustainable competitive advantages might reflect idiosyncratic resource-orientated biases of family vis-à-vis non-family firms, enabling them to offset any overarching threat of imitation.[7] Patient capital, leading in turn to longer-term stewardship and sustained innovation, emerges as one such critical advantage, though this has not always been the case.[8] Barriers to imitation derive not only from technical, but also social complexity; families approach business relationships differently. They may benefit from unique trust-based connections and knowledge creation processes,[9] especially in 'low trust' societies such as France, Italy, and China, sometimes marred by government interventions. Institutional factors matter. Historically, family businesses have flourished in less developed, more regulated economies reflecting less perfect market-mechanisms.[10] Familiness may motivate idiosyncratic strategic behaviour, in turn affecting performance.[11]

Arguments regarding patient capital are borne out by evidence of family firms' remarkable long-term commitment: inspired leadership (even over generations) has often led to tighter knit cultures and strong performances.[12] Others though have highlighted family firms' inward efficiency orientation and lower emphasis on strategic planning, resulting in lower growth and participation in global markets.[13] Family firms sometimes do face trade-offs because of constrained resources or family interests and can thus favour lower capital intensity.[14]

Performance debates have proven inconclusive. Some found evidence of higher profitability ratios in family vs non-family firms; others found the opposite; whilst Storey found no difference either way. Country and scale may also matter. Among United States (US) *Fortune* 500 companies, family-influenced firms achieved higher returns on assets and sales growths between 1994 and 2000, though better performances were confined to 'only businesses with a lone founder'.[15]

Studies controlling for levels of family control, though generally equally inconclusive, indicated a non-monotonic relationship between family control and performance among large US firms: performance first increased as family ownership increased (up to about one-third of the firm's outstanding equity), but then decreased: we adopted Ward's definition that, to qualify as a family business, the family had to own over 50% of the business in a private firm or over 10% of a public company.[16]

Numerous contexts and variables potentially impacting on performance are almost impossible to control for, whilst simultaneously responding to calls for research across more countries.[17] Taking a global perspective, we focus here on family firms' actual international strategies, which have been less researched.

INTERNATIONAL STRATEGIES' IMPACT ON PERFORMANCE

Based on studies of French small and mid-sized enterprises (SMEs), Sirmon et al. (2008) further developed their RBV theoretical perspective by proposing internationalisation and research and development (R&D) as two critical mediating factors, offsetting imitability, thereby impacting on performance. Arguably branding investments (better reflected in sales and general administration expenditure ratios), and capital expenditure levels would be more important in sectors such as services where R&D is less important; but all three variables merit consideration. Global involvement may also be moderated by *strategic factors, family issues*, and *top management attitudes.*[18]

As to whether family firms do or do not internationalise less rapidly, corroborative evidence has been mixed. Spanish and US family firms have been slower to internationalise, focusing more narrowly on customer needs in local markets;[19] Simon (1996) though identified many thriving family 'hidden champions', particularly in Germany, where strong global orientations and levels of internationalisation have often related positively to the percentage share of family ownership, as discussed in Chapter 7. Global strategy per se has been so hotly debated that we need to explore this further for top family firm potential oligopolists too. As elaborated in Chapters 4 through 6, we again utilised Rugman and Calori/Configurations Performance Analysis (CPA) classifications, allowing us to compare family and non-family top worldwide firms and to assess performance outcomes.

Our theoretical model, adapted from Sirmon et al. (2008), is summarised in Figure B.1. We substitute our broader concept of innovation in place of R&D. We further accentuate patient capital and social capital effects, reflecting idiosyncratic approaches to relationships.

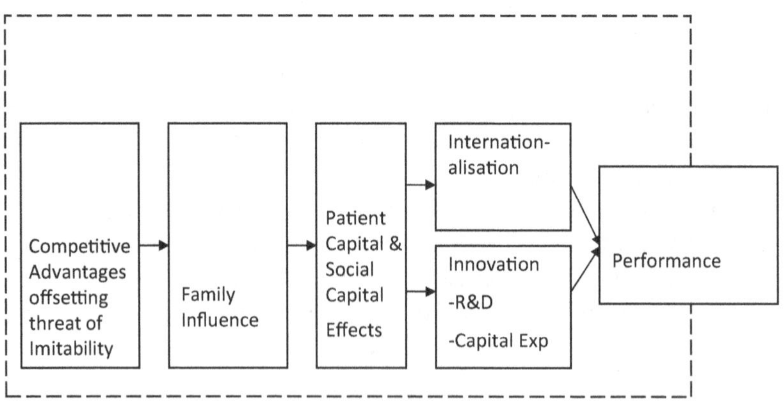

Figure B.1 Global top family firm competitive advantages conceptual model.

METHODOLOGY

Our sample of the world's largest family firms was mainly selected from the *Fortune* Global Top 500 (2003) and *Forbes* Top 2000 (2003), according to turnover. They were defined and identified in line with Ward's criterion, whereby a family had to own over 50% of the business in a private firm or more than 10% of a public company. We adopted Ward's four group classification: family ownership less than 30%, family ownership between 30% and 50%, family ownership greater than 50%, and lastly where the family had raised capital from the stock market.[20]

We then paired these 65 family companies with peer non-family firms. Thomson One Banker Analytics was chosen as our primary data source, since it had comprehensive data on global companies in all countries and for its analytical tools, in turn, enhanced by specialist Excel-based macros we had recently developed. For each selected family firm, Thomson's 'peer' function identified those most closely matched on market segment/activity (primarily, but not exclusively on Standard Industrial Classification codes). Secondly it then allowed identification of the closest match, based on turnover to provide for a size match. We also checked that selected 'peers' were under no form of family ownership. Comparative details are shown in Table B.1.

We analysed the international strategic configurations of all 130 sample companies according to our Calori-based CPA criteria detailed in Chapter 5. Data were obtained using secondary information from an extensive range of industry reports, academic articles, and websites, in addition to Thomson One Banker, our prime source of comparable financial data. Such demanding secondary-based analysis constrained our overall sample number, but statistically, we wanted roughly 30 for each of Calori's two main groups central to our argument (*worldwide players* vs *international challengers*), and for both family and non-family groups. After excluding secretive firms, such as Mars, we classified 65 top family firms as shown in Table B.2.[21]

Company performances were assessed using comparable ratios from Thomson One Banker for all key performance ratios. Our primary dependent performance variable was the 5-year return on capital employed (RoCE) between 1998 and 2003. We assessed longer-term performances for a slightly smaller sample of 56 from each group, examining 5-year averages for the last 20 years, for RoCE and sales growth (our secondary dependent performance variable). This contrasts with other researchers' use of more frequent, subjective stock market metrics (including 'Tobin's q'), but international strategic success often can only be judged over decades. Addressing this longer-term performance time horizon radically reduces the number of data sets and explanatory variables that can

Table B.1 Categorisation of top family firms selected by ownership levels

Publicly Traded			*Private*
Less than 30% ownership	*Between 30 and 50% ownership*	*Above 50% ownership*	*Completely private*
Ito-Yokado	J. Sainsbury	Molson	Robert Bosch
Motorola	Karstadt Quelle	Carrefour Group	Bertelsmann
Novartis	Walmart	Pinault-Printemps	Publix Supermarkets
Bouygues	Ford	Viacom	Otto Group
Gap Inc	BMW	Roche	Boehringer – Ingelheim
Groupe Danone	LVMH	Weyerhaeuser	Heraeus Holding
Anheuser-Busch	Comcast Corp	Bombardier	H&M
Marriott Int	Sodexho Alliance	L'Oréal	Levi Strauss
Dollar General	Winn-Dixie Stores	Lagardere Group	
Nordstrom	SAP	General Dynamics	
Pernod-Ricard	FEMSA	Magna	
Masco	McGraw-Hill	Heineken	
Grupo Financiero	Carnival	Henkel group	
Cemex	Swatch	Illinois Tool Works	
	Albert-Culver	Dillard's	
	Fiat	Thomson Corp	
		Interbrew	
		Ass' British Foods	
		Estee Lauder Cos	
		Bollore	
		Porsche	
		Wm. Wrigley Jr	
		Hyundai Motor Co	
		Tyson Food	
		Clear Channel Comm	
		ERG	

Source: Carr, C. and Bateman, S. (2009). 'International strategy configurations of the world's top family firms: another factor affecting performance,' *International Management Review*, 6(6), pp. 733–758. Reprinted by permission.

be reliably controlled for. We have therefore focused sharply on key variables most pertinent to our study, limiting control variables to include: sector, country of origin, level of ownership (in the case of the family sample), and revenue. We also examined pre-tax profit margins and further benchmarks, including: R&D/sales, capital expenditure/sales, and sales and general administration costs/sales, taking up points raised by Sirmon et al. (2008) and RBV theory.

Our study compares the complete population of the 65 largest accessible family-influenced companies worldwide, alongside non-family peers. They are not statistical samples, purporting to represent smaller companies whose behaviour may well prove different. Yet there is a sense in which we too are modelling processes which influence behaviour and performance: from this perspective we can still treat our two groups of matched

Table B.2 Configurations of all family and non-family firms selected

	Country-centred players	*Geographic niche players*	*Opportunistic international challengers*	*Continental leaders*	*Global luxury niche players*	*World-wide specialists*	*Quasi-global players*	*Transnational restructurers*	*Global shapers*
Family	Publix Supermarkets, Winn-Dixie Stores, Dillard's, Dollar General Corp, Nordstrom, FEMSA	Sainsbury's, Karstadt Quelle, Molson, Comcast	Fiat, Hyundai, Tyson, Masco, Clear Channel Comms, Grupo Financiero, Cemex, ERG	Pinault-Printemps, Bollore	BMW, LVMH, Porsche, Carnival, Levi Strauss	Michelin, Bombardier, General Dynamics, SAP, Estee Lauder, Swatch	Ito Yokado, Motorola, GAP, Magna, Otto Group, Sodexho Alliance, Thomson Corp, Pernod Ricard, H&M, Albert-Culver	Ford, Carrefour, Viacom, Novartis, Bouygues, Roche, Bertelsmann, Weyerhaeuser, Lagardere, Danone, Heineken, Henkel, Illinois Tool Works, Marriott, Boehringer Ingelheim, Interbrew, Ass British Foods, Heraeus GmbH, McGraw Hill	Walmart, Robert Bosch GmbH, L'Oreal, Anheuser-Busch, Wm Wrigley Jr

(*Continued*)

Table B.2 (Continued)

	Country-centred players	*Geographic niche players*	*Opportunistic international challengers*	*Continental leaders*	*Global luxury niche players*	*World-wide specialists*	*Quasi-global players*	*Transnational restructurers*	*Global shapers*
Non-family	Aeon, Albertson, Conagra, Daiei, Loblaw, EchoStar, Great A&P, Family Dollar Stores, Ross Stores, S-oil Corp, Kohl's	Safeway, Kawasaki Kisen, VF Corp, Companhia De Bebidas das	Koninklijke, Mitsubishi, Gus Plc, Asahi Breweries, Kao, JS Group, Allied Irish Banks, CSM NV, Daihatsu, Meiji Seika Kaisha	Renault, Kirin, Merck Kgaa, S&N Plc, Carlsberg	Christian Dior, Compagnie Financiere	Textron, BAE Systems, Apple Computers, Royal Caribbean	Ericsson, Pearson Plc, TJX, Compass, Mitsukoshi, Quebecor World, Heidelberg cement AC, Avon, Allied Domecq, Revlon	Metro, DaimlerChrysler, Nissan, Delphi Automotive, Time Warner, Bristol Myers Squibb, Vinci, Wolter Klumer NV, Georgia Pacific Corp, Goodyear, General Mills, Denso, Ingersoll-Rand, RTL Group, Citizen Watch Co	Astrazenca, Hilton Hotel

Source: Carr, C. and Bateman, S. (2009). 'International strategy configurations of the world's top family firms: another factor affecting performance,' *International Management Review*, 6(6), pp. 733–758. Reprinted by permission.

companies as 'samples' of a notionally larger population, provided we are very cautious. Going beyond descriptive statistics to naïve testing, as, for example, t-tests, neglects synchronous effects even from those multiple factors, identified as critical.

Multi-linear regression analysis was used additionally, just to handle the issue of synchronicity, distinguishing key drivers for high performance within the family and non-family data samples. Family influences or chosen international strategy configurations must here be considered against other key alternative factors responsible for good performance. Our statistical analysis aimed to identify correlations between performance; ownership (in the case of the family sample); international strategy, and country of origin and industry segment. Although statistical modelling is often viewed as the most reliable way to handle multiple variables, it only delivers explanations up to a point (roughly 14% of the story as suggested by our R-squared figures). Since several variables 'sample' numbers are inevitably low in some categories, these results must be interpreted cautiously. It would be wrong to overplay the significance of results from multi-linear regression or to underplay the relative importance of simple averaged statistics: the latter do, after all, represent the *whole* population of extremely large family-influenced companies and their peers.

FINDINGS: FAMILY VS NON-FAMILY INTERNATIONALISATION CONFIGURATIONS

We first analysed Rugman's (2005: 242–254) four international classifications for 17 family and 16 non-family firms, where our companies coincided with Rugman's global top 500 companies. Only one non-family firm (BAe) was classified by Rugman as other than home-region orientated (being bi-regional); this compares with four of our family firms – LVMH (global), Sodexho Alliance (host-region), and Michelin and Motorola (both bi-regional). On Rugman's criteria, our family firms emerge as more globally orientated. However, sample sizes of companies classified as non-home-region orientated are statistically low: these classifications do not do justice to the spread of firms' subtler international strategic choices.

We therefore moved on to a more comprehensive investigation of all nine international configurations, suggested by the alternative approach using Calori-based CPA classifications. Figure B.2 analyses configurations for both (full) samples of family and non-family firms, for the period 1999–2003.

Focusing on essentially the same ratio – the number of firms pursuing these five *worldwide configurations* divided by the number pursuing Calori's four less worldwide *international challenger* configurations – Figure B.3 examines these ratios for non-family and family firms categorised according to ownership level. This depicts a positive trend with regard to level

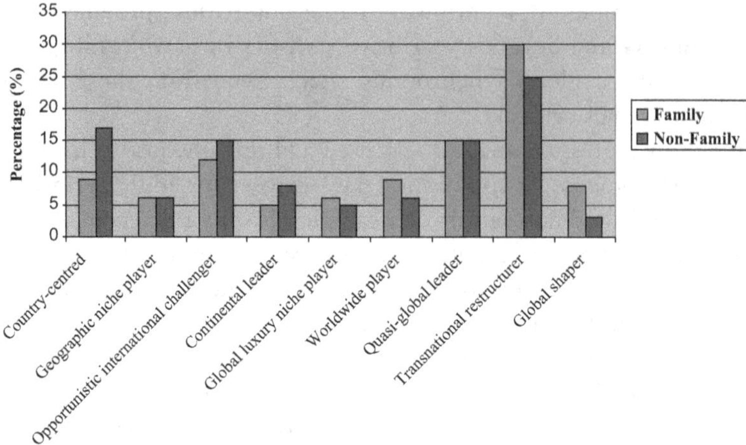

Figure B.2 Global top family vs non-family peer international configurations.

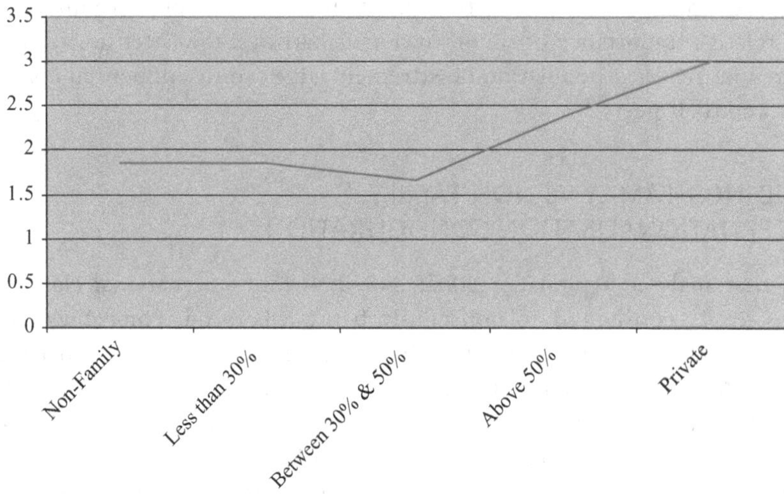

Figure B.3 Global players/international challengers ratios by family ownership levels.

of family ownership at higher levels and international activity; but there is a slight dip in levels of global participation when family ownership lies between 30% and 50%.

PERFORMANCE IMPACT

Family firms exhibited such distinctive and worldwide strategies, but has this factor resulted in better performance? Table B.3 provides some longer-term performance assessment (over a full 20 years) based on our slightly more restricted samples.

Table B.3 Averaged RoCEs: family vs non-family firms, 1983–2003

5 Yr Periods	*1983–1988*	*1988–1993*	*1993–1998*	*1998–2003*
Family	14.9	13.2	12.1	11.0
Non-family	11.2	11.2	12.3	8.1

Source: Carr, C. and Bateman, S. (2009). Ibid. Reprinted by permission.

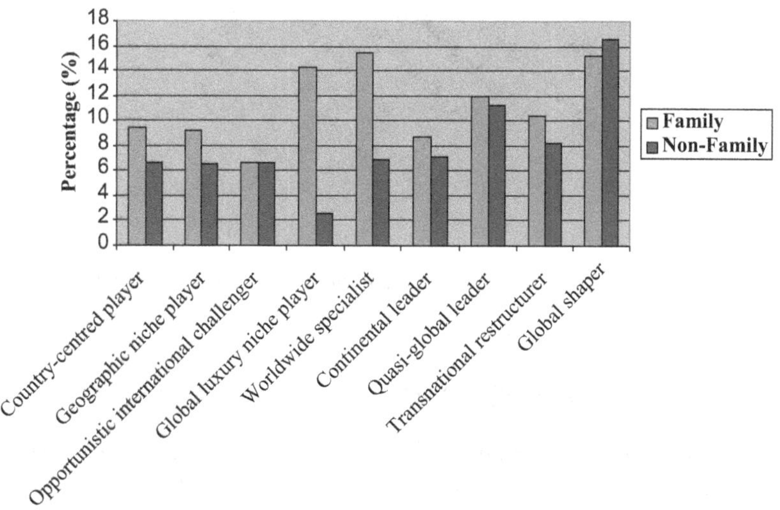

Figure B.4 Global top family vs non-family configurations: average RoCEs, 1999–2003.

Five-year RoCE averages for family were higher, as compared with non-family firms, for 1998–2003, 1988–1993, and 1983–1988, but virtually identical between 1993 and 1998. For the most recent five years, we split our samples into three turnover-size categories (<$3.5, $3.5–$10 billion, >$10 billion) and found that family again outperformed non-family companies in all three size categories. Figures B.4 and B.5 compare RoCEs, averaged over just the most recent five years, and sales growth for all nine international configuration types in Table B.2.

Contrary to our expectations, family businesses exhibited higher RoCEs for all configuration types, with the exception of global shapers, where non-family firms performed a little better. Family global luxury players and worldwide specialists did much better, perhaps reflecting their dedication to core activities. As shown in Figure B.5, family firm types also displayed relatively faster sales growth overall, though inconsistently as between different configurations; non-family firms grew relatively faster in country-centred and transnational restructurer types.

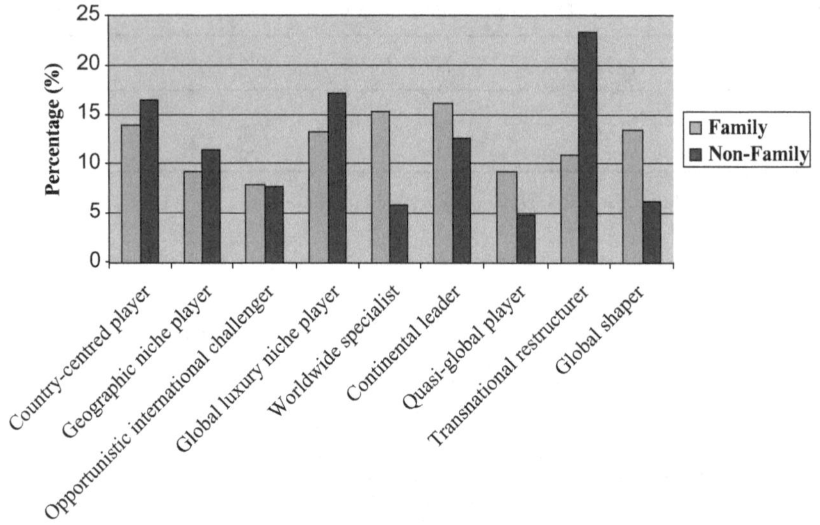

Figure B.5 Average sales growth global top family vs non-family firms, 1999–2003.

MULTI-LINEAR REGRESSION ANALYSIS OF ALL VARIABLES

For the more recent five years, multi-linear regression enabled more systematic performance analysis, taking into account a wider range of key drivers which may have been acting simultaneously. Performance data were investigated on a year-by-year basis for each sample set of 65 companies, using RoCE as the prime dependent variable. The explanatory variables processed by SPSS were: sales ($million) in years 2000, 2001, 2002, 2003 (1999 taken as the dummy variable for SPSS); five types of company ownership/control (including one type for non-family, and using totally private firms as the dummy variable); our international strategy types as above (taking *country-centred players* as the dummy variable); area of origin – America, European, Latin America (taking rest of the world as the dummy variable); and Industry – retailing, media, food/drink and tobacco, household and personal, auto manufacturing, pharmaceutical, and building products (taking miscellaneous sectors as the final dummy variable). Data were analysed on SPSS first using the Enter option to assess the significance of all variables, and then using Forward Multi-linear Regression analysis to establish systematically key drivers only. Results are shown in Table B.4 firstly for non-family firms.

This suggests two main drivers of profitability – sector and broad region – pharmaceuticals and retailing being associated with, respectively, 16.5% and 7% higher RoCEs. The only other statistically significant variable was country of origin: US non-family firms being associated with almost 6% higher RoCEs. However, once these key drivers are controlled for, there is

Table B.4 Multi-linear regression analysis: all variables against RoCE 1999–2003 for 65 non-family firms

Variables correlated with RoCE	*Unstandardised coefficients*		*Standardised coefficients*	*t Score*	*Sig level*
	B	*Std. Err*	*Beta*		
Constant	4.67	1.02	.23	4.60	.000[a]
Pharmaceutical	16.43	3.7	.187	4.44	.000[a]
USA	5.66	1.57	.166	3.62	.000[a]
Retailing	6.88	2.15		3.20	.001[b]

Source: Carr, C. and Bateman, S. (2009). Ibid. Reprinted by permission.

Notes: Adjusted R Squared = 0.150.
a denotes significance level at 99.9%;
b denotes significance level above 99%;
c denotes significance level above 98%;
d denotes significance level above 96%.

Table B.5 Multi-linear regression analysis: all variables against RoCE 1999–2003 for 65 family firms

Variables correlated with RoCE	*Unstandardised coefficients*		*Standardised coefficients*	*t Score*	*Sig level*
	B	*Std. Err*	*Beta*		
Constant	10.45	.71	−.118	14.67	.000[a]
Opportunistic International	−3.60	1.64	.247	−2.10	.029[d]
Challenger	8.93	2.34	−.207	4.39	.000[a]
Global Shaper	−5.78E−05	0.00	.193	−3.65	.000[a]
Revenue	5.07	1.43	.161	−3.65	.000[a]
Retailing	5.09	1.70	.127	2.99	.003[b]
Worldwide Specialist	4.51	1.89		2.39	.018[c]
Global Luxury Niche					

Source: Carr, C. and Bateman, S. (2009). Ibid. Reprinted by permission

Notes: Adjusted R Squared = 0.133
a denotes significance level at 99.9%;
b denotes significance level above 99%;
c denotes significance level above 98%;
d denotes significance level above 96%.

no residual convincing evidence of any link between international strategy configuration and performance: not even for *global shapers* which, in isolation, exhibited markedly higher RoCEs. Table B.5 shows regression results for family firms, controlling for all variables.

For family firms, the most statistically significant effect was the international configuration type pursued. Firms identified as *global shapers, worldwide specialists*, or *global luxury players* were all associated with significantly higher RoCEs: 9%, 5%, and 4.5%, respectively. Conversely, *international opportunistic challengers* were associated with 3.6% lower RoCEs. Just one sector, again retailing, emerged associated with significantly higher RoCEs at just over 5% higher. Here, size as determined by revenue, our other key control variable, was significantly, *negatively* associated with RoCE. Thus revenue, sector, and regions proved key control variables, when comparing family and non-family firms. Once we do this, it is family firms' unique international configuration choices *per se*, which are most strongly associated with our observed performance differences.

DISCUSSION, CONCLUSION, AND SUGGESTIONS FOR FUTURE ENDEAVOURS

Our 'sample', more correctly speaking, constitutes the 'population' of 65 of the world's largest family companies. This comparative study against 65 non-family peers was conceived globally, whereas other studies have generally been restricted regionally, often to single countries. Several national studies provide for larger samples and more numerous control variables (particularly for governance) and so potentially greater statistical robustness. However, these studies have not been validated outside the USA, nor do they completely control for sector, which emerged alongside regions as critical control variables. Our 'matching' principles, based first on industry group and second on size, may though still allow just some regional bias. Whilst US representation is similar for both samples, our family sample contained proportionately more European than Asian companies, just possibly enhancing family firm performance figures. Our international strategic classifications are subtler than other similar studies, but direct field research (though difficult worldwide) would have increased our confidence in judgements based on databases and company websites.

With these reservations, our findings suggest family firms are slightly more internationally orientated than non-family firms, in contrast to studies discussed earlier, more reflective of SMEs. Our results suggest that, after just a slight dip in international involvement when ownership is between 30% and 50%, this increased markedly as compared to non-family firms. Our top world family firms were not less worldwide in terms of international configurations adopted: any relationship with increasing levels of control appeared broadly positive.

For non-family firms, regional and sector effects emerged as important performance drivers, which future studies may need to control for, though once we controlled for counter-factual variables, we found *no* significant relationship between their choice of international configurations and performance.

However, this was not the case for top family firms. Not only did they exhibit different international configurations (as shown in Figure B.2), but these do appear to have influenced performance (even after allowing for these same control variables). Regressing against RoCE for the family firms confirms that three of five worldwide international strategies, *global shapers, worldwide specialists*, and *global luxury niche players*, displayed significantly enhanced performance, whilst the less worldwide *opportunistic international challengers* did less well (as compared with all other configurations). We have expressed some reservations about using multiple regression techniques, particularly given so many potential variables, but there is no better way for controlling for several variables acting simultaneously. We conclude that international configurations as a variable is an important factor bearing on family firms' relatively higher performances.

Possible explanations for our more positive findings for our family influenced firms may lie within some parameters highlighted by studies cited earlier. Long-term commitment was borne out by their surprisingly higher levels of capital expenditure, as compared with sales. Table B.6 shows capital expenditure, sales and administration, and R&D/sales ratios, which were actually lower for family firms. This suggests Sirmon et al.'s (2008) findings may be more confirmation of 'patient capital', than of R&D/sales policies per se (as proposed in their theoretical framework), though our findings concur on the issue of internationalisation. Our 20-year longitudinal results concur with recent historical studies, again highlighting patient capital and long-term commitment. This seems to have been a factor in the cases examined of Walmart and Wrigley. Other explanations lie in the field of governance, though we could not do due justice to all such variables. It may be that other family firms lack the same degree of chief executive officer commitment, allowing other less positive family influences to prevail; nor can we entirely

Table B.6 Family and non-family firm performances and benchmark metrics, 1999–2003

Company	*Average RoCE '99-'03 %*	*Sales growth (simple % p.a.) '99-'03*	*Average profit margin (%) '99-'03*	*Average R&D / sales (%) Y2003*	*Capex/ sales (%) Y2003*	*Sales & gen' admin/sales % Y2003*
Family	*11.1	14.0	*8.0	4.3	5.9	22.2
Non-Family	8.0	11.3	7.4	4.7	4.7	22.1

Source: Carr, C. and Bateman, S. (2009). Ibid. Reprinted by permission. Thomson One Banker.

Notes: Mean differences for RoCE tested statistically significant, based on SPSS, significance level 0.005, based on 2-tailed test, equal variances not assumed (t = 2.84). Similarly for profit/sales margins at significance level of 0.001, equal variances not assumed (t = 3.32). N = 340 for non-family and 325 for family companies, given some data omissions from some companies in particular years. R&D/sales, Capex/sales, and sales and general admin expenses/sales data based on just single years based on slightly smaller sub-samples (56 firms in each) providing fuller benchmark data. Sales growth figures are similarly based on fewer records and were not tested for statistical significance. They should be interpreted as more indicative.

dispense with concerns as to whether the direction of causality runs the other way: i.e., that it is the better longer-term performance of family firms which has facilitated their more worldwide international strategies.

Summarising key conclusions, we found no evidence of family firms adopting more 'inward' orientated strategic choices. Our findings indicate family firms adopt a higher proportion of the most worldwide configurations, as compared to non-family firms. This propensity rises with the degree of family ownership and control. Finally, in contradiction to our expectations and even allowing for control factors, family firms pursing these more worldwide configurations achieved higher, not lower, levels of profitability. In conclusion, family and family-influenced firms' global strategies appear more determined and more successful than hitherto acknowledged. Like emerging market champions, discussed in Chapter 9, they (and their distinctive traits) cannot be discounted among global oligopolists. They, too, are galvanising global transformations taking place and should not be overlooked.

NOTES

1 We acknowledge with thanks copyright permission from *International Management Review* for allowing us to reproduce tables and figures here from our earlier article: Carr, C. and Bateman, S. (2009). 'International strategy configurations of the world's top family firms: Another factor affecting performance', *International Management Review*, 6, (6), pp. 733–758.

2 Miller, D. and Le Breton-Miller, I. (2005). *Managing for the Long Run: Lessons in Competitive Advantage from Great Family Businesses*, Boston: Harvard Business School Press; Miller, D., Le Breton-Miller, I., Lester, R. and Cannella, A. (2007). 'Are family businesses really superior?', *Journal of Corporate Finance*, 13, pp. 829–858; Miller, D., Le Breton-Miller, I. and Scholnick, B. (2008). 'Stewardship vs. stagnation: an empirical examination of small family and non-family businesses', *Journal of Management Studies*, 45 (1), pp. 51–78; Villalonga, B. and Amit, R. (2006). 'How do family ownership, control and management affect firm value?', *Journal of Financial Economics*, 80, pp. 385–417.

3 O'Hara, W.T. (2004). *Centuries of Success: Lessons from the World's Most Enduring Family Businesses*. Avon, MA: Adams Media; James, H., (2006). *Family Capitalism: Wendels, Haniels, Falks, and the Continental European Model*. Cambridge, MA: The Belknap Press of Harvard University Press; Landes, D. (2006). *Dynasties: Fortune and Misfortune in the World's Great Family Businesses*. London: Penguin.

4 Poza, E.J. (2004). *Family Business*. Thomson, South-Western Publishing.

5 Chrisman, J., Chua, J., Kellermanns, F., Matherne, C. and Debicki, B. (2008). 'Management journals as venues for publication of family business research', *Entrepreneurship Theory and Practice*, 32 (6), pp. 927–934; Miller et al., Are family businesses really superior?; Brockhaus, R. (1994). 'Entrepreneurship and family business research; comparisons, critique, and lessons', *Entrepreneurship Theory and Practice*, 19 (1), pp. 25–38.

6 Chrisman, J., Chua, J. and Steier, L. (2006). 'Personalism, particularism, and the competitive behaviors and advantages of family firms: An introduction', *Entrepreneurship Theory and Practice*, 30 (6), pp. 719–746; Chandler, A.D. (1977). *The Visible Hand: The Managerial Revolution in American Business*. Cambridge: Harvard University Press; Chandler, A.D. (1990). *Scale and Scope: The Dynamics of Industrial Competition*. Cambridge: Harvard University Press.

7 Barney, J.B. (1991). 'Firm resources and sustained competitive advantage', *Journal of Management*, 17, pp. 99–120; Sirmon, D. and Hitt, M. (2003). 'Managing resources: linking unique resources, management, and wealth creation in family firms', *Entrepreneurship Theory & Practice*, 27 (4), pp. 339–358; Sirmon, D., Arregle, J., Hitt, M. and Webb, J., (2008). 'The role of family influence in firms' strategic responses to the threat of imitation', *Entrepreneurship Theory & Practice*, 36 (6), pp. 979–998; Eddleston, K., Kellermanns, F. and Sarathy, R. (2008). 'Resource configurations in family firms: linking resources, strategic planning and technological opportunities to performance', *Journal of Management Studies*, 45 (1), pp. 26–50. Strictly speaking the RBV focuses on four aspects of resources and capabilities: their value (V), rarity (R), imitability (I), and organisational (O), known as the VRIO framework, but literature applying RBV to family businesses has tended to emphasise the competitive threat from imitability.

8 Sirmon et al., The role of family influence in firms' strategic responses to the threat of imitation and Carney, M. (2005). 'Corporate governance and competitive advantage in family firms', *Entrepreneurship Theory and Practice*, 29, pp. 249–265.

9 Fukiyama, F. (1995). *Trust: The Social Virtues and the Creation of Prosperity*. New York: Free Press; Sjogren, H. (2006). 'Family capitalism within big business', *Scandinavian Economic History Review*, 54 (2), pp. 161–186; Zahra, S. and Zahra, A. (2006). 'Trust across borders', *Journal of International Business Studies*; Lee, J. and Macmillan, I. (2008). 'Managerial knowledge sharing in chaebols and its impact on the performance of the foreign subsidiaries', *International Business Review*, 17 (5), pp. 533–545.

10 Jones, G. and Khanna, T. (2006). ibid.

11 Arregle, J., Hitt, M., Sirmon, D. and Very, P. (2007). 'The development of organizational social capital: attributes of family firms', *Journal of Management Studies*, 44, pp. 73–93. Empirical findings regarding more specific strategies are, though, more mixed; most studies over rely on statistical associations, raising questions about the direction of causality.

12 Allio, M. (2004). 'Family businesses: their virtues, vices and strategic paths', *Strategy and Leadership*, 32, 4, pp. 24–33; Le Breton-Miller, I. and Miller, D. (2006). 'Why do some family businesses out-compete? Governance, long-term orientations, and sustainable capability', *Entrepreneurship, Theory & Practice*, 30 (6), pp. 731–746; Landes, D. (2008). *Dynasties: Fortune and Misfortune in the World's Great Family Businesses*, London: Penguin.

13 Gallo, M. and Sveen, J. (1991). 'Internationalizing the family business: Facilitating and restraining factors', *Family Business Review*, 4 (2), pp. 181–190; Westhead, P. and Howorth, C. (2006). 'Ownership and management issues associated with family performance and company objectives', *Family Business Review*, 19 (4), pp. 301–316; Harris, D., Martinez, J. and Ward, J. (1994). 'Is the strategy different for family-owned business?', *Family Business Review*, 7 (2), pp. 159–172; Harris et al. found little difference in family firms' strategic management processes when internationalising, as compared with non-family firms. Arthur Andersen/MassMutual's (1997) survey found that 69.4% of American family businesses reported not having written a strategic plan.

14 Friedman, M. and Friedman, S. (1994). *How to Run a Family Business*. Cincinnati: Better Way Books; Gordon, G. and Nicholson, N. (2008). *Family Wars: Class Conflicts in Family Businesses and How to Deal with Them*. London: Kogan Page.

15 Villalonga, B. and Amit, R. (2004). How do family ownership, control and management affect firm value. Miller et al., (2007), ibid. 15th Annual Utah, Winter Finance Conference.

16 Anderson, R. and Reeb, D. (2003). 'Founding-family ownership and firm performance: Evidence from the S&P 500', *Journal of Finance*, 58 (3), pp. 1301–1327.

17 Kellermanns, F. and Eddleston, K. (2006). 'Corporate entrepreneurship in family firms: A family perspective', *Entrepreneurship, Theory & Practice*, 30 (6), pp. 809–830.

18 Gallo, M., Garcia Pont, C. *Important factors in family business internationalisation*, www.cref.ubordeaux4.fr/Noveau%20Site/ARTICLES/Gallo%20et%20et%20Pont%201996.pdf. 988.
19 Ibid.; Zahra, S. (2003). 'International expansion of U.S. manufacturing family businesses: The effect of ownership and Involvement', *Journal of Business Venturing*, 18, pp. 495–512.
20 The *Forbes Rich List* and the *Family Business Magazine* provided details of families' involvement and levels of ownership, which were further investigated through company websites and annual reports.
21 We further analysed Rugman four international classifications (discussed in Chapter 4) for 17 family and 16 non-family firms, where our samples overlapped.

INDEX

Note: Page numbers in italics and bold refer to figures and tables, respectively. Page numbers followed by n refers to notes.